ULENDO

ULENDO

CLAUDE'S AFRICAN JOURNEY INTO WAR AND PASSION

A History of Empire seen through the Life of
Claude Oldfield (1889-1963)
British Colonial Officer, Northern Rhodesia

MALCOLM ALEXANDER

Mark
with all best wishes.

[signature]
November 2018

ALDRIDGE PRESS

First published in Great Britain by Aldridge Press in 2018
www.aldridgepress.co.uk

A CIP catalogue record for this book is available from the British Library.

ISBN 978-0-9520651-5-9

Maps by Helen Stirling
Design and typesetting by Kevin Ancient
Cover design by Kevin Ancient
Typeset in 11/14pt Electra LT Std

Printed and bound in Great Britain by Short Run Press, Exeter.

Aldridge Press
London
www.aldridgepress.co.uk

In memory of my Mother,
Joy Alexander (née Oldfield)

Learn the facts, Steed-Asprey used to say,
then try on the stories like clothes.

John le Carré, *Tinker, Taylor, Soldier, Spy* (1974)

Contents

Part One 1889-1911

The Making of a Gentleman – Claude's Ancestry, Upbringing and Education

Part Two 1911-1932

A Servant of the Empire – Adventure, Warfare and Passion in the Heart of Africa

Part Three 1932-1963

Victory and Valediction – From the Blitz to the Brecklands – Marriage and Retirement in a changing Britain

Foreword by
Archbishop Emeritus Desmond Tutu

Everybody now knows that we are all Africans, and, in this wonderful book, Malcolm explains why we should be proud of our heritage.

I have known Malcolm, man and boy, since the very early 1960s. There is no reason, however, to believe that because '... I can remember the 1960s, I was not really there...' He was my server at St Alban's Church in Golders Green when I was the curate there, and together we built a bond of friendship that still lasts now. In fact it has transcended generations, as I am the godfather to Charles – Malcolm's son

It has been explained to me that the idea of a foreword is to make some sort of explanation of the weightiness of the work under discussion, and that the writer of the foreword should make every attempt to remain in the background while extolling the virtues of the book.

I am no shrinking violet, so I want to step forward and say that Malcolm has captured the bitter-sweet feeling that loving Africa engenders. On every page that he has written, is the sense of place, time, and emotion that can only come from a love of the continent and its people.

It is so good that his exploration of his uncle's life and times has led to our having this brilliant book.

The book contains an explanation of his uncle's life, but, because of the detail we are given, we are allowed to see what Africa was like in colonial times. At this moment, when we are re-examining the legacy of empire, it is imperative that we try and look again at what was driving people. Malcolm gives us that perspective.

The only reason that I have any hesitation in telling people to read this book is that they will spend time over my foreword, instead of steeping themselves in Malcolm's words.

[signature]

+Cape Town

18 April 2016

Acknowledgements

Bend to it, my brothers, reap!
Gather up the speckled grain
Pile the *daga*-bins a-heap
Grain to brew and grain to keep,
Guerdon of the summer's rain

The Song of the Reapers by Cullen Gouldsbury[1]

The majority of photographs and illustrations are taken from Claude Oldfield's albums, with a few from other family sources, including photographs taken by the author. I would like to thank those who have provided photographs from other sources and to acknowledge permissions given for the use of the following photographs:

> St. Paul's School Archives (Ch. 4), Trinity Hall Archives (Chs. 5, 6), Charlie and Jo Harvey at Shiwa Ng'andu for Sir Stewart Gore-Browne's photograph albums and diaries, Elliott & Fry (Ch. 9), the London Transport Museum (poster of Golders Green, Ch.10), the George Grantham Bain collection (Ch. 10), Deutsches Bundesarchiv, Koblenz (Ch. 11), the Martini Henry Society (Ch. 11), Lee Daniel Crocker (Ch. 13), the Norwegian Directorate for Cultural Heritage (Ch. 15), Tony Wright, friend of Ann Jeffreys (Chs. 15 & 29), the National Portrait Gallery and Bassano & Vandyk Studios (Sir Sampson Sladen, Ch. 15), Denis Mayne's collection, courtesy of Colin Carlin (Jack Venning, Ch. 17), Centre for the Study of World Christianity, University of Edinburgh (Mary Moffat, Ch. 18), the Wellcome Collection (lithograph of David Livingstone by S. Hodson after Sharp & Melville, Ch. 19), *The Scotsman* (Dulcie Gray and Michael Denison, Ch. 24), Rich257 (Parker's Piece, Cambridge, Ch. 26), Michael Trendall (Ann Jeffreys, Ch. 29), and the National Archives of Malawi (Kenneth Kaunda, Ch. 30).

I also have many other people to thank. My first debt must be to those who inspired me to 'follow in Claude's footsteps' and then to write it down.

My initial visit as a 13-year old to Bridgham in south Norfolk inevitably brought me closer to my tetchy and circumspect great-uncle, but in spite of staying with him during many of my school holidays over the following four years, I realise now that I hardly knew him. It was his wife, Elveda, who many years later gave me his photograph albums with the encouraging words 'You may remember he spent some time in Africa!' Elveda's family, both back in the 1950s and today, continue as close friends, and I especially want to thank Rosemary Hills (whose house in Bridgham overlooks the Rectory), Sylvia and Graham Barnes, Roy and Audrey Broad and Jennifer Mason. Sandra and Jim Kerr, who farm at Ongar Park Hall near Chipping Ongar, have welcomed me, showing me their house where Elveda worked in the 1920s.

My Norfolk holidays led to the study of agriculture, but without the fortuitous arrival of a young Desmond Tutu at St. Alban's Church, Golders Green in 1962, that path might not have taken me to Africa. Desmond, his wife Leah and their family, especially their son Trevor, have all been inspirational – and I am really grateful for the generous Foreword that the 'Arch' has written. In a remote part of western Uganda, Hélène (my first wife) and I worked with Stephen and Anne Carr, giving us a first-hand understanding of African rural life. Stephen encouraged me to read John V. Taylor's *The Primal Vision* to gain an insight into the social and religious background of the people with whom we were living and working.[2] When resident in Malawi in the early 1970s, we found that attitudes amongst the white (mainly British) expatriate community were extremely varied, but Tony and Erica Standen stood out for their understanding of Malawi and its people.

Over the years, I have been particularly inspired by the writing of Doris Lessing (esp. *The Grass is Singing*), Oliver Ransford's *Livingstone's Lake*, Hilary Mantel (*A Change of Climate*), Christina Lamb (*The Africa House*), Sara Wheeler's *Too Close to the Sun: The Life and Times of Denys Finch Hatton*, Owen Sheers (*The Dust Diaries*, about the maverick priest, Rev. Arthur Cripps), Tim Butcher (*Blood River*), Cullen Gouldsbury, who with Hugh Sheane, wrote *The great plateau of northern Rhodesia*, a treatise on North Eastern Rhodesia in 1911, and Arnold Wesker's play, *Roots*, set in 1950s rural Norfolk.

Like the Woozle's footprints in the snow in Winnie-the-Pooh, where did Claude leave marks or a scent that could be tracked down? The fascination for me has been in following those, at times very faint, marks.

Hélène, starting with the Bluett's ancestral home at Holcombe Court in Devon, has over more than 30 years, unravelled much of our family history. She has also generously read and commented on earlier drafts of this book.

Alex Aslett, the Librarian and Archivist at Claude's school, St. Paul's, found his school reports and related documents and at Trinity Hall, Cambridge, Robert Athol, provided similar support. Fiona Colbert, the Archivist at St. John's College, Cambridge assisted with information on Robert Jeffreys' academic studies, as did Andrew Mussell at Gray's Inn. Amanda Hunt, at the Diocese of Norwich, helped with the history of Bridgham church and related topics. Rupert Wagstaff, now living in Claude and Elveda's old house in Portland Road, Bishop's Stortford, provided local information.

Although I had lived in Africa for more than five years (in Uganda, Malawi and Tanzania) and also travelled extensively, I barely knew Zambia (Northern Rhodesia) where Claude had worked for twenty-one years in the colonial service. In 1990, I made a low-budget attempt to look for Claude's footprints in the African dust, hitch-hiking to Mbala (previously Abercorn) and gaining my first sight of Kalambo Falls. David Moffat at Chengelo School, Mkushi provided hospitality en route to Lusaka where, at the National Archives, I could find tangible traces of Claude in the Abercorn District Notebook. However, it was not until 2013 that I was able to visit all the many bomas where Claude had lived and worked. For this, I owe a tremendous debt of gratitude to Colin Congdon, a retired Brooke Bond tea-planter and expert lepidopterist (and Martin) who took me on a 2,500-mile 'ulendo' from Dar-es-Salaam, across southern Tanzania, stopping at Mufindi and Sumbawanga, before reaching Mbala; from Kasama, via Mporokoso to Chiengi, along the Luapula valley via Kawambwa to Mansa, then back to Mbala, before driving south to Chinsali, and on to Lusaka. Accompanied by my wife Deirdre, we then drove north via Mkushi and Serenje, before Colin conveniently dropped us off at Shiwa Ng'andu. Here we were warmly welcomed by Charlie Harvey (grandson of Sir Stewart Gore-Browne) and his wife, Jo, who generously gave me access to diaries and records. Some eighteen months later, Deirdre and I returned to Zambia, this time to visit Ndola and Livingstone. For help and support in Zambia, I would also like to thank:

In Lusaka, the director and staff of the National Archives, especially Mauro Sanna and Lwendo Chikange; Peter Aagaard; Mike and Prish

Bingham (Leopards Hill) and John and Gretta Hudson. At Mbala, the director of the Moto Moto Museum, Victoria Chitungu and the librarian, Wilfred Chibola; at All Saints' Church, Rev. Alfred Sichone, and Brian Silwimba at Barclays Bank. And during our travels: Kunda Blackson (Go Mufo Hotel, Chinsali); John Bunda (Kawambwa Tea Estate); Barbara Changwe (Livingstone Memorial, Chitambo); Frederick Chisenga (Chief Chitambo IV); Sempela Chanda Havitus (Acting DC, Chiengi) who in 2012 took us to the Congo border at Pweto, and also introduced us to Koti Tarcitius, a retired MP and leader of the Bwili people; Fr. Patrick Kateule and Sr. Patricia Mapesa (Queen of Angels Catholic Church, Kayambi); Bertha Mambwe (Niamkolo Church, Mpulungu); Mike and Lari Merrett (Mutinondo Wilderness Lodge); Stanford and Albertina Moonde and Willie Kunde (Ndola); Ewart and Hazel Powell (Thorn Tree Guest House, Kasama); Jerry and Jan Selby (Mkushi); James Sinkala (Lukwesa, Luapula); Friday Yamba (Mpika) and Craig Zytkow and Elise (Ndole Bay Lodge).

In the 1990s, a number of retired colonial officials willingly corresponded with me, providing their recollections of Claude and his contemporaries. John Orr-Ewing, who died in 2015, generously gave me introductions to many of his contacts, including George Billing, Harry Franklin, James Murray and Charles Stevens. More recently in the UK, I have appreciated the help of the (then) Zambian High Commissioner, H.E. Paul Lumbi and his colleague, Beatrice Mukuka.

The opportunity to unravel the story of Claude's romance with Dorothy Jeffreys started with meeting Gareth Parkes and later his wife, Carol (née Thatcher). This led to a visit to Port Alfred in South Africa to spend some fascinating time with her mother, Janet Thatcher, niece of Robert Jeffreys. David Jeffreys, a nephew of Robert, very kindly provided copies of correspondence between Robert Jeffreys and his brother, Thomas. This led to meeting Michael Trendall, who was married to Gillian Hodgetts, daughter of Ann Jeffreys. I have also been able to talk to Hazel Ogston and Tony Wright, who both knew Ann when she was living in Glossop. Finally, I am also grateful for the opportunity to talk to David Arkley, who had been married to Audrey Jeffreys.

When visiting the Isle of Man with Deirdre, in August 2014, Peter Burgess of the Laxey Commissioners helped us find the house where Claude and Elveda lived in 1939 (then understandably named 'Abercorn'), now the home of Dr. Juan Garcia, who made us extremely welcome. Jack Kaighan helped by looking into the history of the house and its ownership in 1939.

Dr. Anne Samson, an independent historian focusing on WWI in Africa, and coordinator of 'The Great War in Africa Association', has read the MS, concentrating on the chapters covering WWI and the Appendix, giving valuable assistance in identifying relevant sources at the National Archives in Kew. A number of other academic historians with specialist knowledge of Africa have provided valuable comments and encouragement, including:

Dr. Daniel Gilfoyle, The National Archives, Kew; Emeritus Prof. Denis Judd, London Metropolitan University; Prof. Miles Larmer, St. Antony's College, Oxford; Prof. David Maxwell, Emmanuel College, Cambridge; various staff at the Royal African Society; Dr. Juliette Milner-Thornton, Griffith University, Brisbane, Australia; Emeritus Prof. Andrew D. Roberts, School of Oriental and African Studies (SOAS); Emeritus Prof. Robert Rotberg, Harvard University, USA; Fr. Aylward Shorter, Missionaries of Africa; and Dawn Wright, Africa Section, SOAS Library.

Those who have written about Africa and have readily given me insights into their experience include:

Dean Allen, Colin Carlin (esp. the history of Abercorn), Callum Christie, Julie Davidson, Tony Goddard, David Happold, Michael Holman, Richard Jewell, Jonathan Lawley, Chris McIntyre, Edward Paice, Amanda Parkyn, John Reader, David Salmon, Tony Schur, David Stuart-Mogg and Tim Wright.

Many other friends have also given encouragement in a wide range of ways:

John Bannon, David Clifton, Clive Conway, Canon Nicholas Darby, Michael Dunn, Harry Franks, Alessandro Gallenzi, Charlie Grace, Peter Grosvenor, Mark Hopkins, Stanley Johnson, Peggy Jones, Adam Little, Richard Long, Robin and Pat Macdonald, Archbishop Emeritus Walter Khotso Makhulu, Louise Milbourn, Dr. Howard Moffat, Malcolm Moffat, Rev. Sally Muggeridge, Judy Rossiter, Charles Scott-Fox, Laurence Shorter, Jonathan Stedall, Carole Stone and John Walters.

John Parker, who worked with me through several earlier drafts of *Ulendo*, gave me the right mix of thoughtful comment, vision and encouragement. Piers McGrandle followed with copy editing and John Winckler with proof-reading and indexing. The maps have been carefully and accurately prepared by Helen Stirling in Inverness. Throughout all this time, Halina Rabikowska has given substantial help with research and in painstakingly selecting and enhancing (wherever possible) photographs from Claude's albums that are around 100 years old. Lester Crook (of publishers, I.B. Tauris) kindly undertook a detailed appraisal of an earlier draft, highlighting the key issues relevant to an academic readership. Emeritus Professor Denis Judd, Antony Thomas and Sara Wheeler have all generously given their time to read the MS and to provide comments and observations. Kevin Ancient has admirably looked after all typesetting and design issues, including the cover design. Others have helped me assess various publishing options, including George Boughton, Michael Doggart, Jane Tatam and Mark Wilson.

Ten years ago, I met John Aldridge whilst watching a Test Match at Galle in Sri Lanka. Apart from our shared love of cricket, John has a passion for Africa, having worked for eight years as a teacher and teacher trainer in Zambia and then in educational publishing with Macmillan in Kenya. Later, after a spell with Macmillan in the UK, he started his eponymous publishing company and has given me tremendous support and encouragement in bringing this book to fruition.

Finally, I must sincerely thank my wife, Deirdre, for her patience in commenting on many earlier drafts and often putting up with me retreating to my study instead of taking time off to relax with her. Her encouragement and support are truly appreciated.

In the final analysis, however, any errors or omissions that remain are entirely my responsibility. Please accept my apologies if anyone who has given me help and support has inadvertently not been mentioned by name. Anyone who feels they have not been properly acknowledged should contact the author who will be happy to make amends in a future edition.

---

[1] From Cullen Gouldsbury, *Songs out of Exile* (T. Fisher Unwin, 1912). A 'guerdon' is a reward or recompense.

[2] John V. Taylor, *The Primal Vision: Christian Presence Amid African Religion* (SCM Press, 1963)

Glossary

Askari	Local soldier (or armed guard)
Boer	Afrikaaner (farmer)
Boma	District Govn. Office (Township where District HQ situated) (Swahili: enclosure)
Chief Secretary	Most senior member of the Administration (below the Governor)
Central Africa Federation (the Federation)	Federation of Rhodesia and Nyasaland (1953-1963)
Dambo	Low-lying grassland, usually flooded during the rainy season
Governor	Senior representative of British Government during colonial rule
Katundu	Baggage, luggage
Khonde (Chichewa)	Veranda
Machila	A hammock hung on poles, usually carried by two bearers
Makoro	Dug-out canoe
Mzungu	European (white person)
Provincial Administration	The country was divided into provinces, then sub-divided into districts
Rondavel	Round hut, usually made of mud, with thatched roof
Ruga-Ruga	Irregular troops and mercenaries
Stenographer	Short-hand typist (in Government service)
Stoep (South African)	Veranda

Abbreviations

ADC	Assistant District Commissioner	LegCo	Legislative Council (of NR)
ALC	African Lakes Corp. (incorporated in Scotland; originally as The Livingstonia Central Africa Company)	LMS	London Missionary Society
		MiD	Mentioned in Despatches
		NC	Native Commissioner
		NR	Northern Rhodesia
ANC	Assistant Native Commissioner (alternatively African National Congress)	*NRJ*	*Northern Rhodesia Journal*
		NRBB	Northern Rhodesia Blue Book (published annually by the NR Government)
BCA	British Central Africa (Protectorate proclaimed in 1889; renamed Nyasaland in 1907, Malawi in 1964)	NRG	Northern Rhodesia Government
		NRP	Northern Rhodesia Police
BEA	British East Africa	NRR	Northern Rhodesian Regiment
BSAC	British South Africa Company	PA	Provincial Administration
CiC	Commander in Chief	PC	Provincial Commissioner
DC	District Commissioner	PEA	Portuguese East Africa
DNB	District Notebook	PK	Picannin Kia (little house, ie. latrine)
DO	District Officer		
EAMR	East African Mounted Rifles	PoW	Prisoner of War
		SD	Sub-District
GEA	German East Africa	WENELA	The Witwatersrand Native Labour Administration*
GNR	Great North Road		
KAR	King's African Rifles		
KK	Kenneth Kaunda		
IHL	Imprisonment with Hard Labour		

* WENELA was set up by the gold mining companies in South Africa as a recruiting agency for migrant workers. It grew into a large organisation with its own depots, buses and aircraft spread across southern Africa

Place names

Colonial Name	Modern Name
Northern Rhodesia	*Zambia*
Abercorn	Mbala
Broken Hill	Kabwe
Fife (Old Fife; close to Ikawa)	Close to border of NR and GEA, west of Ikawa, near Tunduma (two miles from Nakonde)
Fort Jameson	Chipata
Fort Rosebery	Mansa
Mkushi	Old Mkushi. 'New' Mkushi is some 50 miles to the north of the original boma
Southern Rhodesia	*Zimbabwe*
Salisbury	Harare
Nyasaland	*Malawi*
Fort Johnston	Mangochi
Fort Hill	Chitipa
Port Herald	Nsanje
South West Africa	*Namibia*
Congo Free State (1877-1908) / Belgian Congo (1908-60)	*The DemocraticRepublic of the Congo (prev. Zaire)*
Léopoldville	Kinshasa
Stanleyville	Kisangani
Elisabethville	Lubumbashi
German East Africa (1885-1920) / Tanganyika (1920-64)	*Tanzania, on merger of Tanganyika with Zanzibar in 1964*
Bismarckburg (on Lake Tanganyika; the port was Wissmannhafen)	Kasanga
Alt-Langenburg	Lumbira (on Lake Malawi)
Neu-Langenburg	Tukuyu

Maps

Mosi-oa-Tunya

*The indigenous Tonga name, The Smoke That Thunders,
later known as the Victoria Falls*

In November 1911, twenty-two-year-old Claude Oldfield emerged onto the terrace of the Victoria Falls Hotel and blinked in the bright morning sunshine. Built by the British seven years earlier as accommodation for workers on the planned Cape to Cairo railway, the hotel, with its secluded loggias, lily ponds and elegant verandas, was quite splendid, and despite the heat he had slept well. Perhaps he was starting to acclimatise sooner than expected? Before leaving home in England, the Colonial Office had warned him it might take a while. It was all a far cry from his home in Maida Vale. Since disembarking at Cape Town, and throughout the long journey up country, he had hardly ceased to marvel that he was here at all, in Africa! The sights, the sounds, the smells; the never-ending skies and the sheer scale of the landscape. He had barely clapped eyes on any Africans before, apart from a fellow student at Cambridge, who was reputedly from a wealthy family, possibly the son of a tribal chief. Still, he had been diligently working at his language studies, hoping at least to be able to greet the local Bemba people and to create a good first impression.

Claude knew his history, of how in early November 1855, David Livingstone had travelled down the Zambezi to see for himself *Mosi-oa-Tunya*, the 'smoke that thunders'. Approaching in canoes, the party could see columns of spray and hear the thunderous roar, miles before reaching the Falls. Livingstone's own account continues:

> When about half a mile from the falls, I left the canoe ... and embarked in a lighter one, with men well acquainted with the rapids, who ... brought me to an island situated in the middle of the river ... I believe that no one could perceive where the vast body of water went; it seemed to lose itself in the earth, the opposite lip of the

*The Victoria Falls at Livingstone, Northern Rhodesia, called by the natives
"The smoke that sounds" – Claude, 1911*

fissure into which it disappeared being only 80 feet distant. At least I
did not comprehend it until, creeping with awe to the verge, I peered
down into a large rent which had been made from bank to bank of
the broad Zambesi, and saw that a stream of a thousand yards broad
leaped down a hundred feet, and then became suddenly compressed
into a space of fifteen or twenty yards.[1]

Livingstone continued his epic journey following the Zambezi downstream to the east coast, completing a 3,000 mile trek from the west to east coasts of Africa. Returning to England, his account of his travels caught the excitement and imagination of the Victorian public and his first book, *Missionary Travels and Researches in South Africa*, published in 1857, became an instant success.[2]

Subsequently other Europeans visited the Falls but it is generally accepted that Livingstone was the first European to announce their discovery. James Chapman and Thomas Baines, who had accompanied Livingstone in 1855, visited in 1862.[3] Baines' strikingly beautiful album of prints, *The Victoria Falls, Zambezi River*, was published by Day & Son in 1865, and as the first artist to portray the grandeur of the Falls, he also did much to capture the enthusiasm of the nation.[4]

Crossing the river then had been a daunting proposition. At the most advantageous point, beyond the Victoria Falls at a crossing called the Old Drift, the earliest explorers climbed into dugout canoes. Later, came the luxury of a metal vessel paddled by half a dozen Lozis who now ruled the area. Another option for reaching the north bank of the Zambezi was to be towed across in a barge by a steel cable.

By the 1890s, Cecil Rhodes' British South Africa Company had pushed north over the Zambezi in their pursuit of skins, timber and ivory, and had also begun prospecting for minerals. This activity, coupled with the improvement in river transport, had drawn British settlers to the Old Drift, the surrounding area becoming known as Livingstone, in honour of the missionary and explorer. Mosquitoes carrying malaria brought high rates of mortality, which consequently drove the settlers six miles north to higher ground, Constitution Hill. This became the new, burgeoning town of Livingstone.

The railway had already reached as far as Bulawayo in Southern Rhodesia and was officially opened on 4th November 1897 by Sir Alfred Milner, High Commissioner of the Cape Colony. The man behind the development of the railway, Cecil Rhodes, had contracted a severe bout of fever and could not be present, Milner likening his absence to a performance of *Hamlet* without the Prince. Rhodes sent a telegram:

> We are bound, and I have made up my mind, to go on to the Zambesi
> without delay. We have magnificent coalfields lying between here
> and there, which means a great deal to us engaged in the practical
> workings of railways. Let us see it on the Zambesi during our lifetime.

It will be small consolation to me and to you to know it will be there when we are dead and gone.[5]

The railway was first extended to access the rich coalfields of Wankie (now known as Hwange), 60 miles south-east of the Falls. When the line finally reached the Falls in 1904, a bridge over the Zambezi had already been started. The preliminary surveying of a possible bridge site had started four years earlier, in 1900, at the height of the Second Anglo-Boer War but with communications to the south having been cut, some delay in construction was inevitable.

Rhodes wanted to ensure that his vision was not misunderstood, writing in 1900:

> ... every one supposes that the railway is being built with the only object that a human being may be able to get in at Cairo and get out at Cape Town. This is, of course, ridiculous. The object is to cut Africa through the centre, and the railway will pick up trade all along the route. The junctions to the East and West coasts, which will occur in the future, will be outlets for the traffic obtained along the route of the line as it passes through the centre of Africa. At any rate, up to Bulawayo, where I am now, it has been a payable undertaking, and I still think it will continue to be so as we advance into the far interior. We propose now to go on and cross the Zambesi just below the Victoria Falls.[6]

Rhodes was not a man to pause for breath. Rather than wait until the bridge was finished, he instructed track to be laid in advance on the northern side from Livingstone to Kalomo, and even sent the component parts for a small locomotive across the river on an aerial runway. The Victoria Falls bridge was a crucial link in the route of the railway north. Surprisingly, Rhodes never visited the Falls, yet dared to envisage building a 'bridge across the Zambesi where the trains, as they pass, will catch the spray of the Falls'.

Ewart Grogan and Arthur Sharp, writing in 1900, believed that 'the concept ... was bold, to the point of arrogance: to build a modern steel bridge supported by a single slender span here, in the middle of the deserted jungle.'[7] Rhodes, who died in 1902, never lived to see his bridge completed; a magnificent structure of which he would have been justly proud, an emblem of the Empire and a vital stepping-stone in his Cape to Cairo vision.

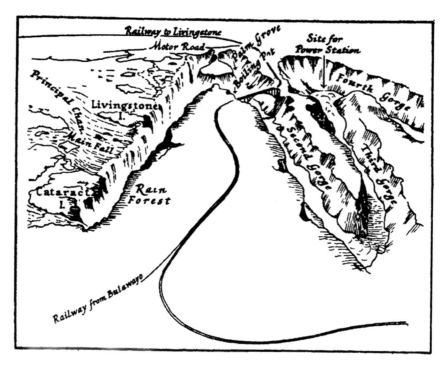

Bridge location map (by H.F. Varian)[8]

Boarding his train, Claude would have wanted a good view of the Falls and would have known of Rhodes' insistence that the bridge should be positioned close to the mighty cascade of water so that passengers could feel the spray. This had meant spanning the river just below the 'Boiling Pot'. As Claude crossed the Zambezi toward Livingstone, the newly-designated capital of Northern Rhodesia, he could contemplate the imminent start of his new life. Just now he could sit back and immerse himself in the sublime, spectacular surroundings unfolding around him, and recall the words of David Livingstone as he had looked down for the first time into the churning chasm:

> No one can imagine the beauty of the view from anything witnessed in England. It had never been seen before by European eyes; but scenes so lovely must have been gazed upon by angels in their flight.[9]

---

[1] David Livingstone, *Missionary Travels and Researches in South Africa* (John Murray, 1857)

[2] Livingstone, ibid.

The Victoria Falls Bridge in 2014 (Author in foreground)

[3] James Chapman (1831-72) had been near the Chobe in 1853 and, like Livingstone and Oswell on their first visit to the region two years previously, had been told stories of the Falls. *In Travels in the Interior of South Africa*, Bell & Daldy, 1868, he writes of his later arrival at the Falls: 'Here the panorama first broke upon us in all its grandeur, and I could not avoid the reflection that, could I but have known of the magnificent sight I lost in August 1853, after being very near it, and how nearly I had forestalled Dr. Livingstone's discovery, I should certainly have made another effort at that time to accomplish the object.'

[4] Thomas Baines, born at King's Lynn, Norfolk in 1820, was well known as an artist, explorer, cartographer and naturalist. He was a member of Livingstone's Zambezi Expedition (1857-59) and spent most of his life in southern Africa. He died in 1875 in Durban.

[5] Peter Roberts, *Sun, Steel & Spray – A History of the Victoria Falls Bridge*, Victoria Falls Bridge Company, 2011 and B. White, *The Trailmakers, The story of Rhodesia Railways*, Supplement to *Illustrated Life*, Rhodesia, 31 May 1973.

[6] Introduction by C. J. Rhodes in Ewart S. Grogan and Arthur H. Sharp, *From the Cape to Cairo: the first traverse of Africa from south to north* (Hurst and Blackett, 1900)

[7] Grogan and Sharp, ibid. and Mark Strage, *Cape to Cairo* (Jonathan Cape, 1973)

[8] H. F. Varian, *Some African Milestones* (George Ronald, Oxford, 1953)

[9] Livingstone, ibid. (Chapter 26)

CHAPTER 1

Camera Obscura

I know Claude would have liked you to have them.
You may remember he spent some time in Africa!

Elveda Oldfield, holding a pair of dusty
photograph albums

Claude entered my consciousness in the way that peripheral relations tend to, as someone simply 'there', a part of the family furniture. At my christening in the spring of 1944, with D-Day and the outcome of the war still in the balance, my father's Box Brownie recorded a fine April day, a small tea party in the garden, with the tall, fifty-something, sombre yet dashing Claude in RAF uniform. Known as 'Uncle Phil', at my early birthday parties he appeared as a rather stilted figure in a tweed sports jacket with leather elbow patches, stiff white shirt collar and old school tie worn with incongruous panache above fraying trousers. Like all adults, he seemed to tower over me and had a natural authority. It was impossible for me to imagine that he had ever been anything other than this rather dull and ancient relative, standing impassive, in the background.

Malcolm, his mother Joy, Claude and Elveda, April 1944

When I was nine years old my father died. Shortly afterwards my mother and I moved in with my maternal grandparents in Golders Green. My grandfather, Charlie Oldfield, married to Maisie, was ten years senior to Claude and his only surviving brother. After a rather frosty period, possibly caused by Claude choosing Elveda to be his wife, I gathered that the two brothers had now drawn closer to one another, Claude and Elveda visiting quite frequently from their home in Bishop's Stortford. Maisie's death only a year after my father's may have precipitated Charlie's heart attack. Afterwards, the doctor warned him against using the stairs, so with no bathroom or loo downstairs, he was for some months confined mainly to the upper floor of the house. My mother coped admirably on two fronts, lovingly caring for her father and raising me.

Beneath his somewhat irascible manner, my grandfather was kind and generous to me, talking cricket and the finer points of football pools: what were the odds of a big prize for eight draws on the Treble Chance, against those for four 'aways'? Was Vernons or Littlewoods better? For modest stakes – a 2/6 postal order sent off each week – the excitement when the results came on the wireless on Saturday evening was intense.[1] I cannot recall us ever winning.

When the talk drifted to family matters, my grandfather sometimes spoke about his brother's marriage, which seemed to have been controversial at the time. The stories about how the couple met varied, casting her either as a 'picture house' usherette or a Lyons Corner House waitress – a 'Nippy' as they were called. Either way I gathered that my great-grandmother had not welcomed Elveda into the family. It was true that Claude and Elveda were a contrast, but this seemed less about their age difference – Elveda was twenty years younger – than their demeanours. As my grandfather enjoyed his whisky and cigar before supper, Elveda would be warm and effusive, while Claude stood always in formal jacket and tie, jingling coins in his pocket. Was he weighing up Charlie's observations on the state of the world, or was his mind somewhere else, inhabiting one of the many chapters of his past of which I knew nothing?

Reserve aside, Claude did not lack a sense of duty, and on numerous occasions he and Elveda came and looked after my grandfather, allowing my mother to take me for happy summer holidays in Devon. By fourteen, I was a keen cyclist and so discovered that there was a world outside London of green fields and winding hedgerows. When Claude and Elveda moved to Norfolk, I asked my mother if I might go and stay with them. In the summer of 1957, I boarded the train at Liverpool Street Station, my destination Harling Road, seven miles beyond Thetford in south Norfolk. With me was my prized black and chrome Hercules Roadster. Claude had taken a lot of persuading by my mother to let me visit. Whether

*The Rectory, Bridgham / Elveda with cats /
Smallholder farming: pigs, geese and turkeys*

knowing this at the time would have put me off I don't know. Like any
boy, all I really thought about as the engine steamed out of London was
the adventure, going somewhere I had never been before, albeit only a
hundred miles up the line.

At Harling Road station I was met as arranged by a Miss Wetherall,
a jolly lady in her mid-fifties who introduced herself as a friend of the
family. Together we cycled past the old ruined church at Roudham and
up the hill, arriving three miles later at the little village of Bridgham.
The Rectory, a large double-fronted Georgian dwelling leased from the
church, accommodated Claude and Elveda, her youngest brother John,
her recently widowed younger sister Jean with her seven-year-old son, plus
an elderly spinster cousin of Miss Wetherall, Gwen Bourne. Completing
the bucolic commune, add Flossie, a terrier/collie bitch, Sam a boisterous
black Labrador, a couple of cats and several very free-ranging chickens.

Only next morning did I realise that the business side of the Rectory was pig farming, a joint venture between Claude and Elveda, her brother John and Miss Wetherall. Eight breeding sows produced 'weaners' – piglets that were sold off at seven or eight weeks of age. Prices that year were good, and the enterprise was doing reasonably well. Help with the day-to-day chores was welcomed, and I was soon filling the water troughs by bucket and shouldering heavy bales of straw. The Norfolk air and hard labour left me dog-tired every night but with a healthy glow.

Elveda was kind and affectionate towards me, and even Claude made conversation when we took a break from our labours. He told me that the day before my arrival, the RAF had staged a thousand-man parachute drop over nearby Bridgham Heath, some of the chaps landing inadvertently on the main railway line, but fortunately there had been no trains running past at that time. As a retired RAF officer, although without much flying experience, the operation had obviously interested Claude, and led on to some discussion of military matters. Warm approval of Churchill and Field Marshall Montgomery seemed the standard line for his generation, but a war that had ended before I was crawling had little significance for me. Now the Soviets were the bogeymen our RAF boys were preparing for. Claude also related stories about his life in Africa, to which I listened inattentively. The leopard-skin rug in the living room, overlaid with muddy footprints, made no connection in my mind, and Claude's reminiscences would be interrupted by Elveda's appearance at the open window to show me a fluffy newborn chick.

Over the next few days, in between pig-keeping duties, I took my Roadster out beyond Bridgham, eclipsing the miles with ease. I discovered the ancient Peddars Way, a probable Roman footpath running northwards to the coast near Hunstanton, and according to legend, haunted by a ghostly dog called Black Shuck.

Back home in London I asked my mother about going again to Norfolk. Apparently Claude was reluctant. What were his reservations? Perhaps it was just the idea of yet another person in the house, even though I had been a willing helper. I continued to badger my mother, until it was agreed that the following spring I might take a friend and camp in the garden. It was early April, clear skies and freezing after dark. After the second night under canvas with inadequate sleeping bags, we were taken pity on and allowed into the house, returning outdoors during daylight hours and cooking our own eggs, beans and sausages on a primus stove.

11

I was allowed to return to Norfolk each year, helping with the pigs and poultry at the Rectory and at harvest time on the local farm. Slowly I realised the kind of work I enjoyed, and a career in agriculture beckoned. This awakening was all down to Claude and Elveda, her uncomplicated warmth an open encouragement to the rural life, his reticence perhaps a spur to prove myself.

Not that Claude lacked consideration. In December 1962, shortly after my nineteenth birthday, he and Elveda took me to the Odeon Leicester Square to see David Lean's epic *Lawrence of Arabia*. One of the first films on wide screen, the cinematography, battle scenes and stirring human drama played out against the sweeping backdrop of the desert and the bloody romance of World War One, made a spell-binding four hours' entertainment. Like many of their generation, my great uncle and aunt were keen cinemagoers, but I did not realise how this film must have had a particular resonance for Claude. A couple of months later, in the freezing February of 1963, at about the time I was milking a dairy herd in Hertfordshire as part of a year's pre-university farming experience, my great uncle Claude died.

Claude had been seventy-three. My great aunt Elveda, still in her early fifties, carried on with the help of her brother and Miss Wetherall to work the smallholding. In between studies I continued to visit Elveda, while Claude receded to the back of my mind as a phlegmatic, slightly-faded Englishman of the old school, who had played no starring role but was worthy of Milton's observation that 'they also serve who only stand and wait'.[2] It would be another twenty years before I had occasion to revisit this view of my great-uncle.

By 1967 post-war austerity was becoming a distant memory as England, still basking in the euphoria of last year's World Cup triumph, won the Eurovision Song Contest, and the Beatles released *Sgt. Pepper's Lonely Hearts Club Band*. Tom Stoppard's philosophically sparkling *Rosencrantz and Guildenstern are Dead* premiered at London's Old Vic. In May, Prime Minister Harold Wilson announced that the UK will be applying to join the EEC, but later in the year is forced to devalue sterling, claiming that it will not affect the 'pound in our pockets'.

By now I had a degree in agriculture, and, tacitly agreed between us, a fiancée. Hélène and I had met while students, she at Christ Church College, Canterbury, me at nearby Wye College. The next logical step, since my family are not farmers, was to find a job as a farm manager. Initially I had assumed this would be in Britain, but through a chance meeting with a young curate at my local Anglican church, I realised that there were other possibilities. The priest, who will become a lifelong friend, was Desmond Tutu.

Talking to Tutu about Africa was a sobering reminder that despite decolonisation, the 'wind of change' observed by Macmillan, had not eased the acute poverty facing so many in that part of the world. In my last postgraduate year at Wye, I had also been enthused by the vision of a former student, Stephen Carr, now working with his wife Anne in western Uganda. The Carrs wanted to show young African school-leavers that it was possible for farming to provide a decent living as a commercial enterprise, a better option than drifting into the shantytowns around Kampala. In due course, this led me to the door of the Church Missionary Society, which recognised that looking after the welfare of their intended flock needed practical solutions as well as spiritual outreach, deploying personnel with a variety of skills on a voluntary basis.

I had never been to Africa, and the recollection that my great uncle Claude had once lived and worked there remained a vague one, occupying little more space in my memory than the faded leopard skin rug at the Rectory. As a young graduate it was the future that drew me, not the past. I asked Hélène one day, 'Fancy living in Africa?' Somewhat to my surprise she did not immediately refuse. A few weeks later we were married and boarding a BOAC VC-10 to Entebbe on the shores of Lake Victoria.

Our stay in Uganda was for two years; our very few European neighbours, volunteer teachers or missionaries. Our existence was frugal, living healthily off locally-caught dried fish, sweet potatoes and other staples from the fertile Ugandan soil, topped up with imported canned goods, corned beef in particular. The earnest missionaries however suggested that in the interest of the cause we could, and by implication should, manage on less than the modest allowance paid us by Christian Aid. Later, noticing correspondence from an investment firm, we learnt that Anne was a scion of a wealthy whisky distilling family. Unlike Saint Martin, it seemed some have rather more than a cloak to share with the poor. We were able to visit Kampala every few weeks, usually managing an evening out with other young couples drawn to work in newly independent Africa. Working on the scheme with us was another Wye graduate, Richard Adams, a rather shy unattached young man, whom we invited for supper on a regular basis, but it struck us that that the volunteering life in Africa could be especially lonely for a single person. This observation would return to me.

This two-year overseas assignment, coming straight out of university, probably made us realise that being missionaries ourselves was not our long-term calling, although from working closely with Stephen Carr I gained a first-hand understanding of subsistence farming and village life in Uganda. A subsequent three-year stint in Malawi, planning agricultural projects for World Bank funding, followed later by management and finance positions, including a lengthy period with Brooke Bond Tea, took me back on a regular basis, and my love of Africa grew. However it was not until 1983, after paying one of my occasional visits to Claude's widow, that my interest in the continent took on a whole new significance.

My great aunt Elveda, by this time in her seventies, had reluctantly moved from Bridgham into the small town of Thetford, initially lodging with a friend, before being offered a newly-built British Legion flat. As my wife and I approached the front door, a mynah bird called out 'Hello, hello!' in an uncanny impression of Elveda, who despite the onset of fibrositis, was the same cheerful, outgoing person I had known since my childhood. She seemed pleased with her new flat, and glad to have regular coffee mornings, Friday night bingo and other social events on tap, and to be only a short stroll from her favourite pub.

Over tea and cake, while enjoying Elveda's convivial East Anglian

Elveda, when living near Thetford, Spring 1982

14

dialect, quite unlike Claude's formal diction, I pondered the nature of their marriage, acknowledging that I ought to know more about the Oldfield side of my family. I had rather assumed that they had been 'metropolitan gentry', as I had been told that my great-grandfather had taught classics in Maida Vale. I believed Elveda's family had been in Norfolk for some generations. In the 1950s I recalled her parents, Walter and Lucy Law, living at a tied cottage, the Gatekeeper's House, on the railway line near Roudham Hall, where they worked the level crossing. If a farmer needed to take his tractor across the tracks, Walter used to telephone the signal box for clearance before opening the gates.

I concluded that Claude and Elveda's relationship had been founded on contrast, a cheerful object lesson in *vive la différence*. I remembered Elveda's family being impressed that her husband was 'well-spoken' and by his oratory on formal occasions. Claude in turn must have appreciated his wife's affectionate, homely qualities. Add a shared interest in football pools and their efforts to produce an income from pigs and poultry, and the recipe for contentment seemed reasonable. What more was there to know?

After a second cup of tea, we told Elveda we ought to be heading back to London, and on the way to the door congratulated her on her new flat with *mod cons*. The only downside in her view was a lack of storage, and she needed to have a clearout. 'Which reminds me,' she said with a twinkle in her eye, 'I've something for you'. From an overflowing cupboard she brought out a pair of large dusty photograph albums. 'I think you'd better take these dear, there's nobody else would value them or make use of what's in them, and I know Claude would have liked you to have them. You may remember he spent some time in Africa!' We both smiled. Taking a polite flick through, I thanked Elveda and promised to take good care of the albums.

That evening I sat down and looked at the photographs more carefully. There were several dozen sepia images, some faded or over-exposed, featuring Claude at various stages of his life, together with snaps of family, friends and acquaintances, buildings, waterfalls, landscape and wild animals. The most immediately striking pictures were those of Africa, scenes of game hunting – hippos, big cats and other prey displayed triumphantly by Africans. Some included Claude, in one frame wearing full colonial attire of pale flannel suit, canvas shoes, collar and tie and pith helmet kneeling proudly beside a magnificent recently-shot leopard. The image of the rug in the Rectory flashed into my mind. Was this that very

Dorothy at Abercorn, 1926

beast? The collection also revealed a man who had rowed at Cambridge and Henley and served in both World Wars. The Africa pictures, all carefully annotated, dated from 1911.

What most caught my eye though, was the recurring presence of an attractive, bob-haired young woman. Captioned 'Dorothy', she appeared in a variety of outdoor settings, sometimes with a man, one assumed her husband, and two young daughters. In other shots she was alone: at the wheel of a car, head lowered and gazing coyly, seductively even towards the lens, then posing coquettishly up to her thighs in a lake, her one-piece costume, for those pre-bikini days daring in front of any man, especially one not her husband. What part had this woman played in Claude's life that he had been moved to capture her obvious charms?

I was intrigued as to why such a rich history had been hidden away, and wished now I had listened more closely to my great-uncle's tales of 'looking after his people' and riding between African villages on a motorbike. I could not remember ever seeing the albums when visiting him. And did Elveda know who Dorothy was, and where she fitted in? What secrets lay here?

I tried to imagine Claude as an elegant young bachelor, burnished by the African sun. When and how did he meet Dorothy, and what of the man who appeared to be her husband, and the two young girls? Oh for the chance to talk with Claude again over the leopard skin rug! With the set of clues now in my possession, how I would have liked to travel back in time and piece together his life. Then, thinking about it at greater length, I decided that perhaps the idea wasn't so far fetched. Working in Africa had given me a head start on its geography and generic past, which would surely assist me in picking up the trail. The fascination crystallized into a plan: to reconstruct the life and times of my great uncle.

The focus of my investigations must wherever possible be the more *ad hominem* testimony of diaries, and any letters, telegrams or other photographs; then perhaps official archive material from Africa and the UK. The chances of finding anyone apart from my mother who had known Claude in the early days seemed slim but not impossible; the two young girls with Dorothy for example, might still be alive. Whatever pieces of the personal jigsaw could be fitted together, the historical milieu that formed its backdrop was also now engaging my curiosity.

Africa I would revisit, retracing Claude's movements, the life that he had led, his friends and associates and the events that had unfolded around him. The scent was in my nostrils, but though eager to begin the exotic part of the adventure right away I knew I must start at the beginning, and with the simple question: where had Claude Philip Oldfield come from? The answer was to provide a further surprise, and it would by no means be the last.

---

[1]   2/6, the abbreviation for two shillings and sixpence, or 'half-a-crown', which was one-eighth of a pound. The half-crown was demonetised on 1 January 1970, the year before the UK adopted decimalised currency

[2]   From the sonnet, *When I consider how my light is spent*, John Milton 1608-74

CHAPTER 2

A Victorian Family

She was poor but she was honest,
though she came from 'umble stock

R.P. Weston and Bert Lee, 1930

Our memories of people are often inextricably linked to places. Like watching a grainy old home movie, I can see my grandfather in his upstairs sitting-room, enthralled by his newly-acquired Bush 14" black and white television as Jim Laker destroys the Australians on a 'sticky' wicket at Old Trafford in 1956. Claude as always is standing, offering occasional laconic commentary on the match. Claude's other backdrop in the 1950s was Norfolk, surrounded by chicken feed sacks and half-completed pools coupons, the *Daily Mail* ever open at the racing page. It was hard to picture him anywhere else before the discovery of the photo albums.

Those faded images would open a door not only to Claude's past, but also to a vanished world that had existed long before him. One clue however suggested that one feature of that world might still survive: a picture of a house. It was a property of an entirely different order to that which any of my family inhabited, being a very large and solid Tudor stone pile, replete with high tower and buttresses, massive transom windows and the suggestion of extensive land. Claude's annotations referred to it as 'Holcombe Court, Devon' and, what was most extraordinary, as the birthplace of his mother. Checking that the building was still standing, and then finding Pevsner's description of the south entrance front as, 'the most spectacular example of the Tudor style in Devon', was enough to whet the appetite. With some further investigation, we might uncover how Claude's mother, Mary Anna Bluett, began her life there.

It was a fine Sunday morning in spring when my wife and I arrived in the village of Holcombe Rogus. The first impressions of the Reverend John Swete, visiting in 1800 seem an appropriate description of what awaited:

I had before me full in view a very picturesque scene formed by the village of Holcombe Rogus, and castellated mansion, long a seat and residence of the Bluetts. This latter I found nearby at the head of the village street, contiguous to the church and to the vicarage house, a most magnificent antient edifice of considerable extent and altogether such a pile (considering it the mansion of a private family) as is not to be paralleled in the country.[1]

Etching of Holcombe Court (c. 1850)

So captivated was Swete that he made a sketch and later a watercolour of the mansion. We noticed that parts of the building to the left of his painting had now gone, but the substantial remainder was no less imposing. As public access to the house was not possible, we walked over to the nearby church, All Saints, where the morning service was just ending. The parishioners gave us a generous introduction to the history of the church, including Bluett's private chapel. Holcombe Rogus was once a large manorial estate, the Court built around 1540 by Sir Roger Bluett, whose noble lineage could be traced back to the Domesday Book, the Bluetts having come over from France soon after William the Conqueror. What though of Claude's mother, born many centuries later, apparently within these grand walls? It was time for some detective work.

A lengthy trawl through parish records later revealed that Claude's mother was indeed the daughter of the then incumbent of Holcombe

Court, Peter Frederick Bluett, though not by his wife, Caroline Bluett (née Lefevre), who had already given him eleven children. Bluett, now in his mid-forties had been conducting a semi-clandestine affair with Claude's maternal grandmother, Maryanne Meech Knowlman, having befriended her when she was only thirteen. Maryanne had given birth to their daughter a year later (Claude's mother, confusingly named Mary Anna) not at Holcombe Court, but in the far humbler surroundings of a small cottage in Weymouth. Although Bluett's marriage to Caroline came to an end with Maryanne's pregnancy, this relationship continued with Maryanne having seven more children with Bluett, living a peripatetic existence between Exeter, Southampton and Clerkenwell, before finally settling in Wembury in south Devon for the next 14 years. While living at Wembury with Maryanne, Bluett started a relationship with their housekeeper Eliza Kingcombe, who became pregnant in 1867. Maryanne

Peter Frederick Bluett, Squire of Holcombe Rogus (c.1850)

departed for London, but Bluett, now on his third liaison, went on to have a further seven children with Eliza, residing at Wembury and Plymouth.

Peter Bluett's behaviour was highly questionable, even by the moral standards of his day, and when Claude's grandmother took him to court in 1873 and secured £300 per annum 'maintenance', a full account of his misdemeanours came out. He had apparently met Maryanne in 1848, when her father was his resident land steward at Holcombe Court, when

> the plaintiff was then about thirteen years of age. The first time the defendant saw her she took a note to him from her father. After this he used to call very frequently at her father's house, gave her fruit, cakes and sweets, took her out in his carriage with her parents, and effected her ruin when she was only about 14 years and three months old.[2]

At that time, the age of consent for a female was twelve, and was only raised to thirteen after 1875.[3] No other marriage had taken place, so bigamy did not apply. In law, at that time, Bluett's only offence was not to have made provision for his long-standing mistress and mother of seven of his children, although he had paid for all the children to be educated.

Claude's mother, who bore the maiden name of Mary Anna Bluett, was from landed gentry, the ancestral stock of Holcombe Court true enough, but being the wrong side of the blanket, apart from the maintenance, it seemed that none of the wealth or estate ever found its way to her or her children. Under primogeniture, the eldest legitimate son would have been in line to inherit, but by 1857, extravagant living and heavy gaming debts forced Peter Bluett to sell Holcombe Court the following year, to the Reverend William Rayer for £57,000 (c. £2.5m today).[4]

Mary Anna, one of numerous siblings between three mothers, was left with nothing but a photograph of the great Tudor house that her paternal forebears had owned for four centuries. It could be argued that her sister Ellen fared better, in marrying John Hallett of Stedcombe, whose family had amassed considerable wealth from sugar plantations in Barbados. Although John's ancestor Richard Hallett had brought a retinue of slaves back to Lyme Regis in 1690, a family coat of arms and ownership of the historic Stedcombe House conferred outward respectability.

It was time to explore Claude's father's background, where a rather different story emerged. Thomas Smedley Oldfield was born in 1844, in the Derbyshire market town of Wirksworth. Involvement in lead mining in the nearby village of Brassington had provided a living for several generations

Mary Anna Oldfield (née Bluett)   *Thomas Smedley Oldfield*

of Thomas's family. Brought up by his great-aunt and grandmother at No. 28 West End, a modest two-bedroom terraced house close to the centre of Wirksworth, Thomas had left home at sixteen to become a pupil-teacher at the National School in Atherstone, a market town east of Birmingham, lodging at the house of the head teacher. Clearly bright, highly motivated and socially mobile, within a few years he had moved to the south coast as an assistant master at Hewitt's School in Rottingdean near Brighton.[5] Though unable to discover where Thomas and Mary Anna met, we were able to ascertain two things: that on 8th August 1876 they were married at the parish church in Edgbaston, and that Mary Anna was already four months pregnant.

Thomas's ambition led him to London and a new appointment as tutor at a public school. On 8th January 1877, their first child, Thomas Robert, known as Robert, was born at 18 Carlton Terrace, Paddington Green, and baptised six months later at St. Peter's Church, Elgin Avenue, a short walk from their home. The couple would have all their children baptised at St. Peter's, but tragically their only daughter Marie died from croup just three weeks short of her fourth birthday, having been baptised the day before. The last of their four boys, born on 6th May 1889, was Claude Philip Oldfield.

Brothers Harold (left) and Claude (right) with their parents

Claude's brothers were Harold, three and a half, Charlie (my grandfather) coming up to eleven, and Robert, twelve. By the time of Claude's birth, the family had moved to a Victorian terraced property in Oakington Road in an area known as St. Peter's Park on the southwest side of Maida Vale. It was from this address that Claude's father, with a Bachelor of Arts from London University, gave private lessons in Latin, Greek and Logic, subjects prized by aspiring young men and their families as a passport to higher education and advancement in the professions. Later to be acclaimed, 'one of the foremost tutors of his day (who) achieved a measure of success, unapproached by any of his contemporaries', Thomas Oldfield was much in demand, a forerunner perhaps of today's 'super-tutors'. His style was of its time, steeped in Victorian notions of rote learning, as he intellectually cudgelled his pupils with an unrelenting discipline. Subtler techniques were also employed, notably the Socratic method, the interlocutor playing devil's advocate to the unsuspecting pupil to reveal the paucity of his logic and thereby tighten it. 'Frequently he would confront budding orators with apparently guileless questions, and disturb the glib note of assurance which characterizes so many political speakers.' His son Harold recalled pupils crying from the severity of the lessons: 'There have been enough tears in our dining room to float a Dreadnought. I have often seen men of twenty sobbing like children.'

Thomas Oldfield's academic pupils included Harcourt Butler, who went on to Harrow and Balliol and became Governor of Burma, Gilbert Frankau, a Jewish convert to Anglicanism who attended Eton, spent time in the family cigar business and wrote poetry, and Samuel Montagu, who founded the bank bearing his name and was a noted philanthropist and

Liberal politician. Most of his scholars were successful in the diplomatic, banking and literary worlds. Oldfield's pupils at Hewitt's School had included Sydney Buxton, who became a radical Liberal parliamentarian and the first Earl Buxton, and Maurice de Bunsen, who after Rugby and Christchurch, Oxford became a distinguished diplomat as British Ambassador to Spain, then Austria between 1913 and 1914.[6]

For Oldfield, the classical world was both a profession and a passion. As his income grew he collected paintings and sculpture, including a *pietà* by Giovanni della Robbia. Finding a picture of the beautiful *pietà*, a representation of a sorrowful Virgin Mary, it struck me that the acquisition might have been in remembrance of his daughter Marie. It seems that following her early death, religion became more important to the family, the boys being afterwards swiftly baptised.

In Victorian England religious and denominational allegiances mattered, and by extension came prejudice. Anti-Semitism was ingrained in certain professional and social spheres, though Hewitt's School had many Jewish pupils whom Thomas would have taught. Maurice de Bunsen, his pupil at Hewitt's, was by contrast from a Prussian family, and Maurice's father Ernest, Prussia's Ambassador to Britain, had written on the shared origins of various religions, including Buddhism, Christianity and the ancient Essene sect of Judaism, though ironically, aspects of his work were later appropriated by Nazi ideologues.

A more positive interpretation of de Bunsen senior's relatively free thinking in an age of orthodoxy, could have been picked up by his son's incisively-minded tutor at Rottingdean. If so, Thomas Oldfield may have been a somewhat eclectic tutor, regarding the purpose of education in its original Latin sense of *educere* – to lead forth, rather than impose. Partly self-taught, his journey from the Derbyshire mining village would have encouraged him to teach all, irrespective of religion or background, his primary duty being the precision sharpening of young minds.

On first discovering my great-grandfather's reputation, I found myself rather sentimentally hoping he had not been as strict with his own sons as with his paying pupils. It seemed most likely though that their intellects would have been challenged from an early age, and any 'sloppy' thinking come down hard upon. Inevitably young Claude, encountering the upper-class boys who came for tutoring – and seeing some leave in tears – would have learned there was no easy route to real learning: rigour, clear headedness, brevity, accuracy and no excuses were imperatives to unravelling the moral, political and philosophical issues explored in

Claude (c. 1897)

Harold (left) and Claude (right) at home
(with aspidistra)

classical literature. By the time Claude was ten, his oldest brother Robert, after studying at the Royal School of Mines in South Kensington, was married and bound for Australia. Charlie remained at home, destined initially for an electrical apprenticeship, followed by a much more successful career in insurance. Harold, now thirteen, still at school and coping with a crippled left leg, was studious, enjoyed the classics and was to develop a love of poetry. What direction I wondered, did Claude take? As youngest child he could well have been doted upon by his mother, the last of her brood, and held in particular affection by all the family.

One would imagine Claude's first steps in education being guided by his father, alongside attendance at a local primary school. But what was his conception of the world? Gazing at his first map he would likely have seen a quarter of its land mass shaded red, denoting the British Empire. Reinforcing the sense of dominion over a vast area of the globe, inhabited by a happy multitude of loyal subjects of many tongues and hues, came Queen Victoria's Diamond Jubilee celebrations of 1897, staged at the suggestion of the Colonial Secretary Joseph Chamberlain, as a festival of the British Empire, the seventy-eight-year-old monarch being also Empress of India. The royal progress set off from Buckingham Palace for a service at St. Paul's Cathedral, and patriotic Londoners turned out in force along the route, hoping for a glimpse of the carriage, or simply to wave a flag, raise their hats and raise the roofs with adulation. Victoria was said to be at first unenthused about the celebrations, but if expecting approbation nonetheless, she was not disappointed, recording in her journal that:

> The streets, the windows, the roofs of the houses, were one mass of beaming faces, and the cheers never ceased … no one ever I believe has met with such an ovation as was given to me, passing through those six miles of streets … the crowds were quite indescribable and their enthusiasm truly marvellous and deeply touching.

The crowds had reason to be cheerful, and grateful to their monarch; the day was declared a bank holiday, and Victoria had reportedly told her advisers, 'If you want a big affair, then get the government to foot the bill.' Corporate philanthropy also funded nationwide street parties, Sir Thomas Lipton of Lipton Tea providing a feast including free beer and tobacco for 400,000 of London's poor. A chain of beacons was lit across the country, and in London eight year-old Claude, his brothers and parents must surely have been among the beaming faces their Queen looked out on that day.

Four years later the mood was very different. At half past six on the evening of 22nd January 1901, after spending Christmas and the New Year at Osborn House on the Isle of Wight, Queen Victoria passed away peacefully at the age of eighty-one. Her sixty-three-year reign had been the longest of any British monarch. Those who had grown up in the previous century, many of them now grown old, had never known a time without her. Yet as Edward took to the throne, little else seemed changed. Despite some embarrassing defeats in an unpopular war with the Boers, Britain still ruled the waves, her empire on which the sun never set still confidently, some might say complacently, intact. As young Claude looked forward to beginning secondary school, his big map of the world was still a quarter red.

[1] Todd Gray & Margery Rowe (eds.), *Travels in Georgian Devon: The Illustrated Journals of the Reverend John Swete, 1789-1800* Vol 4 (Halsgrove Press, 1999) pp 196–9

[2] Devon Lammas Assizes: Maria Ann Meech Knowlman v. Peter Frederick Bluett (Special Jury), as reported in *The Exeter & Plymouth Gazette Daily Telegram*, 31 July 1873.

[3] The Offence Against the Person Act of 1861. See www.historyofwomen.org/timeline

[4] Charles Scott-Fox, *Holcombe Court: A Bluett Family Tudor Mansion* (Charles Scott-Fox for Nigel Wiggins, 2012)

[5] Also known as Field House School, which Hewitt started in 1863. Source: The

history of St. Aubyns school, which was formally founded in 1895, but had origins in educational establishments founded in the 18th century by the then vicar of Rottingdean, Dr Thomas Hooker.

6   Sydney Charles Buxton (1853-1934), later 1st Earl Buxton, went on from Hewitt's School to Clifton and Trinity College, Cambridge. After his parliamentart career, he was appointed Governor General of South Africa (1914-20). See Appendix.

CHAPTER 3

Fide et Literis

from all nacions and countres indifferently
John Colet, Founder of St. Paul's School, 1509

Remembering that Claude's secondary school had been St. Paul's, I turned to the questions of how and why he had gone there. In terms of connections, his father might have taught Latin and Greek privately to some of the pupils or known one of the masters. The logistics made sense, St. Paul's at Hammersmith being easily accessible from Maida Vale via steam train along the Metropolitan Line, the other two top London schools within reasonable daily reach being Merchant Taylors' and Westminster.[1] As Westminster only took boarders, separation issues and the higher fees might have been off putting.

Academic standing would have been the key criterion, and as any lettered man knew, St. Paul's alumni included Milton, Pepys and Samuel Johnson, names that would surely have burned bright in the imagination of Thomas Oldfield during his own schooling. Oldfield senior was now almost sixty and would have pinned great hopes on his youngest perhaps cleverest child. With his eldest son Robert in Australia, Charlie heading for the City and Harold, bright but severely constrained by his gammy leg, he would have felt immensely proud to be able to give the boy the finest possible education.

Claude started at St. Paul's in April 1902, just before his thirteenth birthday. Forty-three boys were admitted that year, seven of them Foundationers, who had won scholarships.[2] Claude was among the 'Capitation Scholars' whose parents paid the £20 per annum fees. The school's founder John Colet (1467-1519), Dean of St. Paul's Cathedral, had wanted pupils 'from all nacions and countres indifferently'. Colet, a renaissance scholar and theologian, took issue with corruption among priests, advocating they be 'beacons of light' rather than figures of darkness prone to 'devilish pride, carnal concupiscence, worldly covetousness

Harold and Claude at home, Penselwood, 37 Oakington Road, Maida Vale

and worldly occupations'.[3] Though citing St. Paul that people must be 'reformed into a new mind', Colet seems in a sense conservative, urging 'back to basics' Biblical tenets against being 'drowned in the delights of the world'.

Cynics might argue that Colet could afford to eschew materialism having inherited a large fortune from his father, a Lord Mayor of London and member of the Mercers' Company. He does, though, seem to have practised as he preached, sharing an interest in Renaissance humanism with Erasmus and Sir Thomas More. With all of his twenty-one siblings dead and no other family of his own, he endowed the new school, opened in 1509 behind the Cathedral, with the bulk of his father's estate. No fees were required from pupils, the only criterion for entry being basic literacy. Although avowedly celibate himself, Colet found 'the least corruption in married men', and appointed the secular Mercers' Company to run the school.[4] On its opening, St. Paul's was the largest school in England, the headmaster's salary thirteen shillings and sixpence a week, believed to be double that of Eton's head. St. Paul's was the first English school to teach Greek, and though Christianity remained central to Colet's world view, his claim in the school statutes as 'desyring nothing more thane Educacion and bringing upp children in good Maners and literature',[5] in particular the reference to 'literature' rather than say scripture, expresses an accommodation if not bias towards more secular thought, marking him out as perhaps a 'Christian Humanist'.

The founder had little regard for less cerebral pursuits. Hugh Mead records 'no organised games: Colet had forbidden "cockfighting" and "riding about of victory", which he thought nothing but a waste of time.' Possibly such proscriptions contributed to what Mead called the 'sometimes stormy' relations between high masters and governors. The Mercers' Company might also have felt at odds with an ivory tower culture turning out brilliant but impractical graduates.[6]

By the 19th century the narrow curriculum was still a bone of contention, but according to the high master of the time, the intransigence lay with the managers rather than the staff. Hugh Mead again:

> John Sleath, High Master from 1814 to 1838, declared that, 'at St. Paul's we teach nothing but Latin and Greek': but he said so not complacently but with ironical regret: he had tried and failed to get the governors to appoint a master to teach writing and arithmetic. In a reforming age St. Paul's was going to have to change.'[7]

Pressure for change, in particular the issues of access and funding, came in 1861 with the investigations of the Public Schools Commission, and later the Charity Commission. St. Paul's however avoided the close scrutiny imposed by the resultant Public Schools Act of 1868, successfully defending its status as technically a private institution, ensuring the continued independence of its constitution. Whether despite or because of such freer rein, the school was achieving notable academic success. From 1886-95, a hundred and seventy-three entrance awards to Oxford and Cambridge were notched up, twenty-six more than any other single institution.

The school had had more than one physical incarnation. The 1666 Great Fire of London destroyed the original structure along with the cathedral, and a rebuild within four years on a similar footprint, was followed in 1822 by a move to nearby Cheapside. By the 1880s, needing larger premises, a third relocation was underway, several miles from the shadow of the cathedral to a sixteen-acre plot between the present day Talgarth and Hammersmith Roads. Alfred Waterhouse, architect of the vast Natural History Museum in South Kensington completed in 1881, was appointed to design the new premises. By 1884 the handsome red brick and terracotta Gothic building at 153 Hammersmith Road was completed, with a preparatory school in similar style opening opposite shortly afterwards. Facilities at Hammersmith also enabled St. Paul's to participate and compete more widely with other schools in the field of sport and athletics.

It was to this four-storey institution with its imposing spires, that Claude would have made his way in April 1902. Close contemporary Ernest Raymond remembered his heart shaking as six hundred boys assembled for *pi-squash* in the hall:

> The morning sun lit the scene through high lancet windows, emblazed with the heraldry of old pupils who'd been famous and enobled during four hundred years. On the far wall, from the side of the great organ, the Dean, our Founder, portrayed in a huge mosaic, looked down upon these successors of his first Tudor boys. High above him, above everything else, in another vast area of mosaic, the Boy Jesus, President of the school, sat and talked with the doctors in the Temple. 'Ipsum Audite', said the mosaic, 'Hear Ye Him.'[8]

The ceremonious, ecclesiastical setting will resonate with public schoolboys and those familiar with Bunter's *Greyfriars* or *Hogwarts Academy*. So, too, will the mood of anticipation during assembly:

> We all waited, shoulder to shoulder and chattering, till a sonority in the corridor without implied the approach – how shall I put it? – the entry of the Principal Figure. Instantly all six hundred of us fell into silence. Even the masters standing in the gangway fell into silence and stood still.[9]

The 'sonority in the corridor' is pure theatre, reminiscent of Sir Donald Wolfit ruffling the curtain to signal his entrance: 'Let them know you're coming …' For Raymond, the sonorous voice ' … emptied any place, corridor or hall, of any thing but itself. It was the voice of the High Master. It was the 'Old Man'. *Oremus* ('Let us pray') he would boom, but on his lips it meant simply 'pray'. We prayed, that is to say we opened our *Preces*, the Latin prayers which boys had said since before the Reformation, and we mumbled in a chorus six hundred strong...'[10]

One imagines the 'Old Man' to be a charismatic, authoritative individual, a recognisable figure in that age of deference. His name was Frederick William Walker, son of an Irishman, born in London and educated at St. Saviour's Grammar School, Southwark followed by Rugby. After reading Classics at Corpus Christi, Cambridge, Walker became a Fellow and Tutor. Aged thirty he was appointed High Master of Manchester Grammar School, where within two years the improved teaching and subsequent growth of applications obliged him to introduce entrance exams; fifteen years later, pupil numbers had trebled to seven hundred and fifty. Succeeding Herbert Kynaston in 1877, Frederick Walker became the first High Master at St. Paul's in over a century not to be in Holy Orders, which may have been incidental or a nod towards modernisation.

Whatever the expectations, it was under Walker that St. Paul's reputation and intake grew significantly. Britain's exponential growth in population – and arguably also in aspiration – during the late nineteenth century would have increased the desirability to parents of any of the outstanding schools, and Walker's undoubted ability and force of personality had placed St. Paul's high, if not top, of the list. According to Ernest Raymond, he was probably ' ... the last of those nineteenth century headmasters who held it their duty to be formidable to the point of terror. He was the last of the school of Dr. Keate of Eton, and in his day, which was my day, probably the most famous headmaster in England.' Such fame, and the degree to which Walker had become synonymous with the institution was evidenced in a Vanity Fair 'Spy' caricature featuring the High Master, published in June 1902 and captioned simply 'St Paul's School'.

Frederick William Walker
by 'Spy' (Vanity Fair, June 1902)

In 1902 some of Claude's classmates were boarders, but most appeared to have lived within five miles of the school, some as close as South

Kensington. Records of the time include the fathers' occupations, which seem typically professional middle class; retired colonels, stockbrokers, corn merchants, schoolmasters, accountants and dental surgeons. Some boys are listed as 'son of Mrs …' or 'Nephew of …' indicating that the intake was not so thoroughly conventional as might be assumed.

Like most public schools, there was a house system. The day boys' equivalent at St. Paul's were five 'clubs', each named after the master in charge, also referred to as A, B, C, D and E, and Claude was assigned to 'D' or 'Wainwright's' run by Mr. L. D. Wainwright.[11] Claude entered the Classics class with some very able boys, the first few months of which must have been a testing time, his performance scrutinised not only by his masters but also by his father, who would be keen to see his son doing well, in the hope that the following year he might pass the Junior Scholarship examinations to qualify as a Foundationer.[12] The scholarship applications, formally announced in the February 1903 edition of *The Pauline*, looked daunting, with candidates subjected to five days of exams, morning and afternoon, covering Mathematics, Divinity, Greek, Roman & English History, Geography & English Grammar, Latin, Greek, French, Freehand and Geometrical Drawing and Elementary Science. Claude could naturally count on a great deal of input from his father in preparation for this marathon, a prospect he might well have had mixed feelings about. To fail would mean further financial outlay for Thomas Oldfield, but more importantly disappointment that his son was not ascending the academic firmament with quite the trajectory he himself had achieved. For Claude, the possibility of letting his father down hung over him like the sword of Damocles.

It would have required talent, diligence, encouragement, intensive coaching and an element of good luck for Claude to pass, but pass he did, no doubt delighting his father, as well as freeing him from the burden of fees until Claude was seventeen, by which time it was doubtless envisaged he would go up to university.

In July of that same year 1903, Claude received the foretaste of a future rite of passage, attending for the first time an Apposition.[13] Instituted by the Mercers as an assessment of the quality of teaching, appositions had had some serious consequences, as in 1559 when High Master Freeman was removed, officially for lack of learning but more likely for holding the wrong religious views. High Master Charles suffered a similar fate in 1748, with an allegation of threatening to 'pull the Surmaster by the nose

'D' Class, St. Paul's School (Claude: back row, 3rd from left; L. D. Wainwright: front row, middle)

and kick him about the school.' The more serious charge it seems was that on Charles's watch the pupil roll had fallen to a mere thirty-five. Other complaints against masters included accepting fees and gifts to take in boarders, the kind of corruption looked into by the nineteenth century commissions. By Claude's time, the Apposition had evolved to become a celebration of academic success cum speech day, with subject prizes and invited guests. In 1903 Claude would have sat in the gallery, while the 'Eighths' were in the main body of the hall. Only one ticket per pupil was issued, available by written application. One can be confident that Thomas Oldfield secured a ticket, eager to see his son, now a Foundationer no less, at such an important event in the calendar of this revered institution. Meanwhile he awaited the next measure of Claude's progress, his first school report.

*St. Paul's Crest, Fide et Literis,
on Claude's cufflinks.*

1   In 1863, the Metropolitan Railway began the world's first underground railway service
    between Paddington and Farringdon with wooden carriages and steam locomotives.
    This route, when fully extended, was electrified in 1906 and later known as the
    Hammersmith & City line.
2   *Dickens's Dictionary of London*, by Charles Dickens, Jr., 1879: St. Paul's School
    (founded 1512 by John Colet DD, Dean of St. Paul's).
3   *John Colet's Convocation Sermon* (1512) quoted in John C. Olin, *The Catholic
    Reformation* (Fordham University Press, 1992).
4   Source: Mercers' Company website
5   From the statutes of St. Paul's School: *Statuta Paulinae Scholae*
6   High Master is the term used to denote the head teachers of two English independent
    schools: St. Paul's and Manchester Grammar. See A. H. Mead, *A Miraculous Draught
    of Fishes: A History of St Paul's School* (James and James, 1990).
7   Mead, ibid.
8   Ernest Raymond, *Mr Olim* (Cassell, 1961). Raymond (1888-1974) was best known
    for his first novel, *Tell England* (1922). His autobiography was published in two
    volumes: *The Story of My Days, 1888-1922* (1968) followed by *Please You, Draw Near,
    1922-1968* (1969). Liddell Hart (1895-1970) writing to *The Pauline* confirmed that
    the character of Dr. Hodder was based on the High Master during Raymond's time,
    Frederick William Walker; and that Mr. Olim was based on Rev. Horace Dixon Elam,
    Remove Master. Source: King's College, London, Liddell Hart Centre for Military
    Archives.
9   Raymond, ibid.
10 Ibid.
11 In Autumn 1903, the other Clubs were: 'A' Botting's; 'B' Walker's (after Rev. R. J.
    Walker, not High Master Walker); 'C' Gould's; 'E' Mathews'. The Houses were run by
    G. G. Loane.

12   Foundation Scholarships:

An Examination will be held at St. Paul's School, West Kensington, on Tuesday, April 21, 1903, Wednesday, 22, Thursday, 23, Friday, 24, and Monday, 27, for filling up five or more vacancies on the Foundation. The Examinations will commence each day at 10 am and 2 pm. If, from any cause, the date of Examination is changed, notice will be given by advertisement in the newspapers. The Scholarships (open to all boys whether now in the School or not) are divided into two classes, Junior Scholarships and Senior Scholarships. The Junior Scholarships are open to boys of under 15 on April 21 (boys under 12 being eligible, if of marked ability), and are tenable to the age of 17. The Senior Scholarships are open to boys over the age of 15 and under the age of 17 on April 21, and are tenable to the age of 19. Foundation Scholars are exempt from entrance and tuition fees. Candidates for Junior Scholarships are examined in the following subjects: 1. Mathematics; 2. Divinity; Greek, Roman, and English History; Geography and English Grammar; 3. Latin; 4. Greek; 5. French; 6. Freehand and Geometrical Drawing; 7. Elementary Science. Candidates for the Senior Scholarships are examined in the first six of the above subjects and also in: 7. Chemistry and Physics; 8. Linear Perspective.

13   An apposition is a public disputation by scholars; a formal examination by question and answer. Apposition at St. Paul's now takes place in mid-May and has become purely ceremonial, but 'formal examination by question and answer' remains its cornerstone, when some four or five Paulines declaim (usually by delivering a summary of an academic paper) and an invited 'Apposer' judges the quality of each declamation. The ceremony is combined with the award of prizes to those in the Eighth Form. Source: St. Paul's School website.

CHAPTER 4

Fight the Good Fight

His classical work is very fair & he is making steady progress
School Report, July 1907

Tracking down Claude's school report of July 1904, I found his Latin judged to be 'Much improved: translation weak.' Greek was 'Quite satisfactory', French 'Good', English 'v. fair', and Mathematics, 'Very fair'. In summary the pupil was deemed to have, '… not quite come up to expectations. Translation careless. Will spend any length of time over interesting work.'

A less than glowing assessment, though in mitigation, standards at St. Paul's were exacting, the bar in classics, one of the most difficult subjects, set high. It also occurred to me that the 'expectations' stemmed from the reputation of his father. Would the words 'weak' and 'careless' have smarted, made Claude despondent? Through his very engagement with the classical canon he could draw comfort. In Virgil's *Aeneid*, a text Claude would have striven to learn by heart, *Sequiturque patrem non passibus aequis*, 'one who follows his father with unequal or unmatched step', might reassure him he was doing his best to please the pater. Ovid meanwhile has a sage warning against over-reaching: *Medio tutissimus ibis*, 'you will go most safely in the middle'. Claude was showing no sign of flying dangerously near the sun, yet the absorption in what he enjoyed, stories that fired his imagination perhaps, rather than the narrow boundaries of curricula, suggests not quite a maverick, but the glimmerings of an individualistic personality.

Given that the charisma of a teacher can have a huge bearing on any pupil's development, I was curious as to who was influencing Claude at this time. I found that in his Remove year he was taught Classics by the Reverend Horace Dixon Elam. Author Ernest Raymond, who described his classroom at St. Paul's as a 'bare, worn, splintered floor, four rows of chipped and ink-patterned desks, and masters on a dais', created a fictional teacher, almost certainly based on Elam:

a thin and scraggy figure with skin like a withered grape. Sixty now, his hair was still more black than grey, and so was his brief, bristly moustache. He wore always a clerical frockcoat, old and greening and rubbed to a shine that almost reflected the sunlight. His gown was even greener and at one place hung in a frayed rag. His toes, treading the floor, turned so far outward that he seemed splay-footed.[1]

Another Old Pauline, Compton Mackenzie, featured a hauntingly similar character, a Mr. Neech in his novel *Sinister Street*. Beneath Elam's scruffiness though was a mind of steel and a sharp tongue. Sarcasm and rudeness, often delivered in Latin was commonplace, ordering boys to construe with the injunction, '*Tityre tu patulae recubans sub tegmine fagi*' 'Go on you bladder of idiocy! Castigating them with, 'You pockpuddings, you abysmal apes, why couldn't you have learned these lines at home?' Bracing for the lash of Elam's caustic upbraiding, Claude and his classmates might be described by the opening of the Aeneid, Book II: *Conticuere omnes intentique ora tenebant*: 'All hushed, and keeping their rapt gaze upon him.'[2] Whether or not Elam's acerbity concealed the tender heart of a Mr. Chips, it is nevertheless telling that when Raymond held a dinner to celebrate the classics master's seventieth birthday, more than forty former students attended to pay tribute.

Christmas 1904 would have found Thomas Oldfield a happy man.

St. Paul's School (c.1900)

Claude had added Divinity to his studies, and his Latin was improving, with satisfactory progress in French, the report concluding that he was 'working admirably and successfully'. The young man was clearly finding his feet and settling in to life at St. Paul's, with academic achievement complemented by sport, in his second year entering the Novices Boxing Competition Light Weights. The school magazine reported on his preliminary bout against R. T. Brotchie: 'Oldfield fought very pluckily, putting in some good straight lefts. Brotchie knew more, however, and won with points to spare.'[3] Brotchie was destined to lose a bigger fight. After qualifying at The Royal London Hospital, Whitechapel as a surgeon, he worked in Tarbert in Argyllshire, among his duties that of 'Certifying Surgeon' under the Factory and Workshop Acts, and in 1915 was killed in action at the age of twenty-seven.

In 1904, as Claude tested himself in the art of pugilism, his appetite for adventure may have been stirred by the experiences of two Old Paulines reported in that year's magazine. Embarking on a two-month journey from Southampton to Fort Jameson in the east of Northern Rhodesia, the intrepid pair had taken the mail steamer from Cape Town to Durban, then a coasting steamer to the Chinde River, the mouth of the Zambezi. There they boarded the *Princess*, a stern-paddle riverboat, travelling in relative comfort for four days until reaching the Zambezi proper. To skirt the virtually impassable Shire rapids, an overland trek of over sixty miles was then required, followed by a barge to Port Herald (modern day Nsanje in the south of Malawi), where they were carried by *machila* (a hammock hung on poles) by African porters to the more hospitable Shire highlands. Crocodiles and hippo abounded in the lower river, an elephant had been shot providing good meat for the boat crew and tales were told of hungry leopards and ferocious buffalo.[4]

If Claude had read this story, he would have realised that in Africa nothing could be taken for granted; sailing on Lake Nyassa, one of the travellers had, 'never been so ill in all my life, I ain't no sailor bold',[5] while at Fort Jameson in June, 'several people regularly have fires in the evening and this is 13½° south of the equator!' The author of the five-page account concluded self-deprecatingly: 'I

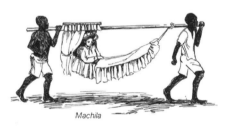

Machila

Machila with carriers. Shirley Sinclair, The Story of Melsetter (M. O. Collins, Salisbury, Rhodesia 1971)

have spun out my tale far longer than I meant, and I will end with an apology'. To a fourteen-year-old boy whose horizons were a few stops on the Metropolitan line, this expedition into the 'dark continent' by two young men from his own school, would surely have fired his imagination on some level.

Claude's third year at St. Paul's, 1905, coincided with a major change, the retirement after twenty-nine years of High Master William Walker. The news, made public in March, lamented the end of an era, 'It would be out of place at present to attempt any estimate of the grievous loss that the School will sustain. The announcement must come as a shock to all friends and well-wishers of St. Paul's'. Walker was to finish that September, and a number of people, some of whom might once have quaked under his rule, were already dewy-eyed at the prospect of his departure. In July, *The Pauline* bore an encomium that Horace himself might have thought purple prose:

> Not even the clear judgment and literary skill of our contributors – to whom we tender our thanks for their work – could fully sum up such a character of High Master … He has seen the masters under him increase in number from six to thirty-six; rank after rank of schoolboys has passed out into the world from moulding of his hands. That there are to-day many men all over the earth who turn with eyes of respect and love to the new School would surely bring joy and gladness to Dean Colet. That we, who may call ourselves the High Master's pupils as proudly as the Victorians spoke of Dr. Arnold, grieve to think that his personality is going from us, must surely be grateful to him, to whose memory we can now only cling with sadness, as to that of a tried but distant friend.[6]

A further tribute from a senior master acknowledged Walker's depth of friendship and encouragement to love learning for its own sake. One anonymous Old Pauline wrote a sonnet in his honour, concluding with the couplet: 'So may you rest as veteran in the sun / Whose work is ended and whose meed begun.'

As A. H. Mead points out, the much-fêted Walker would be a hard act to follow, 'Perhaps it was inevitable that the successor to this gigantic eccentric should seem controversial and rather colourless.' That successor was Rev. Albert Ernest Hillard, arriving at St. Paul's in September 1905 after ten years teaching at Clifton, followed by six as Headmaster of Durham School. Hillard's commitment to scholarship would be seen over the course of his career, in writing and editing numerous educational texts for students, including *A Continuous Narrative of the Life of Christ in the Words of the Four Gospels,* and collaboration on several works with colleague Cecil Botting, including *Elementary Latin Exercises* (1910) and *Graduated Latin Selections* and *Elementary Greek Translation,* both published in the early 1920s.[7]

Equally, Hillard seemed a man of God, tightening the knot of faith and learning with the introduction of Sunday morning school services in Latin, and an annual confirmation service at St. Paul's Cathedral, the first on 9th April 1906. No such ceremony had been held there for twenty years, and the Bishop of London, making up for lost time perhaps, delivered not one but two addresses and confirmed sixty-two boys. High Master Hillard, the Surmaster and Rev. Elam were all robed, the other staff in academic gowns and hoods. The first hymn was 'Fight the Good Fight' and *Veni Creator Spiritus* was sung to the music of Thomas Attwood, an auspicious occasion in the grand setting of the cathedral, and most surely an uplifting and memorable one for sixteen-year old Claude.[8]

One of Claude's most notable fellow pupils was Bernard Montgomery, later Field Marshal and 1st Viscount Montgomery of Alamein. Although a year senior, Montgomery became a good friend with whom Claude often shared a desk for certain classes.[9] Born in Kennington in November 1887, Bernard was the fourth of nine children of Anglo-Irish Anglican priest Rev. Henry Montgomery and his wife Maud. In 1901, after eight years as Bishop of Tasmania, Henry became Secretary of the Society for the Propagation of the Gospel (SPG) and the family returned to London. Young Bernard arrived at St. Paul's in 1902 after a stint at King's School, Canterbury, and enjoyed sport, particularly cricket, rugby and swimming. He did not distinguish himself academically and left in 1906, though remained a private in the Cadet Corps before going on to Sandhurst two years later. A respect for St. Paul's would endure however: 'If you want to work, there is no better school.' Thirty-eight years later he would return to work there again, setting up a planning HQ for the Allied invasion of Europe.

Paul Nash, born on 11th May 1889, five days younger than Claude, had come as a capitation scholar in January 1903, left after one term, and was readmitted in September 1904. The son of a successful lawyer, Nash's home life was tough, possibly explaining the hiatus in his schooling. His mother suffered mental instability and she would die in an asylum when her son was just twenty-one. After failing his exams Nash enrolled at the

Chelsea Polytechnic in 1906, thereafter the Slade. The contrast with Montgomery would become marked during the dramatic times ahead. 'Monty', a soldier to his fingertips, with a blunt approach to leadership and an allegedly obtuse one to diplomacy, seems unlikely to have shared the artistic, or simply human, response that informed Nash's stark depictions of the 1914-18 conflict.

Claude now a middleweight, continued to box. After a walkover in the 1906 Spring Term semi-final (W. de B. Wood had scratched), he fought H. H. R. Gresham, a Wainwright housemate in the final: 'Gresham has the makings of a very powerful boxer; he stands well, is quick with his hands, and hits very hard. Oldfield did his best, but had no chance with him.'[10] Claude's opponent might have been expected to fight in the St. Paul's Boxing Day later that year, but *The Pauline* noted that 'Gresham did not enter, after his promising performance in the Novices'. Perhaps Gresham was resting on his laurels. Claude's third year report suggested he was doing likewise in Latin: 'he has the ability to be higher' and 'I think him easy going.' Claude's overall performance though seems by no means mediocre, his French being 'very fair', Divinity & English good and Mathematics improved to 'satisfactory'. By July 1906 he was considered to be 'An able boy who has done very fairly; but he might take a better place without much difficulty.'

One cannot point to sport or any other activity that was draining Claude's attention. After his defeat by Gresham, he may have abandoned boxing. With no mention in the reports of rugby or cricket, Claude may have started to get interested in rowing, and in September 1906 might have seen a renowned Harvard squad take on a Cambridge crew stroked by D. C. R. Stuart that had beaten Oxford earlier that year. Ernest Raymond in *The Story of My Days* never forgot looking towards Barnes Bridge and 'the flash in the sun of a light blue oar' as Cambridge led the way.[11]

Claude's fourth year Latin was 'Rather good; nice touch in his composition'. 'His classical work is very fair & he is making steady progress. His English, though improving, seems to indicate want of reading.' At the 1907 Apposition on 31st July, Claude would have been very familiar with the proceedings. Hillard had now completed two academic years, and welcomed several distinguished guests.[12] There were numerous achievements to mention; one former pupil with paintings in the Royal Academy, another a Senior Wrangler at Cambridge, a first place in the higher Civil Service, successful careers begun at the Royal Naval College and Sandhurst and several scholarships to universities.[13] Cyril Picciotto was awarded the Governors' Prize for Greek Verse and *proxime accessit* for the High Master's Prize for Latin Elegiacs.[14] Picciotto would have a successful legal career and later write a history of St. Paul's, published in 1939.[15]

The Apposition play that year was *The Frogs*, a socio-political comedy by Aristophanes in which the old and new orders vie for acceptance.[16] *The Pauline* was pleased that 'after an age of dullness impenetrable, the Apposition play had begun to reassert its position.'[17] The magazine considered the piece a good choice for the visitors and less advanced pupils: 'Profiting by the ignorance of Greek among the majority of the audience, the players made the most of the action.' *The Pauline* also reviewed a new play in London, *Attila: A Tragedy in Four Acts* by Laurence Binyon, OP (1881-88). *The Spectator* reviewer admired the verse, but was uncertain about the structure.[18] Binyon would achieve universal recognition with his beautiful and moving poem of August 1914, *For the Fallen*.[19]

Hillard used the 1907 Apposition to discuss the perennial issue of home versus school in the educational equation. Talking up the merits of the recently introduced option of weekly boarding at St. Paul's, he expressed the hope that it would strike a balance between the undeniably important influence of a boy's family, and the opportunity for heightened academic focus when away from it. Claude, still a dayboy, returned to St. Paul's in September 1907 for his last academic year. The school captain was E. G. Mächtig, Claude's classmate, whose Latin it appears might have suffered from the extra responsibility: 'Has kept too narrowly to his subject; and has not been at his best this term.' Machtig's star would ascend though, to a knighthood for services in the Dominion Office, covering Tanganyika and Australia. L. D. Wainwright continued to preside over 'D' Club, captained by P. S. Woolf, another of Claude's fellow Classics pupils, a Jewish boy, whose older brother Leonard became a Cadet in the Ceylon Civil Service and husband of Virginia Woolf.[20] Under High Master Walker, St. Paul's had begun to admit non-Christians, and several of Claude's contemporaries were among the brightest and best of their generation of the Jewish intelligentsia with whom his father was closely associated.

So far as I could ascertain Claude held no special responsibility in his final year. Summer term started on 6th May 1908, and after the Ascension Day holiday and a two-day Whitsuntide break, finished with the Apposition on 29th July. Among the new boys due in September was a neighbour of the Oldfields, Victor Gollancz, later the publisher and philanthropist. Claude's final report suggests he had grown bored with school, familiarity breeding perhaps not contempt but a loss of steam: 'Clever but no enthusiasms. Uneven worker, tho' he has perhaps worked at his books' for Latin. Greek showed uneven composition and was 'never first class; his other work is fairly sound, but lacks sustained interest.' His progress in French appeared lacklustre: 'Dull; no sort of originality. Though some knowledge.' In summary it was felt that Claude had 'made some improvement, but his work remains uneven. He will certainly stagnate unless he extends his interests & his reading: his abilities are sound.'

After over four years at one of the finest schools in England, these were not the kind of parting remarks to send Claude, or his father, dancing into the street. At the same time the boy was far from written off, and what resonates most is a sense of untapped potential. If there were some enemy of promise what was it – indolence, lack of self-belief? We should not discount the effect of puberty. After four years in the frock-coated confines of a Christian school, the boy had become a man, looking for change and the freedom to explore relationships. It seemed all might be in the offing, when Claude learned he had passed the examinations to read Classics at Trinity Hall, Cambridge, starting in the Michaelmas Term of 1908.

[1]   Ernest Raymond, *Mr Olim*, (Cassell, 1961)
[2]   *Conticuere omnes intentique ora tenebant / inde toro pater Aeneas sic orsus ab alto*: All were hushed, and kept their rapt gaze upon him; then from his raised couch father Aeneas thus began. Translated by H. R. Fairclough.
[3]   *The Pauline*, No. 147, July 1905
[4]   Ibid., No. 143, December 1904, p 221
[5]   'I ain't no sailor bold, and I never was upon the sea.' (Traditional sea shanty)
[6]   *The Pauline*, ibid.
[7]   Bolchazy-Carducci Publishers, Inc., USA
[8]   *Veni Creator Spiritus* ('Come Creator Spirit') attributed to Rabanus Maurus in the ninth century. When the original Latin text is used, it is normally sung in Gregorian chant. As an invocation of the Holy Spirit, it is sung when celebrating the sacrament of Confirmation. Thomas Attwood (1765-1838) was an English composer and organist.
[9]   Discussion with Roy Broad, Claude's nephew by marriage, November 2015.
[10] *The Pauline*, April 1906, p 36
[11] Raymond, *The Story of My Days: An Autobiography 1888-1922* (Cassell, 1968)
[12] *The Pauline*, October 1907
[13] The Senior Wrangler was the top mathematics undergraduate at Cambridge, the person who had achieved the highest overall mark among the Wranglers, students

who gained first-class degrees in mathematics. The position was once regarded as 'the greatest intellectual achievement attainable in Britain'.

[14] *proxime accessit*: runner up

[15] Cyril Moses Picciotto (1888-1940), son of Lelio Raffaele Giacomo Picciotto and Mary Miriam (di Isaac) Picciotto (née Benoliel). On admission to the school, the records show '*Picciotto*, Cyril Moses (July 28, 1888), son of Mrs., 54 Warrington Crescent' (in Maida Vale).

[16] *The Frogs* was performed at the Lenaia, one of the Festivals of Dionysus in Athens, in 405 BC. The play tells the story of the god Dionysus who, despairing of the state of Athens' tragedians, travels to Hades to bring the playwright Euripedes back from the dead.

[17] *The Pauline*, No. 162, October 1907

[18] *Attila* at His Majesty's Theatre: *The Spectator* 7 September 1907.

[19] Including the best-known verse:

> They shall grow not old, as we that are left grow old:
> Age shall not weary them, nor the years condemn.
> At the going down of the sun and in the morning,
> We will remember them.

[20] Leonard Sidney Woolf (1880-1969), husband of Virginia Woolf, was a political theorist, author, publisher and civil servant. Attended St. Paul's 1894-99, before winning a classical scholarship to Trinity College, Cambridge.

CHAPTER 5

Blade on the Feather

A straight oar looks bent in the water.
What matters is not merely that we see things,
but how we see them

Michel de Montaigne (1533-92)[1]

Claude went up to Cambridge in the sixth year of the long Edwardian summer. The supremacy of the Empire had been bolstered by the launch in 1906 of the first of the Dreadnoughts, a new super battleship designed to outrun and outgun any rival. The burgeoning middle classes, secure within the precious diadem of their island, and following the example of their fun-loving monarch, lived above their means in the pursuit of pleasure. The lower orders had to be grateful for what they got, or in the case of the striking Belfast dockworkers who asked for more than ten shillings a week, be shot at.

Many found pleasure in nature. Lovingly recording the flora and fauna of the British hedgerows in words and pictures, Edith Holden's *Country Diary of an Edwardian Lady*, never intended for publication, became a posthumous bestseller seven decades later. While collecting flowers at Kew in 1920, Edith had fallen in the Thames and drowned.

Brought up in inner London, close to Paddington station, Claude must have found the rural surroundings of Cambridge pleasing. Then there was the whole picturesque social side of varsity life – punting on the Cam in boaters and blazers, parties, balls and theatre trips, with aristocrats and Indian princes among his peers.

Trinity Hall was older even than St. Paul's, having been founded in 1354 by Bishop Bateman of Norwich to promote the study of canon and civil law, possibly also to replenish the stock of clergyman and lawyers wiped out in the Black Death.[2] It seems the creation of Cambridge colleges was almost an annual event around that time, with Pembroke Hall, Gonville

Hall and Corpus Christi starting life roughly concurrently, preceded only by Peterhouse (1280-84), Michaelhouse, Clare Hall and King's Hall (later merged in a new foundation). One hopes that Claude felt the same joy on arrival as Thomas Tusser did in the sixteenth century:

> From London hence, to Cambridge thence
> With thanks to thee, O Trinitee
> That to thy Hall, surpassing all,
> I got at last;
> There joy I felt, there trim I dwelt,
> There Heaven from Hell I shifted well,
> With learned men, a number then,
> The time I passed.[3]

Trinity Hall is tucked away behind Gonville & Caius, down Trinity Lane, or for those who know the short cut, down Senate House Passage. The recent history of the college, edited by Peter Pagnamenta, is aptly entitled *The Hidden Hall*.[4] There are not the grand vistas of King's or the romantic facades of Corpus, but Pevsner describes the Front Court with its pleasing regularities as 'comfortable and phlegmatic'.[5]

Trinity Hall

Claude in Trinity Hall 'colours'

Claude soon established himself within Trinity Hall's rowing fraternity, the most successful Cambridge college at that time, in spite of having relatively few students from which to draw. His college had a reputation to keep up; the Hall 1st Eight had retained its place at the 'Head of the River' in the 1908 May Races, followed by two Hall men winning the Coxless Pairs at the Summer Olympics at Henley that year.[6] At the Trial Eights for the Cambridge boat in the Michaelmas Term, the winning crew had three Hall men; C. M. Stuart, C. P. Cooke and G. D. Compston (cox), who would steer Claude's boat the following summer.

Trinity Hall continued to dominate Cambridge rowing, contributing five to the University Boat Race crew in March 1909, although sadly Cambridge were beaten.[7] In the May term, the Hall entered a junior Eight for the Thames Cup at Henley with Claude rowing at (3), the event that year being held over four days, starting on Monday 4th July.[8] The famous stretch of river can be serene on a summer's day, but alas it was not so for Claude's first regatta. Cook says it all: 'The weather was generally very bad except on the last day; when it did not rain it blew.'[9] In Trinity Hall's first race on the Monday against Corpus Christi, they were behind for most of the first half, before eventually winning a close race by half a length.[10]

Claude's Eight had to row their next heat later the same day, against Anglian Boat Club, which that morning had beaten Jesus College, Cambridge by three-quarters of a length. Anglian went well from the start, gaining a lead of three-quarters of a length at the quarter mile and, although Claude's crew tried to fight back, Anglian kept their advantage, winning by three-quarters of a length.[11]

Style has always been important at Henley and perceived breaches of etiquette, on and off the water, were liable to censure. *Vanity Fair*, previewing the 1906 Regatta, expressed concern at the increasing dominance of foreign crews, not always considered strictly amateur.[12] When the Belgians then won the Grand Challenge Cup, Trinity Hall's defeat was attributed to the segmented British club system. The Belgians, it was alleged, were not:

> members of a single rowing club, but the pick of the best amateur oarsmen in Belgium – a sort of Leander Club, in fact. They had worked themselves up to a machine-like perfection in their own peculiar style. As regards that style it is not the first time that it has been seen at Henley. It is based on the principle that the long English swing and the application of strength necessitated in a sharp beginning exhaust a crew.[13]

Two heats in a single day was a tough baptism for Claude, compounded by the disappointment of his crew losing on their second outing, but to row at Henley in his first year must have been a thrill, and encountering sportsmen who challenged the ethos of the 'amateur', an education of another kind.

In that May of 1909, Claude also took part in regattas at Maidenhead and Marlow, sometimes in a Coxed Four, and relaxed with friends, punting on The Backs, the weather thankfully better than at Henley. After the exams, came the balls, plays and concerts, the normally sequestered college opened to the outside world, and family, including sisters if one was lucky enough to have them, which Claude was not, were allowed up. There was also the possibility of romance, and for those who took a girl out on the river and wanted to move things along, the *Eights Week* magazine in 1909 suggested a useful ploy: to knock a hole through the bottom of the punt, so that 'when it sinks, she is sure to embrace you.'[14] Alternatively, budding suitors were advised to simply bide their time, for 'the chaperone, if there is one (bad luck), is sure to go to sleep – soon.' Whether Claude

Friends at Maidenhead, 1909

Punting on a lovely summer's day, The Backs, Cambridge

Coxed four at Marlow Regatta, 1909

Trinity Hall, 1st May Boat, 1910

needed either leaking punts or sleepy chaperones is uncertain, but the available evidence gives us no clues as to whether he had a special amour at this time.

When the new term started in October 1909, Claude gained his 'seat' in the Trinity Hall 1st Eight, rowing at (4). Sidney Swann, who arrived at the Hall that term, made an immediate impact, no doubt helped by his father's illustrious rowing career there some years earlier. In the Lent Races, '... stroked by S.E. Swann as a freshman, (they) showed very varying form. On the second night they caught First Trinity in the Long Reach, but on the third night they were re-bumped at about the same place, and on the last night they rowed over.'[15] In the May Races, the Hall was bumped by Pembroke, and since being 'Head of the River' in 1907 and 1908, had dropped to fourth place – the lowest in twenty years.

Henley Regatta in 1910 saw a poor showing from Cambridge; ten Eights were entered for the Grand, the Ladies and the Thames, none successful. The Hall sent only a Four, which won both the Visitors and the Wyfolds, comprising Claude's fellow oarsmen, W. J. Davy, C. M. Stuart, R. S. Adams and S. E. Swann as Stroke.[16] Claude was a year older than Sidney Swann, but through rowing the two men would have been well acquainted. Swann was one of the most impressive oarsmen of his generation, possibly second only to Robert Bourne who stroked Oxford to victory over four years from 1909 to 1912. Both oarsmen were honoured with caricatures in *Vanity Fair* magazine, Swann on 3rd April 1912 as

S. E. Swann, 'The Light Blue Stroke'
(Vanity Fair, 3 April 1912)

R. C. Bourne, 'A Good Stroke'
(Vanity Fair, 29 March 1911)

'The Light Blue Stroke', who 'As captain of the "Hall" Boat Club he is a great success, and absolutely indefatigable in his attempts to teach the principles of Cambridge rowing to youthful aspirants.'

Swann was the sole Cambridge man in the Leander crew (the others from Magdalen, Oxford) of 1912 who lost to the Sydney Rowing Club in the Grand, only to beat them three weeks later at the Stockholm Olympics, followed by a win against Bourne's New College Eight in the final. After graduating, Swann would enter the church, serve as a chaplain in WWI then return as chaplain to Trinity Hall in the 1920s helping to restore the fortunes of Cambridge rowing.[17]

Did Claude row in the Boat Race and gain a 'Blue'? Family stories were told of Claude being a 'half blue', but these are normally only awarded for minor sports at Cambridge, and as Claude appears to have concentrated solely on rowing, this seems unlikely. There is no hard evidence and, despite many photos in Claude's albums of rowing and of club dinners, we must conclude that he did not quite make the Cambridge crew, although possibly he rowed in one of the trial Eights.[18] His enthusiasm and commitment for Cambridge rowing is not in any doubt, and it seems highly likely that he would have been on the Tideway at Putney in both

On the Tideway: Cambridge make their first appearance at Putney

1910 and 1911 to support the crew as they prepared to take on Oxford. Unfortunately, this coincided with a good run by Oxford, when they won every race from 1909 to 1913.

It was, and I'm pretty sure still is, the habit of many students to put in sufficient academic work in their first year to pass their exams, relax in the second, and generally procrastinate during the third, before desperately cramming for their finals. Claude did well enough in his first year to gain 2nd Class in the University Examinations, and on 21st June 1909 he was 'Elected to Foundation Scholarships – for Classics – C. P. Oldfield £40', a pleasing achievement, and one sure to have gratified his father. The strong rowing record then speaks for itself, but his final year seems to have included a good deal of fun, including the Michaelmas Term when he was invited to play in a football friendly, 'The Hall' v. 'Miss Gibbs'. *The Daily News* of 11th October 1910 reported:

> The worse half of 'Our Miss Gibbs' – we refer, of course, to the male portion – met certain members of Trinity Hall in a friendly game of Association this afternoon. The ladies of the company watched the play, or hobbled about the field in skirts that reminded one of persons attempting to walk in new shoes with the string uncut, and talked vivaciously to leading lights in the undergrad world whom they had known for some four hours. The ladies cheered on their team in shrill little voices, and laughed funny little silvery, ripply laughs, or sang little snatches of their parts. They even kicked footballs about, a dangerous proceeding in a hobble skirt, till the playing members of the Hall positively ached to stop their game and allow the owners of the fairy feet to kick holes in their hearts.

Despite this distraction, however, the game was fast and furious. 'The Hall' had underrated the capabilities of Mary's dudes, and throughout the whole of the first half they had much the worse of it, though there was no scoring. In the second half once or twice Slithers (aka Mr J. Leopold) who kept goal for Miss Gibbs, had stopped one or two shots with great adroitness, but beyond that had no work to do, and then the manager of the company, Mr. Edmund Nogg Beresford, got away, much to the delight of the ladies, and scored. The game ended without further score, and so we have to record a further triumph of the dear little lady from Yorkshire and the sad downfall of 'The Hall'. But the defeat brings no bitterness with it, and means only that Miss Gibbs will get a bigger reception than ever at the New Theatre this evening.[19]

Celebrated oarsmen Swann and Stuart were not so skilled on a football pitch it seems, as to lift the Hall's performance. Their opponents in the jolly kick-about were the male cast members of an amateur production of *Our Miss Gibbs*, a musical comedy playing at the New Theatre, Cambridge.[20] The West End production had already been a great success, notching up 636 performances from its opening at the Gaiety Theatre in January 1909. Possibly the Hall men, in the good-natured spirit of the occasion, allowed the win, though the local newspaper's humorous disparagement of the 'Miss Gibbs' ladies, whom it did not seem to consider might actually play even in a fun match, shows something of the uphill struggle of the suffragettes to be taken seriously at this time.

Actors are usually lively company, and for both sides the occasion was doubtless filled with hilarity and a fair amount of flirtatiousness all round. Meanwhile the Miss Gibbs players were not the only flamboyant characters Claude would meet at Cambridge.

---

[i] The title of the chapter is from the first verse of the Eton Boating Song, written by a master, William Johnson, for the 'Fourth of June' in 1863. The music was composed by Captain Algernon Drummond whilst serving with The Rifle Brigade in Lahore, India.

> Jolly boating weather,
> And a hay harvest breeze,
> Blade on the feather,
> Shade off the trees,

> Swing swing together,
> With your bodies between your knees,
> Swing swing together,
> With your bodies between your knees

2   Charles Crawley, *Trinity Hall: The History of a Cambridge College, 1350-1975* (Trinity Hall, Cambridge, 1976)

3   From *Map & Directions* (Trinity Hall)

4   Peter Pagnamenta (ed), *The Hidden Hall: Portrait of a Cambridge College* (Third Millennium Publishing, 2004)

5   Jonathan Steinberg (in *The Hidden Hall*) quoting Pevsner, *Cambridgeshire* (2nd ed) (Buildings of England: Penguin, 1970)

6   The Fourth Olympiad, Official Report, The British Olympic Association

7   Sources: Stephen Cooper on *Hear the Boat Sing blog*, 2012 and Henry Bond, *A History of the Trinity Hall Boat Club* (W. Heffer & Sons, 1930) p 138

8   'Rowing at (3)' refers to the position in the boat, the 'seat' that the oarsman occupies. The convention is to number the seats from bow to stern, so the rower closest to the front is 'bow seat' or 'bow', the next is '2-seat' or (2), etc. The seat nearest the stern is Stroke. The Stroke can, of course, be seen by all the crew. The Thames Challenge Cup was instituted for eight-oars in 1868, and attracted entries from home and overseas crews of 'club', rather than 'Grand', standard (Henley Royal Regatta website).

9   T.A. Cook, *Rowing at Henley* (OUP, 1919)

10   THIRD HEAT

Bucks Station—*Trinity Hall, Cambridge*: C. C. Dickens 10st 6lb.; M. Nicholson, 11st. 8lb.; C. P. Oldfield, 12st. 7lb.; R. R. Thornley, 11st.; R. S. Adams, 13st. 3lb.; G. G. C. Pigott, 11st. 10lb.; W. J. Davy, 12st.; T. Gilbert (str.), 10st. 10lb.; G. D. Compston (cox.), 9st. 2lb.

Berks Station. —*Corpus Christi College, Cambridge* : E. S. P. K. James, 10st 2lb.; C. J. Hunter, 10st. 7lb.; J. de C. Pook, 12st. 4lb.; M. H. C. Kelham, 11st. 4lb.; C. C. Evans, 11st. 12lb.; A. W Ritchie, 12st. 9lb.; R. A. Leakey, 10st. 9lb.; L. T. Watkins (str.), 11st.; F. L. Cassidi (cox.), 9st. 1lb.

Corpus were rather quicker off the mark, rowing 20 and 39 in the half and minute respectively, and Hall 19 and 38. Corpus led slightly up Temple Island, and were a half-length ahead at the quarter mile. Hall increased their stroke, and were only a quarter-length behind at the half mile, and level at Fawley Court Boathouse (time, 3min. 43sec.). It was a fine race onward, Hall rowing the faster stroke of 36 to Corpus's 34, the first named having a small advantage at the mile. They kept their lead and spurted well at the finish, winning a good race by half a length in 7min. 45sec. Cook, ibid., p 171

11   THIRTEENTH HEAT

Bucks Station – Anglian B.C.   1
Berks Station – Trinity Hall, Cambridge   0

Anglian, rowing in their Belgian style, rowed 23 and 43 in the first half and minute respectively, Hall doing 19 and 37. Anglian went away from the start, having half a length at the top of the Island and three-quarters at the quarter-mile post. Anglian were still rowing the fast stroke of 38, and had gained a few more feet at the half mile.

They reached Fawley in 3min. 41sec., rowing 37 to Hall's 34. The positions did not change much to the end of the race, although Hall spurted below the mile, and went up a little. Anglian managed to keep their advantage, winning by three-quarters of a length in 7min. 44sec.

[12] *Vanity Fair* (4 July 1906) supported keeping Henley confined to English 'amateurs'.

[13] Woodgate in *Vanity Fair* (11 July 1906)

[14] From Thomas Weber, *Our Friend 'The Enemy': Elite Education in Britain and Germany Before World War I* (Stanford University Press, 2008)

[15] Bond, *Trinity Hall Boat Club*, p 139

[16] Bond, ibid, p 140

[17] Henry Bond believed that Swann 'well and truly laid the foundation of several winning crews since the War (WWI), and did much by his coaching to keep the right principles of rowing alive in the Hall'. Bond, ibid, p xxiv.

[18] Claude's album contains a photo entitled 'Cambridge on their first appearance at Putney' taken by Central News. The photo is probably from 1910, possibly 1911.

[19] *The Daily News* reports that the teams were 'Our Miss Gibbs' – Leopold (Slithers), Darrell (Earl of St. Ives), Cavendish, Gray, Goldey, Lane (dudes), Beresford (manager), Burnaby (Hon. Hughie Pierrepoint), Adams and Rowell (substitutes). Trinity Hall – Stuart, Swann, Russell, Adams, Bavey, Oldfield, Armstrong, Giles, Paget, Samson and Ayliffe.

[20] *Our Miss Gibbs* was an Edwardian musical comedy in two acts by 'Cryptos' and James T. Tanner, with lyrics by Adrian Ross and Percy Greenbank; music by Ivan Caryll and Lionel Monckton. Produced by George Edwardes, it opened at the Gaiety Theatre in London on 23 January 1909 and ran for an extremely successful 636 performances, starring Gertie Millar, Edmund Payne and George Grossmith, Jr. The show also had a short Broadway run in 1910.

CHAPTER 6

Marvellous Parties

*Trinity Hall is keeping it silly and relaxed with
fancy dress allowed and encouraged*
                    May Balls Guide (Cambridge, 2017)

Cambridge's theatrical focus was the Footlights, the student company that had been putting on plays since the early 1880s. Theatricality though was not confined to the stage; an equally stimulating time could be had joining in the university debates and mock trials. The *Cambridge* magazine reported from Trinity Hall on 10th November 1910 that 'the debating clubs are busier than ever in discussing the great questions of the moment, and their presidents, S. Adams of the "Owls" and Mr Fraser of the "Black and Whites" are to be congratulated.' A week later it was announced that the 'Owls' and the 'Black and Whites' had agreed to a joint mock trial, and that the two counsels were busy preparing their cases and stocking their witnesses with the necessary lies. The 'cause célèbre' was a divorce case involving the Hon. Vere de Vere. On 10th December, *The Review* gave its own verdict:

> The Mock Trial was a great success. The principal characters of Miss Raybriele Gay and Mrs. Atholton were very well carried out by P. Rodocanachi and Mostyn-Owen; while B. Landsberg, as the Hotel Proprietor, Lockwood, as the Hon. Vere de Vere, and Woodhouse, as the capable guardian, were excellent. Trusted, as the counsel for the plaintiff, conducted his case excellently, and should take care of his gift of oratory. The defence was conducted excellently also by C. M. Stuart and A. P. Cox, while his honour 'me lud' was ably impersonated by S. Adams, who together with Davy, as usher, wielding a formidable club, kept splendid order. Only the plaintiff's cause was finished, the court adjourning until next Sunday to hear the defence.

The Mock Trial (Claude, 5th from left, back row)

One can imagine much high-spirited playacting and boisterous laughter, all the ingredients of a convivial dramatic society, and demanding little in the way of rehearsals. From my investigations, it seems that Claude was well acquainted with at least two of the cast of the mock trial, having attended the grand occasion of Bertie Landsberg's 21st birthday party in 1910, along with fellow Hall students Paolo Rodocanachi and Ronald Firbank. Landsberg, born in Brazil to parents of European and North American descent and blessed with good looks and charm, was an old Harrovian. He was said to have found his vocation in life by the age of

Bertie Landsberg's 21st Party (Claude, 3rd from left)

eleven, which was the study and pursuit of art and beauty in all its forms. Landsberg made a wide range of friends at Trinity Hall and gained a place in the college 3rd Eight, rowing at (7). Landsberg and Rodocanachi seemed quickly drawn to one another, after Cambridge becoming well known among the cognoscenti as a couple, and part of composer Roger Quilter's circle, many of whom were undoubtedly gay.

Rodocanachi took up art criticism, and lectured on the music of Leo Ornstein at the Sorbonne. As a painter and designer of furniture his creations had enduring appeal, a pair of 'Rodo' armchairs, 1939, recently auctioned at Christie's New York, fetched $68,750.[1] Landsberg, drawn by Picasso and photographed by Lord Snowden, was described as a dilettante and poet.[2] After deciding to marry Dorothea, in later life he became better known for his exquisite restoration of the grand Italian house *Villa Foscari* on the Brenta Canal at La Malcontenta near Venice.[3] Bruce Chatwin visited La Malcontenta in the early 1960s, and it became clear that Landsberg had a great impact on the budding writer, teaching him that 'works of art, if they are to live, should never be bought or sold, but given or exchanged. This, to a boy flogging pictures at Sotheby's, was news.'

Landsberg's 'art for art's sake' ethos, echoed in some respects the views of a student at the Hall some forty years before him. Edward Carpenter was a proselytiser for sexual freedom and the simple life, his Rousseau-like *Civilisation, Its Cause and Cure*, advocating a return to pastoral

La Malcontenta

sensibilities.[5] At Trinity Hall he had met fellow student Edward Anthony Beck, whom he would recall with great fondness,

> with his head full of rhymes and verses, which he had written since he was a boy of eight or ten, to the wonderment and delight of his widower father, who prophesied in no uncertain tone, a nook in Westminster Abbey for his poet son. Beck was a bright, capable fellow, with a slight stoop, and a stammer, and a good-humoured way of laughing at his own oddities. He took the University by surprise by carrying off, in his first year, the prize poem on Dante. At the time I mention he and I chummed together a good deal—indeed there was a touch of romance in our attachment—we compared literary notes, went abroad together once or twice, and after he was made a Fellow, had rooms adjoining each other, and spent many and many an evening in common.[6]

The fondness then turns to regret that his friend's

> vein of poetic feeling and romance, possibly too soon ripe, ran itself out, and he never carried on this line of production or published anything. His mind, perhaps from the same cause, took on a slightly cynical cast; he lapsed into the ordinary channels of lecturing and coaching, then married and had a large family, and so gave himself up to the work-a-day routine of College life.[7]

Carpenter's note of disdain for 'the ordinary channels' of life may of course have been sharpened by his intimacy with Beck. The latter's termination of their relationship hurt Carpenter, who for a while sought solace in the hedonism of the Parisian *demi-monde*.[8] After graduation and attempting to conform to Victorian notions of propriety by becoming a curate, he taught the working class in the north of England, appreciating 'the grimy and oil-besmeared figure of a stoker' and 'the thick-thighed hot coarse-fleshed young bricklayer with a strap around his waist.'[9]

Edward Beck meanwhile flourished at Trinity Hall, having been Master for six years when Claude came up in 1908. His apparent respect for Beck is evident in a postcard sent to his mother.[10] Admiration seems warranted: born at Castle Rising, north Norfolk, and a classical scholar at Bishop's Stortford School, Beck had succeeded the long reign of Henry Latham, a generous benefactor to the college. Beck made his own mark, becoming a fellow in 1871, with scholarly achievements including

Edward Beck, Master of Trinity Hall

Claude writing home, November 1910

editorship of a Euripides play, and a reputation according to Crawley, as a shrewd and humorous man, who gave long and loyal service.[11] There were certain authoritarian tendencies, such as keeping during his time as Assistant and then Senior Tutor, a log of misdeeds that included 'speaking to young ladies to whom one is not related', a crime punishable by gating and fining, maintaining the sense of his college as a male preserve. Beck's proclivities, prior to and possibly concurrent with his marriage, may explain the gravitation of artistic young men with homosexual tendencies, such as Bertie Landsberg, to Trinity Hall during his time.

Ronald Firbank, socially awkward and given to hysterical laughter, was described by Crawley as a 'seemingly incongruous figure … the grandson of a working miner, who became a wealthy railway contractor'.[12] Geoff Dibb, who has studied the life of Oscar Wilde, describes how Wilde's son Vyvyan Holland once spotted the famously effete Firbank – he seemed barely capable of sustaining life (he took in little but air and alcohol) – dressed in sporting kit.[13] When the astonished Vyvyan questioned him, Firbank said he had been playing football. 'Rugby or soccer?' asked Vyvyan. 'Oh, I don't remember' replied Firbank. He did though occasionally get a place in the Trinity Hall 2nd Boat. Firbank's attitude to Cambridge

Firbank's Rooms at Trinity Hall[15]

seems largely one of indolence, since he 'never passed or even sat for any examination.'[14]

Firbank was two generations from the pits, but seems to have travelled louchely, cultivating a camp and bibulous lifestyle akin to that of Waugh's Sebastian Flyte, the dipsomaniac who struggles to escape his mother's stifling Catholicism, a faith that the openly homosexual Firbank eventually embraced, under the influence of Robert Hugh Benson.[16] Yet this miner's grandson would leave his mark, writing eight short but resonant novels, partly inspired by the London aesthetes of the 1890s and consisting largely of dialogue, on the themes of religion, social climbing and sexuality. Like the fictional Flyte, ill health and drink finally caught up with Firbank, and in 1926 he died alone in a hotel room in Rome. Although a catholic convert, Firbank was buried in a protestant cemetery until later re-interred.[17]

Whether Claude could ever have been described as an aesthete is, I feel, debatable. There were certainly times, both at home and at Cambridge, when he would have come under the influence of older, decadent individuals of the kind depicted in fellow Old Pauline Compton Mackenzie's *Sinister Street*. As for the spectrum of Claude's sexuality, I can only surmise. At Cambridge, apart from the interregnum for the May Balls, the college authorities went to considerable lengths to keep females away from the campus, which for most students meant abstinence or taking up with town girls or prostitutes, these options being deemed infra dig. Undoubtedly many of Claude's friends were gay, such relationships being not uncommon in the Cambridge (or Oxford) colleges at that time. In 1907, Erich Bethe had written on the openness of same sex affairs in ancient Greece, but other scholars cite homosexuality as the preserve of aristocrats, a gratifying view perhaps for academics of similar inclination.

By way of some contrast Edward Carpenter's *The Intermediate Sex* looked at Eros as a great leveller: 'Perhaps the true democracy rests, more firmly than anywhere else, on a sentiment which easily passes the bounds of class and caste.'[18] Carpenter also used the term 'Uranian', found in Plato's Symposium as an ancient Greek term for homosexuals, and proposed that the word denote a third gender, a female psyche in a male body, sexually attracted to men. If Carpenter believed that physical relations between the classes could bring about social equality, he would perhaps have been rather disappointed at the empirical evidence to the contrary. The exploitation of Claude's grandmother by a landed gent had brought her scant material benefit, let alone a class revolution.

Edward Carpenter, c.1895 (photograph by Fred Holland Day)

Nevertheless, Edward Carpenter's book would play a significant part in sexual politics, his views now being seen as fundamental to the LGBT (Lesbian, gay, bisexual and transgender) movement. Published the year before Claude's arrival at Trinity Hall, and written by a former student and once close friend of the Master, it would be surprising if copies were not circulating. Whether or not Claude read *The Intermediate Sex*, its ideas – free relationships, crossing class divides, affinity with the natural world – would inevitably have filtered through to him.

How would Claude fare in his final year? The challenge was considerable, the examination syllabus set by the University Ordinances in 1908 demanding unprepared translations from both Latin and Greek, and students required an understanding of Greek and Latin prose and verse based on a possible nineteen classical sources. After Claude's tolerably respectable Second Class at the end of his second year, his final results in the Classical Tripos of 1911 were undeniably disappointing: Third Class, Division 2, and out of 102 students, he was close to the bottom, only nine others getting the lowest grade of Third Class, Division 3, in many people's eyes simply an attendance certificate.[19]

Dazzled by Cambridge's colourful social scene, after what must by now have seemed a lifetime studying the classics, was it so surprising that Claude appeared to have run out of steam again academically, as had happened at St. Paul's, that rowing, and perhaps a degree of revelry, may have taken over? The benefits of time spent on the river should not be underestimated. Sir Theodore Cook, Editor of *The Field*, in 1919:

> Rowing is not a game like cricket; it is not a sport like hunting; it does not evoke merely individual excellence like boxing; it makes a combined appeal, which I venture to think unique, to precisely those qualities of courage in comradeship, of discipline in preparation, of initiative in final accomplishment, which have provided the fibre and foundation of our national character in the ordeal through which our Empire has been passing.[20]

Was Claude a typical 'Oxbridge' undergraduate? Compton Mackenzie's Michael Fane in *Sinister Street* identified two types at Oxford:

> Oxford was divided into Bad Men and Good Eggs. The Bad Men went up to London and womanised – some even of the worst womanised in Oxford. The Good Eggs went up to London and got drunk; and if they womanised no one must know anything about it. Drink was the only vice that should be enjoyed communally; in fact, if it were enjoyed secretly, it transformed the victim into the very worst of Bad Men. The Good Eggs never made a mistake in dress: they only wore old school colours or Varsity club colours: they were bonhomous, hearty, careless, and rowdy in large groups.

Cambridge was probably much the same. Claude might not have distinguished himself academically, but this was not the sole objective of the university experience, and by contributing to its sporting and social life he had surely proved himself a 'good egg'. His life in Cambridge would have opened his mind to new ideas, other modes of living and thinking, stimulated him in ways that 'book learning' alone could never do. One can mull over what kind of world he and his contemporaries felt themselves to be living in, and what they thought the future might bring, but if possessed of a crystal ball they might have been disturbed by some of the images therein.

They would have recognised something of their salad days in E.M. Forster's 1908 novel, *A Room with a View*, and the later Merchant Ivory cinema adaptation. Beneath the film's chocolate box beauty, Ivory portrays the England of the early 1900s as a starched and repressive place, implying that love can flower only by escaping from the manicured croquet lawn to sun-drenched hills under southern skies. Despite a considerable broadening of his mind at Cambridge, Claude had not yet escaped. As far as affairs of the heart went there was still no sign of a significant other, and though there may have been attachments, passion was yet to come.

[1]   Sale 3901, 18 December 2015. Paul Rodocanachi (1891-1958) for Jean-Michel Frank (1895-1941), Rockefeller Plaza, New York.
[2]   Valerie Langfield, *Roger Quilter: His Life and Music* (The Boydell Press, 2002)
[3]   Robert Byron, *The Road to Oxiana* (Macmillan, 1937). Byron (1905-41) visited the villa in 1933 and afterwards wrote that Landsberg had, nine years earlier, found the villa 'at the point of ruin, a granary of indeterminate farm-produce' and had made it a habitable dwelling.
[4]   Bruce Chatwin, *What Am I Doing Here?* (Jonathan Cape, 1988)
[5]   Edward Carpenter, *Civilisation, Its Cause and Cure* (George Allen & Unwin, 1889)
[6]   Edward Carpenter, *My Days and Dreams* (Allen & Unwin, 1916)
[7]   Carpenter, ibid.
[8]   The term *demi-monde*, French for 'half-world', was often used as one of disapprobation, for behaviour contrary to more traditional values.
[9]   Theo Aronson, *Prince Eddy and the Homosexual Underworld* (John Murray, 1994)
[10] The card, unfortunately suffering from some damage, had been posted at 9.30am on November ... 1910, and reads: 'Dear Mother, I hope you are feeling much better... The weather ... It has been ... for nearly a week. ... a photo of our Master, Mr Beck. Love to ..., Phil'
[11] *The Heracleidae of Euripides with introduction, analysis, critical and explanatory notes*, by Edward Anthony Beck, MA and Clinton E. S. Headlam, MA, Fellows and Classical Lecturers of Trinity Hall (Cambridge University Press, 1895)
[12] Crawley, *Trinity Hall*, p 179
[13] Geoff Dibb, *Oscar Wilde, A Vagabond With a Mission: The Story of Oscar Wilde's Lecture Tours of Britain and Ireland* (Oscar Wilde Society, 2013)
[14] Crawley, ibid.
[15] Ifan Kyrle Fletcher, *Ronald Firbank: A Memoir* (Duckworth, 1930). A 'shy Narcissus (he) cultivated elegance in dress and food and furniture.' His rooms were 'arranged with old red silks, masses of flowers, and a number of dainty tables, covered with books and statuettes, and, in a place of honour, a photograph of his mother in Court dress. In this room he would sit in curtained and shaded twilight, behind his head the yellow glimmer of candles set in carved and gilded candelabra.'

[16] Crawley, ibid. Robert Hugh Benson was the son of the late Edward White Benson, Archbishop of Canterbury

[17] James J. Conway, *Concerning the eccentricities of of Ronald Firbank*, Online biography

[18] Edward Carpenter, *The Intermediate Sex: A Study of Some Transitional Types of Men and Women* (Mitchell Kennerley, 1912)

[19] A Cambridge degree is known as a 'Tripos'. The term was first used in the 17th century when verses would be read out by someone sitting on a three-legged stool (or Tripos) at graduation ceremonies.

[20] Sir Theodore Cook (1867-1928), art critic and writer, who was Editor of *The Field* from 1910 until his death in 1928, assembled details of all Henley Regattas for the period 1903-14. Cook was, of course, writing in the terrible aftermath of WWI, when 'courage in comradeship' had been so evident as part of Britain's national character. Cook noted that three of the Cambridge University crew of 1914 (Day, Ritson, and Garnett) were killed, together with their cox, Ridley. Swann was wounded in April 1918; Stroke and (7) received the Military Cross. 'Another Cambridge Eight that was well known at Henley and in Belgium was the Jesus crew of 1911. Half the men were killed: Shields, Goldsmith, G. E. Fairbairn, and Crowe; Bow (Henty) and three (Lieut.-Col. H. C. H. Hudson of the Hussars, who particularly distinguished himself) were wounded; Hudson died in Norway.'

CHAPTER 7

Dreams of Empire 1911

*It will, before long, become one of the stepping stones
of continuous British Empire from Cape Town to Cairo.*

Sir Henry 'Harry' Hamilton Johnston

The year Claude came down from Cambridge saw the crowning of a new king, George V. With the royal bloodline and the immutability of the body politic reaffirmed, rumblings in Ireland, anarchists in London, strikes and suffragette activism seemed but ripples on the surface of the status quo. A Festival of Empire at the Crystal Palace welcomed the incoming monarch, and celebrated Britain's continued power overseas. Ever conscious of German ambitions, the Admiralty ordered more battleships and, in May, the White Star Line launched a brand new super fast passenger liner, the *Titanic*.

In this self-assured, forward-looking world, where would a discerning Cambridge graduate set his sights? Unlike many of his contemporaries Claude was not from a family with land or money, nor was he able to rely on a position in the family firm, and although the Oxbridge network and that of St. Paul's might have opened doors, he had to make his own way in life. He had achieved enough academically to follow his father into the field of education, join his oldest brother Robert in going to Australia, or consider insurance like Charlie. A City career would have been respectable and secure, but would it seem dull and Pooterish to the young Claude?

The Empire on the other hand was something of an exotic oyster, open to adventure for the intrepid. Many had done well in Africa in business and farming, some amassing fortunes through trade or outright exploitation, while the missionary movement, responding to Dr. David Livingstone's clarion call for a worldwide holy trinity of 'Christianity, Commerce and Civilisation', sought to forge more equitable and 'improving' relationships with the people into whose land they ventured uninvited. Exploration had led to settlement, and European governments, 'taking up the white man's burden' in Kipling's phrase, sought new territories and valuable resources, recognising the need for an administrative infrastructure. For the Raj, the Indian Civil Service, staffed at the top by high achieving graduates fulfilled this role, while in Africa it was the British Colonial Service, taking young men from the public and sometimes grammar schools, who ran local affairs and enforced the law in an orderly and systematic fashion.

From 1900 the colonial service had expanded considerably. Brighter university men, of whom Claude, despite his disappointing final degree, was surely one, would normally opt for India or Kenya. Knowing that he had joined the British Colonial Service, why did Claude accept a posting to the relatively obscure territory of Northern Rhodesia? Growing up he would have been very aware of the drama of southern Africa through reports of the Second Anglo-Boer War, which had begun in 1898 when he was nine.[1] His imagination could also have been fired by Livingstone's legacy, to follow in the footsteps of the man who had pledged to 'open up the interior, or perish,' the first European to have seen the Victoria Falls, and immortalised in establishing Northern Rhodesia's then capital, Livingstone.

Another inspiration, the name almost synonymous with Empire, would have been Cecil Rhodes. Equally driven, if more venally than Livingstone, Rhodes had also penetrated beyond the Zambezi, the treaties and expropriations wrought by his British South Africa Company's private army, instrumental in bringing land north of the river under British control. Claude's connection with Rhodes, indirect but not perhaps to be underestimated, was through his Master at Trinity Hall. Edward Beck had been educated at the Grammar School in Bishop's Stortford where the six sons of Rev. Francis Rhodes, incumbent of the local parish church of St Michael's, had also been pupils.[2] The Reverend was remembered for his revitalisation of the school, and his youngest son Cecil's attendance had overlapped that of Beck, who would have known the family well.[3]

Claude's destination however was not to be the growing settlement of Livingstone in the south of the country, but rather Abercorn (now known as Mbala), the northernmost outpost of the colony, close to the border with German East Africa (today's mainland Tanzania). Occupying a highly strategic position, Abercorn controlled the southern approaches to Lake Tanganyika and the port of Mpulungu, factors that would assume great significance from 1914. The location was also favoured by colonials for its altitude of 5,400ft, providing a pleasant climate and

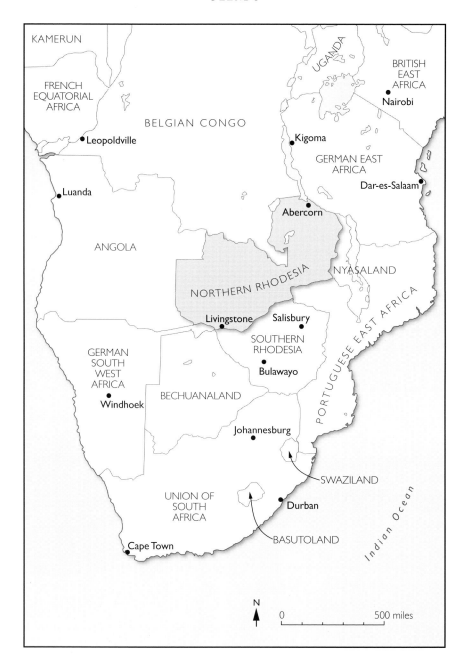

Southern Africa (c.1913)

relative absence of disease. Nevertheless, along with his suits and dinner jackets, Claude would have been advised to take an array of items for a tropical environment, including coloured spine-pads and sola topees for sun protection, mosquito boots and anti-malaria nets.[4]

Although much of the north eastern part of the country where Claude would spend most of his career was populated by the Bemba, the area around Abercorn was home to the Mambwe, with their neighbours the Lungu, living on the shores of Lake Tanganyika.[5] Nevertheless, Chibemba would have been widely understood, except perhaps on the lakeshore. J. C. L. Coxhead, writing in 1914, explains that the Mambwe had occupied their present territory for over 200 years, for when the Bemba themselves arrived from the Congo in the eighteenth century, they claim to have pushed the Mambwe back to the north.[6]

How had Abercorn, Claude's first posting, come into being, and who had trod its soil before him? In the mid 1860s, Livingstone was the first European to visit a village called Zombe. A decade later, Royal Navy Commander Verney Lovett Cameron, while crossing the African continent from east to west, explored the southern end of Lake Tanganyika and is believed to have found some of the great man's papers.[7] Ten years later in the 1880s, the London Missionary Society, inspired by Livingstone, founded a mission at Fwambo, later moved to a better location on the plateau at Kawimbe.

The British South Africa Company (BSAC) was modelled on the British East India Company. Its first directors included the Duke of Abercorn, Cecil Rhodes and the South African financier Alfred Beit and it was incorporated under a royal charter in 1889.[8] This granted the BSAC considerable powers, including the right to maintain or distribute vast amounts of territory, make treaties, establish a police force and set up banking firms throughout south central Africa.[9] The African historian Andrew Roberts explains that copper found in Katanga had initially excited Rhodes, but by 1890 it had become clear that the Belgian claims had prevailed.[10] Furthermore, although establishing clear boundaries with colonial rivals was relatively straightforward, power broking with local people was much harder. By 1891, the BSAC had gained recognition from other European powers, but it was quite another matter to win favour with African chiefs or Arab and Swahili traders.

While certain areas north of the Zambezi might have been less immediately attractive to the BSAC, its acquisitive instinct knew few

THE FIRST BOARD OF DIRECTORS OF THE BRITISH SOUTH AFRICA COMPANY, 1889. Top Row: Horace Farquhar, Esq.; Albert Grey, Esq.; Alfred Beit, Esq. Middle Row: His Grace the Duke of Fife, K.T., P.C.; Hon. C. J. Rhodes (Founder and Managing Director in South Africa); His Grace the Duke of Abercorn, K.G., P.C. Bottom Row: Lord Grifford, V.C.; Herbert Canning, Esq. (Secretary); George Cawston, Esq (British South Africa Company).

bounds. In 1891, responsibility for the area was handed to Harry Johnston, Her Majesty's Commissioner, who was one of the first to comprehend the strategic importance of Lake Tanganyika to Britain.[11] The territory between the lake and the coast had become German East Africa, a yawning gap of almost 600 miles in the chain of British colonies in Rhodes's 'Cape to Cairo' dream. The northern end of Lake Tanganyika was only 150 miles from British-controlled Uganda, and a presence at the southern end of the lake would seem crucial in blocking the territorial ambitions of Britain's European competitors.

In 1893, Johnston selected Hugh Marshall, already serving in British Central Africa (renamed Nyasaland in 1907, present day Malawi), to administer North-Eastern Rhodesia. His letter of appointment, dated 26th July 1893, gave the young man detailed instructions and recommendations and also clarifies the origins of Abercorn's name:

> You will probably find it convenient to make the headquarters of
> your district at a place called Zombe; but as the native name of
> this place might be confused with Zomba (the then administrative

headquarters of British Central Africa, now Malawi), I propose that
your station shall be entitled 'Abercorn', that being the name which
was originally given to the proposed Administration Station at the
south of Tanganyika.[12] The present Abercorn is near Zombe, and is
a station of the African Lakes Company. You will probably also find
it convenient to establish a sub-station at Rhodes Port on Rhodes
Bay at the southeast end of Tanganyika. Zombe itself is situated
at a considerable elevation, and is believed to be very healthy,
whereas the shores of Lake Tanganyika are not quite so salubrious,
and are moreover infested with the tsetse fly. Zombe seems to be a
suitable spot for checking the caravan routes to the east coast and for
defending the European settlements at the south end of Tanganyika
against the raids of the Awemba.'[13]

The passing caravans were presumably checked for human cargo,
as Livingstone's reports in the 1860s of a still flourishing slave trade had
spurred renewed efforts, in particular by the African Lakes Company
(ALC), to eradicate it. There was also a word of warning about the
neighbours:

At present the boundary between the Congo Free State and British
Central Africa has not been conclusively determined; but pending
a definite settlement by H. M. Government, I have always looked
upon the whole of Cameron Bay as being included within the British
limits of Central Africa, on the strength of treaties which I made on
behalf of H. M. Government in 1889. You will, therefore, see that
no aggression is made in that direction by Agents of the Congo Free
State.

While acknowledging the challenges that might be faced living in what
must have seemed, to European eyes, a beleaguered dot on the map,
Johnston waxed lyrical on its attributes, and was unambiguous about its
role in the grander scheme of things. The posting was, he said:

one of the most difficult to occupy in the whole of British Central
Africa; but it is, perhaps, on the other hand, the most interesting from
its geographical position, from the beautiful scenery that surrounds
the south end of Tanganyika, the remarkable native tribes inhabiting
that district, and the fact that it will, before long, become one of the
stepping stones of continuous British Empire from Cape Town to
Cairo.[14]

An unbroken red line, running the length of Africa is seen here not as some hazy ambition, but as a foregone conclusion so strong, in 1893, was the belief in the imperial project. It seems the kind of grandiose idea the Romans might have come up with, possibly explaining its appeal to the classically-educated elite of the British Empire. Marshall, encouraged by the notion of creating a vital steppingstone on the Cape to Cairo route, protected by a squad of Makua police and a few Sikhs, set about erecting a large stockade next to Zombe on the right bank of the Lucheche river.

The position of the Abercorn boma would change four times from the original site on the Stevenson Road. In 1896, following a visit by Lawrence Wallace (later the Administrator of North Eastern Rhodesia), Marshall was persuaded to move nearer to the ALC site at Mandala on a hill above the left bank of the Lucheche.[15] Abercorn continued to expand and in 1902, at a public meeting on 26th June, it was decided that there should be a tangible memorial to Queen Victoria, which led to building the 'Tanganyika Victoria Memorial Institute'. In 1912, the boma was moved again to the centre of the town at the junction of Marshall Avenue.[16] Finally, in the late 1950s, the boma offices were rebuilt up the hill, 200 yards to the south.[17]

In 1895, after two years on secondment from the British government, Marshall was 'handed over' to the BSAC, with his personal doubts about the calibre of some of their officials. He took his role of Magistrate under direct royal warrant very seriously and deplored the behaviour of most colonial recruits. Vigilant about the reputation of his court, it was plain that he, not the missionaries or the commercial company agents, was the 'political' boss.[18] An able linguist and a good listener, he would certainly have had the edge over the more confrontational BSAC types. His nickname among local Africans, of 'Tambalika', refers to a place 'where elephants lie down', possibly a tribute to Marshall's hunting prowess; or less charitably, 'his wont for stretching out natives on the ground for caning'.[19]

Marshall became one of a group of pioneering officials who, through sound administration brought peace, breaking the grip of the Arab slavers, and curbing the raids and brutalities of the Bemba. As well as Consular Officer and the first official Magistrate, he was also the first Postmaster, establishing a mail service to Cape Town via Nyasaland and Chinde on the Mozambique coast. The postmen, forty of the fittest locals dressed in smart red flannel tunics, red shorts and red fezzes, and known as the 'Scarlet Runners', were highly renowned for their punctuality. Communications

'Tambalika' Marshall

were further enhanced during Marshall's tenure, with the construction by Africa-Transcontinental Telegraph, of a line along the Nyasa–Tanganyika corridor.[20] This ambitious scheme, attributed like much else to Rhodes, and all part of the Cape to Cairo master plan, would bear messages, orders and instructions speedily back and forth through a seamless string of British colonies and on to the heart of the Empire in London. In Rhodes's vision, the railway would carry people and goods swiftly and securely over the same vast distances.

Marshall comes across as an ambitious man, determined to satisfy his superiors, becoming in 1910 Acting Administrator for the last days of North-Eastern Rhodesia's autonomy, and moving to Fort Jameson (today's Chipata in eastern Zambia) to preside over the merger with its North-Western counterpart, in the new capital Livingstone. Thereafter he continued in Fort Jameson (founded as an HQ in 1899) as District Commissioner and Magistrate through the First World War, before retiring to his home in Bournemouth in 1922.[21] But it was in Abercorn, after eighteen years of pioneering service, that his memory would live on, the main street continuing to be known as Marshall Avenue.

Reports of Marshall's stabilizing achievements in Northern Rhodesia might well have encouraged the more adventurous European leisure travellers to the area. In May 1905, Gordon Lobb and his friend Hugh Cleaver were among them. Fifty years later, Lobb recounted how they caught a ferry from Harwich to Rotterdam then boarded the German *The Margraf,* paying £22.10s each and sharing four to a cabin for a voyage via Suez to Beira in Portuguese East Africa. Here, taking the overnight train to Salisbury, the travellers repaired to the Avenue Hotel for a few days, before taking another train to the Ayrshire Mine.[22] Knowing 'nothing about Ulendo in those days', Lobb said that they were pleased to find more experienced Europeans to advise them, and to assist in finding bearers to take them overland to Feira (now known as Luangwa) on the west bank of the Zambezi, and the border between Southern and Northern Rhodesia, where they stayed a fortnight with 'a nice crowd in the hotel.'[23]

Moving northwards to game country, Lobb shot a hartebeest at 500 yards, soon realising it was a sheer fluke, 200 yards being regarded as a reasonable sporting chance. At Fort Jameson, he and Cleaver spent some time with C. P. Chesnaye, the Native Commissioner (NC), who would later head up the administration in Abercorn. By foot and machila they pushed on, climbing through the Muchinga Mountains to Mpika then Kasama, until eventually reaching Abercorn.[24] In Marshall's absence, Weggerle, the Assistant Native Commissioner (ANC) welcomed them, arranging baths in which to their surprise, Weggerle 'made his boys pour water over them'. Relaxed after three days' sojourn, the pair continued on through hilly country for a further 28 miles to meet C. N. Blyth at Jericho Farm.

Seeing the kind of life that a European could enjoy, Lobb decided to settle, and immediately acquired a farm. Hugh Cleaver seemed similarly charmed, as he too decided to stay, though any expectation of seeing out his days in Africa were fulfilled rather too soon, when just two months later a bolt of lightning struck him dead on Lobb's veranda.

Unaccompanied women visiting Northern Rhodesia tended to be frowned upon. Colonial officer, writer and poet Cullen Gouldsbury complained of invading 'lady travellers' such as Helen Caddick, who by 1898 had already journeyed widely in Asia and South America, before venturing into central Africa in her early fifties.[25] Carried by machila from Karonga, she was pleased to chance upon 'a lovely little lake, Lake Kilwa' (Lake Chila), and was told it 'was dry ground only a few years ago. He had many times walked over the part where the lake is now.'[26]

After a three-hour trek from the London Missionary Society (LMS) mission at Kawimbe, she paused in Abercorn just long enough 'for the men to have a rest, and then as they were willing, and indeed anxious, to get to Kituta that night, we set off for our journey of five hours', descending 3,000 feet to the shore of Lake Tanganyika. Her memoir, *A White Woman in Central Africa*, describes an impressive trek by any standards, even if she was carried for much of the time.[27]

Another female literary 'invader' was Charlotte Mansfield, already an established romantic novelist when she set off in 1909, aged twenty-eight, on a much-publicised 'Cape Town to Cairo' tour, aiming to complete it within a year.[28] Equipped with cameras and rifles, she travelled by rail to Broken Hill, there hiring forty-nine porters for the onward journey. Three days before reaching Abercorn, her carriers' wives and children came out to greet them, and even though it was bitterly cold, 'all seemed happy, healthy, and very merry.' Thus, already enchanted, on arrival in Abercorn, Mansfield was equally taken with the architecture, finding the Magistrate's residence, 'a charming house, surrounded by a large garden, with a fine view of Lake Tanganyika in the far distance.' Commenting on the government offices, post office and postmaster's house, recently-built Victoria Memorial Hall, doctor's house, government dispensary, two stores, and even the gaol, she was surprised to find that, 'with all these advantages only about eight white people live in the boma, three of whom are women.' Five miles before reaching the town, she had also appreciated a night spent at the thatched shooting box by the Uringi Pans.

Gouldsbury described Abercorn more prosaically than the English romantic novelist, emphasising its status in the area:

Main Street (1917)

The Magistrate's House (1913)

Post Office

Picture a congeries of buildings, thatched or tin-roofed, comprising three or four dwelling houses, a boma or office (palatial enough to one accustomed to the south), a surgery, a gaol like the toy forts which, in our youth, we received as Christmas presents, and a brick sentry-box roofed with slabs of iron.[29] That is Abercorn – which you will be pleased to note, is **the** city of the Plateau, the metropolis of the north.[30]

View from 'Old' Native Commissioner's House

Boma Office

Abercorn gaol (1912)

Many buildings at that time were of simple construction, using local materials for a timber framework, wattle and daub walls and a thatched roof. Having lived for two years in such a house in western Uganda, I can confirm, that if well made, and with adequate windows to allow a breeze to blow through, such houses can be extremely comfortable even on the hottest day.[31]

Charlotte Mansfield described her experience as a guest at Abercorn in five-star terms:

> several days with Mr. and Mrs. Hugh Marshall, and what a pleasure it was, after five weeks spent on a hard camp bed, to seek slumber again with the comfort and cleanliness of fine linen! Mrs. Hugh Marshall is certainly an example to be cited in evidence of how happy and up-to-date a woman can be in the wilds and 540 miles from a railway station. The house is made beautiful by her wood-carving, and everywhere one finds evidences of a cultured and active mind; it was good to see all the dainty toilet arrangements and the table appointments dear to the heart of a woman.

After such hospitality, to press on through many miles of harsh landscape towards Cairo would take some motivation. In the event Mansfield abandoned the plan, allegedly due to a sleeping sickness outbreak and consequent travel restrictions, compelling her to reluctantly 'proceed with my caravan via Nyasaland to Chinde.'[32] Here she boarded the *Kronprinz* for Marseilles, and thence returned to England. Whether sleeping sickness was the whole truth, or a version for her loyal readers we shall never know, but Charlotte clearly fell in love with Abercorn, both of the Rhodesias and Africa as a whole. It was an affection she was eager to share, and in 1911 she replied in *Via Rhodesia* to the frequent question, 'Why did I wish to visit Rhodesia?' that she had found the daily pressure of life in London quite suffocating, and hearing of Africa's vast empty lands had wanted to see them for herself.[33] Having done so, she could dispel some popular myths: 'Darkest Africa? – oh, how he who has been there must laugh at this description! Africa, with the sun always shining, Africa, with the free air for all!' Speaking in hindsight, she said that her journey had been to research 'from a woman's point of view (to) ascertain the possibility of Rhodesia as a good settling-ground for women.' To emphasise the depth of her study, she dismissed the efforts of two earlier travellers, Ewart Grogan and Mary Hall, who although completing the Cape to Cairo route, had in her view missed a great deal along the way: 'neither had given the reader any idea of what lay beyond the railway terminus ... and that both had in fact somewhat neglected Rhodesia.'

Claude may never have met Charlotte Mansfield, as she later settled not in Rhodesia, but in South Africa, where she married a mining engineer. However, if Claude had been reading her observations on Abercorn's suitability for women, he could well have pictured himself there with a wife in the not too distant future.

---

[1]   The conflict is usually known simply as the Boer War, since the First Anglo-Boer War (December 1880-March 1881) is less well known. The Second Anglo-Boer War (October 1899-May 1902) was fought between the British and two Boer states, the Republic of Transvaal and the Orange Free State, over British influence in South Africa. Initial Boer attacks were successful, and though British reinforcements later reversed these, the war continued for years with Boer guerrilla warfare, until harsh British counter-measures brought them to terms.

[2]   Later known as 'Goodman's School'. See also Charles Crawley, *Trinity Hall*, ibid

[3]   The Old Grammar School (Source: *Bishop's Stortford History*)

[4]   The spine pad, which gave protection from the sun, has become a dull museum piece, yet to those living in the tropics in the early days, memories may be evoked of a piece of cloth of cotton, silk or wool, plain or quilted, attachable to the shirt or coat along the spine. Sola topees (or pith helmets) were made of pith or cork, covered in a lightweight cloth. These two items were routinely issued to European military personnel serving overseas in 'hot climates' from the mid-nineteenth to the mid-twentieth century.

[5]   William Watson, *Tribal Cohesion in a Money Economy: A Study of the Mambwe*

People of Northern Rhodesia (Manchester University Press, 1958)

[6] J. C. L. Coxhead, *The Native Tribes of North Eastern Rhodesia*, Royal Anthropological Institute, Occasional Papers, No. 5, 1914

[7] See Verney Lovett Cameron, *Across Africa* (Harper & Brothers, New York, 1877)

[8] James Hamilton, 2nd Duke of Abercorn (1838-1913), styled Viscount Hamilton until 1868, then Marquess of Hamilton (1868-85). The Dukes of Abercorn and of Fife, respectively chairman and vice-chairman, were appointed to give the company prestige but took little part in running the company. Neither had any previous interest in Africa, and Fife had no business experience. Source: J. S. Galbraith, 'The British South Africa Company and the Jameson Raid', *Journal of British Studies*, November 1970

[9] Source: Bodleian Library, Oxford

[10] Andrew D. Roberts, *A History of Zambia* (Africana Publishing Company, New York, 1976) p 162

[11] Sir Henry 'Harry' Hamilton Johnston (1858-1927), a key player in the 'Scramble for Africa'.

[12] Named after the Duke of Abercorn, a President of BSAC (1890-1913). The location of the original Zombe village is eight miles to the west of the current Chief Zombe village and seven miles from Mbala.

[13] The British Central Africa Protectorate (BCA) was proclaimed in 1889, ratified in 1891. In 1907, it was renamed Nyasaland, now Malawi. See W.V. Brelsford, '"Tambalika" Marshall: Letter of Appointment to Abercorn' (Explained by the Editor) *NRJ* Vol. II, No. 5 (1954) pp 47-49

[14] '"Tambalika" Marshall: Letter of Appointment', ibid.

[15] Hope and Marion Gamwell, 'The History of Abercorn', *NRJ*, Vol. IV, No. 6 (1961), p 520. Confirmed in the Abercorn DNB, see Letter from G. Stokes, DC, 29 January 1949.

[16] Abercorn DNB: Abercorn District Notes by Humphrey Nash, District Assistant

[17] The oldest building still standing is the prison, built 1912. The original streets are the main roads from Lake Chila passing by the prison, the Anglican Church and the TVMI, going out to Mpulungu; and the road between the prison and the police station to St Paul's Mission. The original road to Abercorn was from Fife (now Nakonde), running past Kawimbe Mission.

[18] Marcia Wright, 'Tambalika: Perspectives on a Colonial Magistrate in Central Africa', *African Affairs*, Vol. 85, No. 338, Jan 1986

[19] *NRJ*, Vol. II, No. 5 (1954), ibid. See also Flexon Mizinga, Director of the Moto Moto Museum, Mbala, in *The Lowdown* Magazine, May 2001.

[20] Marcia Wright, ibid. The ambitious scheme of the African Transcontinental Telegraph Company, formed in 1892, was almost entirely a creation of Rhodes's forethought and private capital. The chief objective was a forerunner to the railway, but there were commercial possibilities in competing with the owners of the submarine cables between Britain and South Africa. To secure the route, Rhodes had begun negotiations with Germany for wayleaves through German East Africa, having also obtained from Lord Rosebery's Government a treaty with the Congo State for the

telegraph to run along the western shore of Lake Tanganyika in exchange for the lease of the Lado Enclave.

21 R. I. Rotberg, *The Rise of Nationalism in Central Africa: The Making of Malawi and Zambia*, 1873-1964 (Harvard, 1965)

22 Gordon Lobb, 'My First Ulendo from Salisbury to Abercorn 1905', *NRJ*, Vol. II, No. 6 (1954), pp 79-82. For 'ulendo', see Chapter 8 below.

23 Feira, on the west bank of the Zambezi, and Zumbo on the east, were both founded by the Portuguese in the 18th Century.

24 *Machila*: a simple hammock suspended from a long pole, or a pair of poles carried by two men. More sophisticated versions could be shaded and curtained.

25 Helen Caddick was one of a number of middle/upper class women who travelled extensively at the turn of the century. She had a long-term interest in education, travel and anthropology and in 1900 became the first woman member of West Bromwich Education Committee. Source: Library of Birmingham

26 Helen Caddick, *A White Woman in Central Africa* (T. Fisher Unwin, 1900)

27 Ibid.

28 Charlotte Mansfield (b. 1881) also wrote *Torn Lace, The Girl and the Gods* and *Love and a Woman*. After her return to South Africa (c. 1911), she married Vladimir Raffalovich, a mining engineer.

29 Congeries: from the Latin *congerere*, to heap up; a disorderly collection or jumble.

30 C. Gouldsbury & H. Sheane, *The great plateau of northern Rhodesia, being some impressions of the Tanganyika Plateau* (Edward Arnold, 1911; reprint, Negro Universities Press, New York, 1969) p5

31 Wattle and daub is used for making walls, in which a woven lattice of wooden strips called *wattle* is *daubed* with material usually made of some combination of wet soil, clay, sand, animal dung and straw.

32 Chinde, some 40 miles south of Quelimane, became the main entry point for BCA. Ocean-going ships were met by small river steamers which took passengers and goods to the head of navigation on the Shire River at Katunga, the closest point to Blantyre.

33 Charlotte Mansfield, *Via Rhodesia: A Journey Through Southern Africa* (Stanley Paul, 1911)

CHAPTER 8

Eulogy and Ulendo

When all is said and done, in the lands of Eternal Sun
There are tasks, but half begun, men give their lives to learn;
Pitiably underpaid, with promotions long delayed,
They work for the love of their trade and not for a cash return

From The Administrators by Cullen Gouldsbury

The scarecrow may rest o' nights, but never the watcher of men

African proverb

Claude left Southampton on 26th August 1911, travelling second class on the *Balmoral Castle*, at 13,360 tons the pride of the Union Castle line, having completed her maiden voyage to Cape Town the previous year in just sixteen days. She was also the first Union Castle ship to be fitted with Marconi wireless telegraphy. Claude would have steamed down the west coast of Africa to Cape Town, taken the train to Johannesburg, then north to Salisbury, crossing the Zambezi on the bridge opened five years earlier in 1906. Quite likely, he would then have broken his travels for a few days on the other side at Livingstone, before continuing north to the end of the line, at the evocatively named Broken Hill. From here the journey to Abercorn was overland, walking or carried by African bearers, and partly by canoe along the waters of the *Chambeshi River*.

Knowing that the *Balmoral Castle* would have reached Cape Town around 11th September, Claude could have arrived in Abercorn by the end of that month. Seeking confirmation of the dates, on my first visit to Lusaka, I looked into the Colonial Service District Notebook for Abercorn, on microfiche in the Zambian National Archives. The first page begins:

> This book consists of a compilation in September 1911 by H. C.
> Gouldsbury of the various Reports, copies of letters to Headquarters
> and extracts from the former (small) District Note Book compiled in
> 1906-7.

The Balmoral Castle at Cape Town

Each set of handwritten notes is dated and initialled in red ink by its author, in this case Cullen Gouldsbury or C. P. Chesnaye, the latter, as magistrate for Abercorn, Claude's immediate superior. The page carries the stamp of the Central African Archives, dated 25th July 1950, when it was first microfilmed and signed by the Deputy Archivist, T. Baxter. Some pages are missing, and there is no record of Claude's arrival date. Possibly he stopped off en route in Cape Town or Johannesburg to visit friends from England or to look around.

The excitement of Africa must have stirred even Claude's phlegmatic disposition. The greatest danger in Maida Vale in 1911 might have been a runaway horse and cart. Lurid tales from the 'dark continent' featured appalling diseases, lethal snakes and scorpions, man-eating big cats and barbarous spear-wielding savages.

However Claude viewed such stories, a gruesome event just two months before his arrival, would remind any newcomer that Africa was still an untamed land. One of the two men involved, Paul Graetz, a lieutenant in the colonial army in German East Africa was no newcomer.[1] Whilst supervising road building in a remote area near Dodoma in 1907, he requested leave to drive from Dar-es-Salaam to the Cape, hoping to prove to his superiors the value of mechanized transport in Africa. With a friend and a mechanic, he crossed German East Africa to Lake Tanganyika at Ujiji then brought the car by lake steamer to Kituta. With the January rains

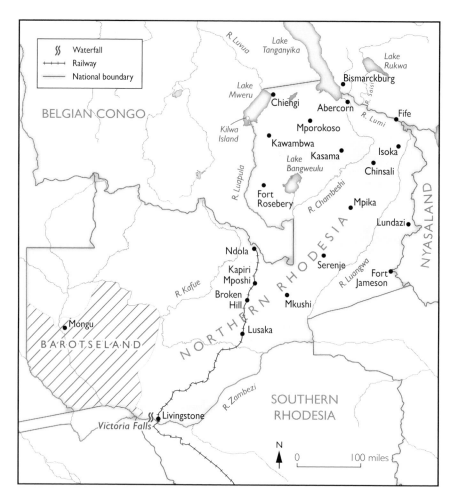

Northern Rhodesia (c.1913)

starting, the trio dismantled the car and had the components carried up the escarpment to Abercorn. The original plan to take the Stevenson Road to Lake Nyasa was abandoned, and they set out to drive south, following the carriers' route to the railhead at Broken Hill. The 500-mile journey included crossing the Chambeshi River in full flood, and numerous nearby swamps. Graetz had allowed a year to reach Swakopmund in South West Africa (now Namibia), but at an average of six miles a day, did it in three months.

Four years later, in 1911, Graetz invited, the French cinematographer Octave Fière, on a journey across the continent by motorboat. Having progressed up the Zambezi and Shire rivers then headed north on Lake

Nyasa to Karonga, they brought the boat overland up the Stevenson Road, eventually reaching the Chambeshi river, that had proved such an obstacle to road travel. On 3rd September during a hunting break, a buffalo that they had wounded came 'charging at Graetz, who just managed to fire a shot at the raging beast... Fière shot the buffalo in the head, but the buffalo had gored Fière three times before it dropped dead.'

Fière also dropped dead. Seriously injured, Graetz struggled on down the Chambeshi river, the Luvua and the Congo. Although clearly intrepid and probably the first European to travel the Congo from its headwaters to the sea, Graetz has been regarded in some quarters as quixotic, the big geographical mysteries including the origin of the Congo having been unravelled many years earlier.[2]

A hidden danger for Claude was sleeping sickness (African *trypanosomiasis*), carried by tsetse flies, although being confined to certain known areas sensible precautions could be taken. As for savagery, Gouldsbury wrote in 1911 of the risks of entering the country of the Bemba people from the East:

> long after the Nyasa-Tanganyika trade route was opened up, the Wemba country was closed and impenetrable to Europeans. The grim barrier of severed heads staked on poles on the Stevenson Road, near Zoche village, was left by Chitimukulu, as the natives say, to terrorise European pioneers and to warn them not to trespass within the Wemba domain.[3]

The courteous reception given to Livingstone in 1867 aside, attitudes to outsiders could never be taken for granted. Professor Andrew Roberts believes that the Roman Catholic 'White Fathers' played a small but significant role in winning over the Bemba, by gaining a foothold among those in the north, under the aegis of Makasa, allowing both the British and the Bemba to learn more of each other without resort to conflict.[4]

Young men like Claude, imbued by education and culture with a sense of leadership and service in the great colonial enterprise were unlikely to be deterred by third-hand stories of severed heads and savage buffalos. Moreover, the British approach was not simply that of *veni, vidi, vici.*[5] The Colonial Service recognized the value of communication in good governance, and required its officers to learn local languages fluently. It's likely that Claude would have started studying Chibemba before leaving England and I was able to gain evidence to support this assumption, when in 1990, shortly after my first visit to Zambia, I was fortunate to meet Harry

Franklin, then in retirement in Hampshire. In 1928, Harry had gone out as a cadet officer to Northern Rhodesia, and recalled his superior, Claude Oldfield, giving him language lessons and reciting poetry in the vernacular.

With the unification of NE and NW Rhodesia completed just as Claude's posting began, he would have felt confident of having chosen a secure region in which to embark on his career, a place where the organizing, ever steadier hand of the colonial service would strengthen and maintain a civilized, quasi-British way of life for the British, in reasonable harmony with the indigenous people. With the systems and practice of laws, tax gathering, rents and labour use established, the administrative machine that kept them running was applied with a relatively light touch. According to Terence Ranger, 'the colonial government made minimal demands and offered minimal services'.[6] He also points out that the minimalist approach of the British towards the host peoples, 'demanded no sort of exclusive loyalty ... and ... abstained from any thought of social engineering.' On this analysis, the colonisers had no desire to change (perhaps with the exception of some Christian missionaries) or integrate with the colonised, simply to keep them content, paying their taxes and peaceable in their own sphere.

During Claude's time in Abercorn, the District Notebook records the work of smoothing relations with and between local people. Chief Fwambo 'ran away to German East Africa in June 1911 and on his return was called to account'. In June 1912, he ran away again 'taking all his cattle ... on 15th October, as Fwambo had not returned the Mambwe chiefs decided that Fwambo's younger brother should act as his deputy in his absence'. Following a report to the Administrator, a written warning was sent to him, giving him 14 days to return. Eventually the Chief returned in February 1913, with all his cattle, promising to do his duty as a chief, and expressing regret for his behaviour.[7] The dynastic line of chiefs continues to this day. In December 2015, the Government was 'saddened at the untimely death of Chief Fwambo of the Mambwe people of Mbala. Chiefs and Traditional Affairs Deputy Minister, John Akufuna said the late Chief Fwambo worked in a cordial relationship with the government and will be missed for his contributions to the development of his chiefdom and the nation.'[8]

Literary endeavour flourished among Claude's colleagues. Encouraged by his superior, Robert Codrington, Christian Chesnaye's report on *A Journey from Fort Jameson to the Kafue River* was published in 1901 by

W.E.M. Owen (colleague of Claude; signatory to report on Chief Fwambo)

the Royal Geographical Society.[9] The thirty-year-old Cullen Gouldsbury, born in Darjeeling, had already achieved distinction as a poet and writer, with several works to his name, including *The Great Plateau of Northern Rhodesia*, a topographical collaboration with Hubert Sheane, published the year of Claude's arrival. Physically Gouldsbury and Sheane were chalk and cheese, the former of medium height, fit and spare built, while Sheane was a far more sedentary individual, 'tall, bulky, soft,' who when cycling, 'usually had a native running behind with a forked stick all ready to connect with the cycle just under the saddle so as to give a push when an uphill bit of path occurred.'[10]

Claude's strong, lean physique, honed by days of rowing at Cambridge, would get plenty of exercise at Abercorn, accompanying his superiors on ulendo, long walks to the small outlying villages to visit tribal leaders; hearing grievances, advising or tactfully admonishing. Ulendo is usually taken to mean a journey or safari, but Gouldsbury suggests an extraordinary variety of meanings.[11] As an adjective, it describes all the accoutrements of the journey: the buckets, folding-tables, camp furniture, even the cans of 'Ulendo beef'. Collectively, ulendo represents the various human beings who go on the journey. Going 'on ulendo' became the norm for the district official during the drier half of the year, when life would become 'a nomadic existence in the barest meaning of the term'.

Preparations for ulendo generally followed a well-known routine, with mental checklists not dissimilar from mandatory pre-flight checks. Anything of value would be packed away at home, and only items considered strictly necessary would be taken, such as frying-pans, enamelware and folding tables. Gouldsbury outlines two approaches to packing, 'one being to do it yourself, in which case your temper will suffer, and you will probably lose money over underweight loads; the other is to take a pipe and a book on to the front veranda, and leave your boys to distribute loads as they think fit.' Having selected your machila-team, allotted carriers to your personal 'boys', and chosen muscular persons to carry your tent, you would be recommended to retire to rest, warning the men that an early start is essential.

In spite of prudent planning, the next morning may still be frustrating, as 'three men will be sick, half a dozen will evolve invalid grandmothers, and one or two will have disappeared. This will necessitate an entire redistribution of loads, and you will probably move off at midday, ruffled and heated.' After the first night's camp, a more consistent pattern would emerge, but perhaps it was not surprising that Africans wondered why European officials always seemed to be scurrying around their districts as if their very lives depended on it.

The objective would be to visit every village once a year, allowing a full day for mission stations or larger villages, with chiefs and headmen, where there might be as many as 400 huts. If three or more villages were to be visited in a day, the tent and sleeping gear would be sent ahead to the last village of the day, to make the camp ready.

Just for one night a patch of forest would be transformed into a dwelling place for 60 or more people, but not far away 'in the middle distance, a pall of bluish grey smoke, low-hanging, marks a village.' The spacious Edgington tent would have been pitched on cleanly-hoed ground under the shadow of a tall, gnarled tree, the clearing encircled by a hastily-made fence of cut branches.[12] A temporary office would have been built of:

> freshly lopped stakes roofed with grass and leaves … and, in the cool, dim depths, one can just discern a table, a chair, and a tin box – which, for the time being, represents to the native mind a concrete exposition of Government.

Temporary grass shelters would have been erected to make the dining-room 'equipped with tables and chairs, venesta-wood boxes, a bottle or two.' The kitchen behind, open to the elements, would be surrounded by rows of 'blackened, polished pots, or glistening gourds, brought by the women of the village … to be reclaimed by them after the exodus of the white man.' In the night, the official might wonder what could be lurking in the shadows. One of the carriers might have caught:

> a glimpse of a long, low form gliding round outside the circle of fires – perhaps a hyena only, perhaps a leopard or a lion. But, somehow, though lions are sometimes heard, though their spoor is found often enough in the vicinity of such a camp, it is but rarely that night attacks occur.

A ulendo party would typically comprise ten machila-men, thirty carriers, native messengers and askari, personal boys, and even several women and babies; may be sixty in total. Exchanging gifts, soon after arrival at a village, would be an important part of the proceedings, with the headman bringing baskets of flour and a few chickens, even a goat. The headman would expect something in return and might receive a yard or two of calico. The main objective was to get closer to the people in their villages, as well as attending to administrative matters: checking the census, the enumeration of stock, enquiries into the condition of crops and the promulgation of any new decrees or by-laws. With the work completed, the party is ready to move:

> the machila-men with much expostulation clear a way through the crowds; the long, unwieldy hammock swings through the lines of scattered huts, over stumps, through gaps in rickety fences. Then come the gardens, where the unfortunate passenger is … bumped like a shuttle-cock upon the raised beds which line the winding path – out into the open country once more, the shrill cries of the women growing fainter in the distance, the song of the machila-men waking the echoes in the quiet land.

In more populated areas a two-day halt might be made. Life then would, relatively of course, become more luxurious. Proper shelters would be built and flannels would replace the 'ulendo kit' of khaki shorts and shirt, socks, boots and a helmet. In the evening or early morning, time could be found for shooting game. The headman might come for an informal evening chat, while the carriers, around their fires, gossip about the day's march. Gouldsbury believed that on ulendo the 'native character is, undoubtedly, seen at its best'. The visiting official has to adjust his outlook to the necessities of their life and 'finds the native in the very midst of his household gods; questions of village policy, of boundaries and of garden sites, of marriage and giving in marriage'. Conversations might cover a wide range of grievances, such as someone losing his wife to another's superior attractions. Advice would be given, witnesses and his erring spouse produced and the case would be heard. The arrival of the official would also cause concern for those who had not paid their taxes!

Gouldsbury extols the virtues of the touring season, comparing it to the excitement felt by a young adventurer of the Middle Ages when setting forth from the comparative security of mediaeval England into France or Italy. He looks forward to days of:

> honest, steady tramping through tangled forest-land – nights that throb and hum with the song of insect life, or, maybe, with the raucous voices of evil beasts – just so long will the life of a district official upon the Plateau of the Great Lakes be one of the lives that is best worth the living.

When not on ulendo, Claude would have spent his evenings dining in his own house with only a servant (or 'houseboy') for company, unless invited to join colleagues, single or married. Other Europeans in the district were mostly farmers or ranchers, who after the Second Anglo-Boer War had arrived from the south, bringing with them exotic bulls to cross with native cattle, while imported horses were used for occasional race meetings in the Saisi valley. Some combined their farming enterprises with game hunting and supporting the labour recruitment for South Africa's mines.[13]

There was much to appreciate in the splendours of Northern Rhodesia's landscape, which since the advent of Kodak technology were easy to capture. Claude's impressive pictures of Kalambo Falls taken in 1913, suggest he accompanied his superior Chris Draper and local farmer Lionel Smith when they were the first to measure the height of the falls. Smith had:

> climbed down into the gorge by crossing the lip of the fall, and scrambling down the cliff face on the northern side. Draper, at the top, tied a piece of calico onto a stone and lowered the stone on a long string held over the gorge with a chiwale palm pole.[14]

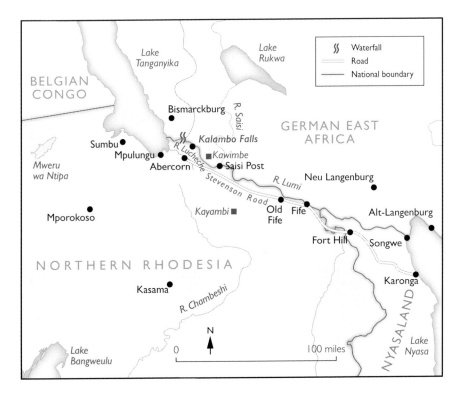

Northern Rhodesian border with German East Africa (c.1913)

When the stone touched the water, Smith fired a shot from his rifle. They measured the string at 701 feet. Smith 'found the gorge to be an eerie place, dark and damp with spray. In the swirling pool was a dead wild pig, that must have fallen over the edge, just being churned round and round.'[15]

John Desmond Clark who would excavate the site some forty years later and find evidence of human activity dating back 250,000 years old, described the Kalambo Falls as: 'one of the unforgettable sights of Africa ... a single, perfect, example of the beauty that is to be found in falling water, in a setting of unsurpassed grandeur.'[16]

At the beginning of March 1913, Claude was promoted from Cadet to Assistant Native Commissioner and JP, on a salary of £325 per annum. That Christmas he celebrated with a large group of fellow settlers, including three wives and two small babies, the married element probably missionaries from the LMS. The highlight of the calendar though was the annual May party. As Gordon Lobb would recall, the tradition was well established among the young, pioneering farmers of Abercorn:

The "Kalambo Falls – Abercorn S.D. 1913. The river flows into Lake Tanganyika, and is the border between Rhodesia and German East Africa. I have climbed down to the pool below, and was scared stiff.

The Kalambo Falls – Abercorn S.D. 1913.

Claimed to be the highest fall in the world over 1000 feet, it runs into Lake Tanganyika five miles away.

Tambalika Marshall and Mrs. Marshall asked everybody in the district on these occasions. It lasted three to five days, and was the great social event of the year. The first one I ever attended was in 1906. We used to have a shoot on the range … On the way down I met an ostrich. I had never met one before, and had been told they could rip you open with their spurs, so I ran like the deuce and, looking over my shoulder, ran into a tree and fell to the ground. The bird stood and looked at me with a peculiar expression on its face, and I stayed down until I was rescued by a boy who knew the bird. I did not know till afterwards that it was a tame one belonging to Tambalika. I might have been even more frightened if I had known that ostriches do not inhabit the Northern Province.'[17]

Chris Draper and family

Christmas, Abercorn, 1913 (Claude 2nd from left)

*Abercorn: Sir Lawrence Wallace (Administrator of Northern Rhodesia, Mr.
Richard Goode (Provincial Commissioner), Mr. 'Tambalika' & Mrs. Marshall,
Mr. & Mrs. C.R. Draper, Mr. Averay Jones*

In 1914 Gordon Lobb proposed that he could stage the May Party 'to give the Boma a rest' and offered:

> a steeple-chase course on the farm, two and a half miles long with eight jumps plus a water jump and a nine-hole golf course and tennis court … everybody wanted to ride, but as we had not enough horses to go round we did the best we could to let as many as we could ride. We had four to five days of party altogether. None of the missionaries accepted our invitation as I suppose horse racing was not in their line.

The conviviality was doubtless enhanced, and Lobb's memory perhaps impaired, by the liquid refreshment:

> We managed to get some quite good beer over from Kasanga, in German East Africa, from the Indians. Beer was more or less unheard of in those days, but one could get plenty of whisky from Broken Hill at £5 a case (good days those). We ended up the last night with a fancy-dress dinner. The beer past lasted out. So ended a good party.

Over the several days of the event, a variety of guests looked in:

> The Boma people took it in turns to come: C. P. Chesnaye, C. P. Oldfield, Mr. and Mrs. Draper and son Dick, Mr. and Mrs. Gouldsbury and son Guy, also Miss Brunton, Mrs. Gouldsbury's companion, Woods, the Vet., John F. Sealy, Lionel Smith of Mpanga, Gerald Morton of Chereshia, who afterwards joined the Boma, Beird of the African Lakes Companies, John Deacon, a trader, Mr. and Mrs. C. W. Blyth and daughter and son, 'Scot' Brown, a cinematograph operator to the Lelsea Expedition, and myself, wife and two daughters.

Another young Englishman, destined to play a prominent role in the political life of Northern Rhodesia, had arrived in the country around the same time as Claude. Schooled at Harrow and the Royal Military Academy, Woolwich, Stewart Gore-Browne had first sought adventure as an officer in the Royal Field Artillery, but reached South Africa just as the Boer War was ending. Uncertain about a career, he pursued his passion for motor racing, until in the spring of 1911, after a round of golf at Byfleet and a conversation with a sapper working in the War Office, he signed up with the Anglo-Belgian Boundary Commission.[18] The Commission had been established by Britain and Belgium in May 1894 to determine the border between Northern Rhodesia and the Congo Free State, the creation of the highly ambitious Belgian King Leopold II, who from an

The May Party   [*Photo: G. Lobb*]

Standing (*left to right*): Messrs. Woods, Scott-Brown, Sealey, Miss Brunton, Mrs. Draper,
   Mrs. Gouldsbury, Mrs. Munro, Mrs. Lobb, Mrs. Blyth.

Sitting (*left to right*): Lionel Smith, C. Gouldsbury, Gordon Lobb, Messrs. Morton, Charlie
   Blyth, Baird, Draper, Deacon.

Source: NRJ, Vol. II, No. 1 (1953) p 78

initially idealistic vision, had turned his 'vast property, amounting to nearly 900,000 square miles, into what was practically a huge slave farm, contrary to all the treaties under which he held his powers.' Largely through the influence of Britain and America, the Belgian Chamber voted on 9th September 1908 for measures that might bring about a more humanely-run colony.

The British cohort of the Boundary Commission, sent out in 1911 to undertake the mapping, comprised five officers and five NCOs, with a corresponding group of Belgians. Gore-Browne recalled: 'Major R. A. Gillam, Royal Engineers, in command; Captain Everett, Welsh Regiment; Captain Walker, Royal Engineers; Lieutenant Wynne, Royal Engineers and myself. My own presence *dans cette galère*, was entirely due to chance.'[19]

Gore-Browne explains that the southern end of the boundary between the two countries is near Kalene, in Mwinilunga district, where the

Major R. A. Gillam, Royal Engineers (SG-B collection)

Muwa Beacon (SG-B collection)

territories of Rhodesia, Angola and the Belgian Congo all meet on the line of longitude on the meridian 24° East. He describes how the boundary first follows the watershed for over 550 miles between the Zambezi and Congo rivers, before coming to the 'Panta-point meridian', close to the headwaters of the Mkushi river, some thirty miles from Serenje.[20] There the border turns sharply north, as an imaginary straight-line, to the Luapula, following the river until entering Lake Mweru; thence to Mpweto at the north of the lake, before becoming a straight line again, eastwards to Lake Tanganyika.

At appropriate intervals, Gore-Browne and his colleagues would erect permanent markers, frequently large wooden beacons thirty to forty feet high. Much of the work was undertaken in the dry season when it was easier to camp, with staff and labourers granted leave during the rains. One difficulty was the area known as the pedicle, that part of the Congo protruding into Northern Rhodesia. The Commission had suggested an exchange of territory to obviate the inconvenience of this protrusion by simply drawing the boundary line across rather than around the area. Partly due to the potential for copper mining, the proposal was not accepted and the pedicle remains to this day.

The Boundary Commission completed its work in January 1914, but Gore-Browne felt a strong inclination to stay on and see more of the country; he had often dreamed of owning an estate, but never had the means to make this possible in England. Hearing glowing accounts of Lake Shiwa, he arrived there in June and was not disappointed:

> We suddenly came upon the most beautiful lake I had ever seen, I was surrounded by hilly country, and along its shores were groves of rare trees, of a kind sacred to Africans. Friendly folk inhabited the one big village on the lakeshore, and there were a dozen different herds of wild game. The surrounding land seemed to be reasonably fertile, judging by the crops that were ripening there. I knew at once that I had found what I was looking for.[21]

Miss Brunton seems to have been the only unattached woman at the May party in 1914. Who knows, perhaps Claude was thinking of her when, sitting at his desk a few days later, wearing a pullover against the slight chill in the clear air, he found his concentration wandering from his monthly reports. Looking forward to a light lunch followed by a nap, and afterwards walking over for tea with Mrs. Draper, he was interrupted by the unexpected arrival in the compound of Gore-Browne and his party. With both bosses, Chesnaye and Draper away, he realised that he would

178 SATURDAY, JUNE 27, 1914. 26th Week

(178-187)

Suddenly arrived at abercorn.
Received hospitably by taciturn
Cambridge youth (Oldfield) who
said he knew me by sight in O.T.C.
days.
Draper out at Saisi.
P.M. called on Mrs Draper, & walked
to Lake Chila.
Dinner with her, & Oldfield.
Wire from Secretary saying K. & B.
might go home with me.

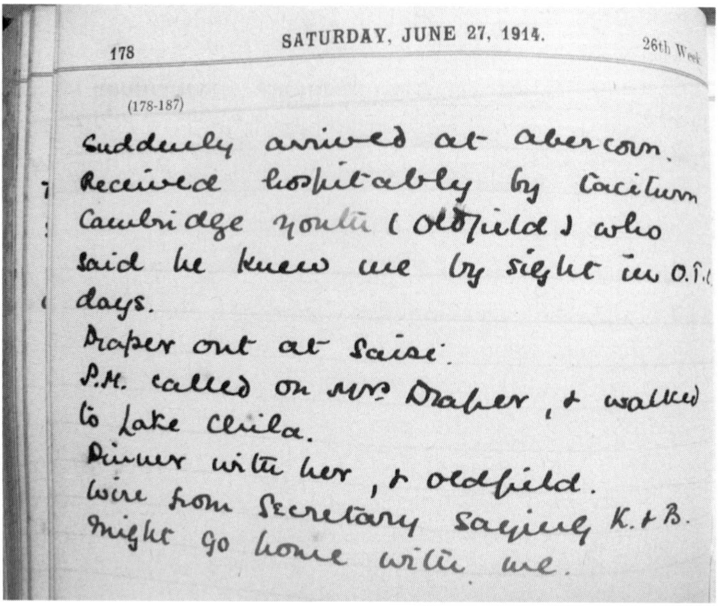

Extract from Gore-Browne's diary

have to 'front-up' and make plans for their stay. He recalled meeting Gore-Browne, who was five or six years his junior, on officer training, back in his Cambridge. Gore-Browne may have remembered Claude, as he kept meticulous diaries throughout his life. After penning the lyrical portrait of Lake Shiwa a few days earlier, he now recorded his visit to Abercorn in a few terse notes, his impression of Claude not entirely flattering:

> Saturday, June 27, 1914
>
> Suddenly arrived at Abercorn. Received hospitably by taciturn Cambridge youth (Oldfield) who said he knew me by sight in O.T.C. days. Draper out at Saisi.
>
> P.M. Called on Mrs Draper, & walked to Lake Chila. Dinner with her, & Oldfield. Wire from Secretary saying K. & B. might go home with me.
>
> Sunday, June 28, 1914
>
> Draper came back today. Most kind. Having all my meals there.
>
> Monday, June 29, 1914
>
> A.M. Business
>
> P.M. To the place cleared for the Cairo to the Cape aviator's landing

Stewart Gore-Browne, Abercorn, June 1914

– when he comes.

Tuesday, June 30, 1914
Gave lunch to the Boma and also incidentally to Dr Wareham.
P.M. Given tennis party.

Wednesday, July 1, 1914
Photographed the telegraphist's child. Sold my tent. Said goodbye, &
then off with Draper about 12 noon. Fed on the way, and left bicycles.
Ghastly road. Drop of 4000' in 15 miles. At last saw Tanganyika. It is
truly a wonderful sight. Camped at the A.L.C. building.
P.M. Paid off carriers, and so on. Sad.

Thursday, July 2, 1914

At about 9 a.m. we saw our steamer.

Got on board & met Chesnay (sic). Very nice but horribly progressive. Under weigh about 12.[22] Disembarking (at Bismarckburg) 2.30. Went to the Boma & then for a walk.

Meanwhile territorial issues elsewhere were coming sharply into focus. As Gore-Browne enjoyed the hospitality of Abercorn and dreamed of a house on Lake Shiwa, in Europe a series of dramatic events was about to unfold. The prelude took place on 28th June, when the Austrian Archduke Franz Ferdinand and his wife Sophie, having narrowly escaped an assassin's bomb in Sarajevo earlier in the day, were shot dead. A touch paper had been lit that in a matter of weeks would engulf large parts of Europe in flames. Among the British, a spirit of patriotic adventure quickly stirred. Gore-Browne left Abercorn and embarked ship at Dar-es-Salaam, pleased to be going home 'just in time to join my regiment and go to France with the Expeditionary Force in August 1914'.[23]

Africa was a long way from Europe, yet the conflagration would leave the continent far from untouched. In Nyasaland on 31st July, Governor Smith asked Captain C. W. Barton to prepare for hostilities. The 5th August, the day after Britain's declaration of war on Germany, saw the formation of the EAMR, the East African Mounted Rifles. On the 6th, the German battleship *Konigsberg* captured and sank the first casualty of Britain's merchant fleet, the *City of Winchester* in the Gulf of Aden. On 7th August, the first shot was fired in Togoland and on the 8th, Dar-es-Salaam was bombarded from the coast. Meanwhile, for Claude and his compatriots in the sleepy outpost of Abercorn, it would soon be something other than beer coming over the border.

---

[1]   From Roger Daniel, 'The First Trans-African Highway' and 'Crossing Africa by Motorboat', *Great North Road* website (2008). The articles encapsulate two travel books written by Paul Graetz (1875-1968): *Im Auto quer durch Afrika* (1910) and *Im Motorboot quer durch Afrika – vom Indischen Ozean zum Kongo* (1912), both published by Verlag Gustav Braunbeck & Gutenberg, Berlin

[2]   Daniel, ibid.

[3]   Gouldsbury & Sheane, *The great plateau*, p16

[4]   Roberts, *Zambia*, pp 287-88

[5]   'I came; I saw; I conquered', attributed to Julius Caesar who, according to Appian,

used the phrase in a letter to the Roman Senate around 47 BC, after victory against Pharnaces II of Pontus at the Battle of Zela.

[6] Terence Ranger, 'Making Northern Rhodesia Imperial: Variations on a Royal Theme, 1924-1938', *African Affairs*, Vol. 79, Issue 316, July 1980, pp 349-73. And as Lewis Gann maintained, 'British authority rested on a minimum of force' (review of A. D. Roberts, *A History of Zambia*)

[7] Abercorn DNB, p 105. Report signed by W.E.M. Owen, ANC.

[8] From the address to mourners during the burial of the late Chief Fwambo, who died on 27 December in Lusaka, aged 80. The Chief's body was flown from Lusaka to Mbala by the Zambian Air Force. *Lusaka Times*, 30 December 2015.

[9] Sir Robert Edward Codrington (1869-1908) was the Administrator of the two territories ruled by the BSAC; from 11 July 1898 to 24 April 1907, for North Eastern Rhodesia; then from February 1908 for North Western Rhodesia, until his death in London on 16 December 1908 at the age of 39. His work laid the foundation for the amalgamation of the two territories in 1911 and his administration was influential in establishing British colonial government in both Northern Rhodesia and Nyasaland, and in making them different in character from white-settler led Southern Rhodesia.

[10] G. Stokes 'Letter to the Editor' *NRJ*, Vol. II, No. 3 (1954) p 84

[11] Gouldsbury & Sheane, ibid., Ch.10, *The Vagrant Official*, p 143 et seq

[12] Benjamin Edgington was a 19th century tent manufacturer, with customers mainly from the world of travel, sport and the military.

[13] Hope and Marion Gamwell, 'The History of Abercorn', *NRJ*, Vol. IV, No. 6 (1961), pp 515-27

[14] Chiwale palm: *Raphia farinifera*

[15] Lionel Smith, 'Measuring the Kalambo Falls', *NRJ*, Vol. I, No. 6 (1952), p 73

[16] J. Desmond Clark, *Kalambo Falls Prehistoric Site*, Cambridge University Press, 1969

[17] G. H. Lobb, Notes: 'The 'May Party' in Abercorn' *NRJ*, Vol. II, No. 1 (1953) pp 76-9

[18] Sir Stewart Gore-Browne 'The Anglo-Belgian Boundary Commission, 1911-1914', *NRJ*, Vol. V, No. 4 (1964) pp 315-29. Sir Stewart Gore-Browne (1883-1967), called 'Chipembele' by Africans, was a soldier, pioneer white settler, politician and supporter of independence for Northern Rhodesia.

[19] Gore-Browne, ibid.

[20] 'Panta-point' (or Mpanta). The point at the southern end of Lake Bangweulu where the Luapula river emerges from the lake. On longitude 29° 50' East.

[21] Sir Stewart Gore-Browne 'Shiwa Ngandu' *NRJ*, Vol. VI, No. 1 (1965) pp 235-38

[22] 'Under weigh' rather than 'under way', whilst not common usage, reflects the maritime history of the expression, along the lines of weighing anchor to get a ship moving.

[23] Gore-Browne, ibid.

CHAPTER 9

The Battle for Africa Begins

In all the German colonies, though but a few decades old,
a life full of promise was discernible

Paul von Lettow-Vorbeck, *My Reminiscences of East Africa*

The longest campaign of the First World War was fought not in Europe, but over the vast area that was German East Africa, which today comprises Tanzania, Rwanda and Burundi. While the first shot and fatality in Africa is believed to have occurred in Togoland, it was in German East Africa that events quickly escalated.[1] The British 'Cape of Good Hope Squadron' used a light cruiser, HMS *Astraea*, to shell Dar-es-Salaam on 8th August 1914, and a week later 200 German and askari troops invaded British East Africa (BEA), later Kenya, at the Holili/Taveta border claiming the first fatality of the East African campaign, a corporal of the Maragoli tribe.[2]

How had this now enemy territory, whose southern border lay so dangerously close to Claude's post at Abercorn, come into being? German East Africa (GEA) had developed under the impetus of Carl Peters who was instrumental in forming the German East Africa Company in 1885.[3] The Anglo-German Agreement signed on 1st July 1890 gave the country 'protectorate' status. When the boundaries were drawn under this agreement, the Kaiser's wish to have at least one snow-capped peak within his empire resulted in an irregularity in the southern line to accommodate Mt. Kilimanjaro within German territory. Lake Tanganyika formed a western border with the Belgian Congo, while to the north, Lake Victoria bordered BEA near Nairobi. To the south, Nyasaland and Lake Nyasa bordered the territory of a third imperial power, Portuguese East Africa (PEA).

The Anglo-German agreement also provided that Heligoland, a small archipelago in the North Sea, should belong to Germany. Britain would gain control of Zanzibar, the former slave market island in the Indian Ocean, situated at an important strategic position opposite the German port of Dar-es-Salaam.[4] This began the extraordinary process by which territories were blocked out with lines drawn on maps far away in Europe. Only later were the boundaries actually tested on the ground, with the war effectively becoming the last stage in the 'Scramble for Africa'.[5]

GEA was a big country, some three times the area of present-day Germany, with a population in 1914 of some five million. Its economic success would require a growth in commerce, which in turn depended on good transport. The new colony had two significant ports, Dar-es-Salaam and Tanga, and two railways were constructed, starting in 1888: the Usambara Line from Tanga to Moshi, where coffee was being grown on the slopes of Kilimanjaro, and the Central Line running 780 miles west from Dar-es-Salaam, via Morogoro and Tabora, to reach Lake Tanganyika at Kigoma, in February 1914. Agricultural plantations were developed, based on sisal, rubber and cotton, but despite trade escalating from 36 million marks in 1906 to 89 million by 1913, GEA never achieved a profit for the German Empire and was subsidised by the Berlin treasury. Nevertheless, it was a possession that the Germans could be expected to defend fiercely and, if they got the chance, enlarge.

At the beginning of the war, Britain and Germany had opposing objectives. Germany wanted to open up the war to divert Britain's attention away from Europe. From their colonies, including GEA, the Germans could pursue this strategy on several fronts – on land, sea (in both the Atlantic and Indian Oceans) and on the inland lakes (Victoria, Tanganyika and Nyasa). However, it was in Britain's interest to try to close the down the war so that it could concentrate its efforts in France and Belgium.[6] The historian Huw Strachan explains that Britain's strategic aims were also influenced by the ambitions of others; with South Africa wishing to enlarge its boundaries in southern Africa, only a decade or so after the end of the Boer War, could Britain rely on their support? France with its west African colonies might also be a rival in the rush for territorial expansion.

While Britain and her allies were working on a strategy to conduct the war in Africa, the Governor of British East Africa, Sir Henry Belfield, stated that the colony had no interest in the present war.[7] There were also severe tensions in GEA, where the Governor, Dr. Heinrich Schnee, an experienced colonial official, ordered that no hostile action should be taken.

The colonial governors, who had often met in the pre-war years, had discussed these matters and wished to adhere to the Congo Act of 1885,

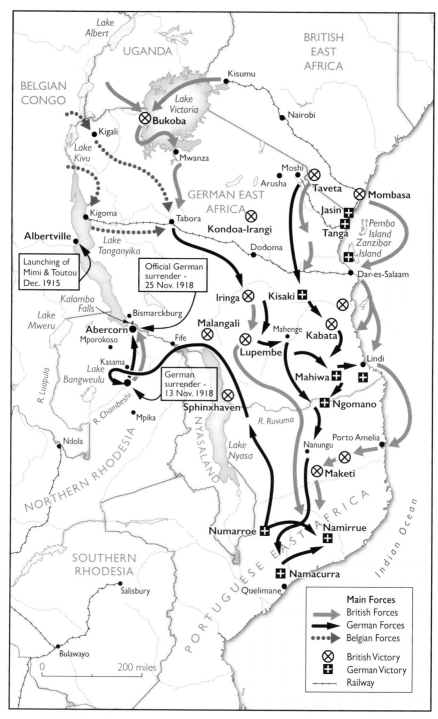

World War One in German East Africa and neighbouring territories

106

General von Lettow-Vorbeck and Dr Heinrich Schnee, Governor, German East Africa

which called for overseas possessions to remain neutral in the event of a European war. Neither colony had many troops. The commander of the German *Schutztruppe*, Paul Emil von Lettow-Vorbeck, appointed in January 1914, saw things differently and was prepared to disobey his legal superior, initially being 'seen as lacking judgement and being dangerously aggressive'.[8] By the end of the campaign, Lettow-Vorbeck had won the grudging admiration of Claude's contemporary Bernard Montgomery, who observed that the general had caused 'a nuisance to the Allies out of all proportion to the size of his force.'[9]

The first substantive action of the campaign in East Africa was an amphibious landing at Tanga in early November 1914, by British Indian Expeditionary Force 'B' under Major Aitken, which was wholly and unexpectedly repulsed by the Germans. Although the British force was far superior in numbers, they were woefully under-prepared and had no idea that the Germans were keen and ready to fight. The encounter became known as 'The Battle of the Bees' as the 98th Infantry broke up when attacked by swarms of angry bees. British propaganda transformed the bee interlude into a fiendish German plot, but many years later, Lettow-Vorbeck described how the machine gunners of one of his companies had been equally affected.[10] When the Allied Indian contingent returned to Kenya, they were subject to some ridicule, and it took time before reputations were restored. Covered extensively in the press, even a song was composed, *Steaming Down to Tanga*, about the debacle.[11] The German victory raised their morale and after witnessing such a miserable British performance, they realised that value might indeed exist in confronting the British in Africa.[12]

Meanwhile, in the Indian Ocean there was a threat to Allied shipping from the SMS *Königsberg*, the lead ship of her class of light cruisers. She had initially attempted to raid British and French commercial traffic in the region, but only destroyed one merchant ship, and had been hampered by coal shortages. The *Königsberg* had harboured stealthily in the Rufiji delta, but on 20th September 1914 she came on the attack, disabling HMS *Pegasus* and the packet ship *Helmut* at Zanzibar, before retreating back to the delta to repair her engines. Three British cruisers, unable to steam into the river to destroy her, set up a blockade of the delta whilst attempts were made to locate the *Königsberg* using seaplanes. Following several attempts to sink the ship during the 'Battle of Rufiji Delta', in July 1915 the British sent two monitors (HMS *Mersey* and HMS *Severn*), who managed to get close enough to severely damage the *Königsberg*, forcing her crew to scuttle the ship. For tying down at least twenty-seven British ships during the 255-day blockade, Max Looff, the captain of the *Königsberg*, received the Iron Cross, First Class.[13] The surviving crew salvaged various stores and all ten of her main guns, and then joined Lettow-Vorbeck's campaign on the mainland.

So what had been happening in Abercorn since the outbreak of hostilities? In embattled times, the island of Britain had always had one great advantage, the English Channel. In 1914, German forces could not attempt to simply march in, as they had on 4th August when they swiftly overran 'plucky little Belgium' in order to attack France. The small British community in Northern Rhodesia could draw no comfort from any natural barrier. Their northern border with the Germans, the thinnest of red lines, was just over 200 miles long, with three straggling outposts: Abercorn, Saisi and Fife.

The southern end of Lake Tanganyika is some 25 miles north west of Abercorn. The parallel shores of the long lake run 400 miles almost due north, with the Belgian Congo to the west and GEA directly opposite. Gaining dominance on Lake Tanganyika was clearly a strategic imperative and, steam vessels being up to ten times faster than the native dhows, would be the first quarry in the sight of any aggressor. With war declared, the Germans lost little time in seizing the initiative. By the end of August 1914, Abercorn was buzzing with the news of the sinking of the 90-ton Belgian steamer *Alexandre del Commune* by the *Hedwig von Wissman* at Lukuga on the Belgian side of the Lake.[14] German superiority on the lake was further strengthened when the African Lakes Corporation's steamer *Cecil Rhodes*, an obvious symbolic target, was disabled in a raid in November 1914.

Some Abercorn residents had taken the sinking of the steamer as good news, making it more likely to galvanise further support from their Belgian neighbours; others remained unsure. The one certainty was that the war had arrived on their doorstep. Following discussions between local commanders in October, the Belgian administration had agreed to place 225 native police on the border to strengthen security.

Whether the War would become a full-blown affair and seriously imperil the Abercorn community, or fizzle out after a spell of diplomatic wrangling, remained to be seen. Being also the closest British settlement to the German stronghold of Bismarckburg, many in the community feared they were a prime target for an attack, and sorely unprepared. But 'cometh the hour, cometh the man', in this case Claude's boss, Christian Chesnaye, who as Abercorn's NC and Magistrate became responsible for its defence.[15] A. E. L. Barnshaw, a scout with the Northern Rhodesian Police working in the Abercorn Telegraph Department, noted that with only a dozen district police, Chesnaye acted decisively, evacuating women and children and putting native and European volunteers, Claude among them, on watch patrols. The news of the war took several days to reach the German post near the border. There was no enemy action until late August 1914 when sporadic raids cut the telegraph line between Abercorn and Fife. These were not pointless exercises; in the first days of September, askari troops under German command were spotted, and estimated to be worryingly strong in number. When the residents of Abercorn heard the rat-a-tat of a Hotchkiss Revolverkanone, a 37mm machine gun, they knew an attack had begun.

This first assault on Northern Rhodesia was led by General Kurt Wahle, a 59-year old retired officer on holiday in Africa with his son when war had been declared. After volunteering to Lettow-Vorbeck, Wahle had

Claude on Border Patrol

mobilised towards Abercorn with a force including 100 askari, 250 'ruga-ruga' and sixty armed porters.[16] The unequal odds were serious enough, but the ruga-ruga also had a reputation for looting and rape. Lieutenant J. J. McCarthy held the enemy at bay with just forty askari of the Northern Rhodesia Police and the local prison was turned into a fortification. But Wahle was not going away.

Chesnaye requested urgent support from Kasama, where a contingent of 100 Northern Rhodesian Police under Major Stennett, ordered up to the northern border from Livingstone, had only just arrived. Learning that Abercorn was under siege, Stennett marched the reinforcements ninety-nine miles in sixty-six hours, reaching Abercorn on 9th September. Three hours later a German field-gun shell came whistling in. More followed, sporadically, but too close for comfort, forty being counted by the end of the day. The defenders held firm, with the loss of two Africans: Privates Chasea and Madi. The following morning, seeing the Germans withdrawing, McCarthy ran with the advantage, and with Abercorn's prison inmates volunteering to carry the Maxim machine gun, gave chase, pushing the enemy to the border at the Lumi river.[17] In Abercorn that evening, Claude and friends must have surely raised a whisky and soda to McCarthy, Stennett, and perhaps Sir Hiram Maxim, without whose invention they might all have been lying in the corner of a foreign field that was not destined to be forever England. Privates Chasea and Madi had found their resting place in the land of their birth. The war however, in the shape of Lettow-Vorbeck, was not yet done with Abercorn.

The boma at Abercorn would meanwhile be further shored up. Around 9th September, news of the attack had also reached Kawambwa, prompting the magistrate to dispatch the Belgian troops from Pweto, at the northern end of Lake Mweru. The first were in Abercorn by the 26th, with more to follow, along with another Maxim. The inhabitants could now feel more secure with the added comfort of being on home ground. Friends caught on enemy soil found themselves in a very different position. Gordon Lobb had received disconcerting news about one of his guests who had attended his May Party only a few months earlier: 'The day war broke out our boys told us that "Scot" Brown and two other white men had been interned at Tabora. This turned out to be true. The natives must have got the news by bush telegraph (drums).'[18]

The drums were efficient. Tabora, a small junction settlement on the central railway line across GEA, was way up country. Back home in England the drumbeat of war had been swiftly muffled by the confident prediction that it would be 'all over by Christmas', and Claude's parents, though doubtless perturbed by news of the Abercorn attack, might reasonably have hoped that once the Germans had been sent packing, the danger would pass. Those closer to the front line of the Empire were less sanguine. On 24th September, German forces had been in action to the north, seizing Idjwi Island on Lake Kivu from the Belgians. The reported reactions of the soldiers supposedly guarding it, gave little reassurance of Belgian commitment or competence:

> The Belgian garrison, somewhat implausibly by this stage, said that they had not realised there was a war on. Their uncaptured compatriots behaved rather as though they subscribed to the same belief. They claimed that they were confronted by 2,000 Germans, when by October, Lettow's concentration of his forces to the north had reduced the strength in the west to twenty-four Europeans and 152 askaris.[19]

The Defence of Abercorn

Machine gun placement

Hospital and Blockhouse (with staked trench)

Trenches and dug-outs

*Gaol with
fortifications*

*Ruins of
Abercorn gaol*

*Military transport,
outside ALC Store*

Ford lorries

The Northern Rhodesia front remained under the control of the Colonial Office, rather than the War Office. In Abercorn, Claude and his colleagues continued their patrols. Dropping guard after the September attacks would have been dangerously premature. Unlike mainstream infantry, the *Schutztruppen* were accustomed to 'hit and run' warfare, successful against local rebels in their own territory. What might appear as retreat and defeat to their opponents, was often a calculated, tactical withdrawal, safeguarding their men and munitions to regroup and plan the next strike.

A recurring concern at Abercorn was the cutting of the telegraph line to Saisi, a vital means of communication. Further anxiety was in the offing. With the German strength in Bismarckburg building up, the Belgian troops, who had bolstered morale were needed to support their comrades at Mporokoso. On 11th November 1914, Governor General Sydney Buxton of South Africa, having been advised of the plan, sent an urgent telegram to the Colonial Secretary, which concluded:

> It is not unlikely that withdrawal will be followed by attack on Abercorn which I fear is in some danger. In October the telegraph line between that place and Fife was destroyed. Unless however you are prepared to suggest to Belgian Government that withdrawal of these troops should be postponed for a time there seems to be no course but for the Commandant General to be left to do the best he can with his own forces.[20]

A series of telegrams – replies, pleas and demands – went back and forth, the Governor General, of course, completely oblivious to the fact that the son of one of his prep school masters was living in Abercorn![21] Meanwhile,

Bismarckburg (on promontory overlooking Lake Tanganyika)

Sydney Buxton

the Belgian troops had left Abercorn, much to the consternation of
its residents. When negotiations eventually allowed the order to be
countermanded, the troops had already reached Mporokoso, where they
would remain for the time being. Uncertainty was the prevailing mood,
and the security and survival of Northern Rhodesia might well depend on
the role of the Belgians. An historic agreement, dating from 1885 between
the European powers, decreed that the Congo would remain neutral in any
conflict, and even after the sinking of the *Alexandre Del Commune*, there
had been mixed messages on the extent of her forces' involvement.[22] By the
end of November, it had been agreed that the Belgian forces in Northern
Rhodesia would defer to British command. Guarding the Abercorn-
Fife border would be a British responsibility, the southern shore of Lake
Tanganyika that of the Belgian troops, who in due course would return
from Mporokoso to be based at Abercorn.

Buxton's rather resigned take-it-or-leave-it ending to his telegram to
the Colonial Secretary suggests, that to many in high office, warfare at
a distance was less a worry than an invigorating diversion: 'These early
battles in East Africa were described by Lewis Harcourt, the British
Secretary of State for the Colonies, as "all very thrilling".' Edward Paice

maintains that: 'beneath the Gilbertian veneer the fighting had assumed a seriousness which few would recognise until much later. Longstanding, and intense, imperial rivalries had been rekindled; colonial ambitions were being reappraised; and the insouciant atmosphere of the first weeks of August was fast evaporating.'[22]

Spirited posturing among the colonial powers, events suggested, was coming to an end. The Germans now dominated Lake Tanganyika and they had set ablaze the ALC stores, after appropriating 150 miles of telegraph wire, later used for their own line from Neu Langenburg to Iringa. In December 1914, German troops from Neu Langenburg launched two attacks on Fife, and though unsuccessful, these repeated attempts on the border showed the German resolve and tenacity. For the British, native loyalty was now at stake, which with relatively few European troops to call on, might soon become an issue of survival: 'the attacks led to growing concerns about British 'prestige' among the African population on the 200 mile border, particularly the 'warlike' Angoni who had rebelled against British rule in 1897-8 in the Fort Jameson area.'[24]

Whether or not influenced by Buxton's telegram to the Colonial Office, a further column of Northern Rhodesia Police was sent to reinforce Abercorn, this time from Schuckmannsburg, in the Caprivi Strip, where the Germans had surrendered on 22nd August.[25] Under the command of Major J. J. O'Sullevan, they moved first by truck and by rail to Sakania, on the border with Northern Rhodesia and the Congo, before starting an epic march, covering 430 miles in pouring rain, in just twenty days. After a few days at Abercorn, O'Sullevan explained that:

> Colonel Hodson, who commanded the forces on the border, sent my column to Saisi, which is on the frontier … We made a fort and trenches, and removed long grass … then we proceeded to patrol, and were practically in touch with the Germans daily … though they were often ten to one … we seemed, by some great good luck, to snatch a victory when defeat seemed almost certain.[26]

Christmas that year for Claude would have been subdued and uneasy. Since the evacuation of the women and children, Abercorn had become an oddly male preserve, perhaps reminiscent of his university days, but with no jolly parties. One couldn't stroll into Cambridge for a leisurely night out or enjoy choirs singing seasonal carols. Instead one listened for the native drums, hazarding a guess at their message, or for the sound of gunfire. With no Belgian soldiers, and their return not certain, the boma

Belgian troops at Abercorn, joining in native sports

must have seemed a very small place:

> The mistaken withdrawal of the Belgian battalion ... left the
> Northern Rhodesia Police unable to undertake anything beyond
> the passive defence of Abercorn and Fife. Consequently the enemy
> raided freely and carried off and destroyed large quantities of the
> telegraph line, in this way completely isolating Abercorn.[27]

On 26th January 1915 the Belgian troops at Mporokoso returned to
Abercorn. Now more confident of the odds, the Belgians planned a two-
pronged movement: a solo expedition into Rwanda and Urundi and, with
the British if willing, over the border of Northern Rhodesia into GEA.
However, with the Belgian forces scattered, supplying such an operation
looked problematic. As for the joint venture, the British Colonial Office,
wary of Belgian competition for a potential Cape to Cairo route beyond
Northern Rhodesia at some future point, demurred.

By April 1915, while Anglo-Belgian diplomatic talks meandered on,
the charismatic figure of John R. Lee entered the stage. A Boer War
veteran and big game hunter, Lee approached the British Admiralty
with an intriguing piece of intelligence concerning a large and unusual
consignment, which for the last few months had been travelling from
the German port of Dar-es-Salaam, across the central railway to Kigoma.
Comprising 5,000 separate crates, the contents when assembled by skilled

German engineers, would amount to a 220ft long ship, 32ft across, with a displacement of 1,575 tons. Once reconstructed, armed and launched on Lake Tanganyika, the *Graf von Goetzen* would render all opposition null and void, and allow the Germans to mount large scale attacks on both Northern Rhodesia and the Belgian Congo.[28] Lee stressed to the Admiralty that this development could seriously undermine Britain's hold over the Africans, and rebellion would quickly follow.[29]

With Churchill's plan for the Dardenelles assault on Turkey stretching resources, how could the British Navy compete? Lee had an idea: rather than trying to outdo the Germans in terms of size, why not dispatch a smaller but faster vessel, armed with a long-range gun? The logistics would still be daunting, but Lee convinced the Admiralty and was sent off to Cape Town to prepare the route, while a vessel and personnel were found. A couple of 40-foot craft, under construction for the Brazilians by Thorneycroft, were commandeered; and to lead the team the Admiralty selected Lieutenant-Colonel Geoffrey Spicer-Simson.

Describing Spicer-Simson as 'something of an eccentric' is an understatement.[30] Others have highlighted his lack of modesty, tact and luck. He had twice been beached for incompetence: once for ramming a liberty boat with his destroyer and then for allowing a German warship to sink a coastal defence vessel under his command as he watched from shore while dining with his wife. To his failings as a naval officer were added braggadocio and condescension.[31] The naming of the motorboats became an issue with the Admiralty, who eventually agreed on *Mimi* and *Toutou*, sounding like a pair of pet Pekinese. Spicer-Simson's more relevant credentials for the forthcoming mission included fluency in French and German, and a four-year stint on survey up the Gambia River. We shall return to *Mimi* and *Toutou* later.

In the spring of 1915, three Belgian battalions were supporting British troops and police along the Northern Rhodesian border, but by June the Belgian Colonel Tombeur had ordered them to deploy north into GEA. In the event, two of the battalions tarried, one at Abercorn, the other at Pweto on Lake Mweru. The fearsome *Graf von Goetzen* had now been launched on Lake Tanganyika, and 700 additional German troops and reservists had arrived in Bismarckburg. From here, they marched with two field guns to Saisi, where at dawn on 28th June, in dense mist, they began a bombardment. Major O'Sullevan's defences had been well thought out, and after a forty-eight hour siege, proved impregnable. Among the German fatalities was one of their company commanders, Karl Proempeler. Closer examination of what appeared to be graves dug by the retreating enemy however, revealed them to contain not bodies, but stores of ammunition, indicating another tactical, temporary withdrawal.

There followed a few weeks of sporadic shooting, until on 25th July came another full-scale assault, led personally by General Wahle. This time the Germans did not retreat and the 450 British and Belgians were outnumbered more than two to one. From Abercorn, Major de Koninck set out with Belgian reinforcements, but was held back by enemy fire. The Germans were pushing steadily closer to the outpost, while those pinned down inside, in dire need of water, were creeping out under cover of darkness for fresh supplies. Eventually, a dusk charge that brought the enemy within seventy yards of the first trench looked like a make-or-break moment. For the Germans it proved the latter, and by the beginning of August they were gone.[32] So too was Gordon Lobb's nearby farm:

> The Germans burnt my place down in the war. All my good furniture, made by Bernard Turner and Freshwater of the London Missionary Society, of local wood, which one does not get these days, went up in flames. Thinking that 'Mula' was our home for our lifetime, I had spent a lot of money on it. 'Scot' Brown's collection of photographs were taken from him so we never saw the photos of the races taken by him, or of some taken of me driving my tandem in a dog cart that I had bought at Fife Boma from the Government.[33]

Lobb had invested his life in Africa, but the memory of happy times would endure: 'The traditional "May Party" was not renewed after the war.

Race meeting at Saisi, 1914: G.H. Lobb, C. Blyth, H.S. Wood, L.M. Smith

Abercorn took a long time to recover.' No doubt Claude shared some of those memories, but his life was still unfolding, the richest, and perhaps most difficult part of it, yet to come. By September 1915, in spite of the war, he was allowed to take his first home leave in four years, leaving Abercorn to head south for Durban and a berth on the *Llandovery Castle*.

[1] Following the declaration of war, the Gold Coast Regiment entered Togoland, advancing on Lomé. An advance patrol encountered the German-led police force on 7 August 1914 at Nuatja, near Lomé, the police force opening fire. Alhaji Grunshi returned fire, the first British soldier to fire a shot in WWI. https://livesofthefirstworldwar.org/lifestory/1492566

[2] Anne Samson, 'When two bulls clash, the grass suffers: World War I in East Africa', Talk at British High Commission, Dar-es-Salaam, 23 July 2014

[3] The Deutsch-Ostafrikanische Gesellschaft

[4] The Heligoland archipelago gave Germany control of the new Kiel Canal and the approaches to their North Sea ports. In exchange, Germany gave up its rights to Zanzibar.

[5] The one boundary which had been walked before it was drawn on a map was between British and German East Africa, with the work of the joint Anglo-German boundary commission starting in July 1885. Lord Kitchener, the British member, recommended that Mt. Kilimanjaro should belong to Germany. By November 1886, the report was complete and the result was agreed with the other major colonial power, France. Source: *The London Gazette*. 6 November 1885 and the historyworld website

[6] Hew Strachan, *The First World War in Africa*, Oxford University Press, 2004

[7] Byron Farwell, *The Great War in Africa*, (W. W. Norton, New York, 1986) pp 121-22

[8] The *Schutztruppe* (protection troops) were the German colonial armed force, under the control of the German Colonial Office. They comprised German volunteers, reinforced by native troops (askaris), and enjoyed the support of local police forces. See Ross Anderson, *The Forgotten Front: The East African Campaign 1914-1918* (The History Press, 2004)

[9] *Later Field Marshall* Bernard Montgomery, 1st Viscount Montgomery of Alamein. See Montgomery of Alamein, *A History of Warfare* (Collins, 1968) p 490

[10] Farwell, ibid., p 171 and Paul von Lettow-Vorbeck, *My Reminiscences of East Africa* (Hurst & Blackett, 1920)

[11] Thomas A. Crowson, *When Elephants Clash – A Critical Analysis of Major General Paul Emil Von Lettow-Vorbeck* (Pickle Partners Publishing, 2014)

[12] Peter Baxter at http://peterbaxterafrica.com

[13] Farwell, ibid., p158

[14] Alexandre del Commune (1855-1922) was a Belgian officer of the armed *Force Publique* of the Congo Free State who undertook extensive explorations of the country during the early colonial period. By the start of the war, the Germans had two warships on the Lake: the 60-ton *Hedwig von Wissman*, and the 45-ton *Kingani*. *Hedwig von Wissman*, armed with four pom-pom guns from the scuttled survey ship

Möwe, sailed to Lukuga, where she sank the *Alexandre del Commune*.

[15] Christian Purefoy Chesnaye (1870-1943), born in Simla, India, was made CBE in October 1918 for his efforts in WWI. On leave in 1901, he was living at 'La Chesnaye' in Bournemouth, but on retirement, moved to California and then to Vancouver Island, where he died. His parents, George and Mary, were from Ireland, but the name suggests that the Chesnayes were descended from Huguenot refugees. Source: *Imperial Vancouver Island: Who Was Who, 1850-1950* by J. F. Bosher (Xlibris, 2010)

[16] Askaris were local soldiers (or armed guards) serving in the armies of the European colonial powers in Africa. The 'ruga-ruga' were irregular troops and mercenaries, drawn from local tribes.

[17] Also known as the Kawimbe river, from its source at Kawimbe Mission, it is a tributary of the Saisi.

[18] 'The "May Party" in Abercorn', *NRJ*, Vol. 2, No. 1 (1953) pp 76-9

[19] Strachan, ibid., p 112

[20] Received, Colonial Office, 12.25am, 11 November 1914 (The National Archives, London CO 417/543 44283)

[21] Sydney Charles Buxton (1853-1934), later 1st Earl Buxton, educated Hewitt's School, Rottingdean (where he was taught by Thomas Oldfield), Clifton and Trinity College, Cambridge (see Ch. 2).

[22] The Berlin Conference of 1884-85, also known as the Congo Conference, regulated European colonisation and trade in Africa during the New Imperialism period, and coincided with Germany's sudden emergence as an imperial power. The outcome was the General Act of the Berlin Conference, which can be seen as the formalization of the 'Scramble for Africa'. The conference also ushered in a period of heightened colonial activity by European powers, which eliminated or overrode most existing forms of African autonomy and self-governance.

[23] Edward Paice, *Tip and Run: The Untold Tragedy of the Great War in Africa* (Weidenfield & Nicolson, 2007) p 33

[24] Paice, ibid., pp 98-9

[25] Schuckmannsburg, South West Africa. Now known as Luhonono, Namibia.

[26] J. J. O'Sullevan, Lecture to the African Society, February 1916, quoted in W. V. Brelsford (ed), *The Story of the Northern Rhodesia Regiment* (Galago, Bromley, Kent, 1954; reprinted 1990), pp 53-7

[27] Brelsford, ibid., p31

[28] The *Graf von Goetzen* had been constructed at the Meyer Werft shipyard at Papenburg, before being disassembled for the journey to Africa. Named after Gustav Adolf von Götzen (1866-1910), a German explorer, particularly of Rwanda, and first Governor of GEA.

[29] Paice, ibid., p 99

[30] Crowson, ibid.

[31] See Giles Foden, *Mimi and Toutou Go Forth: The Bizarre Battle for Lake Tanganyika* (Michael Joseph, 2004) and also Paice, ibid.

[32] Paice, ibid., p 109

[33] The 'May Party', ibid.

CHAPTER 10

Home Fires

Keep the Home Fires Burning,
While your hearts are yearning.
Though your lads are far away,
They dream of home

Composed by Ivor Novello in 1914, lyrics by Lena Guilbert Ford

Sailing from Durban in September 1915, Claude would have known that in May that year the Cunard liner *Lusitania* had been hit by a German torpedo off southern Ireland, with the loss of over 1,000 lives, 283 of them American. After the subsequent sinking of the SS *Arabic* off Liverpool, killing 44 passengers and crew, the German ambassador had reassured the United States that its ships would no longer be targeted without warning. As Claude's ship steamed steadily northwards up the African coast, there must have been some uneasiness on board. America might still be neutral, but the *Llandovery Castle* was unmistakably a British vessel, and one can imagine the collective sigh of relief as she entered Southampton docks.

Now twenty-six, Claude had returned to England with four years' experience of a very different landscape and culture. There had been the shock of the attack on Abercorn, a starker lesson in the realities of warfare than a dog-eared copy of Thucydides. Apart from security drills and long-forgotten afternoons of cadet force exercises at school, Claude had had no military training. During the drawn-out siege, as the Northern Rhodesia Police held the line, he must have wondered if and when he might need to shoulder a rifle and take his place among them.

Meanwhile, Stewart Gore-Browne, his plans for his African estate postponed, was *en route* to the Western Front. Paul Nash, Claude's contemporary at St Paul's, had enlisted as a private for home service in the Second Battalion, the 'Artists Rifles', a reluctant participant in the horrors he would later immortalise on canvas.[1] An older Pauline, Laurence Binyon, inspired by the dramatic scenery of the north Cornwall coast,

*Golders Green, A place of delightful prospects (Poster, 1908 © TfL
from the London Transport Museum collection)*

composed his poem, 'For The Fallen', which was published in *The Times*
in September 1914.

In October 1915 a warm and heartfelt welcome would have awaited
Claude in Maida Vale, from his ageing parents and older brother Harold.
He had also come home an uncle, to Peggy, born on 23rd November 1912
to his older brother Charlie and wife Maisie. They had moved from a flat
in Wymering Mansions, Maida Vale a few miles north to a modest house
in Highfield Avenue in the expanding suburb of Golders Green with
Maisie now expecting their second child.[2] The family would be eager to
hear about events in Northern Rhodesia, first-hand accounts of the recent
border skirmishes. They in turn could tell him how the war had affected
them in London. On the night of 31st May that year, a huge shadow had
fallen across the Thames. At 650ft long, the Zeppelin was larger than any
flying machine ever built. Previously used for leisure, this one brought
death, dropping ninety incendiary bombs and thirty grenades. Thirty-five

people had been injured and seven killed. The other loss, along with the realisation that the 22 miles of the English Channel was no longer an impregnable defence, was psychological. In the words of the German Commander Peter Strasser, 'Nowadays there is no such animal as a non-combatant, modern warfare is total warfare.'[3] It seemed that H.G. Wells's *The War in the Air*, published seven years earlier, had been uncannily prophetic.

Yet on the home front, the full, sinister significance of these visitations was slow to register. Many viewed the airships as they might a dramatic thunderstorm, and commentators noted a cognitive dissonance between the spectacle, and the horror for those on its receiving end:

> all the windows rattled and we became conscious of the booming of guns getting nearer, 'At last the Zeppelins' said Sidney with almost boyish glee … From the balcony we could see the shrapnel bursting over the river … it was a gruesome reflection that while we were being pleasantly excited, men, women and children were being killed and maimed … There was apparently no panic, even in the crowded Strand. The Londoner persists in taking Zeppelin raids as an entertainment.[4]

How was Claude's personal life at this time? Charlie had been free to marry when he chose, but Claude's first three years in the Colonial Service had obliged him, under a rigidly enforced rule, to remain single. The rationale was that young officers should immerse themselves in their work and the local culture and that, particularly with a shortage of suitable accommodation, British-born women rarely adapted well to the lifestyle. Judging by a 1909 directive from Lord Crewe to members of the Colonial Service concerning concubinage, Claude was unlikely to risk consorting with local women: 'Gravely improper conduct of this nature has at times been the cause of serious trouble among native populations … diminishing authority to an extent which will seriously impair his capacity for useful work in the Service.'[5]

Ronald Hyam believes that this change of official attitude was 'tangible evidence differentiating the post-Edwardian empire from what had gone on before'. He also notes that the British policy was markedly different from the more relaxed attitude of the French in West Africa, where concubinage was encouraged as 'the easiest, pleasantest and surest means of gallicising West Africa'.[6] Crewe's position was criticised by Leicester Beaufort, arguing that some of the best officers in North East Rhodesia had emerged from concubinage to become good husbands and effective officers, being more knowledgeable of the language and local customs.[7] Before becoming Chief Justice for North Eastern Rhodesia in 1901, Beaufort had been Governor of North Borneo where he would have learnt about 'sleeping dictionaries' as inter-cultural sexual relations were often known.

The Colonial Service policy must have made it difficult for young officers to find a suitable wife. Girls they may have befriended back in England, perhaps during their university years, might not have waited three or four years for their return. Young men like Charlie Oldfield, living and working in London, had uninterrupted time for courtship. How could a chap in Claude's position expect to meet, attract and build a mutually respecting relationship with a woman, which both might confidently expect to withstand the strains of married life in Africa? As Anthony Kirk-Greene suggests, couples could make hasty and perhaps unwise decisions either way, 'Might the imminence of the end of a four to six months' leave be a spur to an accelerated wedding or would the happiness of meeting survive the apartness for another two or three years?'[8]

Claude had now served his requisite three years as a bachelor, and speculation about his marital prospects would inevitably have been in the air. Back in London, with six months of freedom ahead of him, the onset of war had sharpened the public's appetite for entertainment, which was seen as good for morale. In the autumn of 1915, the enigmatic Lally, who features in Claude's album, one photo inscribed on 13th September of that year 'Yours Lally', perhaps accompanied him around London. Possibly she was invited to take tea with Claude's parents in Maida Vale, afterwards strolling down the Edgware Road to Hyde Park or taking the underground into the West End. They could have enjoyed the latest Charlie Chaplin film, going on afterwards to one of the new supper clubs like the *Four Hundred*, to dance the night away.

Claude and Lally could have first met during his student days at Cambridge and, parting when he sailed for Africa, absence may have made their hearts grow fonder. If there were any dreams of a romantic reunion, did it ever come about? In the time Claude and Lally spent together during his home leave, did they discuss the future? Did the idea of being a colonial wife in Africa appeal to Lally, or might that have been a step too far? Marriage may have been the last thing on her mind.

By December, with the Gallipoli campaign aborted after heavy losses, British morale in the field and at home was in need of a boost. The New

Lally

Year began in a mood of serious intent. The British Army, relying until now on volunteers and regulars, instituted the Military Service Act in March 1916, rendering unmarried men and widowers between the ages of 18 and 41 liable for conscription. Grounds for exemption included those normally resident in the Dominions, and ill health or infirmity, which applied to Claude and his brother Harold respectively.[9]

On 12th February 1916, Claude's brother Charlie and Maisie, had celebrated the birth of their second child, Joy, the author's mother, but on 28th April, his leave at an end, Claude boarded the *Kenilworth Castle* at Plymouth, bound for Cape Town.[10] The danger in European waters had edged up since his incoming voyage. A few days after his arrival, the Italian passenger steamer SS *Ancona*, flying the Austro-Hungarian flag, was sailing off the coast of Tunisia *en route* from Messina to New York when, without warning she was torpedoed by a German U-boat. Of the two hundred lost, nine were American, which coming six months after the sinking of the *Lusitania*, added to growing outrage in the US over unrestricted submarine warfare. In closer proximity, shortly before Claude sailed, the cross-channel ferry *Sussex* had been hit, claiming at least fifty lives. The *Kenilworth Castle* arrived in Cape Town without incident, and Claude made his way by train to Broken Hill and onwards to Abercorn to resume his duties.

The war in Africa had not stood still in Claude's absence. Spicer-Simson's mission to take on the German Navy on Lake Tanganyika with his two miniature battleships, *Mimi* and *Toutou*, had after clever modifications to the vessels, set off in earnest. All involved had been sworn to secrecy, but John Lee, accompanied by Frank Mcgee, an American journalist, in a bid to restore Britain's prestige with the natives, had then inadvertently allowed details of the expedition to leak out. Reports of the pair's drunken escapades in Katanga, offending the Belgian authorities, contributed to the termination of Lee's contract even though Spicer-Simson recognised his value in terms of local knowledge.

A loose tongue aside, Lee had indeed fulfilled his brief, laying out a 150-mile route for the convoy, which consisted of the two gunboats, lorry, trailer and 130 tons of ammunition and supplies. This leg from Fungurume took the convoy six weeks, reaching Sankisia on 28th September 1915. Here, Arthur 'Ginger Dick' Davison took over and on 24th October 'Spicer's Circus', also known as the 'Tanganyika Tits', reported to Commander Stinghlhamber of the Belgian garrison at Albertville on the shores of Lake Tanganyika. The entire journey from Cape Town had been accomplished in four months, covering a distance of 3,000 miles by rail, river, road and track, a Herculean achievement, outstripping even the Germans' transportation of the *Graf von Goetzen*. Now all they had to do was sink it.

Mimi and *Toutou* were launched in December and were soon in action, with their first engagement on the 26th, hitting the *Kingani* below the waterline, forcing surrender. Once repaired, and renamed *Fifi*, Spicer-Simson took the vessel as his flagship, and in February 1916 used her to score a second success by sinking the *Hedwig*. When the *Graf von Goetzen* returned to look for her, Spicer-Simson held his crew off from an attack, and went off to Stanleyville to look for a bigger boat. He found the *St George*, which was being used by the British Consul at Banana Island (situated in an Atlantic inlet to the Congo), and the home of the main Belgian Naval Base. The steel vessel was dismantled, transported and reassembled, ready for service on Lake Tanganyika.

Lieutenant-Colonel Geoffrey Spicer-Simson

By the time Claude arrived back at Abercorn in May 1916, the British were busy planning a strike into GEA from Northern Rhodesia. This decision, made by the Colonial Office, which was still in charge of local military operations, had been spurred on by native instability in the area, not helped by a reduction in administrative staff since the onset of war. The German attacks on the border had required not only more defensive troops, but also a great deal more ancillary local labour. Stretched resources had led to food shortages and discontent. Brigadier-General Edward Northey, the new British commander, began the push northwards into GEA on 26th May 1916. Lt. Colonel Ronald Murray led two companies of British South African Police (BSAP) and a large number of volunteers in a unit known as 'Murray's Column'. On 8th June, a request for the surrender of the fort at Bismarckburg was firmly rejected, but this was misunderstood and a group of BSAP troopers, led by Dr. Harold, a former Irish rugby international, marched up to their door.

HMS Mimi, 1915

Claude's view of the British Fleet, Lake Tanganyika

In the ensuing skirmish, lives were lost, and many obvious questions asked in the *post mortem*.

On the lake, the enlarged British flotilla, under the authority of Spicer-Simson, had set sail to attack the harbour side of the German base, in what could have been a highly effective pincer movement. When Spicer-Simson sighted their heavily armed fortifications, he erred on the side of caution and withdrew, allowing the Germans to escape over water in dhows, much to the ire of the British commander. To the far greater chagrin of Spicer-Simson, the guns on the German fort turned out on closer inspection to be wooden imitations, and he would not have enjoyed his subsequent severe dressing-down by Colonel Murray.[11]

Supplying such a large number of troops across the northern border over difficult terrain was an enormous logistical challenge, with the nearest railhead several hundred miles south. The rough, recently hewn, road to Kasama and Abercorn was unsuitable for lorries or wagons even in the dry season, and oxen quickly succumbed to tsetse fly. The only workable option was to bear goods laboriously on foot. Some 200,000 men from Nyasaland and almost 100,000 more from North Eastern Rhodesia had, since April 1915, been taken into service as porters. This included a contingent from Abercorn, and on his return, Claude had found that the African male population of 8,000 had dwindled, reaching 2,500 the following year.

This huge mobilisation of labour prior to the offensive, viewed as a solution to native unrest, would prove greatly detrimental to food production. With few left to work the land, famine soon set in, putting a further strain on food supplies. Thousands of porters, unable to find food *en route*, were obliged to carry their own rations in addition to supplies for the troops. Pondering this massive inefficiency, Northey looked to the pedicle of the Congo, and the secluded swamplands near the railhead at Ndola. From here, to lighten the load on the porters, he began to organise large numbers of canoes to ferry food and munitions over the waters towards Kasama. By June 1916, British forces had secured the northern border areas of both Nyasaland and Northern Rhodesia, and Northey had taken Neu Langenberg, a good forty miles into German territory. On 7th July, the South African General, Jan Smuts took Tanga, after the Germans evacuated the town, and on 6th August captured Morogoro. But these modest British successes were not being replicated elsewhere.

Further north, at about the time Spicer-Simson was sinking the *Hedwig*, Brigadier General Wilfred Malleson was at Salaita near Taveta, pitting 6,000 men against 1,300 Germans, led by Major Georg Kraut. Malleson, who had seriously underestimated the German armoury, ordered the bombardment of a hill-top position, while missing the machine-gun filled trenches at the bottom, which disposed of two waves of his troops. Malleson, who had made his career in administration, had little tactical experience; moreover, he was considered arrogant and supercilious, inspiring little respect.[12]

On 19th February 1916, General Jan Smuts had taken command of the Allied forces in East Africa, headquartered in Nairobi. After the losses at Gallipoli, Loos and Mesopotamia, a victory was sorely needed, and Smuts put together a force of 27,000, including the Legion of Frontiersmen, led by Lt. Col. Daniel Patrick Driscoll. The Frontiersmen, who formed part of the 25th Royal Fusiliers, were a group of 'adventurers', some with previous operational experience, but with little formal training. This contingent had some colourful characters, among them big game hunter Frederick Courtney Selous, the millionaire William Northrup, naturalist Angus Buchanan, an opera singer, Russians from Siberia, a Honduran general, a circus clown, an Arctic explorer and a lion tamer afraid of lions.[13] Joining this seemingly chaotic group were the 129th Duke of Connaught's Own Baluchis, made up of Indians and sepoys.

The German withdrawal to the south east of the country increased the significance of Portugal's entry into the War on 9th March 1916, but its impact remained local and limited. Strachan stresses Portuguese incompetence, also explaining that it was not in the British interest for Portugal to be able to extend its territorial aims north of the Ruvuma river.[14] In mid-March, Smuts's force, with South Africans and Rhodesians advanced on Salaita, Longido and Moshi. The *Schutztruppen* under Lettow-Vorbeck merely retreated, avoiding an open fight. On 18th March, Smuts attacked at Kahe, but the enemy had taken a strong defensive position, and after inflicting heavy casualties, withdrew that night. As the tropical rains came, Smuts's army started to fall sick.

On 2nd April, General Jacobus (Jaap) van Deventer was sent south to take the Central railway, but after winning a small victory at Lolkisale, lost half his men to disease, was slowed by rain and mud, and half his horses and mules were killed by tsetse flies. On 9th May, with 3,000 surviving troops, van Deventer was attacked by a 4,000-strong force under Major Kraut at Kondoa Irangi; it would take van Deventer a month to recover. Meanwhile the German supply ship *Marie von Stettin* had slipped through the British naval blockade to reach the coast near Lindi, affording badly needed supplies for Lettow-Vorbeck.

Back in Abercorn, with the German threat in abeyance, the inhabitants could feel safer leaving the confines of the boma. During 1916, probably while on patrol or some official duty, Claude carrying his camera, headed for Lake Tanganyika. Reaching the shores he took a detour, arriving at Niamkolo, just east of Mpulungu. He was walking in the footsteps of some remarkable people. The London Missionary Society (LMS), founded by a group of evangelical Christians in 1795, had made their earliest expeditions to the distant islands of the South Pacific, but in 1875 Robert Arthington, turning his eyes towards the 'dark continent', had funded the Livingstone Memorial Mission to Lake Tanganyika.[15] The missionaries travelled overland from Bagamoyo, establishing centres at Urambo and Ujiji. Their calling was neither congenial nor safe, and many died from disease, some at the hands of slave traders.

In spite of the hardships and danger, the missionaries clung to their vision of a permanent home in Northern Rhodesia. Captain E. C. Hore, a leading mariner with the LMS, explored the southern end of the lake, searching for a suitable site to assemble the first steel steamboat. In 1887, the missionaries had returned to Niamkolo, and embarked on further teaching and practical work in Fwambo's village (Kawimbe) on the plateau. In 1895, Alfred J. Swann had arranged for the purchase of a plot at Niamkolo and the cornerstone of a church was laid. The building work was undertaken by Adam Purves, a Scottish industrial assistant and teacher, and comprised a main hall of approximately thirty by eighty feet, with a fifty-foot three-storey tower, which would serve as a landmark for

The ruined Niamkolo church

boats heading into the harbour. Originally the whole roof, including the tower was thatched, while the roughly dressed sandstone, bonded with mud or anthill material stood up well. Purves later moved south to the LMS mission at Mbereshi, where he died of fever in 1901 aged only thirty.[16] By 1908, as sleeping sickness descended on Niamkolo, the inhabitants took to the hills and the mission was abandoned.

When Claude photographed the church in 1916 it had already become derelict, the roof gone, the beams charred by fire. Why did he visit it that day, and record its desolate, forlorn image? Perhaps he was engaged in something more profound than sightseeing, seeking some kind of spiritual sustenance. If he had received the news from England that his niece Peggy had died in July, just four months before her fourth birthday, he could have felt the need for some kind of pilgrimage, a gesture to show his love for Peggy – 'too fair a flower to stay' as her epitaph put it.

Nor, at that juncture, would Claude have known that his name had been 'mentioned in a despatch' from the High Commissioner's Office in Cape Town addressed to the Colonial Secretary in London, The Right Honourable A. Bonar Law. The letter, dated 19th July 1916, reporting on military affairs in Rhodesia from 1st April to 31st December 1915, stated

Peggy's grave, Hampstead Cemetery

that, Certain officers and men have already been the subject of special mention, e.g. those engaged in the defence of Saisi last July. Apart from these, I desire to bring to your notice the names of the following as having rendered valuable service in the course of the period under review… (and went on to cover) Operations on the West, Operations on the Northern Border, and For assistance to the Military Authorities', C. P. Oldfield being one of eight names in the third category (together with C. P. Chesnaye). Andrew Bonar Law, who served as Colonial Secretary from May 1915 to

Andrew Bonar Law

December 1916, went on to be Prime Minister from 23rd October 1922 to 20th May 1923, when he became seriously ill with throat cancer and died later that year.[17]

Faith on all sides would certainly be tested further in the coming months. The recent British military successes, heartening for the small community in Northern Rhodesia, could not be taken for granted. The Germans had lost a few minor battles, but they had far from given up. Brigadier-General Northey's expeditionary forces, with their tenuously slow supply route, and scattered across a wide area of enemy territory were now dangerously exposed. They had also yet to reckon with the daring, enigmatic maverick, the 'Lion of Africa', General Paul Emil von Lettow-Vorbeck.

[1] Following the formation of the Territorial Force in 1908, the Artists Rifles was one of 26 volunteer battalions in London and Middlesex that combined to form the new London Regiment. It was a popular unit for volunteers, particularly from the public schools and universities.

[2] Golders Green station was opened by the Charing Cross, Euston & Hampstead Railway (CCE&HR), now part of the Northern Line, on 22 June 1907. It was one of two northern terminals, the other being Archway. Golders Green had been a small rural hamlet, but the opening of the railway stimulated a rapid boom in house building. The line was extended to Hendon Central in 1923 and to Edgware in 1924.

[3] Peter Strasser (1876-1918), chief commander of the German Imperial Navy Zeppelins, the main force operating bombing campaigns from 1915 to 1917, was killed when flying the War's last airship raid over Britain.

[4] Beatrice Webb, *Diaries, 1912-14*; BBC History website: *The Home Front in World War One*, Peter Craddick Adams

[5] Concubinage: an interpersonal relationship in which two people engage in an ongoing sexual relationship without being able to be married to the full extent of the local meaning of marriage.

[6] Ronald Hyam, *Empire and Sexuality: The British Experience* (Manchester University Press, 1990) pp 157-8

[7] Sir Leicester Paul Beaufort (1853-1926), educated at Westminster and Oxford

University, before serving in Northern Rhodesia from 1911 to 1918. Retired to the Cape.

[8] Anthony Kirk-Greene, *Symbol of Authority: The British District Officer in Africa* (I. B. Tauris, 2006)

[9] The Act, effective 2 March 1916, specified that men from 18 to 41 years old were liable to be called up for service unless they were married, widowed with children, serving in the Royal Navy, a minister of religion, or working in one of a number of reserved occupations. A second Act in May 1916 extended liability for military service to married men, and a third Act in 1918 extended the upper age limit to 51.

[10] *Kenilworth Castle* (12,975 tons) was built by Harland & Wolff, launched 15 December 1903, completed 19 May 1904; scrapped 1936.

[11] Byron Farwell, *The Great War in Africa* (W. W. Norton, New York, 1986) pp 244-9

[12] Ross Anderson, *The Forgotten Front: The East African Campaign 1914-1918* (The History Press, 2004) p 77

[13] See Farwell, ibid., p 258 and C. S. Nicholls, *Red Strangers: The White Tribe of Kenya* (Timewell Press, 2005).

[14] Hew Strachan, *The First World War in Africa* (OUP, 2004) p160

[15] The London Missionary Society (LMS), a non-denominational missionary society, was formed in 1795. The majority of their missionaries were lay people, including basket-makers, blacksmiths, cobblers, carpenters.

[16] Source: 'Missionary Biographies' in Robert I. Rotberg, *Christian Missionaries and the Creation of Northern Rhodesia, 1880-1924* (Princeton University Press, 1965)

[17] Andrew Bonar Law (1858-1923), usually known as Bonar Law, is the only British prime minister to have been born outside the UK (in the then British colony of New Brunswick, now in Canada). He was the shortest-serving prime minister of the 20th century (211 days in office), often referred to as 'The Unknown Prime Minister'.

CHAPTER 11

A Tale of Two Lions

*The ferocity of the Northern Rhodesian lion has become a
by word on a par with the deadliness of the mamba
of South Africa*

Charles Pitman, A Game Warden takes Stock[1]

Born in 1870 into minor nobility in the Prussian Rhine Province, Paul
Emil von Lettow-Vorbeck had, like his father before him, made soldiering
his career. His early achievements had not been especially noteworthy.
Deployment with a multinational force in 1900 to deal with the Boxer
Rebellion in China had disinclined him to guerrilla warfare, regarding it
as bad for military discipline. Arriving in German South West Africa amid
native uprisings in 1904, he was subsequently wounded in the arm and eye,
and taken out of the field. Promotions to major in the 11th Army Corps,
then Commanding Officer of the 2nd Sea Battalion at Wilhelmshaven,
were followed in late 1913 by appointment as Lieutenant-Colonel in
command of the *Schutztruppe* in the German colony of Kamerun. But, it
was to be on the other side of the continent, in the harsh, unforgiving East
African theatre of war, that his enduring legacy as a brilliant tactician was
to be forged.

The remit Lettow-Vorbeck framed for himself even before hostilities
began was simple:

> When I landed at Dar-es-Salaam in January 1914, I hardly suspected
> the nature of the task that was to confront me in a few months'
> time. But during the last ten years the universal war had seemed so
> imminent … Could we, with our small forces, prevent considerable
> numbers of the enemy from intervening in Europe … or inflict on
> our enemies any loss of personnel or war material worth mentioning?
> At that time I answered this question in the affirmative. It is true
> however that I did not succeed in interesting all authorities in this

Paul Emil von Lettow-Vorbeck

idea to such an extent as to cause all preparations which a war of this
kind rendered desirable to be carried out.[2]

The apparent indifference to this vision on the part of his superiors had
not dented his enthusiasm. Having won the Battle of Tanga in November
1914, Lettow-Vorbeck had swiftly gone on the offensive, targeting the
railway lines in BEA. His successes were won at significant cost to the lives
of his troops, including officers. The high body count points to the strong
commitment of those under his command. Like the British, he knew the
crucial importance of native support, and the versatile nature of their
loyalties, and quotes one African's frank admission that they would always
side with the more powerful party. With the *Schutztruppen* numerically
far smaller than the British, the task was to generate the impression of
superior strength and capability. There was though another factor: Lettow-
Vorbeck spoke fluent Swahili, and made a point of promoting Africans.

'It is probable that no white commander of the era had so keen an appreciation of the African's worth not only as a fighting man but as a man.'[3]

One of the major turning points for the Allied efforts was the two-pronged attack on Tabora in September 1916, planned to push Lettow-Vorbeck further south. It became a race between the British and Belgian forces. Commanded by Brigadier-General Charles Crewe, the Lake Force set out from Kisumu, with a number of small craft, to sail across Lake Victoria, successfully attacking Mwanza. Further west, Charles-Henri Tombeur, CIC Belgian Forces, was coming down the east side of Lake Tanganyika, taking Kigoma, then following the line of rail eastwards towards Tabora, the war-time German capital. General Schnee and his wife were ensconced in Governor's House, supported by Major General Kurt Wahle with 5,000 men. After 10 days of hard fighting, the Belgians entered the town, but the Germans hadn't hung about, retreating south-east in three columns. Unfortunately for Crewe, having encountered stiff opposition at Mwanza, difficult terrain and lack of supplies caused further delays. Despite the best efforts of his troops, he had failed to engage the Germans and limped into Tabora six days after Tombeur. This marked the end of Crewe's military service and he retired to his native South Africa to resume his political career.[4]

At the southern end of Lake Tanganyika, Bismarckburg was now in British hands, and the focus of the war had moved away from Abercorn. Nevertheless, continued vigilance and border patrols remained standing orders, and Claude took his turn at these in addition to his paperwork and daily duties around the boma. Though unlikely to win medals or glory, the role was arguably as important to Britain's war effort as that of her armed forces, and no one knew when the Germans might return. Even being a soldier did not guarantee a heroic end. Claude's former colleague, the renowned author and poet Cullen Gouldsbury, had been commissioned in the Royal Berkshires in March 1915, and three months later embarked for East Africa, on attachment to the King's African Rifles. After 10 months on frontline duties in Uganda, he was promoted to Military Landing Officer at Tanga, where he contracted malaria, dying in the local hospital in August 1916. Buried with those who fell in the first attack on Tanga, he was posthumously mentioned in despatches by General Smuts 'for meritorious service in East Africa'.[5]

Towards the end of 1917, after losing over 500 men at Mahiwa – the

Eric William Vellacott

British lost almost 3,000 but could more easily recoup them – Lettow-Vorbeck retreated south into Portuguese East Africa. Their supply lines now non-existent, the *Schutztruppen* had adopted guerrilla tactics, seizing what they needed to survive; a raid on the Portuguese garrison at Ngomano yielding a substantial haul, while a steamer carrying medical equipment provided enough quinine to fight on for several months.

By way of contrast, may we now introduce Eric William Vellacott, the middle of three sons of William Vellacott, a successful chartered accountant in London. His parents lived in Tufnell Park, before moving out to Eastcote, but by the time Eric was four, the family had sought the fresh sea air of Budleigh Salterton, presumably coinciding with his father winding down his accountancy practice. Eric was a pupil at Marlborough College from 1900, where his older brother Arthur was in the same boarding house.

Arthur followed in his father's footsteps, becoming a chartered accountant in London, while Eric, after an apparently undistinguished school career, went up to Oxford, taught for a while at The Grange prep school in East Sussex, then applied to the Colonial Service. His first posting was for three years to the relatively cosmopolitan Livingstone, before being transferred to Mporokoso on 13th December 1913. Gouldsbury had been running the station with, until a few weeks earlier, the support of Claude, who had been on secondment since March.

On 1st January 1915, within a month of Vellacott's arrival, Gouldsbury had resigned, in order to become more directly involved in the war effort.[6] His successor was Geoffrey Stokes, for whom Vellacott would work as his ANC for some months before taking two months' 'sick leave' in Ndola in August 1915. Stokes would recall him, somewhat ambiguously as 'a dark-complexioned most attractive fellow, though I doubt whether he could be called good-looking. He was certainly very highly strung.' On 1st December, Vellacott was transferred to Abercorn, according to Stokes to 'take charge of the wartime Boma on Uringi Pans – the idea of that Boma being that native work could be carried on without natives having to enter the "more or less" military camp at Abercorn.[7] Returning to Mporokoso at the end of April 1916, coinciding with General Northey's advance into GEA, Vellacott was promoted to NC, taking over from Stokes, who moved to Fife. From the reports of contemporaries, Vellacott was particularly diligent, appeared to have earned his promotion, and was continuing to apply himself, but by April 1918, he had been working virtually without leave for over two years.

On one of those bright cloudless days that come at the end of the rains, Claude, sitting at his desk in Abercorn, was asked to go immediately to Draper's office, where he was informed that the NC for Mporokoso had sustained an attack from a lion. Oldfield was to make haste there immediately, and give all possible assistance. In fact Draper was not excessively worried about Vellacott, '…I got the impression that his wounds were not too serious…' while Stokes, whom Draper also telephoned, would recall, '…in addition to expressing my regrets, saying he will make a d—d bad patient!'[8]

As Claude hurried out of Draper's office and scrambled onto his motorcycle, the terrifying accounts of 'man-eaters' would have flashed through his imagination. Such tales had long excited followers of colonial life in Africa. The ravages of the man-eating lions of Tsavo during the building of the railway from Mombasa to Nairobi, with stories of a death toll ranging between thirty to over a hundred, remained potent in the memories of old Africa hands. Closer to home, Claude would have known that in 1898, at Ilabo Stream, the district official W. R. Johnstone had died from wounds inflicted by a lion. In 1911, the NC for Mporokoso noted that an average of ten people were taken by lions every year, typically on the outskirts of villages at dusk.

Claude was about to see the effects of such natural savagery for himself. Meantime, Draper had got a message to Dr Harold in Fort Rosebery, the Provincial HQ to the south of Mporokoso. Harold had arrived and dressed Vellacott's wounds, but decided it was not feasible to move him. From the information available, it seems there was little that could be done. Claude's handwritten entry in the District Notebook several days later was stark: '1918, May 3rd. E W Vellacott, NC, died from injuries from a lion received on 19th April.' Vellacott was buried at Mporokoso boma, his memorial stone 'subscribed for among his personal friends in the Tanganyika District.'

Various reports circulated as to exactly what had happened. Amplifying the basic facts were the memories of those involved, recalled some thirty years after the event. *Man-Eaters at Mporokoso* appeared as an anonymous piece in the second issue of the *Northern Rhodesia Journal (NRJ)* in 1950, introduced with a quote from Captain Pitman's, *A Game Warden takes Stock*: 'The ferocity of the Northern Rhodesian lion has become a byword on a par with the deadliness of the mamba of South Africa.'[9] There followed a list of tragedies covering two pages, deaths of Africans interspersed with lions shot or speared. In 1907-08, Yamutenga and his people destroyed an animal that had killed no less than six natives. In 1909, man-eaters were still a source of terror, killing two women on the Kasama Road, and in 1910, four women and seven men. Buffalo and leopard attacks added to the human fatalities.

In 1951, the third issue of the *NRJ* described the deaths of Johnstone and Vellacott:

> At some point in his struggle, Johnstone climbed a tree and was on a branch that was afterwards measured to be over 15 feet from the ground. The lion jumped straight from the ground on to the branch and knocked Johnstone down. That is a very big jump even for a big cat.

The *NRJ* editors claimed that Vellacott was on the ground and armed, but immobilised by the sight of the beast: 'just as he was about to fire at the lion that was charging him, he was struck by such a violent attack of nerves that he was unable to squeeze the trigger of his rifle. "Buck fever" usually causes a trembling but nothing more, so this must have been a real terror.'[10]

Eighteen months later, the *NRJ* apologized for the allegation of extreme buck fever, the retraction prompted by a letter from Draper addressed to Stokes, NC at Fife:

> during the war many Bomas were shorthanded. Vellacott was alone and in sole charge of Mporokoso District: had been for a long while, ... being overdue for leave ... I well remember one of my official visits to Mporokoso. I was much perturbed by his manner when walking. Swinging his arms about and prancing along in a most peculiar way. I was convinced then he badly needed a rest ... I have put this down to make clear Vellacott's physical state at the time.

Vellacott was in his office and a native came along and said a lion had attacked a woman in a nearby garden and had 'treed' her. Thereupon Vellacott dropped his work, came out of the office, saw one of the prison warders with a Martini Metford, told him he wanted it immediately hastened off … Arriving at the garden he took the Martini and when doing so asked, 'how does it work?'… and started to follow the lion … fired at it – whether he wounded it or not I am uncertain. Anyway, the beast charged and Vellacott grabbed his shotgun, which had been brought along, and at very close range – I seem to remember I made it out to be three or four yards only – Vellacott then shot at it again with the shotgun, but the lion came on and got him down and, thereupon, Ntambanshika intervened and shot the lion. I think it was speared as well – anyway, it was killed. Vellacott was taken back to his house.

To say the man was terror stricken so that he could not squeeze the trigger is sheer nonsense and absolutely inaccurate. He did his best and shirked nothing, although I know he was in poor health owing to overwork. Also he was naturally and always a bit strung. I am pretty sure I held the inquest and, if so, the record should still be in Abercorn office. If not, then Oldfield must have heard it at Mporokoso and I saw the record, for I know that the facts as here recorded are substantially correct. This tragedy left a pretty lasting impression on myself. I don't think I need add any more. But let the bloke who wrote about it in the paper know that he is under sheer misapprehension and he would be wise in the future to make sure his facts and not spread wrong impressions about which might well cause distress to others.[11]

Militaria expert John Richards comments that the Martini Metford, known as 'the Africa gun', was a conversion of the Enfield from the Zulu Wars era, re-chambered to take the new British .303 cartridges.[12] The Metford's cocking mechanism, collecting dust and grit if not cleaned regularly, was prone to jamming. Someone not familiar with the gun, faced with the sudden emergency of a rampant lion, might well struggle to fire the weapon.[13]

Draper's scrupulous concern for the truth, and a man's reputation, is laudable. His frank admission of the effects on himself, suggests that the twenty-nine-year-old Claude, who looked after the wounded man and witnessed his slow and painful death, would have similar enduring memories. Eric Vellacott had died defending a woman from a highly dangerous animal. According to Stokes, Vellacott had known more carefree days, though always tempered by principle, 'When he was leaving Oxford, Gordon Selfridge sent for him and offered to dress him free provided Vellacott, who was a social sort of fellow, fond of dancing, continued to go about and, when opportunity offered, mention Selfridges as being his outfitters. Vellacott turned down the offer.[14]

The destiny of Vellacott's younger brother, Paul, had unfolded rather better. He had made his mark at cricket and hockey at Marlborough, before going on to Peterhouse, Cambridge, gaining a hockey blue in 1914. Serving with the South Lancashire Regiment, he was severely wounded in March 1918, having attained the rank of Major, and with a DSO. If Eric had received word of this by the time of his encounter with the lion, perhaps he had been inspired to act with equal courage?

After Vellacott's death, Claude stayed on at Mporokoso for a further two months until 3rd July 1918, when his acting role was transferred to Bertram Matthews. Developments in the European war had meanwhile moved on apace. German attempts to suborn Mexico with a promise to help reclaim lost territories had, in April 1917, brought America into the conflict, dispatching naval resources across the Atlantic to help safeguard Britain's convoys, and US Marines to France. Germany had responded with a spring offensive in 1918, coming within seventy-five miles of Paris and shelling the inhabitants with heavy, rail-mounted Krupp guns. Heavy casualties and anti-war sentiment in Germany were taking their toll on resources and morale. An Allied counter-offensive at the beginning of August marked the turning of the tide, and on 11th November 1918 – the eleventh hour, of the eleventh day, of the eleventh month – in a railway carriage at Compiègne, France, the Armistice was signed. But had anyone told the 'Lion of Africa', General Paul Emil von Lettow-Vorbeck?

---

[1] Captain C. R. S. Pitman, *A Game Warden takes Stock* (J. Nisbet, 1942). Charles Robert Senhouse Pitman (1890-1975), b. Bombay. After serving with the 27th Punjabis (1910-21), retired to farm in Kenya. In 1924, appointed Game Warden, Uganda, serving until 1951, interrupted by three years (1931-33) as Acting Game Warden in Northern Rhodesia.

[2] Paul von Lettow-Vorbeck, *My Reminiscences of East Africa* (Hurst & Blackett, 1920) Ch. 1

[3] Charles Miller, *Battle for the Bundu: The First World War in East Africa* (Macmillan, 1974). Rapport with the askari doubtless helped with recruitment, eventually enlarging the *Schutztruppen* to an overall force of approximately 14,000.

[4] Byron Farwell, *The Great War in Africa* (W. W. Norton, New York, 1986) pp 288-89) and Ross Anderson, *The Forgotten Front: The East African Campaign 1914-1918* (The History Press, 2004) pp134-5.

[5] *London Gazette*, 10 February 1917

[6] Source: The Mporokoso DNB (where these entries have been retyped at a later date) shows Gouldsbury resigning on 1 January 1914. The author believes the actual date was more likely January 1915, as the obituary for Cullen Gouldsbury in *African Affairs* states that 'from the outbreak of the war until February, 1915, he rendered valuable assistance to the Chartered Company, and especially to the Belgian contingent which was quartered for some time at his own station of Mporokoso.' After unsuccessful applications to join the Rhodesian forces, he resigned and returned to England to offer his services there. *African Affairs*, Vol. XVI, Issue LXII, January 1917.

[7] *NRJ*, Vol I, No. 6 pp 63-64

[8] *NRJ*, Vol I, ibid.

[9] *NRJ*, Vol I, No. 2, pp 71-73

[10] Hunters, if they succumb to nervous excitement at the approach of game, can get '*buck fever*', meaning they miss that small window of opportunity for a good shot, then possibly get off a poor shot and may miss, or fail to shoot at all.

[11] *NRJ*, Vol I, No. 6 pp 63-64

[12] The .303 British is a .303-inch (7.7mm) calibre-rimmed rifle cartridge first developed as a black-powder round and put into service in December 1888 for the Lee-Metford rifle. The cartridge was later adapted for smokeless powder and became the standard British and Commonwealth military cartridge from 1889 until the 1950s.

[13] With thanks to John Richards, formerly with the MoD, militaria collector and owner of an original Boer War Martini Henry (September 2015).

[14] *NRJ*, Vol I, No. 6 p 64

CHAPTER 12

Aftermath

The father is at the front, the mother mills grains for the soldiers,
while the children are carrying the food to the front

A Belgian missionary in the Congo

The silent years go drifting by
As clouds, and yet you do not mind,
Lonely, yet not alone, you lie:
You live in hearts of those behind

Malcolm Humphrey, The Lonely Graves[1]

Early in 1918, Lettow-Vorbeck, deep in the heart of Portuguese East Africa, evading British forces coming from two directions, was heading south amid the rains. His nomadic campaign offered little access to telegraph communications, and with reports via runners and drums subject to rumour and misinformation, reliable intelligence on the war in Europe was slow to reach the remote towns and outposts of Africa, let alone the bush. Operating incommunicado conferred one advantage: the British were often uncertain of Lettow-Vorbeck's position. Any incoming intelligence was gleaned either by his own scouts and patrols, the hit-and-miss reception of the company's wireless set, or scraps of paper – telegrams, Reuters bulletins, scribbled orders – found at abandoned or captured enemy outposts. Information on troop movements, supplies and fighting strength could be precious, but also for the *Schutztruppen*, fighting their own spirited but isolated war, never knowing what tomorrow might bring, any grain of positive news about the Fatherland, or the progress of their comrades on the Western Front, was welcomed. In March 1918, holed up near Nanungu, as the rains cleared and the wireless set began to crackle again, they heard that close to Amiens, German troops had launched a major attack, and advanced over thirty-five miles.

Eager to follow suit, the Lion of Africa was ready to spring again.

Fearing the *Schutztruppen* would now try to push north, General Jacob van Deventer, a South African who spoke little English but was skilled in guerrilla warfare, was now in overall charge of British forces. Van Deventer made plans to seal his enemy off, drawing a 350-mile defensive line on the map from Porto Amélia (now Pemba) on the eastern seaboard of Portuguese East Africa (PEA) to Fort Johnston (now Mangochi) in Nyasaland; simple enough in theory, but with the resources at van Deventer's disposal, almost impossible to implement.[2] This difficulty notwithstanding, the British appeared more than capable of keeping their enemy on the back foot at least, with a fierce engagement near Maketi on 22nd May depriving the *Schutztruppen* of 70,000 rounds of ammunition, and 30,000 rupees, useful cash for purchasing the services of askaris, porters and other vital supplies.

Lettow-Vorbeck retreated further south, scouting out any opportunity to replenish his supplies, and recording:

> In the reports that reached us by the runners of Müller's detachment, the name Kokosani was now perpetually recurring. Considerable enemy depots, strongly protected by hostile troops, were to be found there, so it was said. But where was this Kokosani? The word could not be found on our maps.[3]

In mid-June by a stroke of luck, he stumbled across a clue in some captured documents: 'Kokosani was the same place that featured on Portuguese maps as Namacurra.'[4] With all intelligence suggesting this to be the most promising objective, he set his course. He seemed both fatalistic and intrepid: 'We had no means of knowing whether it would be possible to capture this place, probably very strongly fortified, with our relatively limited resources. Only the attempt itself could enlighten us on that point.'[5]

In the first week of July the attempt was made. During the three-day attack the *Schutztruppen* lost nine men, but the Portuguese and British casualties numbered some 200, many drowned or eaten by crocodiles while trying to escape across the Namacurra river. The battle was a resounding triumph for Lettow-Vorbeck, with 500 prisoners taken, the most valuable prize ten machine guns, 350 rifles and ample quantities of food and ammunition. It was decided that non-essential booty must be denied to the enemy by all available means:

> Unfortunately it was not possible for us to get away the whole stock of excellent wine we had captured. After a sufficient quantity had been

Poster calling for donations to the military, using Lettow-Vorbeck and his troops to raise support. The title reads 'Colonial War Donations'

set aside as a restorative for the sick, the rest had mainly to be drunk on the spot. The risk of a wholesale 'jollification' that involved was gladly undertaken, and everyone was allowed to let himself go for once, after his long abstinence.

Replete with wine, on encountering the local factory's large store of fine schnapps, the conquering heroes were forced to concede defeat: 'With the best will in the world it was impossible to drink it all, so we had to empty a large number of the casks into the Namacurra.'[6]

Van Deventer, expecting Lettow-Vorbeck to march east to the strategic port of Quelimane, pushed on there. But the *Schutztruppen* leader was not inclined to do the obvious. Resting at Namacurra, he lay low till van Deventer's men overshot his position, then turned northeast. Towards the end of August he reached Lioma, where an engagement with the King's African Rifles inflicted heavy casualties on the Germans, their askari and porters. The blow to morale was compounded by an outbreak of influenza in the ranks. Around mid-October at Ubena, Lettow-Vorbeck received reports that Germany's ally Bulgaria had surrendered, Damascus had fallen to the British and the Fatherland was looking to make peace. Lettow-Vorbeck took it all with a large pinch of salt and soldiered on. The British, now expecting the *Schutztruppe* to make for the Central Railway across GEA, were busily strengthening their defences around key points. Instead Lettow-Vorbeck turned west toward British territory, and what he hoped would be rich pickings of supplies and ammunition from the depots along the Kasama to Fife road. His timing was fortuitous as British authority had lately been compromised in Northern Rhodesia, with the Colonial Service, mindful of a recent uprising across the northern border, forbidding the enforced use of native labour. The BSAC, alarmed by the spiralling cost of the war had stopped paying porters, leaving Northey's army largely immobilised and the *Schutztruppen* free to move unhindered; within a fortnight they had covered 100 miles.

Advancing swiftly towards Fife, Lettow-Vorbeck sent Colonel Spangenberg in to attack. The Northern Rhodesia Regiment, made up of the former NR Police, put up a staunch defence, and held the boma for several hours. The engagement teetered on a reversal of fortune for the Germans: Lettow-Vorbeck, narrowly escaped death, and called a withdrawal. The British judged that he would now move on Abercorn and Lake Tanganyika, and quickly sent troops to intercept. With news of the German advance and attempt on Fife, and the likelihood of an imminent attack, Claude and his colleagues were now on high alert. They would also have been aware that the war in Europe appeared to have entered its closing stages and an armistice was likely, but given their position, was this any guarantee of safety? With Lettow-Vorbeck's reputation for defying orders and nothing yet signed or sealed, it was possible that this audacious leader might be spurred on to snatch a small but devastating local victory.

The Lion now confounded his enemy again, turning southwest towards Kasama. With looting rife, the NR Police believed to be on the point of mutiny, and troops dispersed elsewhere, the town lay virtually undefended. There was widespread panic throughout the country. If Kasama fell, who could say the *Schutztruppen* may not turn again and march on Abercorn? When Lettow-Vorbeck's advance guard under Captain Spangenberg arrived at Kasama on 9th November however, they found a ghost town. The British population had been evacuated south to Mpika, save for just nine men, who had mounted two Maxim machine guns on the Chambeshi bridge, though with little idea of how to use them. Spangenberg was looking for ammunition, and finding only a few hundred cigarettes, marched swiftly in the direction of the bridge. On the opposite side lay a rubber factory where Hector Croad, the District Officer, was keeping the ammunition and other supplies. Three days later on 12th November, as Lettow-Vorbeck reached Kasama and Spangenberg overran the bridge, the *Schutztruppe* rearguard under Kohl was engaged by 750 of the King's African Rifles commanded by Major E. B. B. Hawkins. After almost half a day of fighting – the last hostilities of the war – Kohl's men dispersed, hoping that once Spangenberg had taken the rubber factory they could all cross the river and escape south.

On the morning of 13th November, as Kohl's detachment regrouped at Kasama, Lettow-Vorbeck set out alone on a bicycle looking for a place to camp. Just as he had found a suitable site, Captain Müller appeared post-haste with the news that the detachment had just captured an English motorcycle dispatch rider, although other accounts refer to Sergeant Frank Rumsey driving a car:

Photo: *W. V. Brelsford*

Frank Rumsey at Mbesuma 1940

When the news of the Armistice finally came through, Rumsey was instructed by Mr. Croad (the magistrate) to take the news to von Lettow Vorbeck; rather an unpleasant job, as although his car bore a white flag on its bonnet, this meant nothing to the German askari, each picquet making a point of firing a few shots as he passed … For this exploit he was awarded the D.C.M.[7]

Dated 12.11.18, the important telegram read:

Send following to Colonel von Lettow-Vorbeck under white flag.

The Prime Minister of England has announced that an armistice was signed at 5 hours on Nov. 11th and that hostilities on all fronts cease at 11 hours on Nov. 11th. I am ordering my troops to cease hostilities forthwith unless attacked, and of course I conclude that you will do the same. Conditions of armistice will be forwarded you immediately I receive them. Meanwhile I suggest that you should remain in your present vicinity in order to facilitate communication. – General van Deventer.[8]

Lettow-Vorbeck remained unbowed: 'I felt convinced that the conclusion of hostilities must have been favourable, or at least not unfavourable to Germany.' What though if the armistice should suddenly collapse, and the order to surrender be countermanded the next day, or sooner? Ever ready with a contingency plan, Lettow-Vorbeck marshalled his troops by the Chambeshi for a rapid flight south as originally envisaged. Just before midnight, a telegram from Salisbury, delivered via Fife, did not suggest any imminent reversal of fortune: Germany had agreed to the unconditional surrender of all her forces in East Africa by 11th December. Even now there seemed little reason for the *Schutztruppe* to give up, Lettow-Vorbeck believing that this could only be explained by 'the desperate situation of the Fatherland. Nothing else could account for the surrender of a force still maintaining itself proudly and victoriously in the field.'[9]

Confusion reigned on both sides. John Bannon, an RSM in 1/4 KAR, recorded that it was:

reported to me that a white man on a motor cycle carrying a white flag had passed along the road going in the direction of the Huns Camp. We did not know what to think of this; some of our people said it was perhaps a German white who had got a motor cycle and was making for his camp; others said perhaps its peace at home, which seemed too good to be true.

Bannon describes the next day when it was decided:

to again attack the Huns ... but when we reached the road to our further surprise we met two German Askaries with a large white flag with a message to our Commanding Officer stating the war was over and that an armistice had been signed at home. We nearly all went mad with joy.[10]

Although Captain Spangenberg had gained the Chambeshi bridge two days earlier, he had only just begun to fire on the rubber factory when the news of the armistice had arrived. At eight o'clock on the morning of 14th November, Hector Croad now emerged from the building and crossed the river to speak with the *Schutztruppe* commander. Croad's report that the Kaiser had abdicated and quit Germany, and that the country was now a republic, was met with disbelief by Lettow-Vorbeck, the whole turn of events coming as a complete shock to him: 'All our troops, natives as well as Europeans, had always held the conviction that Germany could not be beaten in this war, and were resolved to fight on to the last.'[11]

Lettow-Vorbeck was instructed to proceed immediately with his troops to Abercorn, citing it as the nearest place for them to be supplied with food. All arms and ammunition were to be handed over to the British military representative. Claude, briefed on these plans, was as curious as anyone to meet Lettow-Vorbeck. This was the man whose four-year campaign, but for the mettle of the Northern Rhodesia Rifles in 1914, the continuing contribution of the border patrols, and now the fortuitous ending of hostilities in Europe, might have entered Abercorn as victor rather than vanquished. The name, already well known in the colony, would certainly enter legend.

The War Memorial at Chambeshi Bridge (2012)

John Bannon describes his role:

We then camped along the road … on 15th November, I was chosen
to go into Kasama to the German Camp and take over all allied
prisoners from the Huns. There were seven officers and seven other
ranks; these poor fellows were in a terrible state as they were very
badly treated by the Huns. They had hardly any clothes – only what
they stood in and their boots were tramped off them. It was the
custom of the Huns when they got a white prisoner to take all his kit
and give him their old clothes and boots in return.

Bannon's regiment, in parallel with Lettow-Vorbeck's troops, also
marched to Abercorn, a distance of over 100 miles, arriving on 24th
November. Bannon recounted how:

the following day all the Huns arrived and all their arms were taken
from them. They were then marched to an internment camp, which
we had to find very strong Guards for the following and a summary of
the surrendered – Officers 3, Other Whites N.C.O. lot 152; Askaries
1,168; Carriers 1,522; Women 400. One big gun, 40 shells, 23
machine guns, 14 Lewes Guns, 1,071 Rifles, mostly Portuguese, and
a few English Rifles, 547 bayonets.[12]

On the morning of Monday 25th November, the sky swollen with rain
over Abercorn's parade ground, as the British flag fluttered in the wind
and a contingent of Northern Rhodesia riflemen and askari formed up
as guard of honour for the signing of the surrender, they could see the
Lion of Africa for themselves. Colonel Hawkins, who a few days earlier at
Kasama had fought the *Schutztruppen*, in what turned out to be the last
battle of the Great War, was surprised:

Von Lettow himself turned out to be a very different man from what
we had expected. A little over medium height, and wearing a short
pointed beard, with fair hair turning grey, he is a fine looking man
of forty-nine … instead of the haughty Prussian one had expected to
meet, he turned out to be a most courteous and perfectly mannered
man: his behaviour throughout his captivity was a model to anyone in
such a position.[13]

As a professional soldier, an officer and a gentleman, it seems Lettow-
Vorbeck saw his first duty to behave as such in victory and defeat, although
he and his men had not, as he was adamant to point out, been defeated.

If the armistice had not happened, or if he had chosen to ignore it, he could have continued south and probably reached Broken Hill ahead of either van Deventer or Hawkins and, availing himself there of stores and ammunition, fought on. Sufficiently reinforced, he might have turned and confronted his pursuers, and even pushed back north, and taken the ground on which he now stood as prisoner. Instead he was obliged to endure not ignominy, but a noble acceptance of the fortunes of war. The British officers who received him at Abercorn reciprocated his courtesy, declining to accept his sword when offered, and even allowing other German officers to keep their swords and revolvers.

The *Schutztruppen* commander also made clear his responsibility towards all who had played their part in his campaign, not least his askaris, who were owed money he did not have: '... it was a matter of honour for us to see that these people, who had fought and worked for us with such devotion, should receive their rights.'[14] He maintained that the arrears,

The Surrender Parade, Abercorn, 25th November 1918

Those inspecting the Parade are:- General Edwards, Col. Dickenson, Major Alport, Captain Wardroper, Captain James (all Northern Rhodesian Regiment), C.P. Oldfield, J.P., Political Officer and Magistrate

The author understands that these are the only photographs extant of the Parade in Abercorn on 25th November 1918. On close examination, one can see the six men, as there is another man walking immediately behind (but hidden by) General Edwards. Claude is the last but one in the group. In his album, Claude lists the six names, but other senior officers (on both sides) were probably present on that day. Further information is given in the Appendix.

African drawing of final surrender of Lettow-Vorbeck at Abercorn

though stretching back years and amounting to around one and a half million rupees, were relatively small in European terms, and asked several times if the British would kindly settle the debt on his behalf. While the War Office remained non-committal on the matter, Lettow-Vorbeck itemised what was due to every askari and porter, and issued each with a 'certificate' showing his dues.

Three days later Lettow-Vorbeck and his men were bivouacked by the Kalambo Falls. From here they would be escorted to Bismarckburg, to sail north on Lake Tanganyika to Kigoma, thence by rail to Dar-es-Salaam and the voyage back to Europe and repatriation. As the train rattled eastwards, looking out at the vast terrain the *Schutztruppen* had fought so long and hard to hold, there seemed little certainty under whose flag it would now lie. As the governor of GEA, Heinrich Schnee, observed, 'Only the gods knew what the future holds for Germany.'[15]

Back in Berlin a hero's welcome awaited. On 2nd March 1919, Lettow-Vorbeck led a 'Victory Parade', marching through the Brandenburg Gate to be received by the Weimar government. He and his men had earned the distinction of being the only German force to occupy British territory during WWI, fighting the last battle on African soil on 13th November 1918. His mobile campaign compelled Britain to commit significant resources to a relatively minor colonial theatre throughout the war and inflicted upwards of 10,000 casualties. Eventually the weight of numbers, especially after the attack on Mahiwa in October 1917, had pushed them out of GEA into PEA and Northern Rhodesia, but their forces had

Victory Parade, Berlin

remained active throughout, even though the sustained defence of GEA was only for some 20 months (March 1916-Nov 1917). By 1920, Lettow-Vorbeck had published his own story, translated into English as *My Reminiscences of East Africa.*[16] With the war over, the newly-established League of Nations awarded mandates to the winners, obligating them to report back annually on the development of the territories and their inhabitants. These mandates split the former German colony in two: the mainland of Tanganyika to the British, and Rwanda and Burundi to Belgium.

The war in East Africa had been on an immense scale. It was certainly not, as some have implied, just a 'sideshow'. On both sides, troops and civilians, native and expatriate, had been drawn into the conflict, from at least twenty-five countries: British and German East Africa, Congo, Uganda, Nyasaland, Northern and Southern Rhodesia, South Africa and the protectorates (Bechuanaland, Swaziland, Basotholand), Portuguese East Africa, India, Britain, Germany, Belgium, China, Sierra Leone, Gold Coast, Nigeria, Seychelles, Gambia, Jamaica, Australia and America. In the first two years, the conflict involved mainly white and Indian soldiers, while the subsequent two years saw black troops doing most of the fighting. Over the four-year period, the German forces consisted of approximately 3,000 white and 12,000 black and Arab men, opposed by some 127,000 British, including white, Indian, black and Arab; in all 11,189 men died, with 10,811 incapacitated through disease and wounding, and more died of illness and starvation than from battle injuries.

The armies could not have functioned without the work of black African porters, carriers and labourers, bearing loads of up to 60lb. Many were volunteered by their communities, as well as commandeered as the need arose, and over one million men were estimated to have served in this capacity, though not all armies kept records. An estimated 95,000 black support service men died, the majority, 41,000, coming from GEA. The African population also provided all the fighting forces with food, initially paid for but later commandeered, and what was not eaten was often burnt to deny it to the enemy.

Despite all the horrors of war, there were some positives: employment opportunities improved for some, the value of organisation became apparent and the mixing of cultures led to a sharing of ideas and knowledge which helped future political developments, probably hastening the struggle for African independence. Even if any such benefits were quantifiable, they had been bought at a ridiculous price. In the early days, it seems that Africans did not believe the war was a reality, suspecting that it was a ploy on the part of the colonial rulers to take a firmer grip on their conquests. Then the realisation dawned that they really were fighting one another! 'Why would rich white people fight one another?' But with Africans drawn into the conflict, when they had actually killed white men, it was impossible to maintain unthinking respect.[17] Missionaries themselves felt that their moral authority had been diminished, but in the long-term, for the White Fathers, missionaries and African christians were drawn closer together. They became less of a mystery to each other, with friendships forged in conditions of hardship making a strong tie.

As demobilization got underway, a further calamity for the African population was gathering pace. Several among Lettow-Vorbeck's itinerant army had already been stricken by influenza while still on active service, and by October 1918 its prevalence, at first difficult to distinguish from other complaints, particularly in wartime, had escalated. Shortly after their surrender at Abercorn in November, twelve of the Germans, including Captain Spangenberg, and 279 of the askari and porters died from it. British soldiers in the area were also succumbing at an alarming rate. By far the highest number of fatalities would be among black Africans. In the words of Mulenga Chisanga Paulo, a young survivor of the pandemic who lived near Lake Mweru, 'After the end of the White Man's War catastrophe fell upon us. A bad air fell upon our country. People died like flies. No village or family was spared. There was death everywhere.'[18]

Africans long familiar with dreadful afflictions of one kind or another held the will of God responsible. With only palliative medicine available, European definitions and responses were perceived to be of little help in halting the lethal onslaught. There was also widespread suspicion that the white man's war, which had undoubtedly brought much misery already, had also created the disease, and in a culture long steeped in mysticism, a mistrust of the white man's medicine too. As an LMS missionary at Kambole pointed out: 'Owing to the strong influence of witchcraft and superstition, a great many natives, did not avail themselves of hospital treatment ... A naturally dangerous and fatal disease was rendered doubly so by the indecent panic which prevailed.'[19]

The outbreak was said to have begun in Sierra Leone in the late summer of 1918, from where the constant movements of men and supplies during the latter months of the war accelerated its spread throughout the sub-Saharan region. Later known as 'Spanish Influenza' and *La Grippe*, the Secretary for Native Affairs in Northern Rhodesia would describe it as the most fatal epidemic that ever visited the territory. Rapid containment measures would have seemed essential, but whilst visitors to neighbouring Nyasaland were detained on entry pending medical examination, the Northern Rhodesian administration apparently believed border quarantine pointless, the Preventive Medicine Officer asserting that '... no precaution which can be instituted can be expected to be sufficiently perfect to exclude the disease.'[20]

Bafflingly, the influenza, normally a killer of the young and elderly, hit those in the prime of life. The virus struck with amazing speed, killing around four per cent of the East African population, and an estimated 20-40 million worldwide. The loss of so many able-bodied males left fields untilled and crops neglected, resulting in acute food shortages. Spanish flu was reported by the Catholic White Fathers in all their sub-Saharan vicariates and in Northern Rhodesia, people were immobilised on government orders. The Bishop of Bangweulu testified to a silence enveloping the mission stations for three months.[21]

The massive mobilisation of Africans left a legacy of bereavement and destitution, and no amount of heartfelt tributes to the courage and loyalty of askaris could compensate for the huge death toll of carriers, or the desperate plight of those who survived. As the Colonial Service struggled to readjust, conditions in many cases were made harsher, with local taxes increased to cover shortfalls elsewhere. Some of the worst droughts on record added to the shortage of food.

Father Aylward Shorter expresses the widespread hardship and extensive loss of life from famine and disease; around Lake Bangweulu, villages were deserted, with people foraging in the forest, appearing as 'walking skeletons'.[22] Once an African was known to have the illness, their relatives were encouraged to move them to remote locations and tend to them in isolation in temporary, airy huts called *mitanda*, which, as the virus flourished amid dense poorly-ventilated housing, had some positive effect. The Administration at Abercorn, as in other parts, endeavoured to curb social gatherings, sending out notices to missionaries and churches restricting services and house visits, while local chiefs received similar warnings in their tribal language.

Mitigating the impact of the Spanish flu was not the only headache for the Administration. The Watchtower millennial movement had become stronger in last years of the war, spreading criticism against the colonial authorities and its hated collaborators, the boma messengers, Watchtower offering the only credible outlet for wartime grievances against white rule. Edmund Yorke explains that opportunities for limiting the Watchtower movement were often missed by insensitive handling of the situation and by giving local chiefs permission to use unnecessary force against the its adherents.[23]

In 1919, LMS missionaries at Kambole reported the resurgence of the clandestine Butwa secret society, a cult particularly followed by peoples living near the Luapula river and Lake Bangweulu. The missionaries were particularly disturbed by the sexual excesses of Butwa, which included widespread adultery and incest, but of greater concern to the authorities was the danger of having a 'virtual state' within a state. A major crackdown was implemented, with penalties of imprisonment or lashes for possession of membership, which had some effect, although the society may have simply become more secretive.[24] Perhaps, not surprisingly, demobbed askari could also be a disruptive force.

At last, when the flu pandemic finally appeared to be tailing off, Claude must have drawn a breath and wondered at his own survival over the past four years. Had he not joined the Colonial Service, he might now, like so many of his contemporaries, be dead. He had also been spared the war at sea – the *Llandovery Castle*, on which he had sailed for home in 1915, had been torpedoed in June 1918.[25] Now he had escaped a disease with no apparent cure that had killed thousands, including many of the Germans who had surrendered and stood within yards of him on the rain-soaked parade ground at Abercorn. There, but for the grace of God, he went. Claude might have crossed his heart and offered thanks for

Total Eclipse of the Sun, Abercorn, 29th May 1919

his existence. On the afternoon of 29th May 1919, as the sky quickly darkened, many across Africa, in fear or supplication, began doing just that.

The darkness, to paraphrase Old Pauline, John Milton, was visible throughout the day, beginning at dawn in Brazil, travelling across the Atlantic and reaching East Africa as the sun began to set. Lasting almost five minutes, it would be longest solar eclipse of the twentieth century, instrumental in establishing a scientific theory put forward four years earlier by a little-known patent office clerk, Albert Einstein. Cambridge astronomer Sir Arthur Eddington, charged with refuting Einstein's work, photographed the eclipse from an island off the west coast of Africa. Comparing the images with those taken under normal skies provided proof of Einstein's proposition of the bending of light from stars by the sun's gravity. Newton's two-hundred-year-old hegemony in the scientific firmament was toppled. Einstein's General Theory of Relativity was accepted and he became a celebrity overnight. Claude's snapshot of the eclipse at Abercorn might not win any photographic prizes, but he later recalled: 'as I was able to tell the natives of my District that this was going to happen two months earlier, I acquired an undeserved reputation as a "Medicine Man". They called me a real "Witch Doctor".' Claude's disposition would have been further enhanced when two months later he received a letter from Lawrence Wallace, the Administrator for the BSAC in Livingstone, commending his 'hard work with greater responsibility during the time that Mr. Draper has been on tour, and during the invasion by Von Lettow and the evacuation of the prisoners.' We know that Claude had been 'Mentioned in Despatches' in the report by Sydney Buxton from Cape Town in July 1916 (Chapter 10), this information becoming public knowledge in *The London Gazette* of 13th July 1917, with the report from the High Commissioner's Office, dated 10th March 1917.[26] The contribution from local people is at least partially recognized with the words: 'In supplying carriers, the native tribes of Northern Rhodesia have loyally played their part.'[27] Claude's individual contribution was recognized after the war in an official certificate signed by Winston Churchill, Secretary of State for War.

14. I also desire to bring to notice the services of Major A. Boyd-Cuninghame, Northern Rhodesia Rifles, and Surgeon-Captains Kinghorn, White, and Chisholm.

15. The maintenance of supplies and transport for the troops on the border has been throughout a most difficult and onerous task. From 1st April to 31st December, 1915, 20,000 carriers were employed in carrying over 1,000,000 lbs. of supplies from distant bases, and an additional 50,000 in bringing grain from adjacent districts. But for the indefatigable efforts of the District Officials a breakdown would have been inevitable. The military authorities are especially indebted in this connection to Mr. C. P. Chesnaye, Magistrate and Commissioner of the Tanganyika District. The following officers also rendered valuable assistance :—Messrs. H. G. Power, C. P. Oldfield, G. P. Lyons, A. E. Copeman, and A. Croad. Mr. R. Goode, Secretary to the Administration, and Mr. N. Nightingale, Controller of Stores, are equally deserving of mention for their work in forwarding supplies from Livingstone. In supplying carriers, the native tribes of Northern Rhodesia have loyally played their part.

Extract from Supplement to the London Gazette, 13th July 1917

'Mentioned in Despatches' signed by Winston Churchill

Please Quote

No................

ADMINISTRATOR'S OFFICE,

LIVINGSTONE,

NORTHERN RHODESIA.

8th July, 19 19.

My dear Oldfield,

Mr. Marshall has told me that Mr. Draper had
spoken very highly of the work you have done on the
border since your return, especially the hard work with
greater responsibility during the time that Mr. Draper
has been on tour, and during the invasion by Von Lettow
and the evacuation of the prisoners.

Your name was brought before the Board for
good work during the first trying months of the war.
It is very gratifying to me to be able to do it again
and to the Directors to get the District Commissioner's
appreciations of work done by one of his District
Officers when all have been known to have worked so well
during the very trying time of the war.

I am trying hard to get more probationers to
help in the Districts and to enable those overdue for
leave to get their leave as soon as possible, but it
still seems difficult to obtain men.

Believe me,

Yours very sincerely,

LAWallace

C.P. Oldfield, Esq.,

*Letter to Claude from the Administrator of Northern Rhodesia,
Lawrence A. Wallace, 8th July 1919*

[1] The last verse of 'The Lonely Graves' by Lance-Corporal Malcolm Humphrey, AOC (BEF, Nairobi, BEA), published 1916.

[2] Porto Amélia, named after the Queen of Portugal, was founded by the Niassa Company in 1904. Renamed Pemba at the end of Portuguese rule in 1975. Not to be confused with Pemba Island which forms part of the Zanzibar Archipelago (off the Tanzanian coast).

[3] Paul von Lettow-Vorbeck, *My Reminiscences of East Africa* (Hurst & Blackett, 1920) p 272

[4] Lettow-Vorbeck, ibid.

[5] Ibid.

[6] Ibid., pp 276-77

[7] Captain R. W. M. Langham, M.C 'Thornton and Rumsey of Mbesuma Ranch', *NRJ*, Vol IV, No. 4 (1960) pp 369-76. See also Edward Paice, *Tip and Run: The Untold Tragedy of the Great War in Africa*, (Weidenfield & Nicolson, 2007) p 386 et seq.

[8] Lettow-Vorbeck, ibid., p 315

[9] Lettow-Vorbeck, ibid., p 317

[10] 'Experiences of an R.S.M. in The East African Campaign, 1914-1918', by RSM John T. Bannon, DCM, 1/4 King's African Rifles, edited by his grandson, John Bannon, September 2015

[11] Lettow-Vorbeck, ibid., p 318

[12] Bannon, ibid.

[13] Quoted in Paice, ibid., p 387

[14] Lettow-Vorbeck, ibid., p 319

[15] Paice, ibid. From Governor Heinrich Schnee's, *Deutsch-Ostafrika im Weltkrieg* (Leipzig: Quelle et Meyer, 1919)

[16] In Germany, published as *Meine Erinnerungen aus Ostafrika* (Hase & Köhler, Leipzig, 1920)

[17] Joseph Maze quoted in Aylward Shorter, 'African Recruits and Missionary Conscripts: The White Fathers and the Great War (1914-1922)', *Missionaries of Africa History Project*, 2007, p 149

[18] Quoted in Mwelwa C. Musambachime, 'African reactions to the 1918/19 Influenza Epidemic in Northern Rhodesia and Nyasaland', Department of History, University of Zambia, Lusaka, 1998

[19] Musambachime, ibid.

[20] Quarterly Reports for the period ending 31 March 1919, from Musambachime, ibid.

[21] Aylward Shorter, African Recruits and Missionary Conscripts: The White Fathers and the Great War (1914-1922), *Missionaries of Africa History Project*, 2007

[22] Ibid., p 147

[23] Edmund Yorke, *Britain, Northern Rhodesia and the First World War: Forgotten Colonial Crisis* (Palgrave Macmillan, 2015) See Ch 8 'Reconquest and Reconstruction', p 212

[24] Kambole Mission Annual Report, 1919, quoted in Yorke, ibid.

[25] HMHS *Llandovery Castle*, built in 1914 in Glasgow as RMS *Llandovery Castle* for Union-Castle, was one of five Canadian hospital ships that served in WWI. On a voyage from Halifax, Nova Scotia to Liverpool, she was torpedoed off southern Ireland

on 27 June 1918. Twenty-four people survived, while 234 doctors, nurses and patients lost their lives. The incident became renowned internationally as one of the war's worst atrocities and was one of six British cases presented at the Leipzig trials.

[26] On Friday 13 July 1917, the Second Supplement to *The London Gazette* is devoted to the report from the High Commissioner's Office, Cape Town, dated 10 March 1917, signed by Sydney Buxton. *The London Gazette* is the principal 'journal of record' of the British government.

[27] Ibid., Part II, para 15

CHAPTER 13

C.P. Oldfield, Native Commissioner, Chiengi

A place of singular natural beauty

James Thomson, Native Commissioner, Chiengi, 1929

Back in Britain the flu pandemic, brought home by returning soldiers, had swept through Europe and across the Channel, reaching London by June 1918. Hospitals had been swamped, masked officials walked the streets spraying buses and pavements with disinfectant, and cinemas, theatres and public houses closed their doors. During this horrific time, Claude's elderly parents had been anxious for news of him, and likewise keen to reassure their youngest son that so far, they remained in good health. Infinitely more cheering for them early in the New Year of 1920 was his arrival home on his second period of leave.

The Britain, in which he had grown up, was changing. Female contributions on the home front during the conflict had helped the suffrage movement, and in the general election of December 1919, women over the age of thirty had been able to vote for the first time. Imported by American servicemen, there was also a new and exciting kind of music in town called jazz, to which one danced in a whole new, and in the eyes of many, immoral way. Whether or not Claude was dancing with anyone is an intriguing question. This time, there are no clues as to whether Lally or any other woman was part of his life, although one would imagine there could have been a sufficient number of maids and war widows in London to entertain the attentions of even the most reticent bachelor.

What we do know is that when Claude set sail again for Africa a few months later in May 1920, he was still a bachelor, about to take up his first independent posting, as Native Commissioner for the District of Chiengi. On his return, he went first to Ndola, arriving on 13th June to provide ten weeks' leave cover for Adam Alexander (no relation to the author).[1] At

Detail of north-eastern area of Northern Rhodesia (c.1913)

the southern side of the pedicle, on Northern Rhodesia's border with the
Congo, Ndola lay amid large deposits of copper. Fashioned by generations
of Africans into bodily adornments, the metal would soon be unearthed on
a far larger scale, feeding the growing worldwide demand in the electrical
and construction industries, and making fortunes for mining companies.
Leaving Ndola on 20th August, Claude took three weeks before reaching

165

Chiengi, a lonely spot in one of the remotest regions of the country, on the northeast corner of Lake Mweru. He would have been impressed with the size of the lake and the overall beauty of the surrounding area.

Opinions vary as to the first European to set eyes on the lake. In 1798, the Portuguese, endeavouring to lay a trade route between their territories in the east and west of Africa, which would pass through Kazembe's village, 30 miles south of Lake Mweru, had sent Dr. Francisco Lacerda to conduct negotiations.[2] Lacerda, who died at Kazembe, may not have reached the lake, but his journal was carried back to Tete by his chaplain, Father Pinto. It was later translated into English by the explorer Richard Burton, who questioned whether Lacerda had actually seen the lake.[3] We do know that in 1867, David Livingstone, having set out from the east coast, reached Lake Malawi and was then forced by ill health to travel on with slave traders. Arriving on the eastern shore of Lake Mweru, he headed south to the northeast tip of the Mofwe Lagoon. Here, at Kanyembo, he met Mwata Kazembe VII, who assured him that 'I was welcome to his country, to go where I liked, and do what I chose. We then went (two boys carrying his train behind him) to an inner apartment, where the articles of my present were exhibited in detail.'[4] Continuing south, Livingstone became the first European to see Lake Bangweulu. On finding the Lualaba River, he first thought it could have been the high part of the Nile, then realised that in fact it flowed into the River Congo.[5]

Chiengi also had a dramatic history. The District Notebook records that 'in 1890 a station was opened at Chiengi by one Crawshay who was commissioned from Blantyre, Nyasaland by (Sir) H. H. Johnson. It is thus the oldest Boma in N. E. R.' (North Eastern Rhodesia). The region then was ruled by Msiri, with whom Britain and Belgium were in competition, both countries attempting to sign treaties to secure the copper-rich deposits of Katanga. In November 1890, Crawshay's colleague Alfred Sharpe met Msiri at Bunkeya, some 120 miles southwest of Lake Mweru, in the Congo. When the terms offered by Sharpe were translated, the enraged Msiri sent him packing.[6]

The following April, King Leopold of Belgium made his attempt, sending a deputation under Paul Le Marinel, who managed to obtain a brief letter, signed by Msiri, which alluded to agents of the Congo Free State (effectively Belgium) being allowed into his territory. This being deemed too vague, Alexandre Delcommune was instructed to obtain a more definitive agreement, but Msiri refused further cooperation. Concerned that the British would seek to exploit his failure, in 1891

*Chief Mwenda Msiri Ngelengwa Shitambi (c. 1830-91)
also known as Msiri*

Captain William Grant Stairs (in 1886)

King Leopold decided on stronger action, and sent an expedition led by Capt. William Stairs with orders to take Katanga, with or without Msiri's consent.[7] The mission was all too successful, and would leave a lasting stain on Belgium's reputation.

According to the Expedition's doctor, Joseph Moloney, with negotiations at stalemate, Msiri reacted to an ultimatum and moved to a fortified village at Munema on the outskirts of Bunkeya. The next day, 20th December 1891, Stairs sent his second-in-command, Belgian Lieutenant, Omer Bodson, with Christian de Bonchamps and 100 askaris, to arrest Msiri. Bodson went into Munema with a dozen men and confronted Msiri in front of about 300 of his warriors. Msiri said nothing but in anger started to draw the sword which had been a gift from Stairs. Bodson drew his revolver and shot Msiri three times, killing him. Bodson was then shot and mortally wounded by one of Msiri's men.[8] In an article published in Paris in 1892, de Bonchamps revealed that having carried Msiri's body back to their camp, the expedition had cut off his head and hoisted it on a pole as a 'barbaric lesson' to the Garanganze.

The sinister, atavistic goings-on explored in Joseph Conrad's novel *Heart of Darkness*, were thought to be based on events in the Congo during this era. Stairs, seen by many as a brutal mercenary, no doubt expected laurels, but poetic justice had the final word, as on leaving Katanga he succumbed to a fatal dose of malaria. Canadian by birth, his atrocities on Belgium's behalf also earned Stairs a legacy as a traitor to the British Empire, especially when the full extent of Katanga's mineral wealth was realized. Meanwhile Msiri's kingdom, Katanga included, became part of Belgium's Congo Free State under Leopold, while Rhodes mitigated his disappointment by investing in Katanga's mining industry. Today, the bravery of Msiri continues to be celebrated by the Bayeke of Garanganze, who value their culture and its origins.[9]

Abandoned by the Colonial Service in 1892 after the attack on Katanga, Chiengi had been occupied intermittently prior to Claude's arrival.[10] There was much to like, the view from the boma, 300 feet above the lake was stunning, and writing of his time there in 1929, James Thomson remembered it as 'a place of singular natural beauty'. The commissioner's house, though far from grand, 'a small cottage with a leaking thatched roof', was situated on a bluff, looking out across the water to the mountains beyond Lukonzolwa and 'the mighty gap near Pweto, where the Luapula leaves the lake as the Lualaba (at this point known as the Luvua), on its way to become the Congo River'.[11]

Native Commissioner's House, Chiengi, 1921

Lake Mweru
from the
N.C.'s house –
Chiengi.
1921.
Dr. Livingstone, when
he discovered this lake.
described this bay as
being like " an
unbent bow."

Motorboat on Mweru Lake, 1921

Lake Mweru's gentle breezes encouraged gardening, photographs from the 1920s showing fruit trees, elegant hibiscus and canna lilies. To the east, lay Lake Mweru wa Ntipa, 'the lake of mud'. This swamp-like expanse of about 800 square miles, of variable depth, in places little more than ten feet, dense with papyrus and other vegetation, marked the limit of Rhodes's drive north, and from the surrounding bomas the slave trade had been pushed back. A variety of fauna proliferated, as Claude was to recall in writing to the *NRJ* in 1956:

> I knew the Mweru wa Ntipa well in the old days. My first visit was in 1913 or 1914 in the company of Gouldsbury (of *The Great Plateau of Northern Rhodesia* fame). My next visit was from Chiengi in 1920 or 1921. On each occasion I found the marsh to be a lake, as much a lake to look at as Lake Mweru, the main difference being that the water was brackish and muddy, whereas Mweru water was very clear and sweet. The marsh was a happy bathing pool for large herds of hippo, and there were a few crocs. Bird life was fascinating, enormous cranes and great flocks of pelican, also a few flamingo.[12]

Claude's first three days at Chiengi were spent on the hand-over from a junior officer, Bertram Matthews, who had been in charge since Stanley Hillier had left in March. Once settled in, his day-to-day duties as NC included attendance at *chakas* (or *Indaba*), meetings with local chiefs to discuss their various concerns.[13] Often the agenda included the contentious issue of hut taxes.[14] These poll tax levies had been introduced

The southern shore of Lake Mweru wa Ntipa, October 2012

by the BSAC to defray administrative costs, but also to encourage villagers to cultivate cash crops, or to seek paid work in the towns or burgeoning mining sector. For the year 1920-21, Claude registered the collection of £1,047 in hut taxes, an increase of £250 on the previous year, possibly a result of his extended travels to numerous villages. In June 1921, he received an 'Inspection Visit' from the DC, Edgar Jones, and Townsend Storrs, the Medical Officer.

The Notebooks provide a wealth of information on the life of a district official, and exemplify the attention to detail. 'Births – European', and 'Deaths – European' are itemised, along with 'Date of formation of Sub-District and historical notes of important occurrences'. In 1921, Claude noted that meal, beans and monkey nuts (peanuts or groundnuts) sold at a halfpenny per lb, 'mealies' (corn/maize) on the cob a penny for 3 lbs; fowls (chickens) three for a shilling, or very large ones at six pence each. Rice and potatoes sold for one penny per lb, and other vegetables such as pumpkins, at a third of that price. Chiengi had a flourishing trade in salt, dried in the local pans and then transported to Kasama and Fort Rosebery. Dried fish, taken from the Kalungwishi river and Mweru Marsh, were available. A sale of ivory by the ALC was recorded at '204 lbs @ 2/6 = £25.10.0.' The prices of staple foods today might be 10 times what they were 100 years ago, but poached ivory can now fetch in the region of £1,000 per lb, 8,000 times the 'legal' price in Claude's day.

The NC was also responsible for an annual census. In 1920, Claude's district records show a population of 12,836, based on an actual headcount of 9,836 to which an estimated 3,000, probably young children, had been added. Claude analysed the population by tribal group, comprising mainly Bwile, Washila and Watabwa, with some 'Swahili'.

Who was included in these statistics? In the early 1960s, Jonathan Lawley was responsible for:

> two erstwhile Native Authorities for the small Shila and Bwile tribes north of Kashikishi (Nchelenge). 'The Shila headquarters was … at Mununga, halfway up the lake. The Bwile HQ was 40 miles further up the road at Puta (north of Chiengi), with its wonderful views of the lake where it turns West towards the Congo … the Shila regard themselves as superior to the Bwile, of whom they would say dismissively *Babwile balalima panshi* or 'The Bwile plant their crops low down', i.e. not on ridges.'[15]

The height of their respective crops had not been the only divisive issue for the two tribes. Robert Cancel, an American researcher, recorded many oral narratives of the Bwile people, in the late 1980s and again in 2005.[16] One such story was told by Chief Puta (father of the current chief):

> Our land, of the Bwile, went as far as the Kalungwishi. And the Shila, they're from the Kalungwishi … where they share a boundary with the Lunda. Very far away there, on the other side are the Lunda, the entire [Lake] Mweru area. Because this territory belongs to Nkuba of Lubemba.

Overseeing the Lunda land was a man called Ntinda, who hunted with dogs:

> It is during his wanderings that he came across the princess [in question]. He liked her when he saw her. He said that, 'This one is suitable for me to marry.' They allowed him to take her. They made him pay accordingly.

The payment for the Bwile princess was to be a portion of Shila territory, which was handed over by Lambwe Mutumpa. This didn't go down well with his people, 'He was nicknamed "The foolish one" because he gave up the land,' and the Shila in turn sought redress:

> So they said [to the Bwile], 'We too will penalize you for this one's misbehaviour, you Bwile' … they took land from the Kalungwishi

River up to the Kalobwa River. Now this became our boundary. Our portion that extended as far as the ... what do you call it, the Kalungwishi, it now became theirs, up to today. As for us, our territory extends as far as the Kalobwa River, because of what transpired.'

With its conflicts and resentments over love and property, the story has the compelling raw ingredients of many a Dickens or Trollope novel. And although it is unclear how far back the drama took place, its oral survival demonstrates the sense of a shared past as much as any European history. The same communal spirit in Chiengi manifests itself each August with 'Ubuilile', a celebration of the harvest and the resilience, strategic thinking and self-sufficiency of the people. Nowadays, visitors are welcome and can climb Kabwe Katenda and visit Ingansa, the salt pan that continues to support the local economy. The finale is the opening of the royal granary, *Chayenkuwo*, which never runs out of food.

Writing in 1911, Cullen Gouldsbury describes a typical government station where Europeans had also to be self-sufficient.[17] Abercorn, for example, was home to a magistrate or assistant magistrate, one or two government officials and perhaps a doctor and a trader, but at a smaller station, an officer might find himself alone, or accompanied by 'if he is lucky, his wife'. Gouldsbury describes an undemanding life, with brick houses neatly laid out and plenty of fresh vegetables, milk and meat. The work could be interesting and varied, with plenty of leisure time for

Chief Puta of the Bwile, talking to the author in October 2012

hunting, shooting, gardening, botany and photography. There seemed few downsides. The District Notebooks referred to certain historical health problems in the area – trypanosomiasis, or sleeping sickness which, recorded in 1907, had recurred several times. A segregation camp set up in 1910, had been moved to Kawambwa a year later, and with the threat now receded (except for Kilwa Island in Lake Mweru), the preventative regulations had been lifted. Malaria, nevertheless, remained an ever-present risk.

The picture of tranquillity evoked in descriptions of the elevated boma, is beguiling. The wildlife of Lake Mweru wa Ntipa with hippos and crocodiles must have been a delight for a photographer like Claude. But when night fell, it was wiser to stay indoors. James Thomson remembered: 'a stout cage of wooden bars on the verandah in which the inmate, if nervous, could sit in safety from the lions which wandered rather aimlessly about the station most nights of the week'. After Vellacott's death, Claude knew never to underestimate lions. Over the next 18 months, he would record no less than ten incidents involving wild animals.[18] A section of the notebook headed: 'Wild Beasts etc. Rewards for killing and deaths from', includes an entry for June 1921, when Shiminkata of Nakabwebwe, armed only with a spear, dispatched a lion single-handedly, and received a £2 reward. Not all were so fortunate. In September, Kaputo Mpumo, heir of Chief Mununga, 'died as result of mauling by a lion at Mununga's old village'. The same month, Sikapambwe of Chimondo's dog, while foraging in the thick bush, inadvertently roused a somnolent buffalo, which, 'at once charged and killed Sikapambwe, goring him in the stomach.'

There was the fearsome legend of 'Chiengi Charlie', who, known for his abnormally pale coat and short tail as 'The Devil,' was believed to have done away with ninety villagers in 1909. Fires and armed guards proved ineffectual, and if the door of a hut were barred, he was known to have broken through the thatched roof, stealing the bait from trap guns and escaping unharmed. It was eventually a mail runner, a retired askari called Galatea, who earned the distinction of putting a bullet in Charlie and ending his reign of terror.[19]

Another potential enemy for a colonial officer, especially in a one-man station, was the insidious problem of loneliness. In a remote location, six months or more might go by without seeing another white person and at this time there were few educated Africans in rural areas. The uncertainty of the mail service and a scarcity of good books could compound the sense of isolation. Gouldsbury had warned of 'days when men dreaded sundown and the dark, when nerves were a-jangle, and the very rats in the roof were welcomed as living things.' Deprived of ordinary human contact, a man might understandably seek the nearest available relief, when 'drink and drugs pleaded their charms … and would not be denied.'

Neurasthenia, with symptoms of listlessness, anxiety, headaches, poor concentration and a depressed mood, had also gained currency in medical circles.[20] Described as early as 1829 as a physical affliction of the nervous system, by the late nineteenth and early twentieth centuries, the term was applied in a more general sense to those who suffered from 'nerves'. The spectrum could be wide, from spells of mild irritability to the paralysing 'black dog', that Churchill famously feared. The current understanding of post-viral fatigue might have explained some cases, but there seemed an almost fashionable preponderance of the condition among the more sedentary, professional and upper echelons of society. Freud naturally offered a sexual explanation for male sufferers, claiming 'uncompleted coitus' for poisoning the system. Abstention was seemingly not for want of opportunity. Harry Franklin, who Claude would meet a few years later, described the advice given to him by a more senior official: 'Don't worry if you have a black girl. You're sure to, but don't let it get on your conscience. Everybody does it. You'll be lonely. It's natural.'[21] It seemed that Europeans had the *droit de seigneur* of a chief among Africans, and the failure of any official or grass widower to exercise it by taking a mistress, was regarded by some as very odd.[22] This ran contrary to the official edict issued earlier by the Colonial Administration but by the time Harry arrived, either the rules had been relaxed, or in the seclusion of the remote bomas, they had always been quietly ignored.

Even if Claude had been prone to depression, his propensity for outdoor exercise, mostly in the course of duty, would have been a natural antidote. During his first ulendo from Chiengi in late October 1920, he walked for 21 days, visiting 27 villages. By February 1922, he had travelled for 146 days, thus spending about a third of his time away from the boma, the longest single trip being in October 1921, covering 54 villages in 29 days. One might expect such long journeys on foot to be undertaken mainly in the dry season, but Claude made tours over Christmas and New Year at the peak of the rains. This would hardly have been congenial, often spending wet nights in a tent, but having camped extensively on the border during the war, he was used to roughing it. The timing may have been deliberate, allowing him more opportunity for socialising with Europeans during the drier months.

There were excursions under sail, across Lake Mweru to the even more remote Kilwa Island, whose fishing community, though close to the Congo side, came under the Chiengi administration. Claude made visits across the border into the Congo and, like others writing during the period, would have observed the more sophisticated lifestyle enjoyed by the Belgian officials. Denis Paine, recalling the late 1920s, lamented the paucity of development on the British side, 'where there are only three Europeans: the NC and ALC Agent (both at Chiengi), and a missionary at Kafulwe.' This was in stark contrast to the Congo where, 'The abundance of fish has attracted European enterprise from the Belgian Congo … and Greeks from Kasenga are fishing at the southern end of the Lake.'[23] The fish catch, estimated at 4,000 tons a year, was transported on ice to Elisabethville.

The unhurried pace of Claude's official trips gave him the time, and the vantage points, from which to capture the area's more photogenic locations. Among the natural features which caught his eye was the 'Wasp's Waist', the narrow stretch of river where the Luvua flows north out of Lake Mweru, with Kashyengeneke Hill on the Congo side opposite, and Kabwe's Rock. According to legend, originally:

> there were two rocks, 'a couple'. Long ago, the couple quarrelled and the female rock was pushed away and moved half a mile into Lake Mweru. The remaining rock is called 'Kabwe Katenda'.[24]

Kashyengeneke Hill and the 'Wasp's Waist', 1921

Returning to the boma after weeks on ulendo, how might Claude have spent the many long evenings, when he found himself alone? At sunset, gazing from the stoep as the light paled over Lake Mweru, were there not moments when he might have dreamed of a warm embrace? It may be simplistic to assume that a conventional upbringing, with church-going at home and formal school chapel, would restrain baser impulses, but perhaps there was also a natural asceticism and sense of upright behaviour. On the other hand, Claude had not become a missionary or joined the priesthood. Celibacy, like the rainy season or a tough government posting, had to end sometime.

[1] Ndola DNB. Entry in Claude's handwriting (District Staff Movements, p 18). Adam Murray Alexander was a close contemporary, whose postings included Kalomo (80 miles north of Livingstone) in 1923. See *NRJ*, Vol IV, No. 3 (1960) pp 297-8.

[2] Francisco Jose de Lacerda e Almeida (1753-98) was a colonial Brazilian-born explorer.

[3] Denis Paine 'Lake Mweru: Its Fish and Fishing Industry' *NRJ*, Vol I, No. 2 (1950) (pp 7-13). The *NRJ* Editor, W. V. Brelsford, comments that David Livingstone should have the honour of being the first European to see the lake on 8 November 1867, although, of course, it was generally well known to Arab traders.

[4] Extract from David Livingstone *The Last Journals of David Livingstone in Central Africa from 1865 To His Death*.

[5] David Livingstone, *Personal Letter to J. Kirk or R. Playfair*, from David Livingstone Online

[6] Chief Msiri (c. 1830-91) founded and ruled the Yeke Kingdom (also called the Garanganze) in south-east Katanga from about 1856 to 1891. Sometimes spelled 'M'Siri' (French) or other variants, 'Mziri', 'Msidi', 'Mushidi'. His full name was Mwenda Msiri Ngelengwa Shitambi.

[7] William Grant Stairs (1863-92), born in Canada, was educated there and in Scotland. Joined the Emin Pasha Relief Expedition in 1887 and appointed 2iC after Capt. Barttelot was shot in July 1888. Died on the Lower Zambezi.

[8] Joseph Moloney, *With Captain Stairs to Katanga: Slavery and Subjugation in the Congo, 1891-92* (Sampson Low, Martson, 1893)

[9] See kingmsiri website

[10] In the early years the boma was known as Mputa. It was reopened again, when Choma on Lake Mweru wa Ntipa closed, under the name Chiengi. It was again closed and then reopened in 1907-08 by Wenham to deal with the evacuation of villages on the lakeshore due to sleeping sickness.

[11] Justice J. B. Thomson 'Memories of Abandoned Bomas, No. 8: Chiengi' *NRJ*, Vol II, No.6 (1955) (pp 67-77)

[12] F. B. Macrae 'Mweru wa Ntipa: More about Water Levels' *NRJ*, Vol III, No. 2 (1956) (pp 127-30)

[13] *Indaba* (Zulu) means business or matter. Used widely throughout southern Africa and often referring to a meeting or gathering.

[14] The hut tax was introduced by the colonial administration on the basis of a tax per hut (or household). It was variously payable in money, labour, grain or stock and benefited the authorities: by raising money; supporting the currency; broadening the cash economy, aiding further development; and encouraging Africans to look for paid work. Households whose wealth was mainly in cattle, now sent family members to work to raise cash to pay the tax. The economy needed African labour for building towns, railways and for developing mines. Although authorized by the Colonial Office in London, the tax was paid to the BSAC, as agent of the colonial government. Coinciding with confiscations of cattle, the introduction of forced labour and a series of natural disasters, the tax probably contributed to the Shona part of the rebellion in 1896, known as the First *Chimurenga* or Second Matabele War.

[15] Jonathan Lawley, *Beyond the Malachite Hills: A Life of Colonial Service and Business in the New Africa* (I. B. Tauris, 2010)

[16] Robert Cancel, *Storytelling in Northern Zambia: Theory, Method, Practice and Other Necessary Fictions*, (Open Book, Cambridge, 2013)

[17] Gouldsbury & Sheane, *The great plateau.*

[18] Entries in the Chiengi DNB.

[19] W. V. Brelsford 'The fate of Chiengi Charlie, Man-Eater' NRJ, Vol. V, No. 6 (1964) pp 611-612. First recorded in the *Journal of East Africa* in April 1929 by 'Thomas Alexander', almost certainly Thomas Alexander Barns (1881-1930). Barns was an English business man, explorer, big game hunter, author, artist, naturalist and lecturer who spent many years in Africa from 1898. Given the risks he took in Africa, it is ironic that he died in Chicago having been struck by a taxicab.

[20] Neurasthenia. The term first used at least as early as 1829 to label a mechanical weakness of the nerves. Commonly treated by prescribing rest, especially for women, who were the gender primarily diagnosed with the condition at that time.

[21] Harry Franklin, *The Flag Wagger*, Shepheard-Walwyn, 1974

[22] 'Grass widower' refers to a man divorced or separated, or who is temporarily apart from his wife.

[23] Denis Paine, ibid.

[24] With appreciation to the Acting DC for Chiengi, Sempela Chanda Havitus, for confirming this story in June 2013.

CHAPTER 14

Kawambwa: Surrounded by Missionaries

Those who are dead are never gone: they are there in the thickening shadow.

Birago Diop, Senegalese poet

Africa was a special place where God was present, and he was speaking through African voices.

Mabel Shaw, British missionary at Mbereshi

When the rains stopped, Claude's lonely stint at Chiengi ended and in April 1922 he was transferred to Kawambwa, situated high on the edge of the cool plateau, a boma comprising twenty-six Europeans, including ten women and two children. The previous NC, Gerald Morton, had gone on leave the previous August, leaving cadet officer Eric Clough in charge.[1] When Eric stayed on as Claude's assistant, the two men formed a close friendship, with Claude's dog, Dick, becoming playmate for an orphaned bushbuck that Eric had adopted and tamed.

Eric Clough, 1923

The Medical Officer's House, Kawambwa, 1922

The original administrative boma at Kalungwishi in the Luapula valley closed in 1908 on the discovery of tsetse fly, *Glossina palpalis*, the carrier of sleeping sickness. Kawambwa's higher altitude, reducing the risk of disease, attracted a variety of Christian missions, of whom early Victorian opinion was not always flattering. Professor David Maxwell suggests that with some notable exceptions, 'elites and intellectuals have never been particularly kind about Protestant missionaries.'[2] At the beginning of the nineteenth century, the missionary was seen as a kind of tinker, who in the words of Rev. Sydney Smith, 'could not look a gentleman in the face.'[3] Maxwell explained that by the middle nineteenth century, after Livingstone's explorations, missionaries were 'no longer regarded as religious eccentrics but representatives of Victorian values.'[4]

The denominations were diverse in their beliefs, practices and tolerances. When hosting a 'sundowner' party, Harry Franklin would 'in deference to the Plymouth Brethren, refrain from smoking and serve tea to them and lime juice to the disappointed Catholics, who enjoyed stronger drink and were in need of it.' The Fathers though, had been importing sacramental wine in sufficient quantities to arouse the curiosity of the Customs Department.[5]

Claude would have heard such stories from Willie Lammond. The older of two brothers born in Glasgow to a 'Free Church' family, after training as a fitter Willie had sailed to Africa in 1900 aged twenty-three, landing at Benguela on the west coast when 'there was no Lobito, no railway, no wheeled traffic, no road into the interior.' Proceeding inland, his party followed the routes of slave traders and native merchants, eventually reaching the Lualaba river at Johnston Falls, where the Garanganze Mission had been founded in 1895 by another Scot, Dan Crawford, of the Plymouth Brethren.[6] Lammond particularly respected the achievements of another predecessor, Frederick Arnot, who had opened up the hinterland of what is now Angola and part of the Congo, notably the mineral-rich region of Katanga.[7] By 1904, Lammond had a sweetheart, Flora Merry, but unwilling to 'live in sin', the couple walked 250 miles to have their union blessed in the sight of God. On the way back to Johnston Falls, Flora fell ill with black water fever, a complication of malaria linked to excessive use of its only salve, quinine. She made it to the mission, but died from the fever in January 1906. Lammond then sailed for England, where in 1908 he married Dora Gammon of Ilfracombe, returning to Africa with her the same year. In 1910 an outbreak of sleeping sickness in the Luapula Valley forced Lammond to move his mission to Kaleba, forty-six miles southwest of Kawambwa. By 1922, with the restrictions lifted the mission returned to Johnston Falls.[8]

Lammond's sect, the Plymouth Brethren (then known as the Christian Brethren and later as the Christian Missions in Many Lands), took a literal interpretation of scripture, and were fervent evangelists. Robert Rotberg's comprehensive history of the early missions described the uncompromising standards: 'In order to belong, its members were required to give unmistakable evidence of conversion to God and the service of man. They were required to live lives of danger and complete self-sacrifice and denial. They were to depend on freewill offerings for support – the bounty of God's promise.'[9] Alcohol and tobacco were proscribed, and adherents accepted the reality of the Holy Spirit, the Fall of Man, Hell, Satan, and the Second Coming:

> They subscribed to a justification by faith in which good works were the proof and result of a saving faith; eternal salvation existed for the saved and eternal punishment for the lost. They understood the present and conscious assurance of salvation; absolution of sins was available only through the intercession of Christ and through the joyful anticipation of His return.[10]

Willie Lammond had also studied dentistry at Livingstone College, and found his skills much in demand in Africa. When his younger brother George and his wife joined the mission in 1913, George's cabinet-making prowess earned similar renown. In 1951, Vernon Brelsford commended the Lammond families for leaving 'their mark on the Luapula valley in a practical day-to-day fashion as well as in the spiritual sphere' and undoubtedly Willie Lammond improved the lives of many in Northern Rhodesia, creating a school and home for the blind and physically handicapped, within a caring Christian community.[11]

More moderate missions also sought 'to equip Africans as craftsman and technicians, who could operate effectively in the modern economic world', and translated 'the glad tidings' imperfectly into local languages. There were still attempts to censure indigenous culture, particularly where pleasure or sexuality were involved, with women urged to cover their waists and breasts with skins or calico, and traditional polygamy, bride wealth and adultery condemned as sinful. Barotseland was said to be surrounded by 'awful heathenism' and an 'unfathomable abyss of corruption and degradation.'[12] Most missions frowned on beer drinking and even tribal singing and dancing, simple enjoyments, which, not surprisingly, many Africans were reluctant to forgo.

The Roman Catholic White Fathers (*Pères Blancs d'Algers*) wore the hooded robes of the indigenous Algerians to whom they had first preached.

White Fathers Marsan, Monseigneur Etienne Larue (Bangweulu Vicariate)
and Heulin, Shiwa Ng'andu, September 1925

In 1902, Père Foulon and Père Dellalles had started a mission at Luali, which was abandoned a year later, but in 1910 a new station under Father Binkhorst had opened on the Mpoposhi River at Chiboti, about thirty-six miles east of Kawambwa.[13]

The London Missionary Society (LMS) approach tended to be gradualist, preaching the gospel and expanding slowly as it recruited and trained teachers, with newcomers progressing from 'hearers' to 'catechumens', then full church members. The society also provided dispensaries, medical centres and carpentry training workshops. In 1900, Adam Purves, who had designed and built the church at Niamkolo on Lake Tanganyika, which Claude had visited in its ruined state, escaped from the fever-ridden area with his wife and set up a mission on the Mbereshi river, about twenty-one miles west of Kawambwa. Fifteen years later this would become a mission with a difference, being the first in Africa to include an unmarried woman. Mabel Shaw, eldest of five children, had been born to a non-Christian lower middle-class family in Wolverhampton, her first inspiration a Baptist 'granny' who taught her 'how near God was in everyday things in this world.' Intent on serving in India, when the LMS summoned her to Northern Rhodesia, she concluded it 'must be God's will', and prayed she might 'follow worthily' in David Livingstone's footsteps.

Soon after her arrival, Shaw set up the first school for girls in the

Members of the London Missionary Society, 1924

district, and appears to have been loved by her pupils. Her subsequent writings show a deep affinity for Africans and Africa, a land with 'waters of healing for the peoples ... where all lost things were found' and 'God's awful majesty' abounded. Shaw evoked a markedly different place to the Victorian image of the Dark Continent, full of savagery and disease, while her view of African women as fellow human beings rather than mere church fodder, reflected her brand of liberal evangelical theology, committed to uniting Christians with non-Christians, and the belief that Jesus offered his followers primarily friendship. Even more radically, she turned the Euro-centric concept of conversion on its head, claiming that Livingstone did not bring God to Africa, but rather 'found Him here in every village, in every man, and woman...' and that 'Africa was a special place where God was present, and he was speaking through African voices.'[14]

Mabel Shaw's school at Mbereshi, which opened with four girls and by 1932 had 160, became a role model for girls' education, its founder the most renowned female missionary in Africa. When Claude took up his post at Kawambwa in 1922, the LMS had been in Mbereshi for twenty years. It was unwise to rest on laurels, for while some individuals integrated well with the local community, the foothold remained tenuous; new arrivals struggled with the heat, the rains, language and food, often confining themselves to the mission station as 'aliens in the land of their work'. In 1922, the Mbereshi mission was being run by William and Nancy Freshwater, assisted by Mabel Shaw, heading the girls' school, and another single lady, Winifred Bishop. Shaw set an example of integration, speaking

Grave of Adam Purves, Mbereshi, 2012

Chibemba, and endeavouring to meld Christianity and African customs, referring to 'Chief Jesus' as the highest authority in the community. At thirty-four, Mabel was just a year older than Claude, and perhaps a possible match. They were of similar background and experience, yet still of an age to start a family. Mabel's commitment to the religious life however seemed absolute, and she would remain a spinster until her death in a Surrey nursing home in 1973, aged eighty-five. Willie Lammond had an even longer innings, making ninety-two before his death in 1968. Others were destined to toil for only a short time in the vineyard; Adam Purves, who built Niamkolo Church, died from fever in 1901 at the age of thirty-six.

In the District Notebook at Kawambwa, Claude discovered another poignant story:

> Ten miles east of the Kawambwa Boma on the Mporokoroso road and a mile out into the bush lie Mr Johnstone and his wife near an old boma which he was establishing in 1900, known as the Kampanda old boma ... They have cleared round, planted flowering trees, flowers, marigolds, Salvia and 'forget-me-nots'. And, now, the spot looks attractive ... the interest was stimulated by Mr. S. Palmer, Game and Tsetse Officer. The following families also helped: – the Bands, Byrnes and Mr Morton.

Mr. Bertie Bromley Johnstone and his African wife, Namdwala, would henceforward, the writer assured 'be visited often'. Their fate, and also that of Adam Purves and Lammond's first wife, would discourage many Europeans from considering a life in Africa, but for certain muscular Christians the perils might have been an incentive to go and 'fight the good fight.'

James Lawson and Minnie Nutter (married to LMS missionary, Cecil), both died from black water fever at Mbereshi in 1903 when they were only aged twenty-nine; followed in 1907 by Nancy Miller.[15] In his annual review for the LMS, Cecil Nutter, referred to Minnie as being called to higher service:

> Such saddening events cast a gloom over our first gatherings at this new Station but I believe we were all called to re-consecrate ourselves to our Master's Service. We had long prayed that these meetings might be used of God to the conversion of many around us. These prayers have not been unanswered. There are 3 deeply dug graves here, but they are to us the promise of a rich harvest.[16]

By 1919 the Universities' Mission to Central Africa (UMCA) was having difficulty recruiting. Formed in 1857 following Livingstone's appeal at the Senate House in Cambridge, the UMCA (unlike many of the audience, who supported a strong evangelical theology) had emerged from within the Church of England as an essentially 'high church' enterprise, somewhat Anglo-Catholic in ritual and appeal. The universities concerned, Oxford, Cambridge, Durham and Dublin, organized their first mission under Bishop Charles Mackenzie, sailing up the Zambezi and Shire rivers to Lake Nyasa. Mackenzie and three others died of malaria, and the mission was abandoned.[17]

Not until its fiftieth anniversary in 1907 did the UMCA plan a second attempt in central Africa. At Canterbury Cathedral on 31st March 1910, Archbishop Davidson blessed each member of the mission, and the following year Bishop John Edward Hine, previously Bishop of Zanzibar, established the new Diocese of Northern Rhodesia, laying the foundation stone of St. Andrew's, Livingstone. Hine was succeeded in 1914 by Alston May, a younger man who, realising he had only five priests and two laymen, requested a further ten men, 'a modest requirement for so vast a land'. After the disruption of the First World War, the Bishop was still awaiting his reinforcements in 1919. As the original incumbents died or retired, the fate of the mission stations and the African converts was looking precarious, while at Chipili, Father Pulley's poor health had obliged him to return to England, leaving his colleague Charles Leeke to struggle on alone.[18] The building of a permanent church was being planned, but Leeke told the Bishop that without support the station would be forced to close. In 1920, May returned to England, where he managed to recruit six new priests. Meanwhile, Father Herbert Barnes, from the Community of the Resurrection at Penhalonga in Southern Rhodesia, had transferred to Chipili to work alongside Leeke.

In 1922, Claude travelled to Chipili, and met Fathers Leeke and Barnes. Bachelors of similar age and background, the three men had much in common. Herbert Barnes, educated at Wells Cathedral School, had already spent some years in Africa, initially in Nyasaland. At Chipili he would earn his nickname of 'Father Gadget' for his Heath-Robinson contraptions, including a string and banner device to indicate when the outside loo was occupied.[19] Charles Leeke, from a very 'churchy' family, his father sub-deacon of Lincoln Cathedral and his four brothers all priests, had entered the priesthood via Marlborough and Trinity College, Cambridge. Conscious of their isolation and possibly missing the collegiate

Father Leeke, Father Barnes and CPO at the Chipili Bridge, 1922
(Universities Mission to Central Africa)

atmosphere, a small group including Fr. Leeke had obtained Bishop May's permission to form their own 'congregation' of the Oratory of the Good Shepherd, a society established at Cambridge for the mutual support of celibate priests following a discipline of prayer and devotion.[20] Those outside the faith must have regarded this as an unnaturally repressive way of life for ordinary mortals, and predicted cracks to appear at some stage. Harry Franklin, visiting Chipili some years later, observed 'an Anglican Mission of celibate priests who were not on the best of terms with each other.' It transpired that they 'had been upset by the recent arrival of a middle-aged lady educationist and contended with each other for the duty of sleeping across her threshold in order, so rumour had it, to prevent any of those off duty from attempting ingress.'[21]

Physically, Claude was anything but confined, completing seven ulendos between 3rd June 1922 and 23rd March 1923 (over a total of seventy-eight days, covering 707 miles and visiting 245 villages). In nine months he was away about a third of the time, typically travelling

Mporokoso Christmas, 1921: S. Hillier, G.H. Morton, H.C.N. Hill, CPO

nine miles a day visiting three villages, probably all on foot, as he had not learned to drive, and such roads as existed would have mostly been inadequate for motorised vehicles. There were also visits to Mbereshi and Chipili, and attendance at Fort Roseberry to sit law examinations, and he spent Christmas 1921 with friends in Mporokoso. On 8th March 1923, an inspection visit by Edward Tagart found everything in good order and by May, Claude was ready to depart. There had been two rather sad events, the first a poor emaciated lion, caught with a wild pig in its jaws, was stalked for two hours before being shot dead. Nature bit back when a leopard took Claude's pet dog Dick.

[1] DNB, Kawambwa, Vol. III, p 18
[2] Patrick Harries & David Maxwell (eds), *The Spiritual in the Secular: Missionaries and Knowledge about Africa* (Wm. B. Eerdmans, Grand Rapids, 2012)
[3] Quoted in W. N. Gunson, 'Evangelical Missionaries in the South Seas, 1797-1860', PhD Thesis, The Research School of Pacific Studies, Australian National University, 1959.
[4] Harries & Maxwell, ibid.
[5] Franklin, ibid.
[6] The Garanganze or Yeke people (also 'Bayeke') of Katanga established the Yeke Kingdom under Msiri, controlling the trade route across Africa between Angola and Zanzibar.
[7] W. Lammond, 'Fifty Years in Central Africa' *NRJ*, Vol. I, No. 3 (1951)

[8] DNB, Kawambwa, p 192. William Lammond was born in 1876 into a Free Church family in Glasgow. He worked as a fitter for nine years before sailing to Benguela on the Atlantic coast of Angola in 1901, then proceeding inland on the Quanza (or Cuanza) river. Lammond lived in Northern Rhodesia from 1905 to 1963, primarily at Johnston Falls and Kaleba. Source: Robert Rotberg, *Christian Missionaries and the Creation of Northern Rhodesia, 1880-1924* (Princeton University Press, 1965)

[9] Rotberg, ibid.

[10] Ibid.

[11] Willie Lammond, 'Editor's Notes' *NRJ*, Vol I, No. 3 (1951).

[12] Rotberg, ibid.

[13] DNB. At 31 March 1923: J. Tessier, J. Henlin, W. Merkelbach (Br. Walter)

[14] Mabel Shaw, *God's Candlelights: An Educational Venture in Northern Rhodesia*, Edinburgh House Press, 1932. See also Rebecca C. Hughes, 'The Legacy of Mabel Shaw', *International Bulletin of Missionary Research*, Vol. 37, No. 2, April 2013

[15] Cecil Nutter, born Keighley, Yorkshire in 1873, had gone out to Northern Rhodesia in 1901 shortly after his ordination and missionary training at Harley House, an evangelical college at Bow in east London. From Rotberg, ibid.

[16] Annual Report to Foreign Secretary, London Missionary Society, written from Mberezi (sic), dated December 1903, signed by H. Cecil Nutter. From copy held at SOAS Library, London.

[17] The UMCA was established in 1857 in response to a plea by David Livingstone. Firmly in the Anglo-Catholic tradition, it was the first to devolve authority to a bishop in the field rather than to a home committee. The Society established the mission stations that grew to be the bishoprics of Zanzibar and Nyasaland, and pioneered the training of black African priests. By the time of the centenary in 1957, the UMCA was increasingly collaborating with the Society for the Propagation of the Gospel, with the two organizations merging in 1965.

[18] A.G. Blood, *The History of the Universities' Mission to Central Africa*, Vol II 1907-32 (UMCA, 1957)

[19] George Tibbatts, 'The Oratory of the Good Shepherd: The First Seventy-Five Years', *The OGS Almoner*, 1987

[20] H.R.T. Brandreth, 'A History of the Oratory of the Good Shepherd', OGS *Website* (2015)

[21] Franklin, ibid.

CHAPTER 15

Cherchez la Femme

*Il y a une femme dans toutes les affaires; aussitôt qu'on me
fait un rapport, je dis:
'Cherchez la femme!'*

Alexandre Dumas, *The Mohicans of Paris*

Claude's departure from Kawambwa in May 1923 is confirmed in the District Notebook, and we know that he took up his new appointment as NC, Mporokoso on 1st February 1924 succeeding Stanley Hillier.[1]

Surprisingly, we cannot find Claude's name in any shipping records covering that period, although it is most likely that he went to England on leave. A more intriguing, alternative scenario is possible. A month after Claude left Kawambwa, his friend and colleague Robert Jeffreys arrived in Abercorn, where on 20th July he was to take up his post as Native Commissioner. Robert had brought with him his beautiful young bride Dorothy, who was to become the captivating subject of so many of Claude's photographs, and with Robert eager to show her off, it is not inconceivable that they met up en route with Claude in Cape Town. Is it even possible that, as soon as Claude set eyes on Dorothy, he felt less inclined to go home on leave, and even cancelled his passage? But let us return to Dorothy later.

On returning to Mporokoso, Claude must have experienced a profound sense of *déjà vu*, with the indelible memory of being summoned to help the fatally wounded Eric Vellacott in April 1918, and having also been Acting ANC in 1913. Since then, the Mporokoso boma had seen a series of Native Commissioners, including Gerard Morton, who stayed on as what appears to be Claude's unofficial ANC for nine months until June 1923.

The scale of Claude's new district was impressive, covering 10,000 square miles, with an enormous quantity of game, notably in the Sumbu reserve. The lake and swamp systems ran from Lake Mweru in the north, which Claude already knew well, to Lake Bangweulu, draining into the

Luapula River in the south. Cyril Greenall, DC some twenty years after Claude, remembered Mporokoso as 'one of the great experiences of [his] career' where 'the sensations washed over and coloured the images of all that went on around … I was intoxicated with excitement'. Greenall found the countryside 'especially conducive to this euphoria' being more lush and beautiful than many other parts of the country, and described his time there as 'An Idyllic Interlude'.[2]

Like most new arrivals, Greenall had delved into the District Notebook and found that little had changed since the nineteenth century, when:

> The African Lakes Corporation had come … thinly disguised as missions, but managed by agents of whom it was cynically remarked that they carried a Bible in one hand and a bag of beads in the other. Those days had long vanished, but when one was on ulendo … there were still plenty of beads to be seen, sometimes as just about the only item of clothing worn by some of the teenagers.[3]

From this report it seems that even by the 1940s, modernity had not greatly intruded, and in Claude's time, Mporokoso must have felt very much like the old Africa. The scope for hunting is seen in his pictures of a prize hippopotamus landed at Mweru wa Ntipa in December 1924 and at the Mwepwe Falls on the Lufubu River, on the edge of the Sumbu Reserve.[4]

This provided Christmas dinner for the natives and good dripping for me. Natives dancing while dragging the carcase, which was swollen up like a large balloon. They had great fun trying to ride it and slipping off.

Mwepwe Falls in 1925, including fish traps. The pool below is full of crocodiles.

Eland shot near Pembamoto village. The eland is the largest antelope and the meat is very good, 1925.

Claude enjoyed living in 'one of the nicest houses I have had' with the support of two 'very faithful servants: House boys: Njeresani and Bobo Yenga – 'Butler' and 'Boots'. In place of his ill-fated dog, Dick, Claude had acquired a cat called Ginger. Sadly, this feline friend would also be

snatched from him with cruel haste, for 'Ginger disappeared one night and, I fear, was the victim of a wild beast (leopard or hyena).'

The Mporokoso boma was relatively small with few Europeans for company, so 'bachelor bliss' might be stretching things. The District Notebook shows no record of Claude having an assistant, although in the early 1920s there had usually been a 'second official' – Gerard Morton in 1921-22 and Edward Munday in 1927. Claude and Gerard could have ambled away a few late afternoons on the rather rough nine-hole golf course, which may also have attracted some of the local missionaries such as the Hurlows, Seventh Day Adventists at Chimpempe Falls on

Hurlows and Nutters with motorbikes, Mporokoso, 1925

Mr. & Mrs. Nutter on tennis court, Mporokoso 1926

the Luapula river, and Cecil and Ada Nutter, who came across on their motorbike from their LMS station at Mbereshi.[5] Cecil Nutter, now in his fifties, had married Ada (née Wareham), having met her through the mission after the death of his first wife from fever, and they now had a daughter, Ethel. Ada's brother was Harold Wareham, also at Mbereshi, the siblings being 'children of the mission' whose father had served in India with the LMS.

For more stimulation, the Provincial HQ at Kasama, with a reasonable club and better sporting facilities, was accessible by motorbike. It is likely that Claude would have met Robert Jeffreys here in 1914, when Robert arrived as a young cadet officer. However, it's just possible that their paths could have crossed a few years earlier at Cambridge, when Robert was

*CPO with Mrs. Owen & Jean, Mr. & Mrs. Nutter, Miss Ethel Nutter,
Mporokoso, June 1926[6]*

studying law at St. John's College.[7] The two undergrads would have overlapped during Claude's fresher year of 1908-09, although Robert was academically two years ahead and was not an oarsman. Robert had gone on to Gray's Inn in April 1909, described there as 'of St John's College, Cambridge; the youngest son of George Ernest Jeffreys of Cape Town, merchant.'[8] Called to the Bar on 8th June 1910, by 30th July he had sailed from Southampton to Cape Town, accompanied by his older brother Frankie.[9]

Robert and Claude were destined to become good friends, despite differing backgrounds prior to Cambridge. Robert Sydney Jeffreys was born on 11th January 1888 in Claremont, at the time just a village, six miles from Cape Town at the foot of Table Mountain.[10] The opening of the railway from Cape Town to Wynberg in 1864 had spurred the development of large estates in the 1870s, and in 1882 a management board was formed in Robert's village, which in 1886 became the Municipality of Claremont, also running the neighbouring village of Newlands. Later the family moved to Mount Vernon at the foot of the Simonsberg, now the heart of the Western Cape wine-making region. Robert's father was George Jeffreys, his mother Mary (née Herbert), who at thirty-eight gave birth to 'Robbie', the youngest of four brothers: Harry, Frankie, Tommy and Robbie.[11]

The two younger boys were especially close. Writing many years later, Tommy affectionately recalled special memories of Guy Fawkes Day from their years in the Cape, at Blackheath and at Mount Vernon.[12] Robert started at Green and Sea Point School, before moving to the Boys' High School in Wynberg from age nine to fifteen. In May 1904 Robert's parents came to England, sailing on the *Durham Castle*, and after two years at Bedford Grammar School, Robert went up to Cambridge.

How might we compare Claude and Robert's personalities? Stewart Gore-Browne regarded Claude as a 'taciturn' young man, and we know that he was the product of a late-Victorian upbringing, a disciplinarian father, and the prim confines of Maida Vale's terraced villas.[13] Robert, born under sunny colonial skies, appears more self-assured and relaxed. There was though a considerable difference between the ordered white suburbs of Cape Town, and the never-ending 'bundu' of Northern Rhodesia, where Claude's three years' experience would allow him to offer friendly advice to the 'rookie', and in some small way perhaps take him under his wing for a while. Robert's arrival coinciding with the outbreak of war, they could also have been thrown together on border patrols.

Both men were the youngest of four boys and each probably spoilt to some extent in their early years, then later feeling that they must catch-up with, or even try to outstrip, their older brothers. Given the wider age gap between Claude and his brothers, he might have felt more like an only child.[14] As a highly educated last-born, he might also have felt an obligation to provide 'a return on investment' for his parents.

When Robert Jeffreys had arrived on home leave in Plymouth on 17th May 1918, he could boast four years' service as a colonial officer, and some experience of war. Aged thirty, he was also at the point when marriage was permitted by his employers and expected by his family. Following the Armistice in November 1918, Robert was posted to the more remote 'Old Fife', as Assistant to Basil Goodall. With many of the boma buildings damaged or destroyed in fighting with the Germans, temporary quarters had been erected until a new location could be established at Isoka, after which Fife was closed down in August 1921.[15] During this period, both Claude and Robert would have often met in Abercorn.

In February 1923 while on leave, Robert married Dorothy Christiansen in Southwark. Probably they had met in London (we have no record of Dorothy living elsewhere) but when? Unless it was during Robert's

Holy Trinity Church, Oslo, c. 1890

previous leave in 1918, their meeting, courtship and marriage took place within the space of a few weeks. The one certainty seems to be that Robert regarded Dorothy as very special. Alas, Claude was to experience similar feelings.

Dorothy's background was unusual. Her father was Christian Hjalmar Christiansen, a Norwegian marine engineer from Oslo, who had been baptized at the Trefoldighet, the Church of the Holy Trinity, in central Oslo on 18th August 1867.[16] Having come to England apparently for work, he had met Jane Ellen Saunders from Whitechapel, who was two years younger than him. They married on 19th April 1897 at St. Andrew's Church in Plaistow, just across the Barking Road from their home at 42 Hollybush Street, a recently-built two-bedroom terrace.[17] Here on 27th January 1898, Dorothy was born.[18]

Later that year the family moved to Newcastle, where on 3rd February 1899, Dorothy's sister Agnes was born in Heaton, near Byker.[19] With two young children and her husband a skilled man in the burgeoning shipbuilding industry, this young family should surely have been happy. However at the age of thirty-two, only five months after Agnes's birth, Christian took his own life. The coroner reported that on 22nd July he had 'hanged himself while in a despondent state of mind.'[20]

Following the heart-breaking death of her husband, Jane (usually known by her second name, Ellen) returned to London, and by the spring of 1901 was living with her two daughters in the top floor flat of a four-storey house in Kilburn Park Road.[21] In the flat below was a young couple from Belgium, also with two little girls, just slightly younger than Dorothy and Agnes. Ellen was working as a waitress in a local pub. Here there arises a curious coincidence: Kilburn Park Road was just a few minutes' walk from Oakington Road, where the eleven-year-old Claude was living with his parents and older brothers. The two families could easily have met – perhaps whilst shopping, at the recreation ground or at St. Peter's Church?

Later in 1901, Ellen moved again, to 30 Ulundi Road, close to the Royal Naval College in Greenwich. Its terraced houses built twenty years' earlier, the road had been named in commemoration of the last major battle of the Anglo-Zulu war in July 1879, when the British finally broke the Zulu's military power and captured the royal kraal of Ulundi. Symbolizing Britain's imperial status, this was doubtless Dorothy's first connection with Africa. With the opening of the Blackwall Tunnel in 1897, Greenwich became more accessible to Ellen's parents, who lived north of the river in West Ham. In 1902, only three years after her husband's death, tragedy struck again, when Ellen's daughter Agnes contracted tubercular peritonitis and died on 9th March, just a month after her third birthday. Dorothy had just turned four.[22]

As a widow with a young daughter and scant income, life would have been a huge struggle for Ellen. Enter Sampson Sladen, veteran of a ten-year naval career, much of it spent in the Pacific.[23] On his last vessel the sloop *White Swan*, frequently under canvas, Sladen had reached the rank of Lieutenant Commander. In 1896 he had married Fanny Boys and three years later joined the Metropolitan Fire Brigade. By 1909, he was Chief Officer for Southwark and had taken up residence at the Fire Brigade Station house at 94 Southwark Bridge Road. The 1911 Census listed the occupants as: Sampson Sladen (Head), Ellen Christiansen (Housekeeper), Dorothy, aged thirteen, and a maid – another Ellen – Ellen May Butler. There is no mention of Sampson's wife Fanny, and all we know is that she died a few years later on 19th August 1919. Would it be jumping to conclusions to assume that Ellen was rather more than the fire chief's housekeeper?

In his professional role, Sladen spearheaded improvements in the service that would prove vital for those battling the Blitz two decades later.[24] His career continued to progress and in 1919 he became Technical Advisor to the Ministry of Munitions, and the following year, Commissioner for

Sir Sampson Sladen

London Transport, stepping down in 1922, when he was living at 75 Victoria Street, SW1.[25] If Ellen's relationship with Sladen was of an intimate nature, it was not formalised, but a friendship seems to have endured. Elevated to Sir Sampson Sladen, he attended Dorothy's wedding to Robert on 15th February 1923, where he signed the marriage certificate as one of the witnesses.

The ceremony took place in the splendour of Southwark Cathedral (shown on the marriage certificate as 'the parish church of St. Saviour with St. Peter, Southwark'), close to Dorothy's home at 22 Newcomen Street. The marriage was 'By License', probably because Robert was not a British resident, or perhaps had insufficient time to arrange the reading of banns. Although recently returned from Northern Rhodesia, Robert gave his address as Lealeen,

Robert and Dorothy Jeffreys, married
Southwark Cathedral
(from Ann Jeffreys' collection)

55 Balmoral Avenue, Cape Town – doubtless his parents' home – in Bergvliet. There is no evidence that Robert's parents, George and Maria were present, but his father's profession is noted as 'Gentleman'.[26]

Seven weeks later on 28th April 1923, the thirty-five year old Robert took his twenty-five year old bride aboard the White Star Line's SS *Persic* at Liverpool, bound for Cape Town. One can imagine his pride in introducing his lovely young wife to friends and family in the Cape, and Dorothy's sense of romance as the train chugged north to 'Jo'burg', across the Karoo and on to the spectacular bridge over the Zambezi at Victoria Falls.

From the end of the line at Broken Hill, Robert would have escorted his wife by canoe and over rough terrain, carried by porters or walking some of the way.

In June, Dorothy fell pregnant, and by the time they reached Abercorn on 20th July 1923, she could have been experiencing morning sickness. Accommodation would be ready and she could now rest. As the newly-appointed NC, her husband, replacing Stephen Lloyd who had been in Abercorn just three months, was No. 2 in the administrative triumvirate, with James Moffat-Thompson, Acting Magistrate and DC above him, and junior officer H.C. Brooks as his assistant. By November the rains began, and with Dorothy now five months pregnant, the question of where to give birth became pressing. From his time as a cadet Robert had friends in Kasama, but this is more than a hundred miles from Abercorn. Robert's niece, Janet Thatcher, recalled that Dorothy had walked to Kasama, but even if carried much of the way by machila, with Robert taking time off to accompany her, this would have been an exhausting ordeal in the late stages of pregnancy.

Dorothy's daughter, Ann Kathleen Jeffreys, entered the world on 26th March 1924. If Claude had been out of the country on leave prior to commencing his appointment at Mporokoso on 1st February 1924, his first sight of Dorothy could have been in all her blooming, mother-to-be beauty. If adhering to older social mores, she might have gone into 'confinement' early, only re-appearing after the birth at a small gathering of Robert's colleagues and friends to wet the baby's head. Emboldened by alcohol, the normally reserved Claude would not have lacked for conversational topics with the pretty young wife of his friend, and amid small talk about London theatres, tea rooms and trams, he might already have been imagining how much more he would like to share with her.

---

1   Kawambwa DNB and Mporokoso DNB
2   David G. Coe & E. Cyril Greenall, *Kaunda's Gaoler: Memoirs of a District Officer in Northern Rhodesia and Zambia* (Radcliffe Press, 2003). An idyll is a description of rustic life, in the style of the pastoral poems of Theocritus, the *Idylls*.
3   Coe & Greenall, ibid.
4   Mwepwe Falls are some four miles from Chilima
5   From *The Missionary Worker*, 8 January 1927. Mr. & Mrs. H. J. Hurlow were known by their mission as 'Brother' and 'Sister'.
6   Mrs. Owen is probably the wife of William E.M. Owen. Ethel Nutter, born 18 October 1907, was the daughter of Henry Cecil Nutter and Ada Mary Wareham.

From geni.com and *Ancestry.co.uk* janbrownrigg51/Lyndybee/pondfield (Musgrove)

7   Robert Sydney Jeffreys. Born 9 January 1888, Green Point, Cape Town, South Africa; son of George Ernest Jeffreys, Merchant, and Maria Johanna Herbert; m Dorothy. Subject(s): Law; 1908 Law Tripos Part 1/Second Class; 1909 Law Tripos Part 2/Third Class; BA 1909; LLB 1909. Tutor(s): L H K Bushe-Fox. Educ: Green and Sea Point Public School, Cape Town 1896-1897; Boys High School, Wynberg 1897-1903; Bedford Grammar School 1904-1906. Career: Called to the Bar, Gray's Inn 1910; Assistant Commissioner and JP, Rhodesia 1910-1922; Assistant Magistrate 1926; Judge, Protectorate Court, Nigeria 1939. Died 27 December 1959. Source: St. John's College, Cambridge.

8   Source: Andrew Mussell, Archivist, Gray's Inn, 2 June 2014, who advised that: Robert Sydney Jeffreys was admitted to Gray's Inn on 16 April 1907, when he was described as 'of St John's College, Cambridge; the youngest son of George Ernest Jeffreys of Cape Town, merchant'. He was called to the Bar on 8 June 1910.

9   Shipping Records

10 Robert Jeffreys birth date is given as 9 January 1888 by St. John's College, Cambridge

11 George Jeffreys was born on 11 November 1848 in Cape Town and died in 1924 in Cape Town. Mary Herbert was born in 1850 in Cape Town and died in 1911 in Cape Town. Source: Peill Family Tree on *Ancestry* website. Correspondence from Thomas Jeffrey to his brother Robert between 1953 and 1956

12 Letter from Thomas Jeffreys at Chunga on 5 November 1959 to his brother, Robert, in London.

13 Gore-Browne referred to Claude as taciturn, from the Latin *tacitus*: 'silent'. Taciturn came to be used in mid-18th century English in the sense 'habitually silent'.

14 The only child can be resourceful, creative and confident in his independence, but also have much in common with first-borns, or the youngest in a brood. See Gail Gross, 'The Achiever, the Peacemaker and the Life of the Party: How Birth Order Affects Personality', *Huffington Post*, 23 December 2013.

15 G. Stokes 'Memories of Abandoned Bomas, No. 12: Old Fife', *NRJ*, Vol III, No. 4 (1957). Stokes was stationed there from 1909 to 1911.

16 Christian Hjalmar Christiansen was the son of Wilhelm Christiansen and Anne Marie Pedersen. Source: FHL Film Number: 255760. Reference ID: item2, b2, p210, at *Ancestry* website. 'Norway, Select Baptisms, 1634-1927' and Salt Lake City, Utah: Family Search, 2013. The *Trefoldighetskirken* (the Trinity Church) in Hammersborg, central Oslo, is one of the largest churches in the city, situated close to the government buildings in Regjeringskvartalet.

17 Source: Marriage Cert. St. Andrew's Church began as a small mission in 1860 on Whitwell Road, but a permanent church was opened in 1870 and a separate parish assigned to it the following year.

18 Source: Birth Cert.

19 Source: Birth Cert. Agnes Christiansen was born at their home at 37 Spencer Street, Heaton

20 Source: Death Cert. The Inquest stated that Christian Christiansen had hanged himself in the family home.

21 1901 Census, 31 March, for 123 Kilburn Park Road. The other flats were occupied by

Gustave van der Baks, age 31, born in Belgium, his French wife, Augustine and two young daughters; and George Wells, his wife and two teenage sons.

22   Source: Death Cert.

23   Sampson Sladen, born 14 December 1868, Shooter's Hill, south London. His parents were Joseph Sladen (1840-1930) and Caroline Mary French (1845-73). Sampson had two older brothers, Arthur and Lawrence, and a younger brother, Ernest, who died in infancy. In the 1881 Census, when he was 13, he was a 'scholar', living at Soberton, Hants. On 24 December 1896, he married Fanny Harriet Boys (who died on 19 August 1919), who was the daughter of George Sayer Boys, RN. Source: *Burke's Peerage*

On 24 March 1934, Lieutenant-Commander Sir Sampson Sladen, KBE, RNR, is a passenger on the Orient liner *Oronsay*, which called at Fremantle, en route to Brisbane (*The Courier-Mail*, Brisbane). Sladen died 6 July 1940 on the Isle of Man. Source: *Burke's Peerage* (and gravestone)

24   Sladen served in the Metropolitan Fire Brigade (MFB) from 1909 to 1918. Former Royal Navy and Third Officer (Assistant Chief) of the MFB, he was in charge of the Brigade during WWI. Source: London Fire Brigade website.

25   Telephone Directory, 1921

26   Source: Marriage Cert. The witnesses were Sir Sampson Sladen, KBE and Louise Margaret Blakeney.

CHAPTER 16

Coup de Foudre

She is the rebellious and light-hearted 'New Woman'.
She is the Flapper of the Roaring 1920s.

Article in *The New York Times*, 16 July 1922[1]

If a thunderbolt had struck Claude, he could have had little inkling of the length and intensity of the coming storm. The initial flirtation with Dorothy might have been extremely subtle, especially on Claude's part, and it probably never entered his head that the feelings aroused in him by this young woman would ever go beyond fantasy. Would Dorothy have been equally restrained? Though ten years his junior she was not naïve, and the England in which she had come of age had loosened morally. The 'twenties had been 'roaring' for three years when she married Robert and left London, long enough for her to imbibe the rebellious spirit of the flappers and their scandalous propensity for taking the initiative in matters of sex.[2]

Dorothy

Dorothy was twenty when the First World War ended. The *Daily Mirror* described London as 'wild with delight' and living in Southwark she would have seen huge crowds singing and dancing. There were similar scenes the following year at the nationwide Peace Day celebrations on Saturday 19th July.[3] Born at the end of Victoria's long reign, Dorothy was part of a new generation. Driving buses during the war and the subsequent extension of the vote to property-owning females over thirty, had not obliterated the traditional view of women that her mother had taken for granted, but a fissure had opened in the old order. Across Europe and Africa empires collapsed, countries disappeared, and the map of the world was abruptly redrawn. The kind of flag-waving euphoria young Claude had witnessed in London during Victoria's Diamond Jubilee, and the belief that the sun would shine evermore on Britain's vast dominions seemed no longer quite so tenable, as Britain, 'engulfed in a state of collective national trauma', mourned a lost generation.[4]

But there were cheerful corollaries to the gloom. As a young woman in London, Dorothy had been well placed to observe and embrace the new trends, such as frills in dress and architecture and dancing frenetically to imported jazz, which had become mainstream rather than eccentric. Women could now be affectedly demure yet also spirited. The unmarried without means still had to earn a living, and while the working class went into factories, impecunious middle-class women without education or training were far less equipped for the labour market.[5] Many followed the traditional route as teachers, nurses or nannies. Dorothy, probably leaving school at twelve just as the war began could, with her engaging personality, have found congenial white-collar work – as a trainee typist, secretary or telephonist perhaps.

Technological developments were underway. Marconi began broadcasting from Chelmsford, with Dame Nellie Melba becoming one of the first entertainers to sing over the airwaves in June 1920. Within two years, people could listen at home on a crystal set, a simple form of radio receiver.[6] Cinema, encouraged by the advent of colour films in 1922, became cheap and accessible. Motorcars, in mass production and growing in number alongside horse-drawn vehicles, were no longer a male preserve, and at Brooklands, where Claude's contemporary Stewart Gore-Browne had raced before the war, the restrictions on women competitors would soon be relaxed.

Yet some two million women, who might have loved, married and enjoyed the fulfilments of family life, had been robbed of their hopes by the war. Tragic stories of fiancés lost in battle or returning blind, disfigured and shell-shocked, at a time when post-traumatic stress syndrome was unheard of, were commonplace. A girl brought up believing marriage was her ultimate purpose now feared being forever 'on the shelf' and ending up an old maid. In Sybil Neville-Rolfe's succinct description: 'The war left behind it a generation of Eves in an Adamless Eden'.[7] Attitudes towards single women past a certain vintage could be dismissive, often cruel – in the press, in cartoons and on the stage. Noël Coward caricatured the type:

> We must all be very kind to Auntie Jessie
> For she's never been a Mother or a Wife,
> You mustn't throw your toys at her
> Or make a vulgar noise at her,
> She hasn't led a very happy life.

Within this shifting and often unforgiving social scene was born the new breed of outgoing young woman: with short skirts, bobbed hair and a penchant for jazz – the flapper. Wearing the kind of make-up associated with actresses and prostitutes, drinking, treating sex in a casual manner, smoking, driving motor cars and gadding loudly about town, flappers were arguably the product of a number of factors – the progress of the suffragettes, liberalism, a revolt against deference, the modernist movement in the arts, and increased transatlantic cultural exchange after the war.

A lot of girls of Dorothy's age would have aspired to such a lifestyle. The mantra that 'all clothes make a statement' had yet to be coined, but flapper fashion carried a strong hint of rebellion; arms and legs were exposed, long dresses and corsets disappeared and the bobbed hairstyle, frequently seen on Dorothy, became the norm, along with the use of cosmetics.[8] Social commentators applauded the exhibitionist spirit of the flapper, who:

> lives on encouragement, and only because these sweet, innocent boys try to go her one better does she resort to more stringent methods. Of course a flapper is proud of her nerve – she is not even afraid of calling it by its right name. She is shameless, selfish and honest, but at the same time she considers these three attributes virtues.[9]

The flapper was also seen as something of a tomboy, refusing to play the traditional feminine handmaid to her man, offering him instead fun and friendship, on an equal footing:

> She will never make you a hatband or knit you a necktie
> She'll don knickers and go skiing with you
> She'll drive you as well, perhaps better;
> She'll dance as long as you care to,
> And she'll take everything you say the way you mean it…[10]

The rebellious and light-hearted 'New Woman', she is 'the Flapper of the Roaring 1920s'.[11] While perhaps not the kind of earnest radical that typified the suffragette movement, to describe flappers as shallow would be a generalisation. Besides which, who was to say fun and politics were mutually exclusive and that females could not embrace both? For the countless women toiling in factories, sweat shops, domestic service, and like Dorothy's mother at one time, behind the bar of her local pub, this early expression of 'girl power' might have seemed less relevant, and in 'polite' society the flappers' irreverence provoked outrage. Nevertheless, such a cocktail of frivolity and activism enlivened national debate, and even the scandalised relished reading about the scandals.

By the 1920s, ideas about sexual psychology that had circulated in New York before the war began to permeate the mainstream in Britain. The writings of Sigmund Freud, Havelock Ellis and Ellen Key promulgated the view that sex was central to the human experience and more radically that women had physical desires just like men. In Freud's theories, repressing sexual impulses was self-destructive, and could incubate neuroses of one kind or another.[12] Neville-Rolfe described women dispossessed of their needs by the war or societal ignorance as 'starving for love, deprived of homes and denied the joys of motherhood'. In flapper-hood could perhaps be found sisterhood: 'in friendship, one with another, some sort of substitute for these normal but lost relationships.'[13]

Visually, gender fluidity was cutting both ways, as observed in the popular American song of 1926, 'Masculine women, Feminine men, Which is the rooster, which is the hen?'[14] How far did this blurring of identity extend to sexual practices? Lesbianism was unrecognised in law, but men whose love, according to Wilde's amour Lord Alfred Douglas a decade earlier, dared not speak its name, risked severe penalties and were restricted to discreet private clubs, always under threat of a police raid. The liberalism of the 1920s was relative and patchy. *Lady Chatterley's Lover*, published in Italy in 1928, would not appear in Britain in unexpurgated form until 1960, and then to face an obscenity trial. In New York, actress Mae West's 1927 play *The Drag*, portraying the gay adventures of an unhappily married man, was banned after a few performances. In straight sex, petting was in vogue.[15] While parents might censure the practice, equating it with fornication, their offspring could savour intimacy without shame, and 'petting parties' became popular. Marie Stopes had opened her first family planning clinic in 1920, giving an increased opportunity for couples to go further, though for unmarried women to gain legitimate access to contraception would take longer.

For Dorothy, the flapper phenomenon was still in the ascendant when she was plucked from London to the wilds of Africa. The rapidity of the marriage was perhaps a relief for her mother, allaying fears that at twenty-five her daughter's sell-by date was ticking closer. Sampson Sladen, newly ennobled and well connected, might have helped to procure an eligible bachelor. To a girl without money or position, a Cambridge-educated barrister would be something of a catch, and an element of arrangement in the marriage cannot be ruled out.

Once the couple were settled in at Abercorn, Claude's official visits there would have given him the opportunity to see more of Dorothy. One assumes that at first such meetings were in the company of her husband, but as Claude's album shows, this was not always the case. As the mutual attraction between Claude and Dorothy grew, it was doubtless complicated for Claude by his friendship with Robert. A distant but personally significant event for Claude, occurred a few days after Dorothy had given birth, when on 31st March 1924 Claude's eldest brother Robert, now known by his second name, Thomas, had died in New South Wales aged forty-seven. *The Tumut and Adelong Times* (incorrectly stating his age) carried the following report:

> Mr. Thomas Oldfield, a well known mining inspector of Cobar and Broken Hill, passed away at the residence of his mother-in-law, Mrs Thornton, Adelong on Monday. Mr Oldfield arrived in Australia about 25 years ago and served some time at the Gibraltar gold mines Adelong, prior to being appointed mining inspector. He was 48 years (*sic*) of age and was an associate of the Royal School of Mines, London. Deceased had been seriously ill for a long time and his death was not unexpected. He leaves a widow but no family. We extend our deepest sympathy to the bereaved relatives. The remains were interred in the Anglican portion of Adelong Cemetery, the Rev. Pike officiating at the graveside.

In 1897, aged twenty-two, Robert/Thomas had married Sarah Lightowler from Hull, emigrating together to Australia a couple of years later. The marriage had not lasted and it seems likely that Sarah returned home. Robert, apparently without obtaining a divorce, had then married Jean Thornton, daughter of Jack and Emily Thornton, who ran a drapery business in Adelong. Robert had died of silicosis, the result of spending time underground, the risks from constant exposure to dust then less recognized. The family had heard little from Robert in recent years, and

Robert Oldfield on horseback in Australia

The ruins of Adelong gold mine (photographed in 2013)

Robert Oldfield's funeral was held at St. Paul's Church, Adelong (photographed in 2013)

Claude's recollection of his oldest brother would have been hazy. Their last contact would have been in February 1899 when Robert departed for Australia, but inevitably the news would have stirred childhood memories. Claude's experience of bereavement was limited; his older sister had died before he was born, and more recently there had been the loss of his young niece. His oldest brother had now predeceased their father, bringing to mind John Donne's words:

> For I am involved in mankind
> Therefore, send not to know
> For whom the bell tolls,
> It tolls for thee.[16]

'Living for the moment' might be a fine resolution, but how in the 1920s, in the middle of Africa, might an English bachelor in the colonial service go about it? Perhaps Claude could gain some elucidation from older civilisations, in the culture of the vast, untamed land around him. He might have taken from his bookshelf the volume by his late colleague Cullen Gouldsbury, whose untimely death was incidentally another *memento mori*. Looking afresh at the two chapters entitled 'The Plateau Native', Claude would find the quote from Livingstone's *Last Journals* about the physical beauty of the people, the 'handsome and well-chiselled features' of the men, the graceful figures of the women. The Awemba were also admired for their climbing ability, essential for tree lopping when opening up new land, and for the stamina of the mail runners averaging up to twenty-five miles a day, year-round. The treatise advised that to understand the native, empathy was required: 'One must "think black" to bridge the vast gulf between African and European conceptions' and 'ten years of experience among natives … gives far more insight than mountains of monographs or all the wealth of African literature.' Furthermore, the wisdom of the old men was beyond doubt: 'Innumerable talks upon ulendo with chiefs and village elders can only confirm one in a high opinion of their shrewdness and mental capacity.'[17]

Lowering the book at this point, Claude might have wondered what advice the elders could offer to a man in love with the wife of his friend. The Awemba had seemingly a mixture of character traits, being 'perhaps, the most emotional of the Plateau races' yet in whom one rarely observed extravagant outbursts of passion. There was alleged callousness towards the sufferings of others, contrasting with familial affection such as the love of a mother for her children. The Awemba's reliability was questioned: 'Men who have engaged to work for a year on the southern mines will suddenly feel the homing instinct, and, despite the distance and the want of food for the return journey, will escape and arrive safely at their homes.' Such behaviour seems perfectly understandable, except when the reason defied rational (i.e. European) explanation, as when a large labouring gang deserted Fort Jameson after encountering a bad omen.

The section concluded with an observation that might have shocked an English reader, where in 'the intensity of the sexual nature', it was claimed that in young girls over fifteen, chastity was rare. With immoral posturings and late-night dances inflaming the passions, early marriage was seen as the only answer. The authors cautioned that to describe fully some of the sexual practices 'would require the strong realism of Suetonius' as well as a considerable facility for obscure and obscene Latin. Claude was doubtless familiar with Suetonius's *Life of Tiberius*, in which Tiberius, retired to the island of Capri, enjoyed orgies in various woods and groves that became known as the 'old goat's garden', a pun on the island's name. The writers did submit that the Awemba had a very definite code of sexual morality, linked to superstitious belief and clear sanctions, including bodily mutilation, but that this code seemed purely theoretical and was never enforced. In an apparent plea against censure, a quote from Robert Browning was added: 'My business is not to remake myself, but make the absolute best of what God made'.[18] Writing in 1911, much of Gouldsbury and Sheane's exposition was forward-looking, but they could hardly have imagined the changes after WWI or have pictured the Roaring Twenties. Then, how many of us growing up in the austerity of the 1950s could have envisaged the Swinging Sixties?

As yet, Claude probably had little inkling of Dorothy's tough childhood or her father's suicide before she was old enough to have memories of him. Had Dorothy even been given the tragic details? She might have recalled her younger sister, having been four at the time of her death, and had clearer memories of Sampson Sladen and the house in Southwark. Had her mother's relationship with Sladen been explained, and how had Dorothy regarded him – as a father figure, or an uncle-cum-landlord?

Claude's upbringing had stressed the importance of duty, and as a serving officer he could not be so distracted by a beguiling younger woman as to neglect his work. Of growing concern at this time were rumours from neighbouring districts about the Watchtower Bible & Tract Society (later known as Jehovah's Witnesses), which had surfaced in Northern

Rhodesia under the name 'Kitawala', or 'Kingdom'. The movement
had originated in North America, but its founder in southern Africa was
Elliott Kamwana, born in Mzimba in northern Nyasaland, and formerly a
Scottish Presbyterian, then becoming a Seventh Day Adventist. Returning
to Nyasaland in 1906, within three years Kamwana had baptized 10,000
followers, predicting Armageddon in 1914 and that in a Second Coming,
Christ would abolish hut taxes and expel all Europeans.[19] In 1917, six
members who had been thrown out of Southern Rhodesia had come north,
recruiting, stirring up hostility to the white administration and proclaiming
an imminent new order in which the last – the Africans – would become
the first. Converts were urged to prepare through baptism, renunciation
of polygamy and fervent prayer while awaiting the Day of Judgement, the
date of which was successively postponed.[20] This millenarian mindset saw
no point in planting crops or nurturing livestock, especially if owned by
whites, and the disastrous effects on agriculture were plain to see. Not
content with passive resistance, as the First World War came to an end,
Kitawala groups had begun attacking local chiefs. In Fife District the
Police Service Battalion was called in, and the chiefs worked closely with
the Administration, resulting in 138 arrests and convictions in the High
Court at Kasama.[21]

If the accounts now reaching Mporokoso were to be believed, it looked
as if another charismatic religious leader had emerged. Tomo Nyirenda,
also born and raised in Nyasaland, had moved to Northern Rhodesia's
copper belt, where he had become acquainted with the Watch Tower
Movement and been baptized. The colonial authorities had imprisoned
Nyirenda for failing to register as an 'alien native', and on his release he
had declared himself 'Mwana Lesa' (the Son of God). By early 1925 he
was claiming the ability to divine witches and sorcerers.

The threat posed by Nyirenda, compared to that of the German military
campaign a few years earlier, might in hindsight seem negligible. Yet this
apocalyptic faith, with its black American backers, was insidious rather
than overt, and had the potential to undermine the social infrastructure
and authority on which the colony rested; in short, to quote a British
political leader of the 1980s, it was the enemy within.[22] If the movement's
ideas spread to Mporokoso, Claude's job would become considerably
more challenging, the measured ritual of ulendo and conversation with
village elders replaced by a hostile, unpredictable situation.

Knowledge of subsequent events indicates that throughout 1925,
Dorothy was in Claude's thoughts. However, his loyalty to Robert and a

fear of scandal would have been powerful restraints against embarking on an affair, and without a strong sense of *carpe diem*, things may never have gone any further. A possible catalyst was the death on 13th August of his father, Thomas Smedley Oldfield.

[1]   *Coup de Foudre*: literally, a thunderbolt or flash of lightning; figuratively, 'love at first sight'. See 'Flapping Not Repented Of', *New York Times*, 16 July 1922, quoted in George E. Mowry, *The Twenties: Fords, Flappers, & Fanatics* (Prentice-Hall, 1963).

[2]   The word 'flapper' to describe a young woman may be derived from the idea of a young bird flapping its wings while learning to fly. Earlier usage in the north of England referred to a teenage girl with a plaited pigtail 'flapping' on her back.

[3]   The First World War Armistice came into effect at 11am on 11 November 1918, the 'eleventh hour of the eleventh day of the eleventh month'. This marked the end of fighting on the Western Front, but negotiations continued at the Paris Peace Conference, with the Treaty of Versailles not officially signed until 28 June 1919. The agreements over the African territories were not finalised until 1923.

[4]   From worldwarhistory.blogspot.co.uk

[5]   Virginia Nicholson, *Singled Out: How Two Million Women Survived without Men after the First World War* (Viking Books, 2007)

[6]   Mike Smith, 'UK Radio, A Brief History, How It All Began', www.mds975.co.uk

[7]   Sybil Neville-Rolfe, *Sex in Social Life*, (George Allen & Unwin, 1949)

[8]   Carolyn Kitch, The Girl on the Magazine Cover (University of North Carolina Press, 2001)

[9]   Ruth Hooper in 'Flapping Not Repented Of', ibid.

[10] 'Flapping Not Repented Of', ibid.

[11] Andrew Lamb, *150 Years of Popular Musical Theatre* (Yale University Press, 2000) See Chapter 11, The 1920s: The 'Années Folles' p 195

[12] Nancy Woloch, *Women and the American Experience: A Concise History* (McGraw-Hill, 1995)

[13] Neville-Rolfe, ibid.

[14] The song, composed by James V. Monaco with lyrics by Edgar Leslie, featured in Hugh J. Ward's musical comedy *Lady Be Good*

> Masculine women, Feminine men
>
> Which is the rooster, which is the hen?
> It's hard to tell 'em apart today! And, say!
> Sister is busy learning to shave,
> Brother just loves his permanent wave,
> It's hard to tell 'em apart today! Hey, hey!

[15] Kissing or fondling that stopped short of intercourse, allowing erotic interaction without risking pregnancy

[16] *John Donne, Devotions Upon Emergent Occasions*, Meditation XVII

[17] Gouldsbury & Sheane, *The great plateau*, ibid.

[18] From *Bishop Blougram's Apology*, a long poem published in the two-volume *Men and Women* in 1855, by Robert Browning (1812-99).

[19] Mark R. Lipschutz and R. Kent Rasmussen, *Dictionary of African Historical Biography*, 2nd edition (University of California Press, 1986)

[20] Catherine Coquery-Vidrovitch (translated by David Maisel), *Africa: Endurance and Change South of the Sahara* (University of California Press, 1992)

[21] Tim Wright, *The History of the Northern Rhodesia Police* (British Empire and Commonwealth Museum, 2001)

[22] 'We had to fight the enemy without in the Falklands. We always have to be aware of the enemy within, which is much more difficult to fight and more dangerous to liberty.' Margaret Thatcher, on the 1984-5 miners' strike.

CHAPTER 17

The Agony and the Ecstasy

Lovers and madmen have such seething brains,
Such shaping fantasies, that apprehend
More than cool reason ever comprehends

Shakespeare, A *Midsummer Night's Dream*[1]

Thomas Oldfield had died at home in Maida Vale, the principal cause of death cited by a Dr. Hodge as toxaemia following the removal of his appendix, and an operation for an intestinal obstruction.[2] Even if earlier letters had warned Claude of his father's declining health, the news would have been a considerable shock for Claude. There was no compassionate leave, and it would be another eighteen months before he could return to London to offer his mother any support.

Thomas Smedley Oldfield

Meanwhile, how had Dorothy been passing the time? After the birth of her daughter Ann in early 1924, we can assume that servants would have taken care of the household chores and helped look after the baby, and as the young wife of a colonial officer, little was expected of Dorothy other than to await her husband each lunchtime or evening, perhaps with flowers on the table and his favourite drink mixed, ready to hear about his 'day'. Stuck at home, the time must surely have dragged, especially the long mornings. Robert, even if 'on station', would most likely be away at his office from 7.30 to 1.30 without a break, and lunch might not be taken until the early afternoon.[3] When the baby was sleeping and Dorothy sat in quiet solitude in the house, she might have thought back to her former existence as a single woman in London. Did she miss the busy streets, the noise and energy, the opportunity of chance encounters, the sense that her life still had possibilities? Meeting Robert must have excited her, but now she was a young mother thousands of miles from her familiar world. Dorothy may have found it difficult to adjust to her new life in Africa and the limited company of other Europeans might have increased the risk of post-natal depression. The suicide of Dorothy's father's at the age of thirty-two also suggests possible inherited depressive tendencies.

When Robert and Dorothy had stood together at the altar in February 1923, joined in the sight of God in holy matrimony, what had been going through each of their heads? Robert must surely have been pleased to have found such a beautiful young bride, Dorothy perhaps thrilled that a good-looking man, a Cambridge graduate and barrister, wanted to marry her. Freud might have said something about the knight in shining armour filling the void left by the untimely death of Dorothy's father. Whatever their private thoughts, neither bride nor groom could have known that in less than two years their marriage would be compromised by infidelity.

Some writers have suggested that affairs never just happen, and that one or both parties must be hungry – for excitement, novelty or love – even before meeting one another. Was it simply tedium that drove Dorothy within a year of her daughter's birth, to embark on a relationship with Claude? Perhaps there were other factors – emotional or physical needs that Robert did not fulfil – and belying the affable countenance in the photographs, was Robert perhaps a rather cold fish? Dorothy's new life, begun with such promise, may just not have lived up to her expectations. As for Claude, meeting Dorothy could have been the first time he had really fallen in love. All these questions are perforce speculative, but an element of *coup de foudre* seems undeniable.

The practicalities of the affair cannot have been easy. Dorothy was in Abercorn, Claude more than a hundred miles away in Mporokoso, the sole official overseeing his district. Finding time and a credible excuse to visit Abercorn and the Jeffreys's house would require careful thought. Claude would have needed to travel there to converse with his superior, Jack Venning, the Provincial Commissioner, ideally when Robert was out on ulendo. Venning, though, also visited Mporokoso, as in December 1925.[4] Although not exactly mid-way, Kasama might have been another possibility, although the question of how Dorothy would have got there and on what pretext, especially without her husband, and with a young child at home, is intriguing. If the rendezvous was Kasama, where might the lovers have spent time together? With no hotels, the only available accommodation would have been the government rest house or perhaps the club, a rather blatant option one would imagine. Perhaps an understanding friend, dissolute missionary or man-of-the-world settler loaned them a spare room?

Claude, in old school tie and pith helmet, Mporokoso, 1926

Native Commissioner's House, Mporokoso

Jack Venning in his retirement at 'Chisungu' on the Mpulungu road from Abercorn, about 1960. Large frangipani on either side of the steps up to the house. His billiard room and office were behind the centre French windows.

Yet how on earth did they arrange their encounters? Claude had access to mail runners and could send a letter from Mporokoso to Abercorn in three or four days, but a letter marked for 'Mrs. Jeffreys: Personal' would clearly arouse suspicion if seen by Robert. The lovers would have had no direct telephone line and no Leo as their 'go-between'.[5] Initially, Dorothy could have seen Claude as simply a new acquaintance, a good companion, someone whom she could confide in and talk to as she tried to settle into the colonial lifestyle. And while she may have placed an enormous significance on her meetings with Claude, at this stage in the affair, around the middle of 1925, she may also have attempted to be more appreciative of Robert and was perhaps rejected.

By the same token Claude had found someone with whom he could relax and talk to about his life, his hopes and fears. When the line was crossed between friendship and physical love, was it Dorothy who made the first move? In attempting plausible hypotheses, it might be unjust to describe her as a *femme fatale*, yet such women did and do exist. If she was seductive, did she set out to seduce? Would she for her own amusement have led Claude knowingly into compromising or dangerous situations? Claude was in his mid-thirties, surely capable of knowing his own mind, and not one would think completely green in matters of romance. A full-blown affair with a married woman on the other hand was quite different, and must have given him pause for thought, not only in terms of his own sanity and self-interest, but also his friendship with Robert. However as Shakespeare put it, 'the lunatic, the lover and the poet are of imagination all compact' and Claude, for all his learning was as capable of making a fool of himself as any man.[6] Yet was this foolishness? Who is to say that Claude and Dorothy were not made for one another?

If either of the lovers had decided to cast caution to the wind, they must on sober reflection have known the risks. Exposure would have jeopardised both men's careers, although the male contingent might have closed ranks around Robert, leaving Claude ostracised from his fellow officers and friends. A cuckold might once have demanded satisfaction and pistols at dawn, and a variation on the theme could not be ruled out even in 1925. Dorothy was also gambling with her own reputation; the demure young wife who had been made welcome could very quickly, in the starchy, parochial atmosphere of Abercorn, be recast as a scarlet woman. The female contingent in Abercorn was small, making social exclusion absolute and painful. Dorothy and Claude could not expect knowledge of their exploits to pass without any censure, as might have been so with the 'Happy Valley' set in Kenya twenty years later.

This is not to say that affairs were unheard of in Northern Rhodesia. Amanda Parkyn, a young wife in Abercorn in the 1950s, wrote candidly about her experiences in amateur dramatics, when she was 'seduced by the flattery of being so desired by an older married man. Nothing happened between us other than a few clandestine, relatively chaste meetings and, naïve and simplistic as I was, I was sure the whole thing would die down without anyone knowing about it.' People did hear about it however, including the older man's wife who, when her husband refused her demand to pull out of the forthcoming theatrical production, departed in high dudgeon to Mpulungu, 'whereupon the news was around the community in a trice.' Amanda's plea that 'we haven't done anything!' produced only limited amelioration.[7]

Something did however happen between Dorothy and Claude, as by the middle of 1926 Dorothy was pregnant. If she and Robert had not had sex during the relevant time frame, she would have known that Claude was the father. Possibly it was only one night at the end of February that she had spent with Claude, the culmination of a series of flirtatious encounters, an evening of alcohol and abandon. If her marriage was loveless she might not have cared much, perhaps welcomed the pregnancy as an expression of her freedom and hang the consequences. Based on the later, confident opinion of her niece Janet Thatcher, Dorothy's second child was always known to be Claude's, so it appears unlikely that Dorothy herself was ever in doubt. She might have told Robert of the pregnancy almost immediately, whether or not there was any room to prevaricate regarding the paternity. In pre-DNA test days, an unfaithful wife could always hope that a cuckoo in the nest might pass undetected by her husband, her family and the world at large.

*Bob (Robert Jeffreys), Mrs. Nutter, Dorothy, Ann & CPO, Mporokoso, 1926
(Dorothy appears to be 'showing' her pregnancy. The photo was probably taken in
June/July 1926, shortly before the Jeffreys left for England)*

On 6th August 1926 Robert and Dorothy departed for their home leave. Taking their daughter Ann now almost two and a half, they began the long journey south. It seems likely that before sailing on the *Durham Castle* they stopped over in Cape Town with Robert's family, since they did not arrive in London until 1st October. They might have been expected to remain in London with Dorothy's mother, who would be excited to see them and meet her granddaughter for the first time. Instead they made their way to Charmouth on Dorset's Jurassic coast. Kelly's Directory describes the town at that time as:

> a pleasant watering place on the shore of the English Channel, a village and a parish, 6 miles south-east from Axminster on the main line of the London and South Western railway … and 146 from London. It is a place of great antiquity, being on a branch of the trackway called Ikenield Street … The views around are extremely beautiful, especially from the eastern cliff – Cain's Folly. Golden Gap Hill, one of the most lofty, is 600 feet high.[8]

The Jeffreys took temporary accommodation at No.1 The Hillside, one of three Regency villas built in 1827, set halfway up a steep slope with glimpses of the sea between Charmouth's main street and the surrounding

No.1 The Hillside, Charmouth (2016)

hills. On 26th November 1926 this would be the birthplace of Dorothy's second child, Audrey.[9] Why had they chosen this quiet seaside village? The sea air in autumn would be revitalising after the heat of Africa, and the house may have belonged to friends. Dorothy's mother could also have been invited to come down to assist with the birth.

Meanwhile Claude was due home leave, his stint at Mporokoso, three months short of three years, having ended on 1st November 1926. Dorothy had definitely changed his life, but did he now feel roguish or rueful about what had happened? His mood may have altered from day to day. Maybe he felt jealous of Robert and longed to be with Dorothy as his child arrived into the world. Of course, as yet he might even have been unaware that he was the father. As the days went by, whatever was running through his head would almost certainly have remained there; with no close friends or colleagues in whom to confide, the working out of his emotions would be a solitary task.

What about his family though? Anticipating arriving home for the first time since his father's death, Claude knew his first duty of care would be to his seventy-year-old mother, and it is highly unlikely he would want to shock her with intimate confessions. In leafy Golders Green, Charlie, husband to Maisie and father to my mother Joy, now aged ten, might, had Claude chosen to tell him, have lent a sympathetic ear, tinged even with

Harold Oldfield

vicarious pleasure at his brother's raffishness. More likely Claude feared reproach and planned to say nothing of the matter. Still resident in Maida Vale was Harold, Claude's older brother, now aged forty. His disability had recently necessitated the amputation of a leg. A genial, sensitive soul, with interests in poetry and the arts, Harold seems unlikely to have judged his brother, but again uncertainty would probably compel Claude to keep his own counsel. The situation with Dorothy was still too raw, its future unknown. The seeming innocence captured in his photographs of her, carry a faint bittersweet note, yet dare he hope that some day they might be together? Right now, like Aeneas, his future lay 'in the lap of the gods' and until they had decided what his fate might be, he must carry his elation and his burden alone.[10]

[1] Theseus, Act 5, Scene 1, at the palace of Theseus in Athens. *The Agony and the Ecstasy*, by Irving Stone and published in 1961, was based on the 16th century war of wills between Renaissance artist Michelangelo and Julius II, the 'warrior pope'. In 1965, Philip Dunne adapted the book for the film, directed by Carol Reed.

[2] Source: Death Certificate, 14 August 1925. Informant: C. E. Oldfield, son, of 23 West Heath Drive, Golders Green. In the Sub-district of Paddington North in the County of London. Registrar: Frederick J. J., House Registrar.

[3] Olive Champion, *Journey of a Lifetime*, 1994, cited in Anthony Kirk-Greene, *Symbol of Authority: The British District Officer in Africa* (I. B. Tauris, 2006). See Chapter 9, pp 180-206

[4] Mporokoso DNB: J. H. Venning, PC (1876-1963) made an Inspection visit to Mporokoso on 14 December 1925 (when Claude was NC).

[5] Leo acted as the 'Go-Between' in L. P. Hartley's eponymous novel, published 1953, taking letters to and from Marian and Ted in the summer of 1900 in Norfolk.

[6] *Midsummer Night's Dream*, ibid.

[7] Amanda Parkyn, *Roses under the Miombo Trees: An English Girl in Rhodesia* (Matador, 2012)

[8] Kelly's Directory of Dorsetshire, 1915

[9] On 16 September 1837, Miss Harriot Prior of Lyme purchased No. 1 Hillside (then occupied by Mrs. Cleaves) for £875 from Joseph Wilson. The property was then owned and occupied by the Prior and Templer families, the last to live there being Miss L. K. Prior, who sold it to Canon and Mrs. Whittington. On the death of Canon Whittington, it was purchased by the Ecclesiastical Commissioners in 1953 and became Charmouth Rectory. Source: www.freshford.com/charmouth

[10] From Homer's *Iliad* (8th century BC)

CHAPTER 18

Life at Shiwa Ng'andu

Lorna! Yes, you are sweet, but you are not your mother

Thomas Hardy, 'Lorna the Second'[1]

Even with Dorothy departed from the scene, Claude had seemed in no great hurry to get home. Leaving Mporokoso in November, three months after the Jeffreys, he had not sailed from Cape Town until the New Year, arriving on the *Windsor Castle* at Southampton on 24th January 1927. Perhaps it was the first available passage, but if the delay were deliberate it verged on dereliction of filial duty to his mother, widowed for the past eighteen months. Possibly he had waited till the coast was clear, for by the time he docked Dorothy and Robert were ready for their return to Africa in three days' time. For their paths to have crossed now was a prospect he might have wished to avoid, even though a polite veil could have been drawn over any suspicion of Dorothy's infidelity, supposing though that the new offspring bore an uncanny resemblance to Claude? There could be awkwardness or embarrassment and Robert might have felt equally keen to avoid Claude. The other possibility, by no means remote, is that they all met up in London and spent a convivial evening together before the Jeffreys set sail. My mother incidentally, though just ten years old at the time, had an impression of Claude as a bit of a charmer, who 'cut quite a dash' on his visits home from the colonies.

Whichever way things had played out at the beginning of 1927, Claude knew he would not see Dorothy again for at least another six months. Departing from England in August, he would be providing leave cover for his friend Harold Brigham at Lundazi.[2] Situated in the east of the country, away from the Bemba people whom he had got to know so well, Claude's fluency in Chibemba would be of little use amongst the local Tumbuka, Ngoni and Chewa, whose lands straddled the border with Nyasaland. Lundazi, reached via the regional capital Fort Jameson, was some 340

A.N.C.s huts, Lundazi, October 1927

H.L. Brigham - Lundazi, October 1927. Head Messenger Bwembia and Messenger Zakeyu. A nice pair of tusks (when ivory was plentiful)

Harold Brigham, showing off his new Francis Barnett motorbike, Lundazi, 1926

miles from Lusaka, with the last 120 miles along an uneven, mostly dusty, dirt road, leading to a dead end. A resident British Army officer used to looked after the incoming mail, so the postal address was: 'P.O. Box 1, c/o Colonel, Lundazi', but popularly known as *Bokosi wanu, Kanele*.[3]

Claude would not have been expecting much mail, as his tenure at Lundazi ended in November on Brigham's return. October here could be oppressively hot, the Luangwa valley particularly so, and Claude's next move to Chinsali, where he could look forward to running his own patch once more, would be a relief. But what of his main concern – that his and Dorothy's child was to all appearances the legitimate second daughter of Mr. and Mrs. Jeffreys. How did Claude feel about this extraordinary situation – shut out and resentful, or grateful for his pleasure and glad to be off the hook? Beneath a stiff upper lip, was he still in shock?

Claude reached Chinsali on 19th November 1927, allowing sufficient time for a two-day handover with his predecessor, Martin Otter.[4] After so many postings, he knew the familiarization process off by heart; looking through the registers, getting the gist of local affairs, nearby missions, European and Asian businesses and tribal chiefs, taking particular note of any longstanding issues or sensitivities; which friendships to nurture, what enmities to monitor, along with the history of the district. Chinsali boma had been founded in 1908 by 'Bobo' Young, one of the pioneers of North-Eastern Rhodesia. Knowles Jordan, the NC from 1920 until early 1923, related how in 1897, 'Bobo' had first set up an administrative post at Mirongo, not far from a Senga Chief called Chiwale:

> One day, Bobo received an urgent message via Chiwale's runner praying for his assistance as he was being attacked by a mixed force of Arabs supported by a contingent of Awemba. Bobo, being a very plucky man, immediately complied and supported by a small, armed force, repulsed the attackers with severe losses on their side. After this, the Awemba sued for peace, and when the station of Mirongo was abandoned for health reasons, Bobo selected Chinsali for the site of the new Boma, named after the Headman who had lived there.[5]

'Bobo' Young and family

Although Chinsali still lacked many basic facilities, including piped water, it was at least connected to the HQ at Kasama by road. The bridge across the Chambeshi had been built in 1922 at the instigation of Knowles Jordan, with the help of his Assistant, Harold Brigham, described as 'a very capable official'. The bridge was constructed from iron trestles bolted together on land and pulled into position with long cables of bark rope. With 'dambo' areas on either side of the main river subject to flooding, local men and women, using only simple hoes, had created substantial embankments. The bridge proved to be one example of a colonial initiative that was welcomed by the indigenous community, the Awemba remarking, 'Now we are free men and do not have to risk our lives crossing the Chambeshi in frail canoes!'

Situated on high, sloping ground covered with light forest, Knowles Jordan found Chinsali peaceful and attractive, albeit rather lonely. As the senior official, Claude would have lived in the Magistrate's House, with its:

> walled-in courtyard, with a narrow entrance at each side, flanked by a sentry box, a reminder of more turbulent days; at the back of the courtyard were the quarters for the native servants and a kitchen. A short distance beyond, a low ridge covered with large grey boulders among which grew red flowering aloes and various types of vegetation graced the landscape; while in front, and to one side of the house, a fine mango tree flourished.

This pleasing setting was complemented by access to a freshwater stream in a nearby grove, and milk from a small herd of government cattle. If, like Knowles Jordan, Claude had felt isolated, he could always break any veneer of protocol, by spending time with his subordinate, John Moffat, who resided close by in a small bungalow.

John Moffat and Dr. Brown, Chinsali, 1929 (after playing golf)

If preferring one's own company, the front verandah offered 'a grand view of some miles of rolling bush veldt which included a small primeval forest named Chiri, the home of a few elephants, a couple of black rhino, some bushbuck and sundry other animals. Towering above the other trees in this forest were some magnificent specimens of the mahogany tree known locally as Mofu.'[6] With wild bees proliferating in the forest, and the nearby dairy herd, one could be persuaded that this was indeed a land flowing with milk and honey. This particular Canaan though was safer to appreciate at a distance, as one local man found to his cost:

> It was no easy matter entering this forest owing to a multitude of thorny growths of all kinds and long rough grass. A watch had to be kept for snakes as members of the dreaded mamba family made it their home. Once an unfortunate native who had entered in search of honey was bitten by one and died before he could reach his village.

Back within the compound, those who strayed less innocently could be be accommodated in 'a gaol with high walls, and a small building divided into offices with one room which could be used either as a court-room, or for meetings with Chiefs and Headmen.' The overall layout of the settlement was tidy and compact: 'The main road running from south to north divided the boma into two sections; and on the opposite side were the lines, containing neat round thatched huts for the Messengers and Mailmen, and for the Native Clerk who also acted as an interpreter when necessary.'

Head Messenger Shikalima, Messengers Mitimingi, Funduma and Mwanamashika, Chinsali, October 1928

Native staff, Chinsali, October 1928. Shikalima, Benjamin Wake,
Reuben Siame, Robert Wake

Claude was following in the footsteps of numerous well-respected officials since Young's day, including Brigham and Otter. The young John Moffat, who had been in this his first post for just ten weeks, would remain with Claude for a further eighteen months before moving to Luwingu in April 1929. The expanding Moffat clan was well known, having first come out to Africa as missionaries, and in 1845 John's (great) aunt, Mary

Mary Moffat, wife of David
Livingstone, Africa, c. 1845-1860

Moffat had married David Livingstone, bearing him six children, only to die of malaria in 1862.[7] The handful of other Europeans included the Presbyterian missionaries at Lubwa, and the charismatic individual whom Claude had encountered briefly just before the war, the motor racing enthusiast Colonel Stewart Gore-Browne at Shiwa Ng'andu.[8]

Lubwa, established as a mission in 1913, was being run by Rev. and Mrs. Robert MacMinn, members of the Livingstonia Mission of the Free Church of Scotland, supported by Dr. and Mrs. D. M. Brown.[9] MacMinn had served the church since 1893, and would continue working in Northern Rhodesia until 1934, a remarkable forty years, much of the time devoted to the compilation of a Chibemba dictionary and Bible. Visiting the Lubwa Mission in 1927, Claude also met Rev. David Kaunda, who had moved from the Livingstonia Mission to Lubwa in 1905, initially to start a school. The young David Kaunda, born in Nyasaland, was an ordained Church of Scotland missionary and teacher; his youngest son, Kenneth, was then three years old. Who could have foreseen that this boy would, in 1964, lead Northern Rhodesia to independence as Zambia?

Despite the dearth of European company, Claude would have been pleased to be closer to 'Bembaland', the northern part of his new district being true Bemba, while the south included Wisa and Senga people. Claude recorded the dates of appointment and succession of local chiefs: within the Wemba tribe, Sub-Chief Mwawa (Chanda Makasa) died in February 1928, but the appointment of Headman Kaleya, the senior nephew of the deceased, was not approved by the Governor until November of that year. Amongst the Wisa, Chieftainess Mukungule died in 1921, but the heir Mbaloma was a young boy, during whose minority, Chief Mukupa of the adjacent Mpika District acted as Regent. The approval to appoint Mbaloma as Chief was only given by the Governor seven years later in December 1928.

Chiefdom was not always a job for life, and whilst tribal rank doubtless conferred privileges, these did not include immunity from the law under British administration. During Claude's time as Assistant Magistrate, a leading figure in the Senga would forfeit both his liberty and status as a result of misdemeanours:

> Sub-Chief Fulaya (Lameck) was found Guilty of Indecent Assault and sentenced to 2 years IHL. (Magistrate, Kasama, Case No. 6/1928) in June 1928. In February 1928, he was convicted of Larceny and two offences against the Game Ordinance. (N.C.'s Cases Chinsali Nos. 6, 7 & 8 of 1928), and sentenced to 5 months IHL. He was deposed by order of HE the Governor in August 1928. The appointment of Ngalule as Sub-Chief Fulaya is approved by HE the Governor, September 1929.'

IHL – Imprisonment with Hard Labour – continues to be used as a punishment in the region. As recently as 2014, Kennedy Nkhoma, the Head of Malawi's Prison Service, appealed for the practice to be abolished, arguing that prisons should become a corrective facility and not punishment institutions.[10]

The ritual following the death of a chief would be a greater shock to most European sensibilities. To the west, lived the paramount chief of the Awemba, known as the 'Chitimukulu'.[11] The funeral of a Chitimukulu had always been a momentous event, featuring in pre-colonial days the ritual killing of a number of slaves and retainers. With the chief's body swathed in ox-hide, four male bearers – the 'Fingo fya mfumu' – would convey him to Mwalule, a distance of some thirty miles, arriving at a large mushitu, a dense grove of tall trees, through which ran a strong flowing stream, the Mikunku.[12] Knowles Jordan was told that on commencing the journey, a man or woman beloved by the chief had to be slain. When the long, straggling cortege reached the Chambeshi River, a flotilla of skilled paddlers would ferry the party in dugout canoes to the other side, where:

> Shi-Mwalule, the guardian and priest of the sacred burial grove, took charge and on arrival at the graveside, three specially selected young boys and three young girls were killed by blows on the nape of the neck, delivered with a heavy stick; the bodies were lowered into the grave and placed in position. With much ceremony and chanting the body of the Chief was then interred.

Stewart Gore-Browne had first visited this 'remarkable place, with the huts all amongst wonderful great palm trees with thick foliage' in 1914, and described the master of ceremonies, the Shi-Mwalule, as 'a sort of Dean of Westminster Cathedral as it were, except that in the old days he was never allowed to bury more than one king and was put to death himself when the next one died.'[13] Depending then on how long a succeeding Chief might be expected to live, the job of Shi-Mwalule would be either hard to fill, or sought after as a high honour, in this life and the next. The burial area was also subject to absolute respect at all times, and whilst a tourist wandering into the more sanctified areas of an English cathedral might receive little more than a ticking off from a verger, at Mwalule the consequences of intrusion could be dire, as Knowles Jordan explained:

> It was taboo for ordinary people to enter the grove, and no reptiles or wild animals might be killed in its vicinity. A young Native Commissioner, Ford by name, was so foolish as to penetrate the sacred grove accompanied by a native follower. After his transfer to

Kasama, he was one of a group watching the tall iron flagstaff being lowered to the ground: unfortunately he misjudged the distance required for safety, for when it fell it struck him violently on the shoulder causing his death. Being the most unusual type of accident, the superstitious Awemba attributed it to his transgressing the taboo, thereby bringing upon himself the wrath of the Spirits (Mipashi). His native companion, strangely enough, also met with violent death, being killed by a man-eating lion.'[14]

In 1914, before his departure for the battlefields of Europe, Gore-Browne had been enchanted by Lake Shiwa, 32 miles south of Chinsali. Back in England, he had rejoined his regiment as a Captain in the British Expeditionary Force, followed by promotion to Brigadier-Major with the Fifth Division. He saw action at the Battle of the Somme and was awarded a DSO. By 1920, the beguiling memory of Northern Rhodesia had drawn him to return, and brought about a revelation: 'On my first morning back at Shiwa, I walked down to the lake and it suddenly struck me: here I was starting a completely new life at the age of 47, and in all these years I had learned nothing that would be of any use to me now.'[15]

The Old Harrovian, with a private but not unlimited income, knew he would need fresh resources as well as knowledge if he were to realise his dream of creating a farm estate in Africa. Quite apart from the palatial house he was envisaging, roads, bridges, agricultural equipment and basic facilities for a workforce all cost money. Support, both moral and financial, was available from his devoted and childless paternal aunt, Ethel Locke King who, with her husband Hugh, had poured her energies into the Brooklands motor-racing track in Surrey, and the luxurious Mena House Hotel in Cairo. What better choice for their next project, than to become sponsors of their nephew's thrilling Northern Rhodesian scheme!

Assured by the BSAC that he could have 10,000 acres at a nominal cost of one shilling, Gore-Browne recruited three ex-Army friends into the venture, but by early 1922 the relationship with two of them had begun to unravel, Charles Austin and Walter Cowie both alleging inconsiderate treatment.[16] Gore-Browne's brother Robert and his wife Margaret, who had been resident in South Africa and joined the partnership, also found it difficult to share the romantic vision, and left in 1924.[17] By 1927, Hector Croad, having retired as a district official three years' earlier, was supervising construction and road building, supported by Joe Savill, who as foreman played a major role in creating the house, and for a short while, young

Guy St. Clair Rideal, on Chinsali   *CPO and golf caddies, Chinsali, 1930*
tennis court, 1929

Viscount Peter Ockham, son of the Earl of Lovelace.[18] Croad, regarded as 'taciturn and morose', had reputedly initiated the common custom of junior officials never speaking to their DC before eleven in the morning: 'Africans, with their ironic sense of humour, gave him the native name of "Chendanseka" – He who walks with a smile'.[19]

Although now close neighbours, Claude's involvement with Shiwa Ng'andu seems to have been limited, suggesting the two men never really clicked – but civil servants were not Gore-Browne's favourite characters, DCs even less so.[20] However, a number of Claude's junior boma colleagues, including John Moffat, Edward Munday and Guy St. Clair Rideal, would also appear as guests in Gore-Browne's diaries and photographs.[21] For his part, Gore-Browne found Chinsali:

> not thrilling. I spent the day I arrived there & left early next morning. It's very much a backwater & long may it remain so. The magistrate was away, & his very worthy but intensely dull wife entertained me to a very dreary dinner in Bob Young's old house. It was jolly kind of her all the same as she herself was going off the next day.[22]

The wife was almost certainly Mrs. Knowles Jordan, her husband being the Chinsali Magistrate at the time.

Gore-Browne's passion for Shiwa Ng'andu and Northern Rhodesia would be life-long. John Hudson, a long-time resident of the country, paid tribute to his host's achievements:

> Over the years he developed the estate energetically, planting citrus orchards from which he distilled essential oils, and constantly building in local materials – the superb house, with its central courtyard, library, many bedrooms, and family chapel, and staff housing, a hospital, a post office, a network of irrigation furrows, and an airstrip.[23]

Yet Gore-Browne was candid about the challenges of trying to establish a going concern:

> Our early years were something of a disappointment. To counter the frightful cost of freight which my choice of a home 400 miles from any railway involved, we had decided for our principal product to concentrate on Essential Oils whose market value is high in proportion to their weight.[24]

So was Stewart Gore-Browne simply a romantic visionary? The swift departure of his initial collaborators suggests a degree of single mindedness, and that he found compromise difficult. Hector Croad, nonetheless, stayed at Shiwa for several years although in time his boss would rely less on white management support. One old retainer described his behaviour as 'just like Chipembele' the rhinoceros, the most bad-tempered animal in the bush. *De haut en bas* or not, without Gore-Browne's spirit and tenacity this pioneer dream could not have been realised. Teucer's spirit of *nil desperandum* was appropriate, for after experimenting with flowering shrubs, eucalyptus, 'Attar of Roses', and later, geranium oil, peppermint and lemon grass, 'it was not till we got to the Citrus Oils that business began to look up.'[25]

The largesse of Aunt Ethel was also essential for the development of Shiwa Ng'andu. The affection between aunt and nephew was intense, and it was hard to say who was the more doting, with Stewart's letters providing an insight into his feelings and ambitions. Given three wishes, he would likely have used one to appoint his Aunt as gracious chatelaine at Shiwa. He would earn a singular reputation as a host, though one with it a rather overbearing proprietorial attitude. His letter to the NRJ of 1953 averred 'It isn't quite correct to say my estate is on its shores. It's rather the other way, the lake is on my estate.'[26] There had been earlier claimants to the lake, notably David Livingstone's dog Chitane who, when the great man passed by in January 1867, was sadly drowned.[27] The name that stuck, Shiwa Ng'andu, translated popularly as 'Lake of the Royal Crocodiles', the crocodile being the token of the Bemba royal chiefs called Ng'andu.

Claude's posting to Chinsali in 1927 coincided with the arrival at Shiwa of Gore-Browne's bride, Lorna Goldman. His junior by twenty-two years, she was the daughter of his first love Lorna Bosworth-Smith, with whom he had enjoyed a three-year courtship, ended in 1906 when she married Edwin Goldmann, a Polish Jewish surgeon.[28] Tragically both had died by the time their child was eleven years old. Young Lorna, branded 'a bit of a troublemaker', was expelled from a number of boarding schools prior to Sherborne, where she was still a pupil when Gore-Browne persuaded her to marry him. A society wedding was held at St. George's, Hanover Square in July 1927 when Lorna was only nineteen.[29] The poet Thomas Hardy, a friend of her family, was sufficiently moved to compose a humorous, if somewhat edgy, paean to the young bride, Lorna the Second:

> Lorna! Yes, you are sweet,
> But you are not your mother
> Lorna the First, frank, feat,
> Never such another! –
> Love of her could smother
> Griefs by day or night;
> Nor could any other,
> Lorna, dear and bright,
> Ever so well adorn a
> Mansion, coach or cot,
> Or so make men scorn a
> Rival in their sight;
> Even you could not!
> Hence I have to mourn a
> Loss ere you were born; a Lorna! [30]

After a few days honeymooning at Aunt Ethel's hotel in Cairo, the newly weds sailed for Dar-es-Salaam, there taking a train west to Kigoma on the shores of Lake Tanganyika, thence sailing south to Mpulungu, before the final overland leg to Shiwa Ng'andu. How would Lorna settle in? Given the whirlwind nature of the marriage and the age difference, not to mention whispered or imagined comparisons between Lorna and her late mother, the husband and wife were reportedly sometimes awkward in each other's company. There were signs though of a gradual, growing affection, even if Lorna was said to find her husband's 'Lord-of-the-Manor stuff' – sounding the gong for dinner, nightly black-tie attire and hoisting the Union flag each morning, hard to relish or understand.[31]

The Gore-Brownes returned to England for the birth of their first child, Lorna Katharine, on 21st April 1929, at Chertsey, near Brooklands. With Stewart's obsession for the original Lorna, and reflecting perhaps his enthusiasm for motor racing, he referred to the new-born as 'Lorna Mark III'. Claude would have heard all about the goings-on at Shiwa Ng'andu; a luminous marriage, another child and another successful, lucky man who, leading a charmed life, seemed to have it all.

---

[1] From Thomas Hardy, *Winter Words* (Macmillan, 1928)

[2] Source: DNB for Lundazi. The record of 'Changes in District Staff' appears to have some anomalies. H. L. Brigham is shown arriving on 17 December 1926, but an entry on the same line implies that he was made up from ANC to NC in July 1926. Brigham appears to have left Lundazi on 19 November 1928. E. H. Cooke is shown as NC from 6 November 1927 to 15 February 1930, but perhaps arrived a year later?

[3] From *lundazionline*

[4] Martin John Bruere Otter. Served 1913 to 1933. Source: *NRBB*, 1924-45.

[5] E. Knowles Jordan ran the Chinsali boma for two years from 1920 and contributed two articles to the *NRJ* in 1965-66, recalling his life at that time: 'Chinsali in 1920-22', Part I by E Knowles Jordan (*NRJ*, Vol V, No.6, 1964, pp 540-8) and Part II (*NRJ*, Vol VI, pp 82-6)

[6] Knowles Jordan, ibid.

[7] Julie Davidson, *Looking for Mrs Livingstone* (Saint Andrew Press, Edinburgh, 2012)

[8] The Chinsali DNB lists the Europeans in the District as at 31 Dec 1927 as: 'C P Oldfield, Assistant Magistrate / J S Moffat, Cadet / Rev R L MacMinn, Missionary, Lubwa / Mrs MacMinn, Missionary, Lubwa / Dr D M Brown, Lubwa / Mrs Brown, Lubwa / Col. Gore-Browne, Shiwa Ngandu / Mrs Gore Browne, Shiwa Ngandu / H Croad, Shiwa Ngandu / J Savill, Shiwa Ngandu / Viscount Ockham, Shiwa Ngandu'.

[9] Robert Donald MacMinn (1870-1956) served with the Livingstonia Mission from 1893 to 1934 (at Lubwa 1913-33). He contributed to the translation of the Tonga (of Nyasaland) and Tumbuka New Testaments, and made a translation of the whole Bible into Chibemba. His publications included school readers and devotional books in Chibemba. From Robert I. Rotberg, *Christian Missionaries and the Creation of Northern Rhodesia, 1880-1924*, Princeton University Press, 1965

[10] *The Nation*, Malawi, 5 May 2014. http://mwnation.com/prison-chief-calls-for-an-end-to-ihl/

[11] Literally meaning a big or mighty tree. His totem Mwine Ng'andu signified the 'Royal Crocodile'.

[12] E Knowles Jordan, ibid.

[13] Letter from SG-B to Aunt Ethel, dated 6 July 1921 (Private collection, Shiwa Ng'andu)

[14] E Knowles Jordan, ibid.

[15] Source: www.shiwangandu.com

[16] Cowie fell ill and died in Abercorn. Austin eventually decided that he would make his career back home.

[17] Robert I. Rotberg, *Black Heart: Gore-Browne and the Politics of Multiracial Zambia* (University of California Press, 1977)

[18] W.V. Brelsford, *The European Pioneers of Northern Rhodesia – Hector Croad (The Silent One).* As acknowledged by Gore-Browne: 'Perhaps I must finish by mentioning the house here in which I live with my family. The outstanding feature of this good-sized building is that it has been constructed by Africans, under the guidance of Joseph Savill, an Artilleryman who served with me in the First World War.' (*NRJ*, Vol VI, 1966 p 235) Peter Malcolm King, 4th Earl of Lovelace (1905-64) succeeded to the title on 5 October 1929. Source: *The Peerage.com.* Chinsali DNB, ibid.

[19] Brelsford, ibid.

[20] Having read through SG-Bs diaries covering that period, it seems clear that Claude was only an infrequent visitor to Shiwa. See Anthony Kirk-Greene, *The Africa House:* Review for britishempire.co.uk, about 2004

[21] Temporary Lieutenant Guy St. Clair Rideal, RNVR, HMT. John Cattling: awarded DSC, 1940

[22] Letter from SG-B to Aunt Ethel, dated 6 July 1921, ibid

[23] John Hudson, *A Time to Mourn* (Bookworld Publishers, Lusaka 1999)

[24] *NRJ*, Vol VI, (1966) p 235-8

[25] *Nil desperandum Teucro duce at auspice Teucro:* 'no need to despair with Teucer as your leader and Teucer to protect you'. From Horace's *Odes.* And *NRJ*, Vol VI, ibid.

[26] *NRJ*, Vol II, No. 1 (1953) p 76

[27] It is not clear from Livingstone's account whether the dog was taken by a crocodile, but it was lost crossing the stream, where it was quite wide, when in fact, a better crossing place could have been found. Source: David Livingstone (ed. Horace Waller) *The Last Journals of David Livingstone, in Central Africa, From 1865 to his Death* (John Murray, 1874)

[28] Obituary of Lady Gore Browne, *Daily Telegraph*, 27 February 2002

[29] Rotberg, *Black Heart*, ibid.

[30] Thomas Hardy, ibid

[31] Obituary, ibid

CHAPTER 19

A Burnt Out Case

He met a man from Northern Rhodesia, who told
him about the copper mines and the wonderfully high
salaries. They sounded fantastic to Tony. He took the next
train to the copper belt ... The cost of living was high, and
then, everyone drank so much …

Tony Marston in *The Grass is Singing* by Doris Lessing

*Joe, Lorna Gore-Browne and baby Lorna, Rideal, Mrs. Hill, Stanley Clark and
Hope (governess), Shiwa, October 1930 (from SG-Bs album)*

By mid-February 1930, while Stewart Gore-Browne continued to bask in
the glow of fatherhood with his beautiful young wife Lorna and new baby
at Shiwa Ng'andu, Claude was again on leave. Sailing from Cape Town,
the Ellerman Line's *City of Palermo* docked in the Port of London on 21st
March.[1] It seems likely, having examined both shipping records and key
photographs in Claude's album, that Claude went to Tilbury Docks a few
days later to say 'goodbye' to the Jeffreys' family as they departed for Cape

Dorothy, Ann and Audrey on board (probably 16 April 1930)

Town on 16th April on board the *Guildford Castle*. The photograph shows warm clothing being worn, not surprising given the dull, cold weather with northerly winds.[2]

London seemed relatively unaffected by the stock market crash of the previous year, though with the slump in heavy industry, unemployment was rising sharply. Cheaper consumer goods were becoming available at the expanding chain of Woolworths and increasing numbers of men and women were smoking. An estimated fifty percent of the population now visited the cinema every week. Despite worries about the nation's finances, the capital was flourishing with new industries opening up to the west of the city.[3]

That summer of 1930 would have provided a reflective break for Claude, and an opportunity to spend time with his widowed mother, now in her late seventies, still living in the family home in Oakington Road. His brother Harold was also at home, active with the Paddington branch of the Liberal party. Londoners who had never seen exotic animals were encouraged to marvel or recoil at Regent's Park Zoo, and horse riding in

Hyde Park was popular.[4] English sporting prowess though was not at its finest in 1930. The Americans triumphed in almost all the Wimbledon events, with Bill Tilden winning the Gentlemen's Singles, and English cricket faring little better. Don Bradman scored a massive 254 out of the Aussies' first innings total of 729 at Lord's, going on to win the Ashes series.[5]

The leave would provide Claude with some good memories. His brother Charlie had risen to a prestigious position at Harrods, heading up the insurance broking business. With time to enjoy golf and holidays in Broadstairs and Deal with his wife Maisie and daughter Joy, now fourteen, Charlie seemed the epitome of the comfortably off, well-rounded man.

By August Claude was preparing to depart again for Africa, not expecting to see his mother, brothers, sister-in-law and niece for the next three or four years. Awareness of his mother's advanced age must have lent their farewells an added poignancy, more especially perhaps for Claude, unable to reveal that, *mutatis mutandis*, Charlie was not her only son to have given her a grandchild.

On 7th September 1930 Claude arrived in Serenje, further south again, outside Bemba territory, to oversee the Lala people. Perched atop a hill within the high plateau of the Muchinga Mountains, approached only by a very rough track, the government officers here must have felt very isolated, with views as far as Petauke, some 120 miles southeast across the Luangwa valley. The elevated boma was exposed to dangerous electrical storms. John Bowden recalled the head messenger's quarters being hit one year: 'the hut was ablaze, flames leaping high in the air, despite a heavy tropical downpour. The wretched inmate was asleep when the lightning struck and the whole of his left side was paralysed.'[6] Bowden explained that the location, on the direct mail route from the north to Fort Jameson, then the capital of North Eastern Rhodesia, was an ideal resting place after the arduous journey through the Luangwa Valley.[7]

Descending the gentle slopes to the north of the plateau, Claude could reach the swamps surrounding Lake Bangweulu and Chief Chitambo's village, where on 1st May 1873 Dr. David Livingstone, stricken by malaria and dysentery, had died. A memorial marking the spot was erected in 1899 attracting only those visitors prepared for tracks barely passable in the wet season. Livingstone's legend pervades so much of Africa: South Africa, Botswana, Malawi and Zambia in particular. His explorations and efforts to spread the gospel will always be compelling, but the events surrounding his death at Chitambo's are especially moving. In February 1873, having reached the northeast shore of Lake Bangweulu, Livingstone had sought a passage through the flood waters of the Chambeshi river to reach the southern end of the lake. Two weeks after crossing the river, by 25th March, suffering from acute dysentery and persistent haemorrhaging, Livingstone and his party found themselves still wading through swamp.[8] By 15th April, he recorded that: 'I, being very weak, had to be carried part of the way.'

His diary entry twelve days later is less coherent: 'Knocked up quite and remain – recover – sent to buy milch goats. We are on the banks of R. Molilamo.' Our knowledge of what happened over the next five days is taken from the account, delivered later in England, by Livingstone's faithful servants, Chuma and Susi:

> On the 30th April, 1873, Chitambo came early to pay a visit of courtesy, and was shown into the Doctor's presence, but he was obliged to send him away, telling him to come again on the morrow, when he hoped to have more strength to talk to him, and he was not again disturbed. In the afternoon he asked Susi to bring his watch to the bedside, and explained to him the position in which to hold his hand, that it might lie in the palm whilst he slowly turned the key.'[9]

Ministering to his needs as best they could that night, Chuma and Susi left Livingstone to sleep. Some time later, as Coupland wrote 'Livingstone seems to have realized that the end had come; and, since he meant to die

as he had lived, with a last, perhaps a fatal, effort of his unconquerable will he somehow got himself from the bed to his knees.'[10] At around four in the morning, Majwara the watchman woke Susi, and together with Chuma, they found Livingstone kneeling, his head buried in his hands on the pillow. They waited for some movement but 'when they saw none, one went in and touched the kneeling man's cheek. It was almost cold. David Livingstone had been dead for several hours.'[11]

David Livingstone (lithograph by S. Hodson after Sharp & Melville Wellcome)

Given the powerful taboo in much of Africa against handling

corpses, what occurred next is quite remarkable. Livingstone's followers removed his heart and viscera, placed them in a tin box and buried them beneath a tree in the village, where prayers were then offered by one Jacob Wainwright, a 'Nassick' boy who, brought up by missionaries, possessed a prayer book and spoke English well.[12] Wainwright also carved an inscription on the tree, variously said to be either *Mvula* or *Mpundu* where a monument still stands. The remainder of Livingstone's body was dried, salted, wrapped in calico and placed in a cylinder of bark, which was covered in tar. This simple coffin was carried all the way to Bagamoyo on the east coast, taking some nine months, and then across the sea to Zanzibar. The intention was to break the news to the British Consul, John Kirk, although it transpired he was on leave in London.[13] His deputy Captain W. F. Prideaux, therefore ordered the warship HMS *Vulture* to bear the coffin forthwith to England.[14] Livingstone was finally laid to rest in Westminster Abbey on 18th April 1874, with only one African, Jacob Wainwright, present. Chuma and Susi arrived in England too late for the service and had Livingstone known that they would receive no reward from the Government, perhaps he would not have been surprised, it would have been merely the last of many disappointments.[15]

Thirty-four years later in 1908, Livingstone's nephew Malcolm Moffat established a missionary station, hospital, school and church in Chitambo's village. Inevitably perhaps, Livingstone remained a controversial figure who despite his driven nature was criticised by fellow missionaries for not producing more converts. His report of the Nyangwe massacre in 1871 when slave traders fired into a crowded market and an estimated 400 people were killed, shocked the British public. Subsequent government pressure on the Sultan of Zanzibar resulted in the closure of the island's slave market in 1873, just six weeks after Livingstone's death, ending the legal slave trade on the East coast of Africa.

Livingstone could be impatient with Europeans who would not or could not work at his pace, but was nonetheless respected, often loved,

Chief Chitambo with the author, October 2012

by many Africans. Slated as a poor expedition leader, who made crucial strategic and geographical errors and never found the source of the Nile, he was also hailed during his lifetime and since as a courageous explorer. Acclaimed as a Christian martyr who ultimately gave his life in spreading the Word, Livingstone became an inspiration for the large numbers of subsequent missionaries to Africa, and the growth of much of the modern day church in southern Africa.

Claude had been sent to Serenje to relieve Tom Chicken, who was due home leave. Serenje was the first posting for Harry Franklin, who recalled the sight of antelope and buffalo silhouetted in the distance the day he arrived:

The sun behind us was sinking fast. Everything glowed. The track dipped and there was a great belt of reeds, gold-dusted at the tips, reaching far out towards a flash of water. It was very beautiful. 'Lake Moir', Andrew said. 'See the geese flighting down? We'll reach Serenje in ten minutes in those hills. It's a nice station. You'll like it.'[16]

In his amusing autobiography, Franklin rather puzzlingly makes no mention of his wife or his daughter Tony, even though he had probably married soon after arriving in Northern Rhodesia, as Claude's photographs from Serenje in 1930 indicate.[17] Writing more than forty years after the events, Franklin, whether by accident or design, appears to have transposed some of the events at Serenje. He describes boma life with typical dry English wit, relating how after dinner on his first night, his host Tom Chicken:

> already portly at thirty-five, lent me a hurricane lamp ... with which to find my way back to my euphemistic house. It was a small thatched oval building of two rooms, with a little front stoep, a bathroom and a store at the back, and another little stoep at the back on which stood a gauze contraption pretending to be a meat-safe.[18] Out at the back, some eight or nine paces away, was a kitchen and another twenty paces led one to the PK.[19] The roof of the house was full of sanitation-conscious rats who had made half-crown sized holes in the calico ceiling for their convenience. Some of the holes were over the bed ... I was soon drowsy but, remembering the candle, I opened my eyes and saw two rats gnawing at its base. I blew it out and let them have the rest.'[20]

Franklin is somewhat dismissive of Serenje, describing it as 'allegedly a township … of two houses (the DC's and mine), a native store, the Messengers' lines or compound, a gaol with one large communal cell and a guardroom, several tin roofed shacks for housing grain, tools and government stores, a tennis court, a five-hole golf course, The Office, outside which was the flagstaff.'

Franklin was also less than complimentary about one short-term appointee, asked to cover during Chicken's absence. From the District Notebook, this must have been Thomas Sandford, who arrived 'in a bad temper in which he remained for the two months of his stay at Serenje. He was sent after this time to Fort Jameson as Provincial Commissioner, the job which he thought he should have had before.'[21] Equally, the young Franklin was candid about his own deficiencies, giving credit to others where due, when explaining how to deal with livestock:

> 'Handing over' involved counting the cattle, the Boma herd.
> Counting a herd of long-horned native cattle confined in a kraal is
> neither an easy nor a soothing occupation. The beasts get nervous
> and suspicious and mill around with their horns clashing. I had never
> been a cattle fancier but I knew how many beasts there ought to be,
> from Tom's list.

After a period of some chaos, the animals ran out of the compound faster than they could be properly counted: 'At the end of it, with all the cattle stampeding for the bush, I said, "I'm sure the number is correct, Sir. But I'll get the herdsman, he can check."… The new DC strode off to count something else. I gave Tom's list to the native clerk. Tom's lists of things were always roughly right.'[22]

Unlike Gore-Browne, Franklin did not find Claude taciturn, but rather 'an amiable man who refused to count anything but signed everything – stayed rather less than two months and again I was alone, waiting for somebody more permanent and also for my leave.'[23] When I chatted with Harry Franklin many decades later, he recalled Claude's language lessons and recitation of Chibemba poetry. These contrasting impressions of Claude can perhaps be explained by status; Gore-Browne's seniority and authoritative manner might have inclined a younger man to defer or simply clam up. The youthful Harry comes across as straightforward and affable, ready to listen, learn and see the humorous side of life.

Living so close to where Livingstone spent his final days might have helped Claude count his blessings and feel inspired. He was in good

CPO at the Serenje tennis court, 1930

Armstrong Siddeley car outside Serenje Aerodrome, 1930 – and gun-bearer Kasaba, my bodyguard

health, doing reasonably well in his career and might yet marry and have a family. As Pascal observed: 'the heart has its reasons which reason knows nothing of'.[24] Claude's heart might very well have felt torn, unsettled, yearning – for some kind of resolution regarding Dorothy.

In November, as the rains began and the flood waters spread out from Lake Bangweulu and the Chambeshi river, Claude would recall the difficulties of travelling in such conditions and, the risk of lightning aside, have appreciated his hilltop house at Serenje. News would have reached him that the MCC, as part of their South African tour, had come as far north as Livingstone on 11th December to play a one-day match against Northern Rhodesia, but the home side lost badly after being bowled out for 73, Ian Peebles taking a hat-trick.[25] Claude knew that his future lay in the hands of the Administration in Livingstone and that his innings in Serenje would soon be over, but where would he play next? When the directive arrived, he should have been excited: a long-awaited promotion to District Commissioner, bringing substantially more responsibility. The location was Ndola, where for three months in 1920 he had provided sick leave cover for Adam Alexander, visiting 118 villages during a six-week ulendo, and Claude recalled a typical rural boma.[26] He was in for a shock. Over the last ten years, the atmosphere had changed immeasurably, and Ndola was now at the heart of the rapidly expanding copper mining industry, a much more cosmopolitan and far livelier place.

Tom Sandford arrived at Serenje on 27th January 1931 and, after the customary three-day handover to his successor, Claude set off for Ndola.[27] Established as an administrative post in July 1904 by J.E. 'Chirupula' Stephenson, the boma had been named after a small stream, a tributary of the Itawa or Kafubu river. Approved as a site by the Administrator of North Eastern Rhodesia, Robert Codrington, within a year responsibility was transferred from Fort Jameson to Kalomo, the HQ for North Western Rhodesia.[28] When Knowles Jordan arrived in 1910 by train from Broken Hill, the line having just been extended to Ndola, he was accompanied by specialists in cotton and rubber growing.[29] More heavily wooded than the country to the south and watered by the upper Kafue River, the district was inhabited principally by the Lamba tribe. 'Old Ndola' had three 'wattle and daub' thatched bungalows: for the DC, the NC and the Medical Officer. There was also a prison, a long building comprising offices, and rondavels for staff housing. Fronting the boma was a beautiful 'mushitu' (a small patch of forest), in which 'a pair of jewelled louries and other birds had their homes, and at night the savage grunt of a leopard was often heard from its depths.' Knowles Jordan 'walked, cycled and hunted over areas which concealed minerals to the value of millions of pounds.'[30]

With the railway had come commerce. The line to Kapalala on the Luapula River, then by boat to the Chambeshi River, had become the main trade route for the Northern Province, with Ndola established as a key distribution centre. The route chosen for the railway however made

The Slave Tree, Ndola in 1930 and 2014

'the disadvantages of the site on the Ndola Stream more apparent, and by the end of 1911, the boma ... was transferred, bringing with it the name of Ndola to the site on which the town now stands.'[31]

One of the interesting features of modern Ndola was, until quite recently, the 'mupapa slave tree', an ancient pod mahogany, said to have been the meeting place for Swahili slave-traders, including Chipembere, Malilo and Chiwala, who arrived in the area during the 1880s.[32] Donald Chikumbi believes that the tree provided a shaded meeting area within the stockade, where groups of up to seven captives from the surrounding population were occasionally sold to the Mbunda from Angola.[33]

Basic mineral workings at Bwana Mkubwa, six miles south-east of Ndola, date back to the fifteenth century, and an open cast mine, the oldest in the country, had been in operation since 1902.[34] With the exponential growth in electrical appliances and cabling, there were now fortunes to be made from copper. As talk of the mineral wealth gathered pace, and with the railway already in place, the fortune hunters had begun to arrive. The first phase of the Northern Rhodesian copper revolution took off in 1922, when a small mining company called Bwana Mkubwa was dramatically enlarged, raising an impressive capital sum of £1.5m, its new board comprising some of the most powerful mining magnates in South Africa.[35] By 1924 the company had purchased the claim at Nkana, and the following year drilling commenced at a number of sites.[36] The Roan Antelope company was formed in 1927 and within a year was mining underground and embarking on fresh drilling at Mufulira.[37]

There was huge optimism. The mining companies' prime concern was to unearth as much of this treasure as quickly as possible, even if this meant a rough and ready approach to manpower and facilities. Writing in 1961, Rev. (later Bishop) John Taylor describes how 'Clearing the surface, drilling and constructing the pilot plant required a great deal of cheap labour. Huge camps sprang up in the open bush. Living conditions were crude enough for the white supervisors and technicians; for the unskilled African labourers, wages, rations and housing were of a standard which is hard to imagine today.'[38] By 1930, an estimated 30,000 Africans were employed in mining in the area, and Claude would have been aware that men from various parts of Northern Rhodesia, Nyasaland, Southern Rhodesia and South Africa had joined the labour camps. Not surprisingly, when members of these different tribes, far from their homes, began to intermingle there could be tension. The number of incoming white workers and managers was also astonishing, swelling from something like 200 to 300 new arrivals each year in the early 1920s to a total of 3,650 men by 1930. Much of this expansion would have been at the Bwana Mkubwa mine, and the new white communities living in makeshift accommodation in the bush were equally diverse: Texan drillers, hard-bitten Afrikaaners, fitters and turners from South Africa, smelter men from Wales, many of them bringing relevant mining experience – but few would have shared Claude's background or Oxbridge education.[39]

The 'new' African population working for the mining companies had either arrived as 'contract labour', recruited by agents visiting local villages, sometimes using a measure of coercion, or were 'directly-hired' workers who had come voluntarily. Jane Parpart's research stressed that 'men did not bring their womenfolk, and mining companies resented the cost of housing and feeding women and children'.[40] Academics have debated whether there was an 'urbanised' workforce as such, as by the early 1920s some 9,000 Northern Rhodesian Africans were employed just across the border by *Union Minière* in Katanga, and by 1930, almost 50,000 had found employment outside the country.[41] For Claude, this was an aspect of African social and economic life which he had not previously encountered, added to which the mining companies often resented any interference from the colonial administration in the management of their labour force.

So why then had Claude been selected as District Commissioner for this place? Responsibility for the promotion appears to rest with Basil Goodall, who had 'strongly recommended Oldfield to be District Commissioner, Ndola.'[42] The endorsement was surely well intentioned. Claude's degree in classics from Cambridge would have signalled to Goodall, a graduate of Jesus College, that here was a gentleman with a rigorous mind. Having written a paper on the meaning of various Wemba words, Goodall may also have been aware of Claude's language abilities.[43]

We can therefore assume that Claude took up his new appointment as DC with an appropriate degree of optimism and pride. His photographs show that Dorothy certainly spent time with him in Ndola. Whether fleetingly or for longer isn't certain, but the pictures suggest that they had time alone and that their feelings for one another were still very much alive. Since Dorothy's pregnancy and the birth of Audrey, had there been a break, and now they were reunited?

Dorothy at Ndola, 1931

But how could they or did they conduct their relationship? Dorothy now had two young daughters as well as a husband. Other photographs show Claude, Dorothy, Robert and the girls all together in convivial mood, but one imagines that a lifestyle à la *Jules et Jim* would have been hard to contemplate.[44] On top of these strains, Claude was facing an accelerated pace in his work life and having to deal with brash, often abrasive, executives in the bustling mining community of Ndola. He had received his long-awaited promotion and Dorothy was back in his life, but at what cost? Something had to give, and when it did, James Murray put it down to temperament: 'Oldfield was a mild and gentle fellow and the District was grossly understaffed. The wild west atmosphere of four large mining construction camps was quite uncongenial to him and different to anything he had previously experienced and he had a break down.'[45]

Engulfed by circumstance, Claude had burnt out.

---

[1] Incoming Passenger Lists: 21 March 1930. Port of Departure South Africa, Durban, calling at Algoa Bay, Capetown, East London, Madeira. Port of arrival London. Passenger Claude Philip Oldfield, age 40. The Ellerman Line's *City of Palermo*, built

in 1905 at 4,699 tons, was the ex-*Rio Negro* of the Hamburg South America Line. Following war reparations in 1919, she was acquired in 1921 by Ellerman, but was scrapped in 1933.

2   The shipping records show Robert, Dorothy, Ann and Audrey as passengers on the *Guildford Castle*, departing London for Cape Town: *Guildford Castle* (132611) 7,995 tons. With 159 passengers. Master: H.L. Scholfield. *Monthly Weather Report of the Meteorological Office (April 1930)*, Vol 47, No.4 (HMSO)

3   London had a high proportion of new 'sunrise' industries, making electrical equipment, food and consumer goods. Light industry continued to move west: Hoover, EMI and Coty all built smart new factories and Ford opened a mammoth factory at Dagenham in Essex in 1931.

4   London Underground Summer Days 1930 art deco vintage repro travel poster

5   Australia won the 1930 Ashes series, winning two matches and losing one, with two tests drawn.

6   C. J. Bowden 'Memories of Abandoned Bomas: No. 17 Serenje' *NRJ*, Vol VI, No. 1 (1965) pp 153-8

7   C. J. Bowden, idem.

8   J. Desmond Clark, 'David Livingstone's Memorial at Chitambo's', *NRJ*, Vol I, No. 1 (1950), pp 24-33

9   David Livingstone, *The Last Journals of David Livingstone, in Central Africa, from 1865 to His Death, Volume II, 1869-1873* (ed. Horace Waller), *Continued By A Narrative Of His Last Moments And Sufferings, Obtained From His Faithful Servants Chuma And Susi* (John Murray, 1874)

10   Reginald Coupland, *Livingstone's Last Journey*, (Collins, 1945)

11   Livingstone, ibid.

12   Moses D. E. Nwulia, *Britain and Slavery in East Africa*, (Three Continents Press, Washington DC, 1975) See page 115: At Nassick, near Bombay, the [Church Missionary Society] maintained an establishment for slave children. They were taught 'industrial occupations' such as bricklaying, carpentry and smithing, and trained 'as servants fitted to earn their own livelihood in India'. Nine of the Nassick graduates accompanied Dr. Livingstone during his last expedition to Central Africa.

13   John Kirk (1832-1922) was a Scottish physician, naturalist, companion to Livingstone and British administrator in Zanzibar.

14   Tim Jeal, *Livingstone* (William Heinemann, 1973) and Martin Dugard, *Into Africa: The Epic Adventures of Stanley And Livingstone* (Doubleday, 2003)

15   Jeal, ibid.

16   Harry Franklin, *The Flag Wagger* (Shepheard-Walwyn, 1974) p 31

17   When I met Harry Franklin and his wife, Marie, in October 1986, at their home at Warren Lane, Froxfield, near Petersfield, they were both recovering from a nasty car crash three months earlier in July. Mrs. Marie Constance Franklin had been a Mistress in European Education (*NRBB*, 1930). Their daughter, Tony (b. 1929), later Mrs. Tilling, was coming over from Zambia to see them shortly. I met Tony Tilling more recently in November 2012, when she was living in Lusaka; by now in her early eighties, she preferred not to talk about 'the early days'.

18   A *stoep* (Afrikaans/Dutch) is a raised veranda in front of a house.

[19] PK: *picannin khia* or 'little house'; a latrine or long-drop.

[20] Franklin, ibid., p36

[21] DNB for Serenje. Thomas Frederick Sandford, b.1886, Cornwood, Devon. Became NC; helped the war effort by getting supplies to British troops in action in GEA. Awarded Order of St Michael and St George, 1935. Source: http://www. devonheritage.org/Places/DevonCounty/TheSandfordFamilyofDevon.htm

[22] Franklin, ibid., p71

[23] Ibid., p72

[24] Blaise Pascal: 'The heart has its reasons, which reason does not know. We feel it in a thousand things. It is the heart which experiences God, and not the reason. This, then, is faith: God felt by the heart, not by the reason.'

[25] *The Yorkshire Post*, Friday 12 December, 1930. MCC is the Marylebone Cricket Club, founded in 1787. For much of the 20th century, MCC organised international tours on behalf of the England cricket team. A 'hat-trick' is the taking of three wickets in three successive balls.

[26] C. P. Oldfield, NC, was appointed from 13 June 1920 to relieve A.M. Alexander, before Oldfield transferred to Chiengi on 20 August. Alexander had been on sick leave to Kasama (and also in August 1917) and had been appt. NC, Ndola on 18 February 1917, on transfer from Mkushi. From 30 June to 12 August 1920, Oldfield visited 118 villages, including Mushiri, Chiwala, Chitina, Nkale, Nkambo, Malenbeka. Source: DNB for Ndola

[27] Source: Serenje DNB (Typed list of Transfers, copy of page 17 (handwritten) near the end of DNB): '27 January 1931. C. P. Oldfield left on transfer.'

[28] DNB for Ndola, p 484

[29] E. Knowles Jordan 'Old Ndola: Memories of Abandoned Bomas – No. 11', *NRJ*, Vol III, No 3 (1957) pp200-5. The railway from South Africa was built as part of the vision of the Cape to Cairo line, the economic case being made for access to the mining potential of Central Africa. The 3ft 6in gauge line reached Northern Rhodesia in 1905 when the 100-mile Livingstone to Kalomo line was built in advance of completion in September of that year of the Victoria Falls Bridge across the Zambezi. The line was extended to Broken Hill (now Kabwe) in 1906 and to Ndola in 1909. From various sources.

   The Rhodesia-Katanga Railway opened in 1909 to connect with the Beira & Mashonaland and Rhodesia Railways terminus at Broken Hill with the *Chemin de Fer du Haut Katanga* at Sakania. Source: DNB, Ndola, p 391

[30] E. Knowles Jordan, ibid.

[31] DNB for Ndola, p 484, ibid. See also L. H. Gann, *A History of Northern Rhodesia: Early Days to 1953* (Chatto and Windus, 1964)

[32] The tree has fallen, supposedly due to termite damage.

[33] Donald Chikumbi (National Heritage Conservation Commission) addressing a workshop on slavery and the ivory trade held in Bagamoyo, Tanzania in 2008, reported by Edwin Mbulo in 'Tracing slaves from Zambia', *Zambian Chronicle*, 2 February 2008

[34] Bwana Mkubwa, located near the Kafue River, some six miles south east of Ndola, is the oldest mine in the region. As a settlement with no municipal status, it became

a locale due to the abundant copper deposits. The name means 'big chief' or 'great master'. Francis Coleman suggests that the origins of the name are various; most likely is that William Collier and Jack Donohoe were led to the ancient workings, naming the area Bwana Mkubwa after Francis Enilius Fletcher Jones, NC; Coleman *The Northern Rhodesia copperbelt, 1899-1962* (Manchester University Press, 1971)

[35] The Bwana Mkubwa Copper Mining Company was registered in London in 1910. Source: Zambia Mining News, 19 January 2015. See also Gann, ibid.

[36] By 1928, Bwana Mkubwa owned the Baluba, Chambishi, Chibuluma, Mindola, Mufulira, Nkana, and Roan Antelope mining properties. In 1929, Bwana Mkubwa Copper Mining Company had proposed layouts for a public township. However, by 1931, there was limited progress on it and a final proposal was rejected chiefly due to worries of lesser profits if there were local government taxation. Source: Emmanuel Mutale, *The management of urban development in Zambia* (Ashgate Publishing, 2004) p 84 et seq.

[37] John V. Taylor & Dorothea A. Lehmann, *Christians of the Copperbelt: The Growth of the Church in Northern Rhodesia* (SCM Press, 1961) See Chapter 2, The Opening of the Copperbelt.

[38] Taylor & Lehmann, ibid.

[39] Gann, ibid.

[40] J. L. Parpart, *Labour and capital on the African Copperbelt* (Temple University Press, Philadelphia, 1983)

[41] James Ferguson, Expectations of Modernity: Myths and Meanings of Urban Life on the Zambian Copperbelt, University of California Press, 1999

[42] Correspondence in December 1986 with James Murray, when retired and living in Woking, Surrey. Edward Basil Goodall, CBE (1885-1936) had been educated at Jesus College, Cambridge.

[43] Edward Basil Goodall, *Some Wemba words, some meanings and explanations* (Oxford University Press, 1921)

[44] *Jules and Jim* is a 1962 French romantic film, written and directed by Francois Truffaut.

[45] James Murray correspondence, ibid.

CHAPTER 20

None but Thou

More lovely than the monarch of the sky
In wanton Arethusa's azur'd arms
And none but thou shall be my paramour!

*The Tragicall History of the Life and Death of
Doctor Faustus, Scene 13, Christopher Marlowe*

While Claude was struggling at Ndola, Lorna Gore-Browne was expecting her second child, Stewart probably hoping that this time his wife would produce a son and heir to perpetuate his name and inherit his grand African estate. He loved order, formality, parades and dressing-up, his well-stocked

*Very Rev. Wilfred Gore-Browne,
when Dean of Pretoria, 1909-12*

cellar and immaculately turned-out staff the order of the day, not only for special occasions. Although an unregenerate snob there was a thoughtful side to Stewart's character, a sensitivity, indeed love, for Africa's people and a concern for their welfare, temporal and spiritual.[1] A role model was his uncle Wilfred, who had left his Darlington parish for to be Rector (and later Dean) of Pretoria, and was from 1912 until his death in 1928, the first Bishop of Kimberley and Kuruman. Described as a saintly bishop with 'a keen sense of humour' and 'a winning courtesy', Wilfred Gore-Browne would pay several visits to Shiwa.[2] Stewart Gore-Browne felt strongly that religion and its rituals should be seriously and correctly observed. Writing to his Aunt Ethel in July 1921, already enraptured with Lake

Shiwa and full of plans, he had compared his encounters with two of the principal missions, the White Fathers at Kayambi and the Scottish Presbyterians at Kawimbe, and wondered:

> whether the R.C.s weren't nearer the true way of religion. The two priests stood at two altars in their vestments, red-robed native acolytes served, and an intensely reverent congregation knelt or stood, following the whole service with apparently intense devotion. The priests spoke the Chi-Wemba words as it seems only these Frenchmen can, like natives, and all the long responses were given by the congregation. Perhaps it's all superficial, but I don't think so, and it <u>can't</u> be wrong to connect the worship of God with reverent ceremony instead of the sort of familiar, snivelling, shuffling chat at the other place, where everyone sat down, & a conversation at the back of the hall had to be checked half way through.[3]

Robert MacMinn at Lubwa explained to Gore-Browne the importance of his Presbyterian mission creating the kind of civilised environment in which religion might best flourish: 'our view is different to that of the White Fathers. They build a church first of all. We believe in building a station, with school & dwellings houses, & later a church at our leisure.' Gore-Browne wrote approvingly: '… a scholarly old man, in the main busy studying the wemba language (while his wife whom I didn't see runs a hospital & I fancy most else.) Socially I liked him more than most people I've met lately. For one thing he came from Ayrshire & knew of all our folk.'[4]

The chapel at Shiwa Ng'andu, 2012

Gore-Browne's chapel would also receive favourable reports. Eileen Bigland, who stayed at Shiwa in the late 1930s, describes the short service led by the Bwana every Sunday morning: 'It was extremely simple, two lessons from the Bible, the Lord's Prayer, and a second prayer. Always, I noticed, the lessons concerned things which they could understand; always the audience stayed quietly, their brown eyes very round, until the Bwana had finished.'[5] The snobbish, autocratic image of Gore-Browne was further mitigated by his pleasure at any encouragement for his enterprise, particularly from the church, as in his reflections after meeting a local priest:

> He surprised me immensely by coming out with a warm appreciation of us & what we're trying to do here, saying that our influence on the whole neighbourhood couldn't be overestimated, & that he was always hearing natives discussing us & our ways & marvelling. I wish I thought it was true, but it's nice to hear it all the same, from our Rector so to speak, and in view of what father saw of my 'useless' life.[6]

The modesty seems genuine, but it is perhaps the final words, the yearning for paternal approval, apparently denied him, which suggest that beneath any bluster Stewart Gore-Browne was as human as the next man and felt failure as keenly. The grand house at Shiwa could express a desire to prove himself a worthy, indeed prodigal son. In the field of romance it seemed the prize was now firmly his, with Lorna Mark II, daughter of the woman that had snubbed him as a young man, ensconced as his wife. Such was Stewart's pride and devotion to young Lorna, that on her arrival he had had carved above the front door the initials of their Christian names, 'L 1932 S'. On seeing the inscription she had apparently replied, 'Does that mean we have to live here forever?'[7] Was she thrilled or horrified? Time would

Miss Gore-Browne and body guard. 1930. Col. S. Gore-Browne is the biggest land owner in N. Rhodesia and has 37,000 acres.

Shiwa Ng'andu, November 2012

tell, but Shiwa Ng'andu was integral to Stewart's life, and he obviously hoped that Lorna would come to love it too. For Claude, wedded bliss must have seemed something that happened only to other people. As a result of his downfall at Ndola, by May 1931 he had been transferred to Mkushi, an attractive rural area much more akin to his previous postings.[8] James Murray commented: 'Between the years 1911 and 1929, I think the farthest south he had ever been stationed was Chinsali, which is rather like saying of an Englishman that he had never been south of Newcastle.'[9]

Without greater detail of his breakdown, we can only assume that Claude became extremely fatigued and distressed, losing patience with colleagues or the managers from the mining and construction companies. The likely medication on offer would be a few stiff whiskies and some well-meant encouragement to 'cheer up old man'. Any anxiety regarding Dorothy would not have helped, and if observed with her around Ndola, Claude may have felt the opprobrium of his colleagues. The truth might also by now have dawned on Robert Jeffreys, leading to words, a scene, maybe in public. The gossipy European community and sideways glances were enough to put any man on edge, especially during the depressing atmosphere of the rains, when Claude arrived in Ndola.

It was also around this time that the impact of the slump in the world economy started to hit the Northern Rhodesia copper belt. As copper prices declined, mines around the world ran at a loss. Following an international copper quota agreement in August 1931, the Anglo American Corporation and the Rhodesian Selection Trust each curtailed their production in the country to 25 percent, which they decided to produce from their most developed mines at Rhokana and Roan Antelope, respectively. Cutbacks and closures spread. Bwana Mkubwa had already closed in February 1931, followed later that year by a halt in production at Chambishi, Nchanga and Mufulira.[10] Mbozi Santebe explains how the reduction in mining activity was followed immediately by massive reductions in the workforce 'the non-racial axe of the depression spared neither Africans nor Europeans as both were laid off in large numbers at short notice or without notice at all. Due to the layoffs, the population of the Copperbelt was sharply reduced.'[11]

The drastic population decline on the Copperbelt between November 1930 and June 1933 meant that 'the number of Europeans fell from 3,600 to 1,200, while the African population was drastically reduced from 32,000 to 9,300.' Salaries for the remaining mine workers diminished to offset the cost of production. The colonial administration regarded the industry as international property, and feeling that there was very little it could do to stop it crumbling, left resuscitation efforts to the mining companies at both local and international level.[12]

After his escape from the Copperbelt, how did Claude fare at Mkushi? James Murray makes no mention of any rumours, but speaks favourably of his new boss, recalling how they saw 'one another daily for about 8 hours a day in the office and frequently for sundown or supper as well … Claude Oldfield was a good linguist (Chibemba) and I was a keen pupil. We read collections of folk tales together and we collected proverbs and riddles.' Claude being some eighteen years senior, one can imagine a paternal or elder-brotherly affection towards the twenty-four year-old James, who had come out to Northern Rhodesia only a couple of years earlier. Schooled at 'Teddies' (St. Edward's, Oxford), followed by a degree from Christ Church, he was manifestly Claude's type, able to provide cultured company, doubtless a tremendous relief after the miners and money-grubbers at Ndola. At Mkushi, with the next white man seventy miles away and no motor transport other than the official car, Claude and James found themselves pleasantly sequestered in 'an undulated, well-watered and lightly forested plateau not very fertile, and two hot low-lying valleys named the Luano and the Lukasashi.'[13]

In the rainy season the place became even more isolated, as Knowles Jordan, inveterate chronicler of Northern Rhodesian bomas, pointed out: 'When the Mkushi River was full after heavy rains, making it impossible or dangerous to use the drift, a very clumsy dugout canoe was used to ferry travellers and their belongings from bank to bank.' Mkushi lay at the heartland of the Lala tribe, their Chief Shaiwira living to the north of the boma. Knowles Jordan recalled 'the famous Mwana Lesa case in which something like 200 alleged witches were drowned, many of them in the Mkushi district.' Following a sensational trial at Broken Hill, Shaiwira was hanged, alongside the millenarian preacher Tomo Nyirenda, referred to earlier during Claude's time at Mporokoso.[14]

Claude could now write to his family with a chuckle that he was living near Piccadilly Circus. It was true. The crossroads:

> between Mkushi Boma and the Great North Road in the one
> direction and the deserted Mutuga Mine and Fiwale Mission in the
> other' had been so christened, as Gordon Read recalled '... by the
> miners at Mtuka Mine or the Lunsemfwa Claims on the opposite side
> of the river. It is also difficult to say what year it was named. I have
> a note in my diary that on the 15th July, 1923, I started off to find a
> route for a road to Chiwefwe. I remember this, but I did not make the
> road. I left Mkushi on the 5th July, 1924, to proceed on leave and did
> not return there until the 15th August, 1926. I left Frank Brown (later
> Chief Secretary, Nyasaland) in charge, and I think he made the road
> during 1925 or 1926 and it would be named, I suppose, about that
> time.[15]

CPO at Piccadilly Circus, Mkushi District, 1932

To the amusement of many Zambians, Piccadilly Circus remains to this day and features in a recent road improvement programme for the movement of goods and services in the commercial farming area, the Mkushi Farm Block.[16]

Mkushi, in outward terms at least, was a return to normality for Claude. At the end of July he toured the district for two weeks by car, with five messengers and a retinue of carriers, visiting every village in Chief Chitina's country save Nkole. Making a number of enquiries about traditional claims, he also called at Chiwefwe and the Anglican Mission at Fiwila. Over three weeks in October he drove a further 390 miles, taking in fifty-seven villages in Chief Mukonchi's area, as well as inspecting roads and deciding on the strengthening of the bridge over the river Muka. Away from the noise and fractiousness of Ndola, this peripatetic life, meeting the Africans in their homelands was where Claude felt most comfortable. The job was not without its own challenges, but his linguistic and administrative skills, and most importantly his temperament, seemed suited to them.

Meanwhile where was Dorothy? She was not long in putting in an appearance at Mkushi. She would have heard of Claude's untimely departure from Ndola, and even without specific details or his saying as much, would have realised how miserable he had been. As for her own happiness, we can only hypothesise, but here is a possible scenario: time was passing, and with the two girls growing up and the emotional gulf between her and Robert widening, she may have despaired of the future with a husband she now realised she had never really loved. But if she wanted Claude, permanently and properly, how might it happen? Some action on her part might make Claude aware that she was prepared to defy convention, and impel him to seek a home for them together back in England. Such things are always easier said than done, and if Dorothy were indeed struggling with such feelings, her life would have seemed like it was on hold.

G.H. Lobb, Ann and Audrey at Kapiri Mposhi, 1931

The photographic evidence certainly suggests the pair were still close. Dorothy also appears to have had a motorcar, ideal for sightseeing and picnics when Claude's colleague James might be using the official vehicle. In some pictures Dorothy is with Robert, but it looks as if she and Claude also found opportunities to be together privately.

Ann and Audrey, with carriage and pair, Mkushi, 1931

The 'Machila' is a very comfortable method of transport

Time passed dreamily on the river, playing around in dugout canoes, swimming at the 'Mkushi Bathing Pool' and diving off the rocks. Where Robert is absent, Dorothy and Claude might be taken for any happily married couple on a rural station, relaxing at the weekend with their family. They also visited the Salanyama Rapids, walked by the river and could if the fancy took them enjoy a round of golf. In a picture dated later in the year, a tall young bachelor appears frequently with them, along with his dog Peter at Namufyoto Waterfalls. This was Charles Stevens, who followed James Murray after four months, the latter moving to Ndola.[17] Stevens was also of similar background to Claude, on his first posting and eager to learn, described by George Billing as having 'a great deal of talent & many admirable qualities: a hard worker, excellent linguist & delightful sense of humour. His brother, Bob Stevens, was one of our senior District Commissioners.'[18] Billing, who was stationed at Isoka from 1930-33, recalled his DC mentioning Oldfield 'in complimentary terms as one of the senior officers in the administration.' Possibly any rumours had dissipated by now, Claude's otherwise upstanding reputation, good manners and role as mentor, outweighing any questionable aspects of his behaviour. There might even have been sympathy for his predicament, especially in the light of his recent breakdown.

The scenes at Mkushi suggest that Dorothy and Claude wished that these long, languid days could go on forever, with the images projecting a sense of suspended animation. Over six years had passed since their first meeting, and the photographs tell the same story: of two people with a natural, magnetic affinity for one another.

Dorothy might have previously tried to end the affair. After having Claude's child in November 1926, her feelings must have been very mixed, and as far as is known, she had seen little of him for several months after. What thoughts and feelings had been stirred in each of them the day Claude first set eyes on little Audrey? And what of Robert's feelings? If he had learnt that Claude was Audrey's father, might he have been more willing to leave Dorothy, even to insist on a divorce? Such knowledge could have intensified his resentment, making him determined to punish his wife, conceivably taking away the children.

With two men's careers at stake if a scandal came about, we cannot assume that Dorothy was without scruple. Sarah Miles in Graham Greene's *The End of the Affair*, in a marriage without love or passion, stayed with her husband because his livelihood depended upon it.[19] Would it take the equivalent of a German bomb on Clapham Common to end either Dorothy's affair or her marriage? If Robert had also been unfaithful she might have felt far less reluctant to abandon him, or, human nature being perverse, suddenly possessive, who knows? Robert's energies seemed devoted largely to his work, with little chance that like 'Chirupula' Stephenson, he would take up with a local girl.[20] What were the chances of Mr. and Mrs. Jeffreys making a clean, civilised break, as opposed to an ugly, protracted confrontation leaving two young children confused and distressed, their parents unable to know what to say to them? Even a shrewd gambler like my grandfather Charlie would have found it hard to lay odds. For now, it was a non-starter.

The retreat to Mkushi would have given Claude time to meditate, and although not overly religious, a sense of guilt may have troubled him. At Cambridge he would have come across Christopher Marlowe, perhaps in Tucker Brooke's 1910 *Complete Works* with Marlowe's translation of Ovid's *Amores* (love elegies) and the whole of *Doctor Faustus*, a play abounding in psychological insights.[21] Faustus the self-made man, a gifted academic with an understanding of physics, astrology and divinity, yearns for yet headier experiences, omnipotence even, and through the sinister messenger Mephistopheles, makes a pact with the devil: an allotted time to wallow in worldly pleasure and power, before being sent to Hell.

Claude was also a man of talent and accomplishments, and on meeting Dorothy had he too made a bargain? Seven years on, wrestling with his confusion, fears and desires, he would have recalled with a shudder the reply to Faust on asking Mephistopheles how he had escaped from Hell:

> Why this is hell, nor am I out of it.
> Think'st thou that I, who saw the face of God,
> And tasted the eternal joys of heaven,
> Am not tormented with ten thousand hells
> In being deprived of everlasting bliss?[22]

Lying in Dorothy's arms was surely bliss. Was being parted from her a hell that Claude could not bear to comprehend? Yet as Marlowe tells us: 'He that loves pleasure, must for pleasure fall' and if Satan were not now to claim his soul, how would it all end?[23]

---

[1] 'Lions outside the library: The intriguing story of an Englishman who built a feudal kingdom in the African bush', Review of Christina Lamb's *Africa House* in *The Daily Telegraph*, 10 July 1999.

[2] 'In Memoriam: The Bishop of Kimberley and Kuruman', *Church Times*, 23 March 1928, p343

[3] Stewart Gore-Browne, Letters, the Library, Shiwa Ng'andu

[4] Gore-Browne, ibid.

[5] Eileen Bigland, *The Lake of the Royal Crocodiles* (Hodder & Stoughton 1939), (p 117)

[6] Gore-Browne, ibid.

[7] Obituary for Lady Gore Browne, *The Daily Telegraph*, 27 February 2002

[8] Claude was relieved of his position in Ndola and moved to Mkushi on 10 May 1931, his salary then being £780 pa. He succeeded A. S. Chapman, who had only been there for a year and who had also previously been DO at Ndola. Source: DNB for Mkushi

[9] Correspondence in December 1986 with James Patrick Murray, when retired and living in Woking, Surrey. Murray (1906-93), educated at St. Edward's School and

Christ Church, Oxford was DC, then Senior Provincial Commissioner of Northern Rhodesia. Awarded CMG, 1958. Source: afraf.oxfordjournals.org

[10] Annual Report on the Social and Economic Progress of the People of Northern Rhodesia, 1931 (HMSO, 1932) and Roan Consolidated Copper Mines Limited, Zambia's Mining Industry: The *First 50 Years* (Roan Antelope Consolidated Copper Mines, Ndola, 1978)

[11] Mbozi Santebe, 'The Colonial Government and the Great Depression in Northern Rhodesia: Administrative and Legislative Changes, 1929-1939', Dissertation, University of Zambia, Lusaka, 2015

[12] Larry Butler, Copper Empire: Mining and the Colonial State in Northern Rhodesia, c.1930-64 (Palgrave Macmillan, 2007)

[13] E. Knowles Jordan, 'Old Mkushi in 1912 (Part I)', *NRJ*, Vol IV, No 5 (1961) pp 427-33

[14] E. Knowles Jordan, 'Old Mkushi in 1912 (Part II)', *NRJ*, Vol IV, No 6 (1961) pp 583-90

[15] W.V. Brelsford: A Further Note on European Place Names (Recollections of Gordon Read, a retired Provincial Commissioner, previously posted to Mkushi), *NRJ*, Vol I, No. 6 (1952) pp 41-8

[16] 'Italian construction company awarded a 292 km road upgrade contract: An Italian construction company CMC Di Ravenna has been awarded a contract by the Zambian Government through the Road Development Agency (RDA) to work on the Kabwe to Piccadilly Circus and the Mpula to Mansansa roads in Central Province.' Source: *Lusaka Times*, 20 July 2017. Another source implies that Msansa (or Mansansa) is close to Piccadilly Circus: 'At this "Piccadilly spot" is a little town, Msansa with a few dirt roads, no electricity, chickens, children, goats and rural black people on the street.'

[17] Mkushi DNB, p 9. 'C.G. Stevens, Cadet, arrives on first appointment and J.P. Murray proceeded on transfer to Ndola.'

[18] C. G. Stevens' career in Northern Rhodesia included a long period in Barotseland and (together with M.G. Billing) contributed to *The Judicial Process among the Barotse of Northern Rhodesia (Zambia)*, edited by Max Gluckman (Manchester University Press, 1967). Also, personal letter from George Billing, 31 December 1986, when living in retirement at Plettenberg Bay, South Africa.

[19] Graham Greene, *The End of the Affair* (Heinemann, 1951)

[20] 'Chirapula' Stephenson (1874-1955) had two African wives, Loti and Mwapa. In white circles, opinion was divided between those who respected him for his standing in tribal communities, particularly amongst the Lala people, and those who expressed distaste at his 'going native'.

[21] C. F. Tucker Brooke (ed.), *The Works of Christopher Marlowe* (Oxford University Press, 1910).

[22] Christopher Marlowe, *The Tragicall History of the Life and Death of Doctor Faustus*, Scene 3. The play by Marlowe (1564-1593) premiered c. 1592 and was published in 1604.

[23] Marlowe, ibid., Scene 2.

CHAPTER 21

Goodbye Piccadilly

There we will lay down, Under the palm tree
Peace and love and drink, And dream our blissful dream

Heinrich Heine, 1827[1]

In the late summer of 1931, Lorna Gore-Browne gave birth to her second child. If her husband had been dreaming of a son to whom, gesturing across his sprawling estate he might utter the time-honoured words, 'One day my boy, all this will be yours', he was disappointed. New baby Angela was born, like her sister, at Brooklands. On returning to Shiwa, her mother reportedly took to her bed for several days. Was this the 'baby blues', now known as post-natal depression (from which Dorothy also might have suffered), or a sign of broader discontent?

If Lorna had a yearning for adult female company, it was about to be gratified. Audrey Richards, a thirty-two year-old anthropologist from Cambridge, had abandoned her studies and a tumultuous relationship with the charismatic Polish ethnographer and anthropologist, Bronislaw Malinowski, and decamped to Northern Rhodesia. She was destined to become an acknowledged expert on the social customs of the indigenous people: 'Setting up her tent in the middle of the village, Richards observed the daily interactions of the Bemba ... however, Richards never pretended to "go native", and after her long forays in the villages, she would return to the colonial estate of Gore-Browne as her permanent home base'.[2]

Although both women were from well-connected families, they had had different upbringings – and their roles in Africa differed too. Audrey was a highly educated, independent professional, while Lorna was trying to be a conventional wife and mother. They soon struck up a close friendship, Audrey immersing herself in village life, recognising the need to master the local language before engaging in rigorous fieldwork: 'and on the nutritional aspect I had to be able not only to question natives but to listen

Audrey Richards, c. 1930

to their talk when eating and drinking, and to participate in their domestic life'.[3] Distancing herself from the white settlers, officials, missionaries and traders, Audrey's gender seemed to help in her studies and she would earn a prestigious position in the Bemba community.[4]

Although welcoming Audrey into his home, Stewart Gore-Browne became increasingly worried about Lorna being exposed to Audrey's ideas and approach to life. His fears were not groundless, for in 1934 the two women relocated to Cambridge, leaving the Gore-Browne children in the hands of a governess. Lorna studied agriculture, music, German and medicine. Whether there was a lesbian relationship is uncertain, and it was said in Northern Rhodesia that Richards 'preferred porridge to sex'.[5] Lorna may simply have craved her independence and the opportunity to further her education.

For Claude, after the tension and turmoil that he had suffered at Ndola, Mkushi must have felt like a warm bath. The nearby Luangwa Valley, attracting naturalists and sportsmen since the 1920s was home to hundreds of elephant, black rhinoceros, buffalo, impala and kudu. Knowles Jordan thought the best time to visit was between August and October when some of the long grass and jungle had died back or been burnt off, and warned against November and December when the heat was too intense. (Having visited in early November, I can vouch for the sapping temperatures, with little or no breeze to offer any relief).

By the beginning of 1932, Claude had delegated much of the routine district travelling to his cadet Charles Stevens, who made two long tours in February and April.[6] They also undertook expeditions together, enjoying Lunsemfwa Falls 'a beautiful sight, especially towards the end of the rainy season when the river is full to the brim.' From Bell Point they would have looked down into the 'Wonder Gorge' where the Lunsemfwa is joined by its tributary the Mkushi.[7] Journeys to the southern end of the district involved a fair degree of mountaineering, particularly tough for the carriers, with awkward loads to handle.[8]

As Claude bathed in the calming rhythms of nature, still there was the presence of Dorothy. Time spent with her in Mkushi appears to have been particularly agreeable, but the sense of an approaching crossroads must have been ever more palpable. After his breakdown at Ndola, Dorothy knew that her lover would not make Provincial Commissioner and that his career and ambitions could have run out of steam. If they were to stay together, how might it be done?

The Lunsemfwa Gorge, Mkushi, C.G. Stevens

Bob and C.G. Stevens, Namufyoto Waterfall, Mkushi District, 1931

Bob showing his 'wrong end'

Dorothy, in Mkushi Bathing Pool, 1931

Cohabiting in Northern Rhodesia would surely attract reproach from their contemporaries, leading to embarrassing occasions for both of them. Returning to England together might be a seductive vision – setting up home, sleeping in each other's arms each night and enjoying all the untrammelled gaiety and freedom, companionship and love to which surely they were entitled. There were of course any number of flies in this ointment – Robert, the children, Claude's mother and – unless they embraced the stigma of 'living in sin' – the necessity for Dorothy to obtain a divorce.

It seems that Claude could not make a decision. He could be eligible for an early pension, but it wouldn't amount to very much for the two of

Dorothy, Dick and CPO, at Mkushi, 1931

them. If Ann and Audrey were to be with them, would Robert contribute to the girls' upbringing and education? Whatever the arrangement, it would entail a financial burden on Claude for many years to come. Dorothy's love for him might be strong enough for her to cast caution to the wind, but was he of equal conviction? Dorothy may have surmised that he was concerned about his widowed mother, and the possible need to care for her in the future. Did she also think he feared his mother's disapproval, reluctant to confess to the double life he had been leading, fathering a child with another man's wife?

For Dorothy, respectability might have been less important. If it were, returning to London with Claude and putting their relationship on some kind of proper footing could mean a clean slate, a chance for her to recoup her status as a 'good girl'. Her mother, now in her early sixties, was living alone and had moved out of London to the south coast near Bournemouth. Unable to offer financial support, seeing her daughter happy might have outweighed any reservations about her behaviour. In a perfect world Dorothy might simply free herself from her marriage, and thereby gauge her feelings, seeing then if the long affair could translate into some kind of recognised, stable relationship, or whether its forbidden nature had been its key driving force.

Did Claude suffer sleepless nights, guilty about the effect the affair had on both Dorothy and Robert, assuming that after almost seven years, Robert must have had some idea what had been going on? Perhaps here in the tranquillity of Mkushi, Claude attempted to slay his inner demons. Faust and Mephistopheles had rejected God out of pride and would suffer the consequences. Conceivably, Claude felt that any decision over Dorothy was by now too difficult to make, and that fate would run its course. If loneliness and remorse followed, this would be his punishment. But did he not owe Dorothy an answer now, one way or the other? And what about Audrey, their secret child? This living result of their alliance would only grow more present in the world, articulate, and questioning. How might he relate to or make peace with her, with Dorothy, with Robert? Was it even possible?

How was Claude able to address these issues? Any residue of faith instilled in his upbringing had not prevented him from commission of a sin, and his procrastination now was one of omission. Faust had turned his back on God, misinterpreting Christian doctrine to suit his feelings, acknowledging that the reward of sin was death:

Why then, belike, we must sin,
And so consequently die.
Ay, we must die, an everlasting death[9]

Claude might have found it hard to believe that God would forgive anyone who was truly repentant. There were enough missionaries on hand if he wanted to bare his soul, or simply discuss theology in a more detached way. Goethe presents Faust as cold-hearted, cynical and witty, his soul ultimately escaping from Mephistopheles while he is making improper

CPO looking a bit like Mephistopheles

Mephistopheles flying over Wittenberg (lithograph by Delacroix)

advances to the angels that have come to rescue him.[10] This was a much more satisfactory outcome than eternal damnation, and conceivably would have amused Claude's more cavalier side.[11]

Claude's indecision could not continue *ad infinitum*. If the situation became intolerable, someone in the triangle would contrive a withdrawal, Robert perhaps exerting pressure on Claude or Dorothy. At first sight, it might appear as if Claude made the move, as the Mkushi District Notebook states that on 21st May 1932, C.P. Oldfield 'proceeded on leave pending retirement'. In fact, matters had been taken out of Claude's hands.

The German-born historian, Lewis Gann, explains that following the collapse of the world copper price in 1931, the country faced a major crisis which it was ill equipped to handle. Although understaffed at the best of times, the colonial administration had to embark on a major campaign to balance its budget. Civil servants accepted a levy on salaries, and 'some of the more senior officers were retrenched. The district staff for instance was reduced from 110 officers in 1932 to 90 in 1935'. Cuts were made in provincial administration and to technical personnel, whilst the Secretariat seemed unaffected, leading to angry comments and a loss of morale. The salaries of African schoolmasters were cut, putting their real income below that of district messengers.[12] Further evidence that Claude had been retrenched was available at the British National Archives in a 'List of Officers who have retired on Pension since the 1st January 1932' in a despatch dated 24th February 1933. C.P. Oldfield is one of 19 names, including two Provincial Commissioners, seven District Officers (among them Claude's friends Bertram Matthews and Tom Chicken) and a number of senior specialists. Two men were noted as retiring due to ill health, not Claude!

Sadly, the die had been cast and the rural tranquillity of Mkushi would be the backdrop to his swansong:

> Farewell, all joys! O Death, come close mine eyes!
> More Geese than Swans now live, more Fools than Wise.

What though of the ancient Greek belief that after a lifetime of silence, in the moments before death, the swan opens its throat to sing the most exquisite, heart-breaking song imaginable?[13] For Claude, this was retirement, not death, but nonetheless a momentous change – possibly the end of ambition, a loss of power and status, all requiring substantial mental adjustment. He was though an educated and erudite man, taught

C.G. Stevens and Peter, Mkushi, 1931

to think and doubtless doing a lot of it during those final months at Mkushi.

In May he would be leaving for good. Dorothy might have asked, pleaded even to go with him, offering to abandon her husband and children and escape to a new life together. Knowing a decision had been reached, she may have continued to brood. Claude was a part of her that could not be erased, and recently they had seemed so happy together at Mkushi.

The good-humoured Charles Stevens laid on a farewell dinner for Claude, probably for just the two of them, taking the trouble to

Menu for Claude's Retirement 'Dinner' (written on Government Memorandum Pad)

271

draw up a personally signed 'Menu', recording on it Claude's (assumed) date of arrival at Abercorn as 31st December 1911 and his imminent departure date. The meal was eclectic: a crab starter followed by chicken, sausage, beans and potato, then pears and cream, rounded off with sardines on toast; and for good cheer there was whisky, gin, bitters and van der Hum.[14] Charles had selected a number of '78' records for the wind-up gramophone, commencing with Chopin's Preludes 16, 17 and 18, played by Cortot, a renowned Franco-Swiss pianist.[15] The programme was thoughtfully chosen, reflecting Claude's recent mood swings, with Chopin's contrasting tone, tempo and rhythm, haunting and surrealistic at times, moving to dreamy and romantic later; from depths of darkness to songlike tones of warmth and lightness.

The introspective tone continued with Mendelssohn's *On Wings of Song*, Claude perhaps wishing that he might still carry his sweetheart to the fields of the Ganges:

> On Wings of Song,
> Sweetheart, I carry you away,
> Away to the fields of the Ganges,
> Where I know the most beautiful place[16]

The famous *intermezzo* from *Cavalleria rusticana* by Mascagni was followed by Schubert's immortal *Serenade*. The mood of the evening was lightened with a number of arias from Gilbert and Sullivan, and concluded with a Sesotho *Lithoko* or 'praise poem', *Morena Kerefisi*. This is a long piece, with a particularly apposite first verse, which translates as:

> Be quiet and listen to celebration,
> Mixed with cries of weeping.
> Young men, you should give yourselves names,
> When you harvest lustily in the way of young men:[17]

James Murray, Claude's first cadet at Mkushi, who saw the Menu later, observed that:

it was written on Northern Rhodesia Government Internal Memorandum paper and the five courses, except for the chicken, probably came out of tins. It is possible that there were only two people at the banquet; if there was a good excuse it was not unknown for two people on an outstation to put on a coat and tie and make believe they were dining at the Savoy.

So on 21st May 1932, Claude took the train from Ndola, thence via Livingstone, Salisbury and Johannesburg to Durban. His baggage included the skin of the leopard shot in 1917, which would later adorn each of his homes, the same skin laid between us in the somnolent Norfolk rectory as he told me tales of Africa that regrettably bypassed my teenage hearing.

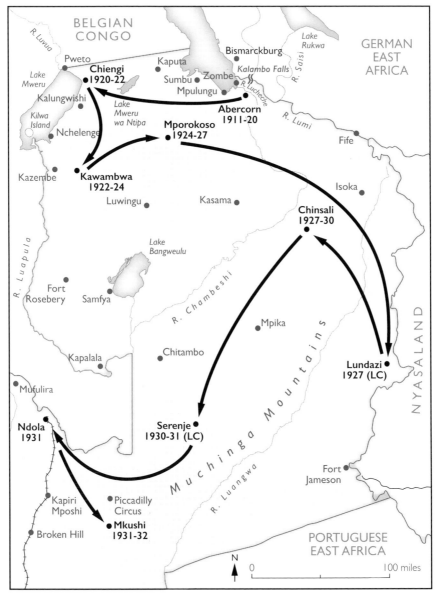

Claude's postings in Northern Rhodesia, 1911-32

Embarking on 13th June on the *Balmoral Castle*, Claude sailed the long route home, with stop overs at East London, Algoa Bay (Port Elizabeth), Cape Town and Madeira, before reaching Southampton.[18]

Claude's final tour had lasted just twenty-one months, during which he had suffered a major breakdown and loss of confidence, yet in that time he had left a good impression. In James Murray's view, Claude Oldfield was 'popular and well liked by his fellow District Officers … a good "native administrator" – if such a term has any meaning to-day … well built, broad shouldered and had been a good oar when he was up at Cambridge.'[19] The farewell dinner given by Charles Stevens would have meant a lot. Now at the age of forty-three, leaving Africa for the last time and on his way 'back to dear old Blighty', what kind of future did he envisage?

> Take me back to dear old Blighty!
> Put me on the train for London town!
> Take me over there,
> Drop me ANYWHERE,
> Liverpool, Leeds, or Birmingham, well, I don't care!
> I should love to see my best girl,
> Cuddling up again we soon should be[20]

But Claude was leaving his best girl behind. Would he ever see her again? And could there ever be another?

---

[1]   Published in *Buch der Lieder* in 1827. Set to music by Felix Mendelssohn (Opus 34-2, 1834). Franz Liszt arranged *On Wings of Song* for solo piano.

[2]   Emily 'Molly' Margaretten in *Audrey Richards A functionalist and devotee of Malinowski. Or something more?* (Yale University Press, 2001). See also Adam Kuper, *Among the Anthropologists: History and Context in Anthropology* (Continuum, 1998) See Ch. 7: 'Audrey Richards: A Career in Anthropology'

[3]   Audrey Richards, *Land, Labour and Diet in Northern Rhodesia*, 2nd reprint (OUP, 1961)

[4]   Adam Kuper, ibid.

[5]   J. Goldstone, 'Audrey I. Richards (1899-1984); Africanist and Humanist', in Shirley Ardener (ed.) *Persons and Powers of Women in Diverse Cultures: Essays in Commemoration of Audrey I. Richards, Phyllis Kaberry and Barbara Ward* (Berg, Oxford, 1992). Malinowski even writes in the preface of Richards' book, *Hunger and Work in a Savage Tribe*, 'I alone have to plead guilty to four books on the subject, two of which have the word sex on the title page' (1932).

[6]   Mkushi DNB, p 9: 'C.G. Stevens, Cadet, arrives on first appointment and J.P. Murray proceeded on transfer to Ndola.' Stevens' career in Northern Rhodesia included a

long period in Barotseland and he (together with M.G. Billing) were contributors to *The Judicial Process among the Barotse of Northern Rhodesia (Zambia)*, edited by Max Gluckman, Manchester University Press, 1967.

[7] The Lunsemfwa is a tributary of the Lukasashi and Luangwa rivers, part of the Zambezi River basin. A popular river for fishing, it contains large populations of tigerfish and bream.

[8] E. Knowles Jordan, 'Old Mkushi in 1912 (Part I), *NRJ*, Vol IV, No 5 (1961) pp 427-33.

[9] Christopher Marlowe, *The Tragicall History of the Life and Death of Doctor Faustus (Act 1, Scene 1)*. See also C. F. Tucker Brooke (ed.), *The Works of Christopher Marlowe*, Oxford University Press, 1910

[10] J. W. von Goethe, *Faust*. The first appearance of the work in print was *Faust, a Fragment*, published in 1790. Goethe completed a preliminary version of what is now known as Part One in 1806. Its publication in 1808 was followed by the revised 1828-29 edition, the last to be edited by Goethe himself.

[11] Mephistopheles is a familiar spirit of the Devil in late settings of the legend of Faust.

[12] L. H. Gann, *A History of Northern Rhodesia: Early Days to 1953* (Chatto & Windus, 1964) pp 251-3

[13] From Orlando Gibbons's madrigal *The Silver Swan*, first published in 1612.

[14] van der Hum is a tangerine-flavoured liqueur produced in the Cape winelands, from a blend of matured potstill brandy, wine distillate, tangerine peel, herbs and spices, with the extracts sweetened with cane sugar syrup.

[15] '78' records, manufactured until the late 1950s, were played at a speed of 78 revolutions per minute. The flat discs were made of a brittle material which used a shellac resin. Alfred Denis Cortot (1877-1962) was a Franco-Swiss pianist and conductor, one of the most renowned classical musicians of the 20th century, especially valued for his poetic insight into Romantic piano works.

[16] First verse of poem by Heinrich Heine, ibid.

[17] David B. Coplan, *In the Time of Cannibals* (University of Chicago Press, 1994).

[18] Incoming Passenger Lists to London: 13 June 1932, Departure: Durban, calling at East London, Algoa Bay Capetown, Madeira. Port of Arrival: Southampton. Passenger Claude Philip Oldfield, age 43. *Balmoral Castle*, Union Castle Mail Steamship Co.

[19] Correspondence in December 1986 with James Murray, when retired and living in Woking.

[20] *Take Me Back To Dear Old Blighty*, written by A.J. Mills, F. Godfrey and B. Scott in 1916. It has been suggested that *Blighty* derives from 'bilayati', a regional variant of the Urdu word 'vilayati', meaning foreign, British, English or European. Source: OED

CHAPTER 22

More than a Brief Encounter

I had loved the country, the great space and quiet of it,
its colours, the smell of the first rains on its parched
baked earth…

Harry Franklin, *The Flag-Wagger*

Claude arrived in the Port of London on 13th June 1932 on the *Balmoral Castle*, the vessel that twenty-one years earlier had borne him to Africa for the first time.[1] One would assume he made his way straight to Maida Vale, to his mother and brother Harold. His mother now eighty, and Harold managing on one leg, the door would be opened by the domestic servant Emily Taylor.[2] As he stepped into the house, all the memories of growing up within its walls would be intense. The spirit of his father, the stern classicist and self-taught connoisseur of art, tutor to future diplomats and statesmen, who had held such bright hopes for his youngest boy, could be felt in every room. The prodigal son was home, but there was no fatted calf, no father to embrace him and say 'well done'.

Claude's family must have been curious about his sudden early retirement. Friends and neighbours in sniffy Maida Vale may have probed Mrs. Oldfield for details as to how her son's career in 'darkest Africa' could have ended, apparently as a result of the world recession and the drastic fall in demand for copper. Perhaps now, over a quiet, homecoming tea with his mother and Harold, Claude might speak of the economic situation in Northern Rhodesia and how he had become an unfortunate victim of the administration's necessity to cut costs. He might have averred to being run-down and in need of a change, of wishing to return to his family, and to England; but he had had little say in the matter. Dorothy could hardly be mentioned – his lovingly-taken images of her, and the complex memories of their time together, locked forever in his heart, would have taken some explaining.

For a well-educated man with administrative experience, one might think London would have offered ample career opportunities. But the recession was deepening and Claude, a tight-lipped fellow with a classics degree, based overseas for over twenty years, could be thought to be inappropriately qualified.[3] There could well be questions as to why he had left the service on 'early retirement', even if the impact of the recession was also beginning to bite in London. This was not yet the age of portfolio careers, of retraining and 'finding oneself'. A man took a job for life – a hiatus aroused suspicion. London did have a number of 'sunrise industries' opening up to the west of London – electrical equipment manufacture, food and consumer goods. Realistically, can one imagine Claude as a works manager, or payroll clerk in the new Gillette or Hoover factory, or at the Ford site at Dagenham. His mother and Harold would have been relying on whatever pension and savings his father may have provided; and although Charlie had a good salary at Harrod's Insurance, he had his own wife and daughter to support.

One would have expected Claude to have eventually settled down into an administrative role – which we know happened at the end of the Second World War – but during the years immediately after his return from Africa, it seems more likely that he lived off his colonial service pension (which was payable on leaving Africa). Being for this period 'early retired', gave

In the Harrow Road,[4]*'Sunny Snaps',*
1935.

From 1936, the Jubilee Year,
Claude, wearing his college tie, with
his Mother

him the benefit of being able to spend time with his mother and brother, Harold – and, of course, to entertain the possibility of meeting someone attractive of the opposite sex.

Claude would observe how London had changed since his youth. The city still exuded a rich atmosphere, physical and figurative, with thousands of coal fires still blackening buildings and thickening the air. The West End had its gloomy back streets and forbidding alleys, but on the main thoroughfares the old gas lamps had been replaced with electric lights. Alongside the trams rattling down Harrow Road, cars and lorries had begun to outnumber horse-drawn traffic, reducing the amount of ordure in the road. In middle class households, telephones were becoming a standard feature for arranging appointments, cabs, workmen, doctors or groceries or simply to gossip.

Claude might have used the telephone to catch up with friends from his *almae matres*, St. Paul's School, and Trinity Hall. He had received automatic enrolment into the Trinity Hall Association, founded in 1904 to keep former students in touch. The more exclusive Aula Club, which only admitted some fifteen new members a year, held a dinner in London during Boat Race week.[5] Claude would certainly have joined The Black & Whites Society, open to Boat Club members who had rowed four or more terms, who were in 1935 able to celebrate winning the Ladies' Plate at Henley.[6]

At his old school, sport had remained important, with improved grounds for rugby and cricket at Ealing, and a new boathouse built in 1929. Claude would also have been impressed by the achievements of some of his contemporaries at St. Paul's.[7] Paul Nash, famous for depicting the horrors of the First World War, had become a pioneer of modernism in Britain, encouraging abstract and surrealist painting in the 1930s and providing the illustrations for *Dorset*, the first of the *avant garde* Shell County Guides, edited by John Betjeman.[8] Percy Fender, two years Claude's junior, became one of the most celebrated cricketers of his day, playing thirteen Tests and captaining Surrey between 1921 and 1931.[9]

Claude could boast no outstanding achievements, but Dorothy and his breakdown at Ndola notwithstanding, he had served his time in Northern Rhodesia dutifully and honourably, and left a good impression on colleagues. Now in calmer waters, there were simple, long-forgotten pleasures to savour, not least with his family. Charlie, Maisie and their daughter, Joy, lived a short walk from the salubrious open spaces of Golders Hill Park and Hampstead Heath, and a stone's throw from the

Golders Green Hippodrome, with its varied programme of plays and musicals, many performed ahead of a West End opening.

For male companionship at home, Claude now had his brother Harold, with whom he shared a background in the classics passed on from their father. Harold, with a keen appreciation of verse, had collaborated on a volume of poems, and Claude would find a renewed admiration for him, his good heartedness and bonhomie in living with disability, an inspiration among his friends. Adapting to his false leg, following the amputation, had dampened none of Harold's enthusiasm for community affairs, notably in his role as a leading light in the Paddington Liberal Association. In the general election of May 1929 he had been agent to the Liberal candidate Reginald Myer, for the constituency of Paddington North. His party came a poor third, the Conservative/Unionist Brendan Bracken taking the seat by a small majority over Labour.[10] The national result was a hung parliament, with David Lloyd George's Liberals holding the balance of power in Ramsay MacDonald's new Labour government. Known as the 'Flapper Election', this was the first time that women, over the age of twenty-one, could vote.

Harold's endeavours for the Liberals were undertaken in tandem with his neighbour, Mr. Cohen. Oldfield and Cohen gained a reputation as an odd couple, provoking 'quiet amusement to many, becoming known as 'the long and short of it', Cohen being very tall and Oldfield, through his disability, the reverse.'[11] Family connections might have helped bring them and the Liberal candidate Reginald Myer together, Myer having married the Hon. Elsie Montagu, daughter of Sir Samuel Montagu (later Lord Swaythling), to whom Thomas Oldfield had taught classics, while Myer's mother was Ellen Cohen.

The Paddington Liberals would doubtless have welcomed Claude with open arms, but as far as we know he was never over enthused by party politics. His spare time was about to be fully, and far more intensely, occupied. Exactly when he met Elveda is uncertain, although Claude's album includes a formal portrait captioned 'Elveda 1932', taken by society photographers Mindel & Faraday of Oxford Street. It is possible that Elveda commissioned the picture herself, perhaps to help in finding modelling or theatrical work. My mother believed that they had met at a West End cinema where Elveda worked as an usherette, after which they had tea together at the Lyons' Corner House near Trafalgar Square. By all accounts, despite an age gap of more than twenty years, it was love at first sight.

'Elveda 1932'

Elveda Law was born on 21st March 1911 in Lower Street, Stansted Mountfitchet, three miles north of Bishop's Stortford, the second child of Walter and Lucy Law, née Bush. Her father was a general labourer, later a truck driver in the timber trade, moving to Norfolk. Walter and Lucy would still be there in the 1950s, working the level crossing barriers from the tied accommodation of the gatekeeper's house on the main railway line to Norwich, close to Roudham Hall. Elveda had left school at fourteen, taking up domestic service at a substantial medieval house known as Ongar Park Hall, some twelve miles south of Stansted. Having been part of a manor around the late thirteenth century, in the early 1900s the property had been purchased by James Kerr, a Scottish dairy farmer, who had moved south 'lock, stock and barrel' to supply fresh milk to the expanding urban population of London. The Marconi Wireless Company, who needed suitable land on which to erect radio masts, then acquired the farm, but granted Kerr a tenancy to continue farming.[12] James Kerr died in 1933, with the tenancy passing to his son Thomas. Jim and Sandra Kerr, the next generation of the family, continue farming there today.[13]

At seventeen, Elveda fell pregnant. As her due date approached, to avoid public disgrace she travelled to Marie Vickers House, a mother and baby home in Finsbury Road, Brighton, where Clifford Walter Law was born on 16th April 1929, just three weeks after his mother turned eighteen. Elveda registered the birth herself one month later.[14] The father was not named on the birth certificate, which has later been appended with the word: 'Adopted'. Use of the term 'illegitimate child' has become almost non-existent today, removed from passports and legal documents

'My darling Clifford' (photograph belonging to Elveda: Clifford, probably with his adoptive mother)

as needlessly insulting to the child, but attitudes in the 1930s were hugely different.[15] Clifford having been adopted, the vexed question of paternity was probably not raised. The Latin dictum *Mater semper certa est* (the mother is always certain) would apply, and biological provenance was unlikely to be pursued unless the issue of inheritance or citizenship was at stake. Elveda might have been fortunate not to have been forced into a shotgun wedding, but the trauma of having to give birth isolated from her family and then surrender her child, while everyone pretended it had never happened, would remain, inevitably affecting the rest of her life. All we know, at the time of writing, is that Clifford is still alive in his late eighties, but does not wish to be in contact with long-lost cousins.

Shortly after this wretched and distressing time, Elveda had moved to 10 Calthorpe Street, just west of Clerkenwell, with Liverpool Street Station a bus ride away, convenient for catching the train home to Stansted or meeting up with friends in Ongar. On 24th May 1930, a new chapter of her life began, when at the St. Pancras Registry Office, she married Joseph Baiden Jackson. Now nineteen, she gave her age as twenty-two. Joseph, whose father was a 'Transport Manager', stated his age as twenty-five, and was a law student, living at the same address as Elveda. Walter Law, Elveda's father, is recorded as an 'Engineer.'

It seems unlikely that Joseph was the father of Elveda's child, who was thirteen months old and growing up with his adoptive parents. The marriage however was not destined to last, and even if they had not already drifted apart, for Elveda, meeting Claude would have been a turning

10 Calthorpe Street in Clerkenwell

point. In addition to the age gap, there was a substantial difference in class and background. Elveda, though not unintelligent, had had a village upbringing, and gained no formal qualifications. Claude, from a sophisticated, middle-class background, had received the finest classical education at a top public school and gone up to Cambridge. Well spoken and well dressed, an older man with a patrician air, solvent and unattached, one could see the attraction for Elveda; but what did Claude see in her? The 1932 photograph shows a stunning young woman, beautifully attired with a ready smile. What man wouldn't fall for her in an usherette's uniform?

Claude could probably have done so and left it at that. But these ships would not just pass in the night. For one thing, Claude, who liked to play the man about town on occasion, would have been proud to have a good-looking woman on his arm. 'Peter', as he puzzlingly called his young amour, looked good on a horse too. Photographs show her riding out on Hyde Park's Rotten Row, following the custom of William III, who had adopted the route as a safer transit from Kensington Palace to St. James's Palace, since when the Row had become the place for the *beau monde* to be seen.[16]

A trophy woman was all fine and dandy, but aside from sex and exhibitionism, what was there to sustain a relationship? One of Claude and Elveda's greatest pleasures was the cinema. A night out at the pictures had become *de rigeur*, particularly since the arrival of the 'talkies'. The intellectual level of the films was not always high, but Claude, like everyone else, enjoyed the cinema for escapism, enchantment and magic. *Sanders of the River* released in 1935, telling the story of DC Lord Sandi's struggle to make peace between rival tribes, while battling slave-traders, would have transported Claude back to his days in Africa and perhaps made him ponder whether he had done the right thing in coming home.[17]

'Peter' riding in Hyde Park, near Marble Arch

Harry Franklin had regretted his decision: 'I should never have left Northern Rhodesia ... I had loved the country, the great space and quiet of it, its colours, the smell of the first rains on its parched baked earth ...'[18] Did Claude also wish he had stayed on now? Ensconced in the 'one and nines', as Elveda slipped her hand tenderly into his, he knew the answer.[19]

In good health, gainfully employed, and with a beautiful young consort who clearly adored him, Claude could count his blessings. His brother Harold had fewer. Back in 1910 at the age of twenty-four, his medical condition had been assessed by the eminent physician, Sir John Broadbent, who had diagnosed syringomyelia, a 'curvature of the spine from birth', causing loss of feeling and an inability to feel pain (anelyesia).[20] Sir John had also noted 'atrophy of the extremities' with trophic lesions on the hands and a trophic ulcer on one foot, probably due to a loss of any sensation of pain. His lungs and heart were however good.[21]

It was now ten years since Harold's left leg had been amputated, and in the latter half of 1936 he became increasingly unwell. That Christmas was to be his last and in February 1937, aged fifty-one, he died in St. Mary's Hospital, Paddington.[22] The cause of death was complex; haemorrhaging from duodenal and gastric ulcers, compounded by the painful, debilitating syringomyelia, in which a cyst or cavity forms within the spinal cord.[23] The obituary in *The Indicator* paid tribute to Harold's stoicism:

A Liberal Worthy of Paddington... Mr. Oldfield was crippled from childhood. His life was despaired of on many occasions and it can be said of him that, 'he lived miraculously'. He bore most cheerfully and good temperedly, sufferings which would have broken the spirit of many strong men ... in death, as in life, people will think kindly of Harold Oldfield and they will miss the sound of his footsteps along the pavement, and his cheery laugh and greeting.[24]

Harold with his dog 'Spot' (some years earlier, Harold had entered a newspaper competition for the best photograph of 'Me and My Dog')

Claude stayed on in Maida Vale, while Elveda remained in lodgings. If they were to marry, they might conceivably live together in Oakington Road, with Claude's mother – one small happy family. Claude was reserved and correct, Elveda spontaneous and effusive, but they complemented one another. Her past was chequered, but then so was his. In 1936, the King, having fallen in love with an American divorcée and commoner, became the first English monarch since 1399 to abdicate the throne. For an anonymous, greying ex-varsity man to wed a pretty young cinema usherette, seemed, by comparison, hardly scandalous. There was only one problem: Claude's mother, and his brother Charlie, felt rather differently.

Perhaps Claude's family felt there must be lots of other charming, unattached young women around for Claude to meet – agreeable, well-brought up girls who never had to work as cinema usherettes, or at anything else. By now though, such girls were waiting in line for the next generation of colonial officers. Twenty-eight year old colonial officer Gervas Clay, on his way back from Northern Rhodesia on leave, had met eighteen-year old Betty on the voyage from Cape Town. Betty and her family were returning from a sightseeing tour of Africa, and Gervas's parents were also on board. In September 1936, the couple married in England, and a month later were heading back to the colony together. Betty's letters home chart the discomfort, and euphoria of her journey: 'All day we travelled through Bechuanaland, with flat scrub land and reddish sand on every side, and when we stopped … the heat was awful, as there was no breeze … the sunset was marvellous … the afterglow broken by continuous stabs of lightning, which is a good sign, as it means the rains are coming…'[25]

At Livingstone, the newlyweds rested for a few days. For Betty, the perilous, sublime presence of the Falls seems to offer a kind of reassurance about her life from this point on:

> We went along to the Devil's Cataract … G and I walked all along the edge … right along to Danger Point and stood up on the huge boulder at the corner, from which you see water on three sides, sheer down on all sides. I had to hang on to G very hard because he's the breed that want to jump over when they look over edges, but luckily he had a very good reason for not wanting to jump over!

When Claude had retreated from the brink at Ndola, he was already going in the opposite direction, his return journey marked, and with no one to steady him. But as he had proved in his relationship with Elveda, there was life in the old dog yet. Might his mother and big brother Charlie not cast convention aside and feel happy for him?

---

[1] The Union-Castle Line operated a fleet of passenger liners and cargo ships between Europe and Africa from 1900 to 1977. Known for the lavender-hulled liners with red funnels topped in black, running on a rigid timetable between Southampton and Cape Town. The *Balmoral Castle*, 13,361 tons, built in 1910, was scrapped in 1939.

[2] 1934 Electoral Roll – 37 Oakington Road

4263	Rw	Ow	Oldfield, Mary Anna
4264	R	–	Oldfield, Claude Philip
4265	R	–	Oldfield, Harold Leslie Francis
4266	Rw	Ow	Taylor, Emily Louisa

Rw: Residence qualification (women) / Ow: Occupation qualification (women)

[3] In 1932, over 20% of the workforce was unemployed; in areas reliant on heavy industry, up to 30%. Total unemployment reached nearly three million, soup kitchens becoming a way of life. The largest National Hunger March started from different parts of the country in September, coming together in London on 27 October 1932, where it was met by 70,000 police, including mounted police using force to disperse the demonstrators.

[4] The Harrow Road is an ancient route from Paddington running north west towards

Harrow. With minor deviations, the route remains otherwise unaltered.

[5] The Aula Club, founded in 1892, was the inspiration of John Fearon and Harold Tingey, as a dining club for old Hall men. (Aula: 'a large place where people can congregate')

[6] The Ladies' Challenge Plate is an event for 'eights' below the standard of the Grand Challenge Cup, first held in 1845, initially as the New Challenge Cup. See also Peter Pagnamenta (ed.), *The Hidden Hall: Portrait of a Cambridge College*, Third Millennium Publishing, 2004 (p 176) and the THBC website.

[7] A. H. Mead, *A Miraculous Draught of Fishes: A History of St Paul's School* (James and James, 1990) p 103

[8] Woolley and Wallis, Auctioneers (On the sale of *Corfe Castle* by Paul Nash)

[9] From 'Cricketer of The Year' in Sydney H. Pardon (Ed.), *John Wisden's Cricketers' Almanack for 1915* (John Wisden, 1915) and Richard Streeton, *P. G. H. Fender: A Biography* (Faber & Faber, 1981)

[10] Brendan Bracken, 1st Viscount Bracken, PC (1901-58), Irish-born businessman, who served as a minister in the Conservative cabinet. Remembered for opposing the Bank of England's co-operation with Hitler and for subsequently supporting Churchill's prosecution of WWII. Founder of the modern version of the *Financial Times*. In the 1929 General Election, the result for Paddington North: Conservative, Brendan Bracken 13,876 votes, 40.9%; Labour, John Gordon 13,348 votes, 39.3%; Liberal, Reginald Myer 6,723 votes, 19.8%. Majority of 528, 1.6%. Turnout 33,947 votes, 69.0%.

[11] Obituary of Mr. H.L.F. Oldfield, *The Indicator*

[12] Harold M. Scott, *Stanford Rivers*, 1974 (Recently rebound by John Glover of Toothill)

[13] James Kerr had been inspired by Primrose McConnell, also a Scottish dairy farmer, who had seen opportunities in Essex. Having moved south, he advised on good agricultural practices and rotations, publishing (jointly with R. J. Halley) an *Agricultural Notebook* in 1883.

[14] Clifford Walter Law: born 16 April 1929, just three weeks after his mother's 18th birthday. Mother: Elveeda Victoria Law, General Servant, of Ongar Park, Wood Toat Hill, Ongar, Essex. At: 11 Finsbury Road, Brighton. Registered: 17 May 1929. Registrar: C. J. Webb. Note: 'Adopted', Horace Burfield, Superintendent Registrar. Source: Birth Certificate

[15] 'Love child' and 'natural child' would be a little more acceptable.

[16] The track was originally known as *Route du Roi* (the King's Road), which was eventually corrupted into 'Rotten Row'. Source: Hyde Park: History and Architecture, *The Royal Parks* website. See also Kathryn Kane, 'The Regency Redingote: Historical Snippets of Regency England: "Rotten Row was Rotten – Kinda" ' at WordPress.com, August 2009

[17] A 1935 British film directed by the Hungarian-British director, Zoltan Korda, based on the stories of Edgar Wallace, published in 1911.

[18] Harry Franklin, *The Flag-Wagger* (Shepheard-Walwyn, 1974) p 103

[19] One shilling and nine pence (1/9). Equivalent to 35 pence in decimal currency.

[20] John Francis Harpin (Sir) Broadbent (1865-1946) MA, DM Oxon., MRCS, FRCP (1904). The elder son of Sir William Broadbent, FRS, FRCP, physician to three

generations of the Royal family and to St. Mary's Hospital, and his wife Eliza, daughter of John Harpin of Holmforth, Yorks.

[21] Hand-written report by Sir John Broadbent: 'Man aged 24'.

[22] Death Certificate: 14 February 1937, St. Mary's Hospital. Harold Leslie Francis Oldfield. Male, 51 years. Of 37 Oakington Road, Paddington, of no occupation. Cause of death: I. (a) Haemorrhage (b) Duodenal and gastric ulceration II. Seringo-myelia. PM. Certified by Aubrey Smith, MRCS. Informant: C. P. Oldfield, Brother, 37 Oakington Road.

[23] Syringomyelia refers to a disorder in which a cyst or cavity forms within the spinal cord. This cyst, called a syrinx, can expand and elongate over time, destroying the spinal cord. The damage may result in pain, paralysis, weakness, and stiffness in the back, shoulders, and extremities.

[24] *The Indicator* was a prestigious local paper covering Paddington, Kilburn, Marylebone, Shepherd's Bush and a large segment of West London.

[25] Writing on Sunday, 18 October 1936 from c/o Mrs. Cartmel-Robinson, PC's House, Livingstone, NR. 'Letters from Betty from Northern Rhodesia (1936-64)' from 'A tribute to Betty St. Clair Clay (née Baden-Powell), 16 April 1917-24 April 2004'. At www.spanglefish.com/LettersFromBetty/

CHAPTER 23

Seven Kingdoms

Off with yon cloud, old Snafell! that thine eye
Over three Realms may take its widest range
William Wordsworth, *Itinerary Poems of 1833*, No. XXI, Tynwald Hill

Mary Anna Oldfield had come a long way from her humble Devonshire upbringing. Settled for most of her adult life in a fashionable part of London, with a housemaid to answer the door and deal with tradesmen, the Dickensian trajectory of her life paralleled that of her late husband, raising a family amid an atmosphere of classical learning, poetry, liberal politics and metropolitan gentility. Although Mary Anna had no noticeable accent, or the stereotypical demeanour of being 'strong in the arm and thick in the head' she had few airs, and light-heartedly described herself as a 'Devonshire Dumpling'.[1] An uncomplaining mother and grandmother, she had suffered the loss of her only daughter barely out of infancy, and

Claude with his mother, Mary Anna - and with his niece, Joy - in the garden at Golders Green

her first-born Robert had left for Australia as a young man, and there predeceased her. More recently dear Harold, crippled from birth, her only companion in the home after her husband's passing, had also died young.

Longfellow's thoughts in *The Rainy Day* may be pertinent, as surely 'the sun still shining behind the clouds' had been her youngest, Claude.[2] Returned sooner than expected from Africa, his pronouncement that he was back for good must have seemed like music to her ears; two of her boys, filling the house with conversation and laughter made it feel like a family home again. When Harold had been cruelly taken, apart from Charlie's regular visits, it was Claude who had kept her company and looked after things. Then this woman, Elveda, had come into his life. Mary Anna could hardly complain about her middle-aged son having a lady friend, especially after all that time out in Africa. Perhaps he might even get married at long last. But this girl was young enough to be his daughter – and she was a cinema usherette. Mary was no snob, but her son had been to Cambridge, mixed with the cream of society, spoke Latin and been a District Commissioner in the Colonial Service. It was all rather upsetting. Why couldn't he find himself someone more suitable? Charlie agreed with her; Claude was making a bit of a fool of himself, and this floozy was probably leading him up the garden path.

Was it Mary Anna's own origins that made her uncomfortable about Elveda? Even if she knew nothing of her adopted baby or the subsequent ill-fated marriage, perhaps she had some intuition. And if her attitudes were conventional, she would regard philandering with common young girls as a weakness, or the prerogative of certain upper-class men, or that of the vulgar lower orders. It did not do for respectable people to emulate them, and when Claude moved in with Elveda at No. 5 Westbourne Terrace, that he had flouted this unwritten rule became undeniable.

Blood being thicker than water, there was no question of Claude and his mother becoming estranged. The slight remove of Westbourne Terrace from Oakington Road was perhaps Claude's attempt to spare her feelings, although he probably knew she would not in any case have tolerated a cohabiting couple under her roof. A marriage certificate would not necessarily have made much difference. Seemingly it was Elveda's age and background that made the relationship out of place in Mrs Oldfield's eyes. Damned either way, why did Claude not go ahead and marry anyway?

On 12th May 1937 in Westminster Abbey, George VI and Elizabeth became King and Queen of the United Kingdom and the Dominions of the British Commonwealth. British subjects living in the Dominions took great interest in such a major event back home and some, like Betty Clay in Northern Rhodesia, wishing they could be amongst the exciting throng as the six-mile-long procession made its way back through the streets of London to Buckingham Palace:

> Oh you lucky people … having such good seats right opposite the Abbey … we read all about it in the papers, which isn't half such fun … Lassie had a letter from a girl who had a seat between Hyde Park and the Marble Arch, and she read it out to us and I read out yours and we are all very excited.[3]

The colony's postmasters must have been equally pleased: 'Total stamp sales during the year amounted to £34,700, £8,000 of which came from the sale of the first issue of King George VI stamps to dealers and stamp collectors.'[4]

Within a month on 3rd June, Edward, the royal brother who had previously worn the crown wed his American fiancée, Wallis Simpson, at a friend's chateau in France, the date coinciding with what would have been his father George V's 72nd birthday. Far away in Claude's old stamping ground, news of the wedding passed without any known official comment, the emphasis being laid instead respectfully on the memory of the former king: 'The seat of government was transferred from Livingstone to Lusaka in 1935, the official inauguration of the new capital being arranged to coincide with the ceremonial celebration of His late Majesty's birthday on the 3rd June.' The same report recorded an apparent concession to the colony's indigenous inhabitants: '… an amending Order in Council, which made provision for a nominated unofficial member to represent native interests …'[5]

Betty Clay, in Johannesburg for the birth of her first child thought the timing of Edward and Wallis's wedding ill-judged: 'I do think it was piggy of them to go and choose that day of all days in the year, wouldn't George have hated it if he had known, and I think they might at least have kept that one day sacred to him'.[6] Edward was a couple of years younger than Wallis, while Claude was some twenty years Elveda's senior. Could the age gap, and the perceived disparity of class, still be causing Claude's mother and his older brother to withhold their approval of the relationship? All we know is that they had still not married.

While the coronation stabilised the nation after the drama of the abdication crisis, on the continent of Europe, the scene was one of actual and growing violence. With greater accessibility to radio broadcasts and a new airmail service, Claude's successors in Northern Rhodesia were more quickly aware of developments back home:

> We listened to the news … heard a bit more about Spain, and those fools on the Deutschland throwing bombs about in the most careless manner, and it seemed very sinister and as if everybody was getting even more war-minded than ever, and we are wondering how long will be able to keep out of it … Is the League of Nations dead, or merely a sleep, (*sic*) or just blind? Has the nonintervention packed (*sic*) being torn up, or merely lost? Surely nobody can really want war, it makes me so CROSS excavation (*sic*) mark.[7]

These were strange, unpredictable times, with the airship *Hindenburg* bursting into flames whilst docking in New Jersey, and the loss of the American pilot Amelia Earhart and her navigator while attempting a round the world flight.

Two years later on 6th May 1939, Claude celebrated his fiftieth birthday. It was seven years since he had left Africa and the Colonial Service, and one can imagine a degree of wistfulness, not just for Dorothy. He would have heard that mining at Ndola had picked up, and that a forty-five mile bituminous road was being constructed to connect Ndola to Luanshya and Nkana. After the experience of his breakdown there, he would hardly have wished himself back among such a madding crowd. It may be a telling detail that in 1938 the colony had appointed an additional judge, who would be stationed at Ndola. The recent establishment of a number of air routes, including from Livingstone and Broken Hill to Ndola would have interested Claude, as well as the introduction of an Imperial Airways flying boat service between Durban and Southampton, and weekly flights by South African Airways from Johannesburg via Lusaka to Kisumu.

Claude's feet though were firmly on the ground, and by this time he may have expected never to go up in an aircraft. Meanwhile fifty was as good an age as any to marry and settle down. Was it then a tragic irony that on 21st June, only a few weeks after his birthday, while Claude was with his mother at Oakington Road she suffered a sudden heart attack and died?[8] On Wednesday 9th August, just seven weeks later, Claude and Elveda were joined in matrimony at the Paddington Registry Office, she now twenty-eight, twenty-two years his junior. The photographs record an unpretentious affair with a few friends, the formalities followed by drinks at a local hostelry. There is no sign of Charlie's presence, but he may have stayed away out of respect for his mother's views, given the degree

Claude and Elveda with friends after their wedding

of haste displayed by Claude. On the register Claude's profession is given as 'District Commissioner (Colonial Office) (Retired)'.[9] Elveda described herself as a 'Spinster', which following her marriage to Joseph Jackson in 1930, she most certainly was not.

The passing of Claude's mother had spared them both the awkwardness and pain of either her outright condemnation, or her feeling unable to confer a sincere blessing upon his marriage. The newlyweds' plans, which they must have been fomenting for some time, were to leave London. Their reason for choosing the Isle of Man was not entirely clear. Popular with holidaymakers from nearby Lancashire, the island attracted far fewer southerners. The simplest explanation is that having visited earlier in the flush of romance, it had become 'their' place. The Isle of Man, reached by ferry from Liverpool or Heysham, also felt like a kind of abroad; it was a Crown dependency, with its own government. The very low tax rates might have appealed to Claude on his limited pension, and cheap cigarettes could be smuggled back to the mainland for family and friends. Celebrated by the romantic for its 'View of Seven Kingdoms' from the summit of Snaefell – England, Ireland, Scotland, Wales, Man, Neptune and the Heavens – there was on the island a sense familiar for Claude of existing at a slight remove from the mainstream, outside of borders, connected yet detached.[10]

There was also an intriguing link with Dorothy, which may not be a coincidence. Sir Sampson Sladen, who had taken Dorothy and her widowed mother Ellen under his domestic wing, and attended Dorothy's wedding in 1922, had retired from being Commissioner for London

Transport to live in Castletown on the southern coast of the Isle of Man. Involved in a number of good causes, Sir Sampson was seen regularly among the congregation at St. Mary's Church, Castletown. He had developed an enthusiasm for motor racing, and also become a Director of British Airships, which was looking to set up flights between London, Blackpool and the Isle of Man, utilising the Avro Avian aircraft.[11] In 1934 he had travelled to Australia, arriving in Sydney on the SS *Oronsay*, *The Sydney Morning Herald* reporting on the visit and:

> his romantic career since he joined the Royal Navy more than 50 years ago … Sir Sampson Sladen said that motor racing was the national sport of the Isle of Man. He had seen Australians in the races, and was still hopeful that some day, one would win. Horse racing and greyhound racing were not allowed, as they interfered with more acceptable fixtures.[12]

Dorothy would doubtless have talked to Claude about Sladen's enjoyable retirement life on a rather pleasant island.

In July 1939, the annual TT (Tourist Trophy) Races took place, which for Claude, familiar with motorcycles from his days in the bush, would be an ideal time to reconnoitre the island with a view to living there with Elveda. At the time, not everyone appreciated the German government's obsession with national pride in sport, and how this 'will to power' would soon explode in the horrors of the blitzkrieg.[13] According to Roger Willis, the signs were all there in the TT of 1939:

> a disciplined force of Nazi NSKK paramilitary storm troopers and regular Wehrmacht soldiers invaded the Isle of Man to seek victory in the world's toughest motorcycle races.[14] Full-scale war against Germany was only three months away and the Third Reich's Führer, Adolf Hitler, was determined to teach Britain a sharp lesson in Aryan supremacy before the guns began to fire in earnest.[15]

Yet even as Autumn 1939 approached, many still expected the storm clouds over Europe to be just a nasty squall that would blow away. The previous September, Mr Chamberlain had flown back from Munich with Herr Hitler's written commitment that the German and British people would never go to war again. Peace for our time was, for Mr. and Mrs. Oldfield, a time for home making. Within weeks of their wedding in August 1939 they were unpacking the china in their first house together.

Our House 'Abercorn' at Laxey, Isle of Man, 1939

They were ecstatic, Elveda recording the occasion in her first photograph album, carefully inscribed with their new address: 'Abercorn, Ramsey Road, Laxey, Isle of Man, August 1939.' More prosaically in his album, Claude mounted a snap of the newly finished property, the builders only just departed, the garden yet to be established.

Laxey was a pleasant village on the east coast of the island, six miles north of the capital Douglas. After leaving the ferry, Claude and Elveda could take the electric tram for a scenic forty-five minute journey along the coast, followed by a short taxi ride up the hill to their house, with its glorious sea views and vista of Snaefell's moorland peak.[16] With an understanding of lead mining from his Derbyshire forebears, Claude was intrigued by the Great Laxey Mine, which had produced lead and zinc from 1780, up until its closure on economic grounds in 1929. After a four-mile ascent by tram from Laxey to Snaefell's summit, on a clear day Claude and Elveda could marvel at the spectacular views of the four kingdoms and, according to folklore, all this and Heaven too.[17]

After seven years in the accelerating modernity of London, reminiscent perhaps of what Claude had found so jarring about Ndola, the other-worldliness of the Isle of Man would feel a welcome relief. Ulendo, the long, unhurried walks he had undertaken in rural Northern Rhodesia, gave space for contemplation, at one with the natural world and the rhythms of one's footsteps. It was a ritual that could be followed in any open space, and within his diary on the Isle of Man might have been found the following entries:

A Good Ridge Walk: It was a glorious day, the day I'd been waiting for. Listened to the early Met forecast and decided that it was a good enough day to start out. Been waiting to do this trip and now that everything in the house seems under control, a good opportunity. Peter (Claude's pet name for Elveda) has already made the trip to the top of Snaefell on the electric tram with me – and enjoyed the views – so she was more than happy to tend the new plants in the garden and have a natter with the neighbours, while I could get some time to relax and reflect on our new life.

Took the tram up as far as 'The Bungalow' then walked briskly up the steep slope, scree-like near the top, to the tram station on the summit. A quick cuppa in the café seemed a good idea, before setting off. The sticky buns looked tasty, but with a thick-cut roast-lamb sandwich in my knapsack, avoided the temptation.

Had looked at the Survey map and talked to some locals, who suggested following the ridge route north. First though, followed the tram track, then down a steep grassy slope, very boggy in places, to the main road. (Was pleased I'd brought the old boots back from Rhodesia, came in handy). Crossed the road where the bikes had sped past in the TT only two months ago. After the pull up onto Clagh Ouyr, the walk started to feel good, up and down along the ridge, with North Barrule beckoning in the distance. Thought about Peter back at our new house and remembered that I'd ordered a coal delivery for the indoor bunker, hoped all would go ok.

Up the final slope, it seemed quite steep, but gosh, I am 50 now! Looking back, realized I was still lower than Snaefell. Scrambled around a bit, thought I'd reached the top, only to find it was another 300 yards to go. Arrived, what a day, just a light breeze. Enjoyed the cold roast lamb. Surveyed a beautiful scene, dropping off the hill towards pastoral land and across to Maughold Head in the east. A few dragonflies on the wing, the odd white butterfly floating by, the peace only disturbed by two bikers trying out their paces on the Ramsey road five miles away. Looked back down the coastline. Laxey village hidden by the hills, but could just see the top of the Wheel. Couldn't see our house, but knew it lay just in the fold of the hills. The first house that really seemed like mine. Hope this was the right move, it certainly feels so, and has made Peter happy, more so than I expected. Pity Mother couldn't have got to know her better, I'm sure they would have got on like a house of fire in time, but there you are. Likewise poor Harold; I feel that in true liberal fashion, he would have brought mother round, and Charlie too. I **was** surprised that Chas was so sceptical, both about Peter and the move to Laxey. Thought we'd be shunned as 'tax exiles'! Colonial Service pension is nothing like as good as his – and reduced because I was forced to retire early – but out here it should suffice, and Peter's not extravagant.

It took longer than I had anticipated, to walk back down. Could see a small farm and a couple of houses at the bottom. Reached there, crossed a small road, then down again, finally to Bellevue and the electric tram home. I was looking forward to tea and cake with Peter.

And what was 'Peter' looking forward to? With a new home in an idyllic setting, with a cultured, undemanding man, two collies and some domestic help, could a girl with no previous money or prospects be said to have landed lucky? Elveda though was still of child-bearing age, and after the brutal surrender of her baby, followed by one failed marriage, she might now long to be a proper mother. In Africa, Claude had spent time with Dorothy's children, Ann, and his own Audrey. How though would he feel about the patter of tiny feet under his own hallowed roof? Laxey could be the perfect place to raise a family.

If such thoughts were on either of their minds, within a few days of their move to the Isle of Man, came a turn of events that would plunge the whole nation's future into uncertainty. On 3rd September, Mr. Chamberlain made his momentous broadcast on the Home Service: Germany, having marched into Poland three days before had given no undertaking to withdraw: Britain was therefore at war. Chamberlain's piece of paper had been worthless. Claude would have been humble enough to admit being taken unawares:

What I hadn't seen was that Hitler was serious, I didn't imagine we'd get to this pitch … Wasn't ever keen on Chamberlain's 'appeasement' policy, seemed a bit of a long-shot, but then again we didn't want another blooming war! With the deadline for Chamberlain's ultimatum passed, and no word back from the Germans, there doesn't seem like any way back now, damn it. What does Laxey hold for us? Was it the right move, but just at the wrong time? What to do

Life on the Isle of Man

now? Might we have to pack it all in, just as we're getting settled?

On 11th September four British divisions left for France, and a month later German U-boats sank the battleship *Royal Oak* in Scapa Flow. The Isle of Man, in the middle of the Irish Sea, seemed suddenly less heavenly, and with Ireland declaring neutrality, effectively denying the Republic's ports to the British Navy, the Manx residents began feeling vulnerable. The hoteliers were instructed to close up and leave in short order, though not simply out of concern for their safety. Estimating that around 75,000 people of German origin were living in Britain, the government had set up enemy alien tribunals to screen those deemed a danger to national security. With Italy entering the war, this figure would almost double. From the first tribunal in February 1940, 569 individuals were judged to be a threat and, seeking a place of marginal military importance in which to inter them, officials decided on the Isle of Man.[18] By the year end, the Manx internee population numbered 14,000. Boarding houses became barrack blocks, with internees working on local farms, running their own newspapers, and even setting up small businesses. There was often a vibrant creative atmosphere, not surprising given some of the individuals, later to be luminous: Sir Nikolaus Pevsner, Lord Weidenfeld, Sir Charles Forte, and R.W. 'Tiny' Rowland. Relations were not always harmonious, with rows flaring up between Fascist internees and their Jewish neighbours, in one instance a riot forcing the intervention of the Home Office.[19]

The holiday island with which Claude and Elveda had fallen in love now a holding pen for thousands of so-called aliens, the railway service from Douglas was suspended and army lorries rattled along the narrow lanes. If an internee went missing, sirens would go off, while planes and military exercises regularly shattered the peace and quiet. Walkers were stopped by patrols or deafened by bursts of ordnance, and the unspoilt beaches were covered in barbed wire. With the shadow of war stalking them, it looked as if the dream of blissful retirement would have to be postponed.

---

[1] Derogatory term for local people, for example: 'I'm a Devonian born and bred, strong in the arm and thick in the head' or 'I'm never going to Tiverton again, it's full of dumb Devon Dumplings.' More affectionately, the Devon Dumplings Cricket Club was founded in 1902 and there are also a number of pubs and restaurants bearing the name.

[2] From 'The Rainy Day' by Henry Wadsworth Longfellow (1807-82):

Be still, sad heart! and cease repining; Behind the clouds is the sun still shining.

[3] 'Letters from Betty from Northern Rhodesia (1936-64)' from 'A tribute to Betty St. Clair Clay (née Baden-Powell), 16 April 1917-24 April 2004.' At www.spanglefish. com/LettersFromBetty

[4] *Annual Report on the Social and Economic Progress of the People of Rhodesia*, 1938

[5] *Annual Report*, 1938, ibid.

[6] Writing on Thursday, 3 June 1937 from 'Northside', 62 Valley Road, Parktown, Johannesburg. 'Letters from Betty', ibid.

[7] Writing on Monday, 31 May 1937, in the filthy Beastly Train, 'Letters from Betty', ibid.

[8] Death Certificate: Sub-district of Paddington West, in the Metropolitan Borough of Paddington. 21 June 1939. Mary Anna Oldfield, 87 years, widow of Thomas Smedley Oldfield, Tutor. Cause: a) chronic myocardial failure, b) auricular fibrillation. Certified by Dr. S. Crown, MRCS. C. P. Oldfield, son, present at the death. W. E. Robinson, Deputy Registrar

[9] Marriage Certificate. Witnesses: M. A. Chadwick and M. A. Good.

[10] The Isle of Man (*Ellan Vannin* in Manx), also known simply as Mann. Some substitute 'Earth' for 'Neptune'.

[11] Lieut. Com. Sir Sampson Sladen, KBE, RN, has joined the Board of British Airships Ltd., *Flight* magazine, 15 March 1928.

[12] *The Sydney Morning Herald*: Thursday 29 March 1934

[13] The will to power (*der Wille zur Macht*) was a prominent concept in the philosophy of Friedrich Nietzsche.

[14] NSKK (*Nationalsozialistisches Kraftfahrkorps*) were the National Socialist Motor Corps, a Nazi paramilitary organization.

[15] Roger Willis, *The Nazi TT: Hitler's 1939 Propaganda Victory on the Isle of Man* (Motobusiness, 2009)

[16] Messrs. Bruce and Saunderson were behind the construction of The Manx Electric Railway, opened in 1893 with a 3ft gauge. The line ran from Douglas to Laxey and was extended in 1899 to Ramsey. The railway is the longest narrow-gauge vintage railway in the British Isles.

[17] Snaefell (*Sniaull* in Manx) comes from the Norse word for Snow Mountain. James, 7th Earl of Derby wrote to his son, explaining that: 'When I go on the mount you call Baroull, and, but turning me round, can see England, Scotland, Ireland, and Wales, I think shame so fruitlessly to see so many kingdoms at once.' The comment made by Earl James has more usually been applied to the higher Snaefell and is the answer to the often-posed question: where can one see seven kingdoms at the same time? The seven Kingdoms being the four mentioned, plus the Kingdoms of Man, Earth (or Neptune) and Heaven. Source: *The Manx Society*, Vol 3, Ch. VII, 'Letter of James 7th Earl'.

[18] At the outbreak of WWII, the UK had become a refuge for those who had fled Nazi persecution, including Jews and political refugees. At first, the authorities interned these refugees with other enemy residents, without distinction. Later, when Italy also declared war, significant numbers of Italian residents were also interned. The Isle of Man, relatively isolated from the mainland and with a useful amount of holiday

accommodation, was used to provide housing for the 'Alien Civilians' (as it had in WWI).

19 Connery Chappell, *Island of Barbed Wire: The Remarkable Story of World War Two Internment on the Isle of Man* (Robert Hale, 2005)

CHAPTER 24

The Balloon Goes Up

Our London Pride has been handed down to us,
London Pride is a flower that's free,
London Pride means our own dear town to us,
And our pride it forever will be

'London Pride', by Noel Coward, 1941[1]

To find themselves suddenly at war had come as a shock to the British. But what did it mean? For the civilian population, the mood following the Prime Minister's announcement was largely one of uncertainty, reading government pamphlets during the listless months of the 'phoney war'. However, as the Germany military machine showed no sign of stopping, let alone retreating, anxiety began to mount, along with calls for tough leadership. King George took notice: Chamberlain the peacemaker, reluctantly gave way so that a new National government could be formed – and in May 1940 came Churchill, seeking not peace but victory.

On 10th May 1940, the Germans extended their *Blitzkrieg* with a massive assault on Holland, Belgium, Luxembourg, and France, whose armies were being supported by the British Expeditionary Force. The scale and ferocity of the German advance pushed the British and French back to the French coast, till by the beginning of June they were pinned down on the beaches. As word spread along the south coast of England, a people's armada of ferries, pleasure boats and fishing smacks set sail to join the Royal Navy in a perilous rescue attempt. In choppy seas, frequently under fire, it seemed an impossible task. When 338,000 men had been brought to safety, Churchill praised the mission as 'a miracle of deliverance,' uttering in the same speech on 4th June, his immortal lines: 'We shall fight on the beaches …'

On 14th June, Hitler's army marched triumphantly into Paris, prompting the French three days later to request an armistice. From across the Channel, it looked as if Churchill's call to civilian arms might soon be put to the test, and on 18th June he stressed the immediacy of the threat: 'Let us therefore brace ourselves to our duties, and so bear ourselves that if the British Empire and its Commonwealth last for a thousand years, men will still say, "This was their finest hour".'

The reference to Empire was not lost on Claude; twenty years earlier he had defended British interests in Africa, now his homeland was in danger. July brought news of a German landing in the Channel Islands. Claude and Elveda, following official advice, decided with heavy hearts to abandon their home on the Isle of Man and return to London. The danger from aerial attacks was greater in London, but at least they would be in familiar surroundings, and not feel alone in the event of a direct invasion. Claude also felt a patriotic desire to be 'where it was at' and do something for the war effort.

That summer in the skies above the Home Counties, the RAF took on the Luftwaffe. For those too young to fight it was an unforgettable experience. Schoolboy John Osborne, later the celebrated playwright, would recall the scene from a sunlit garden in Bognor: 'we were charmed, privileged spectators at the most thrilling spectacular we could ever have imagined ... day after sunny day ... the Battle of Britain exhausted everything, especially our appetite for tea ... we knew our Dorniers from our Heinkels ... and in the evenings ... we listened to the day's tally and moved our pins in the map of southern England.'[2]

The long, aerobatic dance of death ended in the late summer of 1940, 'with the shock of its beginning ... we looked up and saw only the unwarlike flab of barrage balloons.'[3] The British Balloon Command was formed in 1938, as a precaution against the kind of devastating dive-bombing perpetrated by the Germans against the Spanish town of Guernica the year before. Deployed on steel cables over towns and cities, the hydrogen-filled balloons, which if fired on would explode, destroying the attacking plane, restricted the enemy to higher airspace. There were already almost 1,500 barrage balloons, or 'blimps', each the size of three cricket pitches, tethered above the British mainland, about a third of them over London. Claude and Elveda would have felt the full force of the prolonged assaults from high altitude bombers, beginning on 7th September 1940 that would become known as the Blitz. The raids varied in intensity, and took in other cities, but it was to London that the Luftwaffe returned time and again. On the night of 10th May 1941, 515 aircraft dropped over 900 tons of bombs on the city, leaving 1,364 dead and over 1,600 seriously injured.[4]

Recruits, Cosford, November 1941 (W/Cmdr. E.J.
Bradbury, front row, middle; Claude behind)

The raid of 10th May destroyed the House of Commons chamber, a symbolic blow that both shocked and awakened the public. By October 1941, Claude had enlisted in the Royal Air Force Volunteer Reserve, posted to Cosford in Shropshire.[5] At the start of the war, the Air Ministry had used the RAFVR as the principal conduit for RAF recruitment, and by the end of 1941 the unit had produced more than half of Bomber Command's aircrew.[6]

The following year, Claude was sent on a Staff Officer training course at the School of Administration in Stannington, Northumberland. From this intensive programme, newly commissioned officers were expected to assimilate the full range of duties required of them in their future service.[7]

Anxious to do well, on 23rd October he wrote to Elveda:

> We had that exam yesterday afternoon and it was not quite so bad
> as I had expected. I made some mistakes of course, but got quite a
> bit right. They put you in three classes for the results, A, B, C, and I
> think my class was B. I am quite satisfied with that, as I am a bit old
> to go to school & take exams. It seems rather wild outside with high
> wind. It is about 10 to seven, so I expect you and Jean are having tea.[8]

Stannington lay close to the RAF training base at Tranwell (Morpeth),
where on 16th November 1942, a Blackburn Botha took off on the
incorrect runway and collided with another Botha, killing one man and
injuring another.[9] Claude, at last 'doing his bit', was also pleased to learn
that out in Gwelo in Southern Rhodesia, his younger cousin John Hugh-
Jones was also training with the RAF. Chosen for its political stability
and good climate, suitable for flying most of the year, Gwelo, at 4,000ft
above sea level, was also thought to be free of mosquitoes. RAF Moffat,
established there in August 1941, would over the next four years equip
men with specialised skills and know-how 'to swell the overwhelming
force which played such a magnificent and decisive part in the utter defeat
of Germany'.[10]

After his initial training Claude became a Flying Officer with No. 4
Mechanised Transport Corps, based at St. John's Wood, close to Maida
Vale.[11] His principal responsibility was organising women drivers, mostly

Claude, Stannington, October 1942 (Claude, middle row, 4th from right)

John Hugh-Jones, Salisbury, 1942 (in middle) / Gwelo, 1942 (1st left, back row)

part-time volunteers, who after an intensive three weeks of training were posted to a unit or company and assigned to various government departments and agencies.[12] Others took over staff cars for foreign dignitaries whose drivers were unaccustomed to British roads, or drove ambulances during the air raids.[13]

The period from mid-May 1941 until late January 1944 became known as 'The Lull', during which the frequency and intensity of bombing dropped dramatically. The raids were also being hampered by the 'unwarlike flab,' in Osborne's description, of the barrage balloons. Elveda's nephew Roy, nine at the time, recalls being taken by his uncle Claude to his barrage

Officers of No. 4 M.T. Company, October 1943 (S/Ldr. L.J. Gilbert, middle; Claude, 2nd from left). The memorial on the wall to Lord Harris, dating from 1934, clearly shows that the photograph was taken in the Harris Garden at Lord's Cricket Ground

Barrage Balloons over London during WWII

balloon station in London. The RAF's foresight, by pushing enemy aircraft higher, took away much of their element of surprise and compromised the bombers' accuracy. The steel cables provided a further obstacle, material and psychological, to the German pilots.[14] The balloons became a familiar sight in cities, ports and beside factories, and almost 3,000 would be deployed nationwide. It was not always plain sailing; some balloons were struck by lightning or shot down. Claude's role, ensuring that these huge inflatables were properly anchored and at the most effective height, was an essential part of the defence of London.

Without the barrage balloons, anti-aircraft guns and thousands of volunteer ambulance staff, air raid wardens and firewatchers, one dreads to imagine how much greater the devastation would have been. It was bad enough. Sporadic raids on London continued, along with the *Baedeker Blitz* between April and June 1942 on the cultural landmarks of Exeter, York, Bath, Canterbury and elsewhere.[15] On Thursday 7th October 1943, London was hit severely and Claude was most likely working flat out all night dispatching ambulances. From nearby Notting Hill, Vere Hodgson recalled:

> the Ladbroke Square gun cracking out. Donned my tin hat – courage returned and I joined the sightseers. All London was doing the same. Shells bursting and amazing fireworks filled the air above us … Our bombers were on the way out as the Germans came in – sometimes the searchlights caught one of ours, and sometimes the enemy …

30 tons of bombs had dropped. Woodford, Ilford, Grays, Battersea, Hampstead … some say Red Lion Square and Vauxhall Bridge.'[16]

Amid the horror, sandbags, rubble and apprehension, it was British phlegm, cigarettes, lashings of strong tea and good humour that maintained a semblance of routine work and play. Nocturnal renditions of *Roll out the Barrel* on the underground at Warwick Road or Maida Vale might not have been quite Claude's scene, but he very much enjoyed one form of popular entertainment, as shown by surviving pages from his diary. On Tuesday 6th June 1944, he noted: 'The Invasion of France began', followed by a list of film stars that they had seen recently.[17] The diary records several visits to the cinema, followed by drinks in their local *The Alfred* in Formosa Street, and within five days they had seen six films![18] British cinema-going was at its peak, admissions reaching 1.5 billion between 1943 and 1945, ten times greater than today.[19] At the outbreak of war, fearing mass air raid casualties, the picture houses had been closed, but quickly reopened for reasons of morale, the programmes including propaganda newsreels produced by the newly-created Ministry of Information. The cinema became an indispensable source of pleasure for the nation, and the Wartime Social Survey of 1943 found that 32 percent of the British population, mostly the young urban working class, attended the cinema once a week or more.[20]

One Monday evening, Claude and Elveda strolled down the Edgware Road to the Regal, Marble Arch, to see the new British film *Half Way House*. Following the premiere on 14th April 1944, *The Times* columnist wrote: 'an occasional frisson is achieved by acute touches of direction which light up not only depths of human tension and unhappiness, but also unobtrusively reckon with their cause – the war.'[21] Later critics commented that 'the Irishman (Terence), who begins by professing support for his country's neutrality, ends the film by placing humanitarian concerns above national loyalties. As Britain was fully engaged in a war that was essentially over national sovereignty, such issues were an understandable concern.'[22]

On that same Monday evening, after ninety minutes of serious drama, the couple were treated to a classic western, *Oklahoma Kid*, starring James Cagney and Humphrey Bogart. On Thursday, The Grand beckoned with *Purple Heart*, an American propaganda film portraying the Japanese stereotypically as vicious torturers. The review by *Variety* mixed the superlatives: 'an intensely moving piece, spellbinding, though

Dulcie Gray and Michael Denison

gory at times, gripping and suspenseful for the most part.'[23] Sales of US Government War Bonds improved dramatically, and one has to wonder to what degree such widely promulgated images sped the fateful payloads to Hiroshima and Nagasaki.

On Saturday, Elveda's sister Gladys and her son Roy came for the weekend. They all took off to The Odeon for *The Woman of the Town*, a 90-minute Western, with gunfights and galloping horses. What would young Roy have made of the second feature, *Higher and Higher*, a romantic caper starring a young Frank Sinatra, offering a seductive glimpse of the modern American lifestyle?

During this period Claude and Elveda became friends with the actors Michael Denison and Dulcie Gray.[24] Married on 29th April 1939, the same year as the Oldfields, Michael and Dulcie had a one-night honeymoon at the Dorchester, before boarding the sleeper to Aberdeen for Dulcie's professional debut in *Hay Fever*. They now lived just round the corner, having previously occupied separate flats in Dolphin Square, Pimlico.[25] Claude admired the suave and debonair Michael, twenty-six years his junior, typically cast as the quintessential English gentleman.

They shared comparable backgrounds, Michael having been at Harrow then Magdalen College, Oxford. Dulcie, just three weeks younger than her husband, born in Kuala Lumpur where her father was a lawyer, had been privately educated in England before going on to drama school. Michael and Dulcie were also childless, allowing time to enjoy pubs and the cinema. Claude could swap stories of colonial life with Dulcie and talk books with Michael, while Elveda was cheerfully down-to-earth with amusing anecdotes from her usherette days.

War service in the Royal Signals, then the Intelligence Corps, had interrupted Michael's acting career. Meanwhile Dulcie worked in repertory at Edinburgh, Glasgow and Harrogate, before her London debut in A Midsummer Night's Dream at the Open Air Theatre, Regent's Park.[26] In 1943 she played the guileless waitress Rose in Brighton Rock opposite Richard Attenborough, unforgettable as the damaged, monstrous mobster, Pinkie.[27] The play's exploration of sin and redemption may have resonated with Claude, reminding him of past dilemmas.

Gladys and Roy continued to visit on occasional weekends. Claude enjoyed the company of his young nephew, and took him out to visit RAF North Weald in Essex, from where in the summer of 1940 a squadron of Hurricanes had played an important part in the Battle of Britain, seeing action over Dunkirk.[28] Roy has vivid memories of his trips to London, travelling in by train from Stansted Mountfitchet. His father, Charlie Broad, who had acted as Claude's best man in August 1939, was away for most of the war with the 'Desert Rats', the 7th Armoured Division, fighting in the North Africa Campaign and then in the invasion of Italy.[29] After a short home respite, the Rats had then been made ready for the Normandy landings on the afternoon of D-Day.

Charlie Broad (far right) with the 'Desert Rats'

While Claude deployed barrage balloons over London, his school friend Bernard Montgomery was leading the British Eighth Army to victory at El Alamein.[30] The staff and pupils of their *alma mater* St. Paul's had been evacuated to Easthampstead Park, near Crowthorne in Berkshire. The Hammersmith site, damaged by raids in 1940 and 1944, had since 1942 been the headquarters of the XXI Army Group. It was here that Montgomery worked on the D-Day invasion plans and 'On 15 May 1944, King George VI and Churchill attended a final briefing of the Allied Commanders at the School.'[31]

St. Paul's, now only for boarders, under High Master Walter Oakeshott, borrowed nearby Wellington College's playing fields twice a week, as well as a gym and science labs. Little else was shared however, Hugh Mead recalling that, 'Paulines and Wellington boys stayed apart, and enjoyed their prejudices about each other.' Wellington was seen as over-conventional and anti-intellectual and St. Paul's as 'the ragged school'.[32] Avoiding the Luftwaffe was not so easy:

> Wellington College was subject to a devastating air-raid during October 1940, when bombs fell on South Front and the original Master's Lodge. The boys had been evacuated to their air-raid shelters and when the all-clear was sounded, Longden, the sixth Master of Wellington, came out into the porch of the Lodge to go to visit them. The porch had been seriously weakened by the bombing and collapsed on top of him killing him instantly.[33]

Between air raids, life in London was not all gloom. Claude had been pleased to learn in the summer of 1943, that his niece Joy, Charlie's only daughter, was expecting a baby. Malcolm (the author) was born in Hendon on 3rd November 1943. Claude, invited to be godfather, was happy to accept, attending the christening at St. Barnabas Church in Finchley on a warm spring day in April 1944. He could have recalled: *Media vita in morte sumus* (in the midst of life, we are in death).[34]

Claude might not have been leading an Army like Monty, but serving in the RAFVR was dangerous and demanding. The D-Day landings had provoked a further vicious assault on London with the new 'Vengeance Weapons' (*Vergeltungswaffen*). Over 3,000 V1 flying bombs hit the capital and suburbs between 13th June 1944 and 29th March 1945, killing almost 9,000 people and seriously injuring at least 24,000.[35] The V1 had cutters to shear off barrage balloon cables, posing a new challenge for Claude and his fellow volunteers. Elveda meanwhile was working in a factory on the

Edgware Road producing spark plugs.[36]

No one in Britain would ever forget VE Day: 8th May 1945. An estimated one million people took to the streets, the crowds surging down the Mall to see the King and Queen accompanied by Churchill waving from the balcony of Buckingham Palace. A nation at war had been at peace with itself, but how would it fare now that peace had been won? Having helped liberate Greece, Michael Denison would star with Dulcie Gray in over one hundred West End plays and enjoy a sixty-year marriage. Dulcie would also write murder mysteries, radio plays, several volumes of short stories and an autobiography. As if this were not enough, she became a renowned authority on butterflies.[37] But what did the world now have in store for Michael and Dulcie's close friends, Claude and Elveda?

---

[1] London Pride, a species of saxifrage, grew profusely on bombsites.

[2] John Osborne, *A Better Class of Person: An Autobiography 1929-1956* (Faber & Faber, 1981)

[3] Osborne, ibid.

[4] The First Blitz or Night Blitz. The period from 7 September 1940 (Black Saturday) to the night of 10/11 May 1941, including a period from 7 September 1940 of 57 consecutive nights when London was bombed.

[5] The RAFVR had been formed in July 1936 to provide individuals to supplement the Royal Auxiliary Air Force, started in 1925 by the local Territorial Associations. The RAFVR was organised on a squadron basis, with local recruitment similar to the TA regiments. The object was to provide a reserve of aircrew for use in the event of war. By September 1939, the RAFVR comprised 6,646 pilots, 1,625 observers and 1,946 wireless operators.

[6] A civilian volunteer on being accepted for aircrew training took an oath of allegiance ('attestation') and was then inducted into the RAFVR, but then normally returned to civilian life for several months until called up for aircrew training. During this waiting period, a silver RAFVR lapel badge could be worn to indicate status.

[7] Alexander McIntosh (Article ID: A8947010, 29 January 2006) www.bbc.co.uk/history/ww2peopleswar/stories

[8] We can assume from this comment that Elveda was staying with her sixteen-year-old sister, Jean, in Stansted.

[9] The base was home to No. 80 (French) Operational Training Unit. The Blackburn B.26 Botha was a British four-seat reconnaissance and torpedo bomber, built by Blackburn Aircraft in Dumbarton, as a competitor to the Bristol Beaufort, and entered service with the RAF in 1939. It was underpowered and was quickly withdrawn from operations. Source: RAF Tranwell / Morpeth, *The Wartime Memories Project*.

[10] Many from RAF Moffat would also go on to serve in the Far East against the Japanese.

According to Moffat's commander, Group Captain Charles Findlay, the trainees were a cross-section of the RAF, and part of the Empire Air Training Scheme, which prepared the majority of the flying crews that would support the D-Day Landings in June 1944. Moffat's facilities and combined expertise enabled the Rhodesian Air Training Group to turn out complete, fully qualified aircrews – pilots, navigators and gunners. The base was named after Dr. Robert Moffat, missionary and father-in-law of David Livingstone. Moffat's grandson, Howard Unwin Moffat (1869-1951) was the second Premier of Southern Rhodesia, after it became a self-governing Colony. From *The Story of Royal Air Force Station, Moffat: August 1941-April 1945.*

[11] No. 4 M.T. Company was established at 9 Abbey Road, St. John's Wood in May 1941 under the command of F/Lt. C. J. Smith. The unit moved in January 1942 to 20 Langford Place; and again in November 1943 to 116 Hamilton Terrace. Source: RAF MTD website. Flying Officer (F/O) is a junior commissioned rank in the RAF. The rank title does not imply that such an officer flies an aircraft; some flying officers are aircrew, but many are ground branch officers. The insignia consists of one narrow blue band on slightly wider black band, worn on both the lower sleeves of the tunic or on the shoulders of the flying suit or the casual uniform.

[12] All recruits underwent a three-week intense recruit's training course covering vehicle maintenance, map reading, practical (stretcher and respirator drill) and special lectures on gas, driving and breakdown procedure, convoy driving, duties of drivers, vehicle inspection and security. Driving practice was given when necessary. Source: D. Collett Wadge (ed), *Women in Uniform* (Imperial War Museum, 1946)

[13] Collett Wadge, ibid.

[14] Motto *Vi Et Ictu* (by Force and Impact). 'Barrage Balloons for Low-Level Air Defense' *Air & Space Power Journal*, Summer 1989

[15] The Baedeker raids were reputedly carried out after Luftwaffe commanders had consulted the 1937 edition of Baedeker's *Great Britain* guidebook (each target was selected if it had been awarded three stars). Although there were sporadic attacks by small numbers of aircraft in the meantime, London enjoyed a lull in bombing until November 1942, when in retaliation for the RAF's bombing of the historic city of Lubeck, Hitler ordered the Luftwaffe to attack historic cities such as Bath, York, Norwich, Exeter, Canterbury and of course, London. Source: www.blitzwalkers.co.uk/blitz.html

[16] Vere Hodgson, *Few Eggs and No Oranges: The Diaries of Vere Hodgson* 1940-45 (Dennis Dobson, 1976, republished by Persephone Books, 1999)

[17] The Normandy landings (codenamed Operation Neptune) on Tuesday, 6 June 1944 began the Allied Invasion of Normandy. The largest seaborne invasion in history, the operation began the liberation of German-occupied north western Europe and contributed to the Allied victory on the Western Front.

[18] *The Prince Alfred* at 5A Formosa Street, close to the picturesque canals of Little Venice, has fed and watered the residents of Maida Vale since 1863.

[19] In 2014, UK Admissions were 157.5 million. Source: Union Internationale des Cinémas (UNIC)

[20] Mark Glancy, 'Going to the pictures: British cinema and the Second World War', Past and Future, Queen Mary, University of London, 2010

21 *The Times*, 17 April 1944

22 Paul Moody, Studiocanal (quoted by BFI Screenonline)

23 *The Purple Heart*, Variety, 31 December 1943

24 John Michael Terence Wellesley Denison (1915-98); Dulcie Winifred Catherine Bailey (1915-2011)

25 Roy Broad, recollecting his war years, in 2015. Dulcie Gray lived at Flat 505, Hood House with her husband. Earlier Michael Denison lived at Flat 901, Grenville House. Source: www.britmovie.co.uk

26 Playing a feisty Hermia in *A Midsummer Night's Dream* and Maria in *Twelfth Night*, both 1942. Both Gray and Denison remained lifelong champions of the Open Air Theatre in Regent's Park.

27 In the 1947 film version of *Brighton Rock*, Dulcie Gray was passed over in favour of the unknown Carol Marsh. Richard Attenborough continued to play *Pinkie*.

28 The airfield was targeted on numerous occasions by the Luftwaffe during the battle, with the first major raid on 24 August 1940, when more than 200 bombs fell on the airfield; many were killed, and the Officers' Mess and married quarters were damaged. By the end of August both squadrons (Nos. 56 & 151) had to be withdrawn as non-operational due to the loss of pilots and machines. They were replaced on 1 September by Squadrons 249, 46 and 25. On 3 September, just as the planes were taking off, the Luftwaffe again bombed North Weald; aircraft and hangars were destroyed and five people killed. However, throughout the Battle the airfield was never put out of action. Source: www.battleofbritainblog.com

29 In February 1940, the division's name was changed (for the final time) to be the 7th Armoured Division. At that time, the division also received its famous symbol, the Jerboa (Desert Rat).

30 The Second Battle of El Alamein (23 October-11 November 1942) took place near the Egyptian railway halt of El Alamein. With the Allies victorious, it marked a major turning point in the Western Desert Campaign of the War. It followed the First Battle of El Alamein, which had stalled the Axis advance into Egypt after which, in August 1942, Montgomery had taken command of the British Eighth Army from Auchinleck.

31 A. H. Mead, *A Miraculous Draught of Fishes: A History of St Paul's School* (James and James, 1990)

32 Mead, ibid.

33 Quoted in 'Special Features: Wellington College' by Margaret Simons, in the *Berkshire Local History Association Newsletter*, May 2014. Robert Paton Longden (1904-40) graduated from Magdalen College, Oxford and was holding the post of Censor at Christ Church when he was appointed Master of Wellington in 1937 (Christ Church, Oxford). Longden was an old friend of the St. Paul's Master, Oakeshott (Mead, ibid.)

34 The title and first line of an antiphon, attributed to the Benedictine monk, Notker I of Saint Gall, France

35 The first V1 fell on 13 June 1944 on Bow, East London. The V1s were pilotless bombs with a range of 150 miles, powered by an Argus 109-014 pulse engine and launched by catapult from ramps in occupied Europe. Due to design faults and RAF raids on their test facilities at Peenemunde, on Germany's Baltic coast (17-18 August

1943) and on launch ramp sites in Northern France, their use was delayed until June 1944. Each V1 was divided into five sections: pulse engine, control compartment, ball-shaped compressed air tanks, alcohol fuel tank and nose warhead. They flew at around 400mph, guided by autopilot and gyrocompass. After launch from northern France or Holland, V1s could reach London in 25 minutes. A small nose airscrew (air log) measured a set range – every V1 sent against the capital was calibrated for the exact distance to Tower Bridge, after which the droning pulse engine cut out and the V1 dived down, silently and menacingly, onto London. They delivered a powerful warhead: 1,870lb of high explosive. Until their launch ramp sites were overrun by the advancing allied armies, V1s badly damaged the capital.

36 This was most likely to have been the Cricklewood factory of Smiths Motor Accessories (later Smiths Industries).

37 *Butterflies on My Mind* was a scholarly study, written in 1978, with which Dulcie Gray won *The Times* Educational Senior Information Book Award. See Obituary, *The Daily Telegraph*, November 2011

CHAPTER 25

Returning to Cecil Rhodes

Dreamer devout, by vision led
Beyond our guess or reach

Rudyard Kipling, 'Burial', in 1902, in honour of Rhodes

Claude was far from alone in regarding Churchill as a hero. The great man's appearance on the balcony of Buckingham Palace on VE Day had seemed perfectly natural. His stature, rhetoric and steely determination were seen as crucial in the defeat of the Nazis: Winston was not just the Prime Minister – he was the saviour of the nation, a father figure whose future leadership of his country was surely a forgone conclusion.

But from his study of the classics, Claude also knew how suddenly heroes could fall. If Churchill had an Achilles heel it was being upper class. Working people, recalling the troops sent in against striking Welsh miners and decisions made during the disastrous Gallipoli campaign, questioned the legitimacy of such a man in a world of nascent egalitarianism. Claude's late brother Harold had ploughed the middle furrow of politics with the Liberals, whose leader Lloyd George had called for a country fit for heroes after the First World War. Instead there had been depression and poverty. What alternative could Churchill the Conservative now offer? In the 1945 general election, Clement Attlee, in Churchill's acerbic view 'a modest man with much to be modest about' was favoured over the patriotic icon, securing a landslide victory to form a Labour government. Attlee, although a barrister and upper class by birth, had lived and worked among the East End's poor for several years and was committed to the concept of the welfare state.

Meanwhile hardship and rationing remained the norm for most and jobs in 'civvy street' were scarce, with thousands of ex-servicemen willing to try their hand at anything. Claude, now fifty-six, was fortunate to have found a job as Secretary of the British Motor Trade Association (BMTA), at 7 Park Lane, Mayfair.[1] Their membership comprised every British motor manufacturer, importer and accredited dealer, along with a host of related businesses. The postwar steel shortage and a government policy of 'Export or Die', was restricting the delivery of new vehicles to those with essential needs such as doctors. To curb the lucrative black market in cars, the lucky purchasers were required to sign a covenant, drawn up and administered by the BMTA, pledging not to sell the vehicle before an agreed date.[2]

Elveda had also been pleased to continue working, as many women were now expected to make way for the returning men. Soon though, the new National Health Service would be recruiting a women's army of cleaners, nurses, housekeeping staff, clerks and typists. Elveda, outgoing and cheerful, enjoyed the camaraderie of the shop floor, the repetitive work lightened by *Workers' Playtime* on the radio, and a laugh with the

Claude and Elveda on a visit to Ostend, June 1947

girls. Unlike when with Claude's 'posh' friends, or his brother Charlie, there was no risk of committing a *faux pas*.

Claude and Elveda's small flat at 49 Randolph Avenue, Maida Vale was handy for the Bakerloo Line. The imposing stuccoed houses lay close to the eye-catching boats of 'Little Venice' on John Nash's Regent's Canal and Lord's Cricket Ground was up the road, while it was only a short bus ride to see Charlie and Maisie in Golders Green. Charlie, the epitome of modest, middle class aspiration had proved that university was not a prerequisite for worldly success. Since leaving an electrical apprenticeship for insurance, he had consolidated his position at Harrods, enjoyed a happy marriage, and been blessed with his daughter Joy and young grandson Malcolm (yours truly). After retiring Charlie could play more golf and a few hands of bridge at North Middlesex Golf Club, and have a flutter on the horses, his good head for figures allowing him the satisfaction of occasionally beating the bookies. Charlie had never had much interest in acquiring a car, and for holidays, the family often took the train to Broadstairs or Deal, sometimes to Worthing. With Maisie nervous of crossing the Channel, Charlie's golfing breaks at the elegant and fashionable French resorts of Deauville or Le Touquet would probably have been on a 'bachelor' basis.

Now accepting of his younger brother's marriage, Charlie, ably supported by Maisie and their steadfast Welsh maid Nellie, invited Claude and Elveda to Sunday lunch, serving up a very acceptable Aloxe Corton burgundy to accompany the roast beef. The post-prandial forty winks would be followed by a 'constitutional' through leafy Golders Hill Park and across North End Road to the *Old Bull and Bush*.[3] Claude, recalling long African ulendos, might try to encourage the party further, up the hill towards Hampstead and *Jack Straw's Castle*, or beyond to the *Spaniard's Inn*.

Claude and Elveda appreciated the open space around Golders Green, and likewise the countryside when they visited Elveda's family at Stansted and Sawbridgeworth. Agreeing though that a larger flat, or better still a house, would improve their quality of life, they discussed a move to the country, where their limited income would go further. In early 1950 they found a house in Bishop's Stortford and arranged to rent a property at 30 Portland Road, comprising three storeys, a back garden and their own front door.

Bishop's Stortford, a traditional market town in north Hertfordshire, some 30 miles north of London, was becoming increasingly popular with

30 Portland Road, Bishop's Stortford, 2013

white-collar workers travelling into London each day. For the first time in his life Claude became a commuter. In Africa he had recorded his daily routine in the District Notebooks. An entry now, perhaps with a hint of Philip Larkin, might have read:

> Out of the house at 7.15 to catch the 7.26 to town. Only 5-6 minutes to the station, gently down Portland Road, then a left down the hill, the sun just rising over the slate roof of the red brick Baptist church on the right, and the Quaker burial ground on the left – BpS has it all – over the bridge crossing the River Stort, and with station in sight thought best to put on a spurt for the final 400yds. Across the footbridge just as the train comes round the bend. It's on time.

Out past the goods yard, gathering speed. Flat, marshy terrain on the left, open country, more like a dambo. Cross the Stort, then Sawbridgeworth (Gladys and Charlie just up the road). Now it's arable, next year's crop just been sown. On south, past Harlow Mill, then Harlow – oh why make it a 'New Town' – change is not always for the better! Wet, flat land, reminds one of the swamps around Bangweulu, animals grazing, like the old native cattle but with shorter horns. Roydon, narrow boats on the river, looks relaxing. Still flat by the waterway at Broxbourne. Cheshunt. Trinity Marsh Lane level crossing. Another crossing at Enfield Lock. On to Ponders End, still plenty of green.

A longer stop at Tottenham Hale. More open, flat country, but now built up, this must be the Lee Valley. Lovely church spire in the distance on the right. Clapton, then into a cutting, lots of low bridges, then a tunnel, maybe half a mile, Hackney Downs, Bethnal Green, brick walls, shafts of sunlight breaking through the steam and smoke, almost there, another day with the Motor Traders beckons …

Harry Franklin, with whom Claude worked at Serenje, regretted leaving Africa, pondering: 'in London, I should join the ants … in orderly columns as they approached the tunnel that would take them underground to their work, streaming out of it at the other end and jostling, bumping into each other as they dispersed to forage, to work for their food.'[4]

The longer daily absence from Elveda made work more of a necessity than a pleasure for Claude, and stirred tender, uxorious feelings. Shortly after the move, he sent her a telegram from Liverpool Street: 'A HAPPY DAY TO YOU WITH ALL MY LOVE. CLAUDE.' It was 9th August, their eleventh wedding anniversary, regrettably coinciding with a formal dinner that obliged him to stay in town overnight.

Elveda's older sister Gladys was only a bus ride away in Sawbridgeworth, and younger sister Peggy a few miles in the opposite direction at Stansted, where the girls had grown up. Claude's sister-in-law Maisie, fond of her 'Gin and It', was interested to learn that William Gilbey, of *Gilbey's Gin* fame, had been born in Bishop's Stortford.[5]

Claude would also have been aware of the town's other famous son Cecil Rhodes, born on 5th July 1853, his 'genius rooted in the family soil of Bishop's Stortford.'[6] Cecil was the sixth child of Rev. Francis Rhodes and his wife Louisa. Sickly and asthmatic, Cecil was denied the education received by three of his brothers at Eton and Winchester, being sent instead to the local grammar school.[7] Showing worrying signs of consumption, at sixteen he was packed off to his brother Herbert's cotton farm, in the warmer climes of the British South Africa Cape Colony. Claude knew well the story of Rhodes's meteoric ascent from that point on. With the discovery of diamonds in the Kimberley area, it was a propitious time to arrive in South Africa, and the young man used cash from his prospecting to fund frequent trips back to Britain to study classics at Oriel College, Oxford.

The outlay was a drop in the ocean compared to the revenue from diamonds, and when Rhodes graduated at the age of twenty-eight he had acquired immense wealth and influence. Already an MP in the Cape, astute business dealings brought the Chairmanship of the De Beers Diamond Company. Rhodes's impulse was to expand, by diplomacy or force, making treaties with tribal leaders or subduing them with militia. Both strategies required funds, and the discovery of gold in 1884 provided more than enough.[8] By the age of thirty-four Rhodes had monopoly control of the Kimberley diamond fields, netting him an estimated £200,000, and an additional £300,000 from gold. Now one of the richest men on earth, he put his money vigorously to work, acquiring territory and further mining rights in the name of the British Empire.

Cecil Rhodes (c. 1890)

With a Cape to Cairo railway already in his sights, in 1884 Rhodes had persuaded the British government to establish a protectorate over Bechuanaland, inciting antagonism from Boer President Paul Kruger. In 1889, Rhodes's British South Africa Company (BSAC), an autonomous trading and military unit, a private army in effect, was granted approval, and the following year he was elected Prime Minister of the Cape. Although having already obtained mineral concessions from Lobengula in 1888, in 1893 he orchestrated a military expedition by the BSAC into Matabeleland led by Leander Starr Jameson with Sir John Willoughby as his military adviser.[9] Through bribery and some underhand dealing they staked a claim to the country's two northerly provinces, named after him later as Northern and Southern Rhodesia.

Rhodes had long had his eye on the on the mineral-rich Transvaal, and now began hatching a plot to overthrow Kruger, culminating in the infamous Jameson Raid of late 1895. The plan to spark an insurrection among the Transvaal's British labour force against their Boer overlords and then take over failed however, signalling the end of Rhodes's political career. This misadventure was also thought to have played a large part in fomenting the Second Anglo-Boer War in 1899.

Rhodes's most visible achievement, or crime in the eyes of anti-imperialists, was to expand the British Empire in Africa by some 450,000 square miles. In private he was less the all-conquering hero. Never married, theories about his sexuality would divide opinion. Richard Brown argued that there was, 'simply not enough reliable evidence to reach firm, irrefutable conclusions', while Robert Rotberg believed Rhodes to have been 'an emotional if not practising homosexual.'[10] Rhodes certainly held deep feelings towards his male friends, nursing Neville Pickering after a riding accident until he died in his arms, and reportedly weeping at his funeral.[11]

Rhodes's close relationship with the writer Olive Schreiner would be the focus of much debate. Schreiner had looked forward eagerly to meeting Rhodes when she returned to South Africa in 1889, remarking to W. T. Stead that he was 'the only big man we have here', and to Havelock Ellis that he was 'the only great man, and man of genius S. Africa possesses'. When the meeting took place, followed by several more in Matjiesfontein and Cape Town, the rumour mill span, while Schreiner refuted the assumption that she and Rhodes were engaged.[12]

By the early 1890s the hero had begun to tarnish in her eyes. Writing to her brother Will, another Cape MP, Schreiner described the moment on the platform of Matjiesfontein Station when she saw for the first time Rhodes's true venality and began to turn away from him.[13] The Jameson Raid revealed to her the full extent of his moral and political corruption, and in 1897 her novella *Trooper Peter Halket of Mashonaland* carried a damning indictment of the BSAC's part in atrocities against the Ndebele and Shona tribes during the uprisings of 1896.[14]

Rhodes was also embroiled in the scandal of Princess Catherine Radziwill of St. Petersburg, who at the age of fifteen had married a Polish officer in the Prussian army, Prince Wilhelm Radziwill. Estranged from her husband and children, she arrived in South Africa in 1899, setting her eyes on Rhodes or, some said, stalking him. They became friends for a while then Rhodes withdrew, paying her creditors and packing her off to London. Here she was hounded for further debts, incurred by her son Nicholas. Returning to Cape Town in 1900, Catherine, charged with forging Rhodes's signature on promissory notes, was imprisoned for sixteen months.[15]

Rhodes meanwhile was enjoying the good life, evidenced in the huge expansion of his girth and ignoring medical advice to lose weight. On 26th March 1902 at Muizenberg, aged forty-eight his heart gave out. Among the epitaphs, Olive Schreiner judged him a man of great ambition and genius, who had used his talents for immoral and corrupt ends, in her words, 'a great might-have-been'.[16] Princess Radziwill remained an admirer, writing a book titled *Resurrecting Peter: A Reply to Olive Schreiner*.[17] Rhodes's last days were spent with close friend Leander Starr Jameson, who nursed him during his final illness. Jameson would be the trustee and a beneficiary of Rhodes's will, allowing him to continue living in his mansion. Rhodes's final words were typical English understatement: 'So little done, so much to do'.

Olive Schreiner (1855-1920) / Princess Catherine Radziwill (1858-1941)

Cecil Rhodes left a fortune in excess of £3m for scholarships that enabled students, primarily from former British territories to study at Oxford University. In Claude's time, before Empire started to become a dirty word, Rhodes was still lionised. In subsequent years as the biographies stacked up, Paul Maylam has noted three perspectives: veneration, debunking and 'an intermediate view' of the man and his legacy, in which 'Rhodes is not straightforwardly assessed as either hero or villain.'[18] Gordon Cragg, a former student of the University of Cape Town, was concerned about those who have advocated changing names, believing that Rhodes should be looked on as 'a product of his day ... consumed by the ambition of colonial expansion ...'[19]

At the time of writing, the debate rages on. The *Rhodes Must Fall* (RMF) movement started in 2015 with student protests at the University of Cape Town getting the Rhodes statue removed from the campus. The activists' broader objective was emphasising the slow change in racial attitudes in South Africa since the ending of apartheid. An official statement by the University of Cape Town held that 'the behaviour by RMF members is criminal and has exceeded all possible limits of lawful protest action. We are deeply concerned for the safety of students and staff.' [20] A similar campaign has been waged to change the name of Rhodes University in Grahamstown.

The Rhodes Memorial, erected on Devil's Peak on the edge of Cape Town, with magnificent views to the north, has been defaced. Its architect, Sir Herbert Baker, modelled the memorial on a Greek temple, which consists of a massive staircase with forty-nine steps (one for each year of

Rhodes Memorial, Cape Town, 2016

Rhodes's life), leading from a semi-circular terrace up to a rectangular U-shaped monument formed of pillars. Inscribed below the bust of Rhodes are the last four lines from the poem 'Burial' by Rudyard Kipling, written in 1902:

> The immense and brooding spirit still
> Shall quicken and control.
> Living he was the land, and dead,
> His soul shall be her soul!

In Oxford, the anti-Rhodes campaign has called for the removal of the statue in Oriel College.[21] Writing in *The Spectator*, Matthew Parris argued that the statue should stay, and alongside it be placed similar representations of Lobengula and President Mugabe:

> All three did terrible things. All three did great things. All three changed history. All three are among the architects of modern Africa north of the Limpopo. All three were prisoners of their era and circumstances, as we all are. Yet all three transcended their time to some degree. Their spirits will always walk the African bush.[22]

Meanwhile, as Claude made his daily walk through the streets of 1950s' Bishop's Stortford to catch the 7.26 to London, another spirit, very much alive, was walking through the bush in Northern Rhodesia. His name was Kenneth Kaunda.

---

[1] Business card: Mr. C. P. Oldfield, Local Secretary, The Motor Trade Association, 7 Park Lane, W1. Telephone: Mayfair 0186

[2] The scheme commenced in August 1946 with a 6-month resale restriction, increased to 12 months in 1947 and to two years in 1950. From the discussion forum of the *Autosport* website: Leigh Trevail, 'AAGR' and John Elmgreen in June 2012.

[3] *The Old Bull and Bush* dates back to 1645 and forms the title of the 1920s music hall number *Down at the Old Bull & Bush* sung by Florrie Forde; written and composed by A. B. Sterling, R. Hunting, P. Krone, H. von Tilzer.

[4] Harry Franklin, *The Flag Wagger* (Shepheard-Walwyn, 1974) pp 203-4

[5] Gin mixed with Italian (sweet) vermouth. Sir Walter Gilbey, 1st Baronet, DL (1831-1914), was a wine-merchant and philanthropist, born at Bishop's Stortford, to parents Henry and Elizabeth Gilbey.

[6] Robert I. Rotberg, *The Founder: Cecil Rhodes and the Pursuit of Power* (Oxford University Press, 1990) p 681

[7] See Ben Johnson

[8] The first large mining company on the Reef, the Witwatersrand Gold Mining Company, was formed with a total nominal capital of £3m on 14 September 1886

[9] Sir Leander Starr Jameson (1853-1917), also known as 'Doctor Jim', 'The Doctor' or 'Lanner'. Sir John Christopher Willoughby (1859-1918) served in the Matabele War of 1893 as military adviser to Dr. Jameson and in 1895, took command of Jameson's raiding force, for which he lost his commission and (like Jameson) was sentenced to imprisonment. During the Boer War his commission was restored and he served through the Siege of Ladysmith. Also served in WWI under Gen. Jan Smuts and Gen. Jacob van Deventer, returning to England in mid-1917, dying of malaria contracted in East Africa.

[10] Richard Brown, 'The Colossus', *The Journal of African History* (Cambridge University Press) Vol. 31, No. 3, 499-502, November 1990 and Rotberg, ibid., p 408

[11] Robert Aldrich & Garry Wotherspoon, *Who's who in Gay and Lesbian History: From Antiquity to World War II* (Routledge, 2000)

[12] The story of the development of Matjiesfontein, 150 miles north east of Cape Town on the line of rail to Johannesburg, is related by Dean Allen in *Empire, War & Cricket in South Africa: Logan of Matjiesfontein* (Zebra Press, Cape Town, 2015). See also www.oliveschreiner.org

[13] William Philip Schreiner (1857-1919) was a Cape politician and Olive Schreiner's younger brother.

[14] Olive Schreiner, *Trooper Peter Halket of Mashonaland* (T. Fisher Unwin, 1897)

[15] Brian Roberts, *Cecil Rhodes and the Princess* (Hamish Hamilton, 1969). Also Antony Thomas, *Rhodes: The Race for Africa* (BBC Books, 1996)

[16] Source: www.oliveschreiner.org, ibid.

[17] *The Resurrection of Peter: A Reply to Olive Schreiner*, 1900 (i.e. to Schreiner's book: Trooper Peter Halket of Mashonaland)

[18] Paul Maylam, *The Cult of Rhodes: Remembering an Imperialist in Africa* (New Africa Books, 2005)

[19] Gordon M. Cragg, 'Transformation at Rhodes University and the Issues of the Name of our Great Institution' 2015

[20] 'UCT condemns RMF's vandalism and violence' *12 July 2015*.

[21] The College stated that the issue should be 'addressed in a spirit of free speech and open debate, with a readiness to listen to divergent views … (and) has decided that the statue should remain in place, and that the College will seek to provide a clear historical context to explain why it is there.' 'Decision about the Rhodes statue', 28 Jan 2016

[22] Matthew Parris, *The Spectator*, 23 January 2016

CHAPTER 26

Rediens Cantabrigia

Bliss it was in that dawn to be alive
But to be young was very heaven

William Wordsworth, 'The French Revolution as It
Appeared to Enthusiasts at Its Commencement'[1]

As we know, Claude had met Kaunda's father, the Reverend David Kaunda, in 1927 at the Lubwa Mission. When David and his wife Helen, a teacher, had their eighth child in 1924, they named the boy Buchizya – the unexpected one – although he would later be known as Kenneth David Kaunda, adopting his father's name as his middle name. The young Buchizya would have had a dutiful, Christian upbringing, but with some tension from being a 'stranger' with his parents from Nyasaland, whilst trying to negotiate assimilation as a subject of the local Bemba chief, Nkula. However, Buchizya was only but one of several who found fame after attending the mission school at Lubwa, his contemporaries including Simon Kapwepwe and Alice Lenshina, and earlier, Rev. Paul Mushindo.[2] Elias Munshya believes that Chinsali has a justifiable reputation as a point of assimilation for many tribes and epitomizes the character necessary for the founding of the future Republic of Zambia.[3]

Kenneth had followed his parents into education, becoming headmaster of the Lubwa Upper Primary School from 1944 to 1947 and the Mufulira Upper School from 1948 to 1949. Importantly, in between these two appointments, he had worked in a broader social setting in Northern Rhodesia, establishing a farmers' cooperative in the copper mining area and becoming a miners' welfare officer. The mines had previously witnessed strikes, the first by Africans in 1935 having been aggressively stamped out, with six miners killed. Kaunda had also forged links with the European community by becoming in 1949 an interpreter and advisor on African affairs to Stewart Gore-Browne, by this time a member of Northern

74 Argyll Street, Cambridge, 2013

Rhodesia's Legislative Council (LegCo). As yet, few people had heard of Kaunda, but that was about to change.

Meanwhile back in Britain, Claude and Elveda were on the move again, this time to a two-up, two-down Victorian end of terrace, 74 Argyll Street, in a quiet part of Cambridge where town and gown rarely met.[4] The station again was only a short walk for Claude's daily train to London and Elveda would be closer to her family in Norfolk.

At the weekends, Claude could enjoy a stroll into Cambridge, over the Mill Road railway bridge, passing the late Victorian Free Library on the right, down past Gwydir Street, where since 1900 Dales Brewery had been fermenting its 'Champion Ales'.[5] It was only ten minutes to Parker's Piece, where he would be back among the winding streets and ageless college walls he had known so well in his salad days. This was *his* Cambridge. Even after forty years, two world wars and considerable social upheaval since his graduation, it had changed little. Bliss had it been in that dawn to be alive, but to be young and at Cambridge must, in hindsight at any rate, have seemed very heaven. The urge to revisit his old room at Trinity Hall, perhaps to even consider spending the night there when the students went down on vacation, must have been strong.

However, the continuing improvement in the British economy had also affected the Motor Trade Association, whose covenant scheme was cut back as more British marques were freed from resale restrictions, and the scheme was finally wound up in 1953.[6] With the need to reduce staff numbers, the Association's suggestion that Claude might retire, although only in his early sixties, seems understandable. When the day of his departure finally arrived, even if not unexpected, the mental changes required were subtle and less predictable. The severance of routine, the absence of familiar faces on the train and at the office, and the feeling of no longer being a productive member of society, all required adjustment, not to mention the loss of income. On the positive side, Claude was now free to do as he pleased, wandering around the Cambridge colleges, or idling time watching cricket.

Claude describes the scene in 1953, when Elveda was with her relatives in Norfolk: 'Yesterday I had a look at a cricket match on Parker's Piece, and walked about a bit. There were quite a lot of sightseers about, in for the day I expect.' Cricket had been played here, possibly as early as the eighteenth century, hosting the University's regular side on its formation in 1820.[7] The University now played across the road at Fenners where, on 6th May 1953, a star-studded Middlesex team, including Denis Compton and Bill Edrich, made 334 runs against Cambridge, who went on to win the closely-fought game by just three wickets. The University side included Denis Silk, later Warden of Radley College, Raman Subba Row and Robin Marlar.

Parker's Piece, Cambridge (with the well-known gas lamp, erected in 1893, at the cross roads of the paths)

Retirement would give Claude time for reflection, an opportunity to reconsider events, thoughts and feelings from a fresh perspective. He was not alone among his peers in having had a chequered career. Hearing the knock of leather on willow and the gentle applause on Parker's Piece that summer, his thoughts may have drifted again to Percy Fender.[8] Although two years younger, Fender was selected for the St. Paul's First XI in May 1908, Claude's last summer term.

In 1915 Fender was listed among Wisden's 'Five Cricketers of the Year'.[9] After

Percy Fender

service in the Royal Flying Corps in WWI, he had joined Surrey, and was made Captain in 1921. A forceful and sometimes controversial leader, as well as an effective performer with both bat and ball, he inspired the side to compete hard for the County Championship over several seasons. In 1921 Fender had been selected for the England Test team, and the press talked of the captaincy. Sadly, these comments were premature and by 1924, following a clash with the highly influential Lord Harris, his England career was effectively over. Back at Surrey, after continuing disputes with the committee, in 1932 he was replaced as Captain, and three years later retired.

Percy Fender would stand almost alone in cricketing folklore, as a man best known for what he failed to achieve: 'The best county captain who never captained England. No more flexible thinker on cricket ever lived.'[10] There were those who believed he was blocked because he was Jewish. While Fender had always stated he was not a Jew, some maintained that he was simply denying the fact. Speculation persisted even after the 1981 publication of Richard Streeton's biography, but Daniel Lightman, a Jewish barrister and cricket writer, subsequently tracked down Fender's only son, Peter, who confirmed that there was no Jewish blood in the family, but that his father's appearance, in particular his long nose, had led to assumptions. Fender's grandson Guy believes that the deeply conservative cricketing establishment was suspicious of his grandfather, regarding him as some kind of radical, socialist free thinker, a man whom, in the 1920s especially, would be seen as utterly unfit to captain the England team.[11]

In February 1952 the nation mourned the passing of King George VI. In June 1953, Elizabeth II was crowned, the first female monarch since Victoria, under whose reign Claude had grown up. It was the turn of a circle that made Claude even more aware of his years. If there was a temptation to dwell on the past, in particular on Dorothy, the countervailing force was his good fortune that he had met Elveda, whose youth and vivacity had given him new life, dispelling maudlin thoughts or excessive introspection.

During the summer of 1953 Elveda continued to be away intermittently in Norfolk, where her sister Jean was in hospital. Claude was missing his wife badly, hence the daily letters. Replies were answered promptly, with grateful tenderness and a touch of anxiety. June 19th:

> Thank you Darling, for your 'double' letter, it is indeed good news that you will be able to come home tomorrow … lately I have been thinking that Jean was getting a bit fed up with hospital life … I don't quite like the idea of your bringing D with you, as he would be rather a big handicap, and I expect Jean will want to have him with her after so long.

In what way would 'D' be a handicap? Claude's alarm at the prospect of having Jean's five year-old son David around the house for an unspecified period, suggests an antipathy towards children in general, or boys in particular. As for Elveda, she must at some point have given up on the idea of starting a family with Claude. Possibly after her early misadventure and the adoption of her illegitimate baby, she had made it clear that she now had no desire for children. Such a declaration – reassuring Claude that their mutual devotion would never be complicated by bringing up children – may have been what spurred him to marry her as soon as his mother had died.

In the same missive to Elveda, between the endearments, Claude's somewhat self-centred outlook persists: 'Well my Sweet, I can't promise you a rest when you do get back, as although I have tried to keep the place ship shape, there is still quite a bit to do.' Now reliant solely on Claude's pension, it seems that domestic help was not an option. There was still money for an occasional flutter though; after giving the times of three trains that Elveda can catch home from Harling Road, he conveys good news: 'We had quite a nice win on *Sonepi*, £5.10s.0d win and £1.7s.6d place.' Yet with hope and envy mingling eternal in the human breast, he concludes, 'Did you notice that they paid £1,763 for 10/- on the Tote Treble? Someone was lucky!' Off-course betting, prior to a legal change in 1961, and the advent of nationwide betting shops, remained a shadowy subculture of bookies' runners in pubs and workplaces, trying to stay one step ahead of the police. Placing a wager by telephone was however already allowed under the law, and Claude would save his small change for communicating with his turf accountant from the nearest public call box.

Writing on Sunday 2nd August, Claude is pleased that holidaymakers are enjoying good weather in England, and ponders a flutter on the

Scottish football matches beginning ahead of the English season. He informs Elveda that 'the cats shared my dinner, there were some outside pieces I cut off the joint for them, so can wait until this evening for their rabbit.' In her absence, he seems to be saying to his wife, the cats are his only companions, the sentiment further underlined by: 'I am not one of the men who sing, "My wife's gone to the country, Hurrah, Hurrah, I don't care what becomes of me, My wife's gone away!"'[12]

With food rationing not ending until 1954, many householders kept chickens. Claude's four-page epistle the following day tells Elveda that their 'birds are doing quite well.' Money saved on eggs could be 'invested' on horses, and Claude keeps a diligent eye on his bookmaker's accounts, assuring his wife that the latest statement was 'right almost to a penny.' Amongst the talk of runners and riders, he notes one pundit foresees jockey Gordon Richards romping home on no less than four winners that day. The recently-knighted Richards had ridden the sixteen-hand *Pinza* in the Coronation Derby that June, beating the Queen's horse and taking the lead in the final two furlongs to win. Not saying if he is tempted to back Richards, Claude's main concern is to speed his words as swift as meditation to his beloved: 'I must post this before 4.30, so no more now, my sweet. Take care of yourself. I miss you very much. Claude, ILY.'

The next day, Claude's isolation is intensifying and he is impatient for his wife's return. 'Things are very quiet here as you can imagine. Sunday can't come too soon for me.' On the 5th however, she explains that she will be delayed longer than expected with her family. Claude cannot get the pen in his hand again quick enough: 'I can't say that I am not disappointed you won't be coming home till Monday, but I suppose it can't be helped.' He consoles himself with plans to see a George Raft film, but resolves not to sit through *The Bengal Lancer* yet again.[13]

In a further four-page letter on 6th August, Claude ponders the *News Chronicle* racing tipster: 'I think we might give him a trial this week.' A master of trivia, he tells Elveda he has sent a postcard to Don and Ivy, lost his spectacles, and purchased a tin of tongue. The following day his specs have been found, but broken, and he is relieved when the oculist fixes them. We learn that Gladys, Charlie and Roy Broad are planning a day out to Clacton on the Sunday that Elveda was originally due home. Claude might have been tempted to add, 'All right for some!' Instead he goes for a touch of, perhaps ironic, self-pity: 'My old spine has been giving me rather a bad time – old age creeping on, but otherwise I am alright, except that I am fed up with my own company.' When Sunday arrives, the promise of relief is palpable: 'This is to say how thankful I shall be to be able to wellcome (*sic*) you home tomorrow, my sweet. I will expect you at about 8.'

It seems that neither Claude and Elveda, nor her relatives, were among the ten percent of people who by then had a telephone in their home. If Claude's letters are anything to go by, this might have been a blessing for his wife. A third of households now owned a washing machine, and vacuum cleaners had become commonplace, but Claude probably could not, or would not, spend money on such luxuries. Househusbands were unheard of – hence the rueful admission of there being 'still quite a lot' for Elveda to do on her return to Argyle Street.

Claude now had to recognise that he really had reached retirement, and with it, genteel poverty. His colonial service pension, having left Northern Rhodesia after only twenty-one years' service was very modest, amounting to £462.10s.0d., and the Motor Trade Association had provided only moderate remuneration. Although he had joined the RAFVR primarily out of a strong sense of patriotic duty, he had received only a modest honorarium, helping him to keep his savings intact. Eight years had now passed since the end of the war and the money was all but gone. Meanwhile rent, rates, electricity, coal and food bills still had to be paid. Pending a big win on the horses, the Oldfields either had to find a cheaper way of living, or a means of supplementing their income. After some discussion, they agreed on a solution that could perhaps provide them with both.

Throughout 1953, the British government had also been looking for a solution: how to keep hold of their substantial economic interests in central Africa. By August, after protracted talks, they had come up with an answer: the Federation of Rhodesia and Nyasaland. The arrangement left the two territories conquered by Rhodes still bearing his name, and all three largely under British control. The Federation, even with the inclusion of an 'African Affairs Board' which purported to safeguard the interests of the indigenous population, would hold little sway with most Africans. Claude would have followed these developments closely and, in particular, the emergence of Kenneth Kaunda onto the African stage, now Secretary General of his country's African National Congress.

---

1   After graduating from Cambridge in 1791, Wordsworth travelled to France and was

swept up in the ideals of the French Revolution (and, not unconnected, into the arms of the passionately-rebellious Annette Vallon, with whom he had a daughter). The subsequent Reign of Terror and counter-revolution would modify his views on revolution as a Romantic political act, and equally on the enthusiasms of youth. This poem, composed in 1805, was first published in *The Friend*, No. 11, on 26 October 1809.

[2] Simon Kapwepwe, b. 1922; Alice Lenshina, b. 1920; Rev. Paul Mushindo, b. 1896. The Paul Mushindo University, named in his honour, is currently under construction near Chinsali.

[3] Elias Munshya, *'Top Soil': Chinsali and the making of the Zambian nation*, 2014

[4] These terraced 'cottages' fetched c. £300,000-£350,000 in 2014.

[5] The Free Library is now the Bharat Bhavan ('House of India'), used by the Indian Cultural and Community Association and the home of a Hindu shrine for Cambridge. Dale's Brewery was started in 1898 by Fred Dale in Histon Road, but in 1900 was moved to Gwydir Street. When he died in 1930, his son, Lt. Colonel Guy Dale, became Chairman until the firm was taken over by Whitbreads in 1955. Three years later the Brewery was closed.

[6] More marques were freed before the end of 1952, the situation then being that only the fastest-selling products of Britain's 'Big Five' (BMC, Ford, Vauxhall, Rootes and Standard) were still affected, and the compulsory period of ownership was then slashed to just one year. From the *Autosport* website, ibid.

[7] Parker's Piece is also regarded as the birthplace of the rules of Association Football. In 1848, a group of representatives and students from Cambridge decided to draw up a definitive set of rules, which were soon widely adopted. When the Football Association was formed in 1863, they adopted the Cambridge Rules. Various sources, incl. www.espncricinfo.com

[8] b. 22 August 1892, Balham; d. 15 June 1985, Exeter

[9] David Bussey, *John Colet's Children: The Boys of St Paul's School in Later Life 1509-2009* (Gresham Books, Oxford, 2009)

[10] Obituary, *The Times*, 17 June 1985

[11] Richard Streeton, *P.G.H. Fender: A Biography* (Faber & Faber, 1981). See also Daniel Lightman, 'Passing – and failing – the cricket test', *Jewish Chronicle*, 15 July 2013

[12] This reference is to an Irving Berlin number from 1909, which conveys the perceived frustrations of the average middle-class man, yearning to throw off the shackles of conformity, escape from his wife and, if only for a while, enjoy the bachelor life again. From '50 Records That Matter, 1900-1919' at www.aceterrier.com

[13] *The Lives of a Bengal Lancer* is a 1935 American film loosely adapted from the 1930 book by the British-Indian author Francis Yeats-Brown.

CHAPTER 27

The Summer of 1957

On Breckland wide, the bracken waves

Charles Harper, 'Breckland Time-Piece'[1]

A tall, slim, slightly-stooped man in his middle sixties, carrying the morning paper, opens the rickety gate. His cavalry twills and faded sports jacket, patched at the elbow, with pale blue shirt, white collar and stud and old school tie, cut a rare sartorial dash in this rural backwater of Norfolk. The youthful figure of his wife appears, ferrying two large buckets of water. As he waves to her, she laughs cheerily in response.

Approaching the house he passes his brother-in-law John's circular saw, droplets of dew drying to rust marks on the teeth. A sturdy Fordson tractor, rolled out of Dagenham before the war, its blue paint almost gone, the drive-belt half-rolled up on a heap of logs, sits ready by an old fuel can, and the broken glass of a hurricane lamp. Piles of sawdust and chippings, amid the trunks of once lofty oaks, well past their prime, lie heaped behind the saw awaiting their fate. At the door he stops for a moment and looks back towards the broken fence, half hidden in a dense profusion of nettles; it irks him that he has no money to sort it out. He, his wife and her younger brother, John, are doing all they can to make ends meet; pay the rent and keep up the hire purchase on the Ford Consul, a fairly recent model bought in Newmarket.

Picking up the paper today, he will read further comment on Harold Macmillan's recent 'Never had it so good' speech, in which the Prime Minister urged the British people to 'go around the country, go to the industrial towns, go to the farms and you will

see a state of prosperity such as we have never had in my lifetime
– nor indeed in the history of the country.' Did Claude agree
with the Prime Minister's euphoric assessment? His and Elveda's
circumstances could hardly be described as prosperous. A decent
win on the pools would certainly make a difference, and along with
his weekly pension he makes sure to pick up their usual coupon.
In the Post Office he meets Mr. Brown, one of the few neighbours,
along with Kathleen Wetherall of 'The Grove', living in similarly
impecunious gentility with whom he can enjoy an engaging
conversation. He has yet to find anyone else in the area with the kind
of intellect of those that surrounded him at Cambridge, or in the
colonial service. Conversations in the village would understandably
be about the cost of living and 'getting by' on a farmworker's wages –
and perhaps the 21-year old Lester Piggott's second win at the Derby
on *Crepello*.

Although it's early August, a few clouds are already building up
and there is a slight chill in the air. The cool breeze reminds him
of his first African 'winter' starting in May 1912, a few months after
he had arrived in Northern Rhodesia. He had expected to spend his
whole life out there, retired now of course, perhaps owning a small
farm, living like a little lord on his pension.

This was the sleepy, bucolic scene that was to become so familiar to me
in the small village of Bridgham, in Breckland, south Norfolk. Sharing a
large property with Elveda's relations had seemed the perfect solution to
their financial problems. There was also the potential to live off the land
a little, something they had perhaps considered on the Isle of Man before
the war had swiftly curtailed their retirement dream.

Elveda, brought up in rural surroundings, had lost no time in persuading
her husband of the benefits of the move. Next came the idea of rearing
pigs. Elveda's younger brother John Law had offered his practical support,
and Kathleen Wetherall, a friend of the family, agreed enthusiastically to
put up some funds. It had not been difficult to get started; the old buildings
at the top of the field took only a little time to convert into pigsties for the
sows to farrow. Expectations were for eight to ten piglets per litter, twice
a year, then selling the weaners on to another producer for fattening, or
failing that, auctioning them in the nearby market town of Diss. There

Weaners being sold in Diss Market, 1957

would be outlay on animal feed, but with *Ware's* at Harling Road obliging
the fledgling farmers with a credit account, and weaners selling for £8
each, their returns were predicted to exceed the costs by a comfortable
margin.

In terms of living arrangements, there was one essential change for
Claude and Elveda. Since becoming man and wife, from London to the
Isle of Man, London again, and then Bishop's Stortford and Cambridge,
they had enjoyed domestic seclusion together. Now they would be sharing
a house rented by John. Extended families and acquaintances co-existing
under one roof was not uncommon though, and the scale of the property
did afford them some degree of privacy, perhaps as well given the number
and diversity of the other occupants, which included Elveda's youngest
sister Jean, recently-widowed, with her young son David, another brother
Alf and his new wife, Mary, plus Gwendoline Bourne, a cousin of Kathleen
Wetherall.

The Rectory, though neglected of late, was a beautiful, classically-
proportioned Georgian house built around 1770 and enlarged in the early
19th century.[2] When the last full-time incumbent left, the Rev. Theo
Child, Rector of the adjoining parishes of East Harling and West Harling,
was given responsibility for taking services at the church in Bridgham.[3]
With the Rectory vacant, the Diocese of Norwich was willing to accept
a reasonable rent from John Law, who was Churchwarden. Rumours

The Rectory, Bridgham (in 2013)

abounded that Lord Nelson had once stayed at the Rectory, and etched his name on a windowpane. In a comprehensive and deeply researched history of Bridgham, David O'Neale debunks the story, explaining that the window in question was 'an upper one on the right-hand side of the front, and was built in 1804. Nelson's movements from that time until his death are known. The person scratching "Horatio Nelson" was obviously the young Comyn, after all it was his name also!'[4]

'Young Comyn' was the son of Stephen George Comyn, a favoured naval chaplain of Lord Nelson, who had served with him at the Battles of the Nile and Copenhagen.[5] At the height of the Nile engagement, Nelson, sustaining a bloody head wound and convinced he was not long for this world, summoned Comyn to his side. The surgeon however assured the Admiral that all was well, and when victory was won, Nelson requested Comyn to conduct a service of thanksgiving from the quarterdeck of the *Vanguard*.[6] Due to retire from the navy, Comyn now sought Nelson's assistance in finding a living ashore. After putting in a word with the Lord Chancellor, on 24th June 1801 Nelson wrote to Comyn congratulating him on his appointment as Rector of Bridgham. The letter also bore a postscript in Emma Hamilton's handwriting: 'Joy joy to you & Mrs Comyn my dear sir'.[7] Comyn moved into the Rectory in 1802, accompanied by his wife Charlotte and seven-year-old son, George. Their second son, born in 1806, was given the name Horatio Nelson William Comyn.[8]

Rev. Stephen Comyn conducting the thanksgiving service after the
Battle of the Nile (Aquatint by John Augustus Atkinson, 1816)

The Bridge over the Thet, 1957

Bridgham features in the Domesday Book, although there is an earlier reference when Bridgham was gifted to the monks of Ely by the wealthy Anglo-Saxon widow, Aelfwaru, who died in 1007.[9] In 1050 it was known as *Brugeham*, and by 1280 as *Briggeham*, meaning the ham or settlement by the bridge.[10] With its linear layout, running parallel to the river Thet, the southern boundary of the parish, the village probably began life as a crossing point. Other factors may have been its proximity to the ancient Peddars Way, a Roman road much frequented by pilgrims journeying from Suffolk and elsewhere to the *Shrine of our Lady of Walsingham* in north Norfolk, and the prehistoric drove road, crossing the parish, from Hockwold to the Thet.[11]

St. Mary's Church, Bridgham originated as a wooden structure, rebuilt in stone around the fourteenth century. The door to the south was probably thirteenth century, complemented by a northern porch circa fifteenth century. In place of an early tower, believed to have collapsed some 300 years before Claude and Elveda's arrival, was a squat wooden structure housing the one surviving bell.[12] Simon Knott, a contemporary connoisseur of East Anglian churches, describing Bridgham as 'one of those sprawling Norfolk villages, a little off the beaten track, which are always a pleasure to visit' was equally enamoured of St Mary's: 'a delight, and rather different to most other medieval churches in appearance. Its pleasing and curious shape is a result of the buffeting of the centuries.' He was also glad to find the place well appreciated and welcoming to visitors: 'I got the impression that he (the caretaker) was mostly keen for us to see it because he knew it to be beautiful and prayerful. It would not be possible to go into Bridgham church without realising that it was the House of God.'[13]

St. Mary's Church, Bridgham, 1957

In his middle sixties, Claude had found himself in a corner of England often dismissed as visually and culturally barren. Noel Coward had not helped with his droll remark in his play *Private Lives*, with 'very flat Norfolk', becoming a sole point of reference for the metropolitan set.[14] Other impressions of the county, especially from those who have lived there for any length of time, are far more positive. Edward Storey enjoys 'the "still centre" when all around is turmoil.'[15] Lilias Rider Haggard wrote of this corner of England being: 'more lovely than any place on earth. Beautiful with a hint of secrecy which haunts it, as the memory of a dark and tender sadness clouds the brilliance of a summer day.'[16] Dick Bagnall-Oakeley believed that 'Norfolk' is not simply a word to define a county, but 'it also describes a language, a humour and a way of life.'[17]

Claude certainly found it difficult to fully adapt to the Norfolk way of life, where only people born in the county are able to fully penetrate the language. Bagnall-Oakeley believed that 'just as their language, so also the people of Norfolk are tough, resistant and impenetrable.' Arnold Wesker's 1958 play *Roots*, written in a Norfolk dialect, portrayed the region as timeless and traditional, resistant, impervious even to modernity, in which the metropolis of London is thought of as quite another world. But Norfolk is a large county, so what was it really like around Bridgham, in the midst of the Brecklands, whose sandy heaths, among the driest in the country, covered much of north Suffolk and the south of Norfolk?[18] 'Brecks' was used to describe an area of heath cultivated in a number of sections, which after harvesting, was left to revert to nature. Claude would have observed the belts of twisted Scots pines crossing the Brecks, first planted as windbreaks to protect the light topsoil from erosion, and learned the long history of human and animal habitation from the Stone Age; the Neolithic flint workings at Grime's Graves, rabbit warrens and landed estates. The magic of Breckland is perhaps best captured in poems by 'Hugh the Harp', Rev. Charles Hugh Richardson Harper, who was Rector of West Harling, just across the river Thet from Bridgham, from 1899 to 1915, before moving just a few miles to Riddlesworth:

> When I a thousand years am dead,
> I wonder who will be
> Riddlesworth's Rector, in my stead,
> And Harling's after me.
>
> On Breckland wide the bracken waves
> Unchanged since that far day

> When the first flint-men dug Grimes Graves,
> And knapped the boulders gray
>
> What did they know, those ancient men,
> And still less what know we
> Of man's beginnings, and his end,
> On time's uncharted sea? [19]

In his second poem, written during World War Two, Harper reminds us that even the most tranquil places can be visited by harsher elements, both natural, and in the frightening new world that had arisen in his lifetime, man-made.

> Night and day the droning airplanes
> Pierce the deep, dreaming Breckland sky,
> Outpacing the sun as it girdles the globe
> And the startled stars whirling by.
> Is Man's knowledge now a blessing or curse?
> Is Man's modern world for better or worse?
> Again heaven makes no reply. [20]

The 'droning airplanes' of the US Air Force had arrived in 1942, along with some 50,000 military personnel in the build-up to D-Day. By the 1950s they were long gone. The bracken still waved and the Thet whispered to the reeds, the stars recovered their equanimity in the firmament, and though the pilgrims on the Peddars Way might better be described as hikers, Charles Harper would be overjoyed to know that the intrinsic qualities of the Brecklands were largely unchanged.

The community however, had altered in certain respects. Under the deep, dreaming sky, the Rectory had seen the last of its clerical incumbents, and was now home to an assortment of lay people. Religion though continued to play a part, as John Law, in his mid-twenties when his older sister Elveda and Claude moved in, had become closely involved with St. Mary's and it was very fitting that he was appointed churchwarden. Brought up largely in Norfolk after his parents moved their timber business from Stansted, he had left school without qualifications at fifteen, and been toughened up in the 2nd Battalion of the Coldstream Guards, fighting 'communist' terrorists in the Malayan jungle from 1948-50. [21] Back in Norfolk after demob, he had started to earn his living cutting and selling firewood, now supplemented by a share in the pig enterprise and the potato crop from a small field by the side of the house.

John Law with his younger sister, Jean   *Kathleen Wetherall*

A thoughtful, reserved young man, with no known attachments, John Law's involvement with the church had been instrumental in Claude and Elveda forming a strong bond with Miss Wetherall. Kathleen Ada Violet Henniker-Wetherall had purchased 'The Grove,' a lovely timber-framed seventeenth century house, in 1940.[22] Of 'independent means' – she never let much be known about her past – she had immersed herself in village life, the St. John's Ambulance Brigade, numerous other charities and the church all keeping her busy. It was Kathleen who had largely paid for the four sows: two large Whites and two Danish 'Landrace', and they did look good! If only there had been saddlebacks, which Claude knew from Northern Rhodesia, pigs that could obtain a proper protein balance from foraging rather than from expensive formula food.

More importantly for Claude, Kathleen was a good friend and confidante. Both well educated, they enjoyed conversations about art and culture, Claude sharing reminiscences of his Cambridge days with someone on a sympathetic wavelength. Kathleen, a gifted artist and watercolourist, painted an ashtray for Claude with the Trinity Hall emblem: 'Sable, a crescent within a bordure ermine'.[23]

Trinity Hall Crest

Although ten years younger, Kathleen's appreciation of Claude's scholarly background must have revived his sense of identity, and the topics of conversation must surely have included Africa. Claude would have seen the Pathé News footage of the uprisings in Kenya, and the trial of Jomo Kenyatta on charges of Mau-Mau collusion. On 8th April 1953, the BBC reported that Kenyatta and five other Kenyan African leaders had been sentenced to seven years hard labour. In Northern Rhodesia, Gore-Browne and the European community would no doubt be hoping that the recent Federation with Nyasaland and the 'African Affairs Board' might forestall the need for similar measures. The Kenyan Emergency however went a great deal further than locking up six men, and details of the widespread atrocities committed against Africans would take many years to emerge.

Elveda was pleased that Claude had found a kindred spirit in Bridgham, helping him to feel more at home in a setting with which she was already well accustomed, surrounded by her relatives. Cheerful and hardworking, Elveda really was in her element looking after the pigs, poultry and vegetable garden, and playing a full part in the daily and seasonal routines of the countryside. When rationing ended in July 1954, some people were so thrilled that they set fire to their ration books. The Oldfields also hoped that life might get easier, win or no win on the horses. Watching Claude, in his somewhat curmudgeonly way adapting to life at the Rectory, Elveda was looking forward to their first Christmas there together. News received a few weeks later meant that it was not to be.

---

[1] By 'Hugh the Harp,' Rev. Charles Hugh Richardson Harper. Source: David O'Neale (ed), *Harper, Reverend Charles Hugh Richardson, A Breckland Time-Piece: Tales Of Bridgham Folk* (1996).

[2] Bridgham, Tl 98 NE, 6/24 The Rectory, 21.7.51 II. House. c. 1770, enlarged early C19. Flint and brick rendered with pantiled roof at rear and slate at front. Double pile plan with hipped roofs. Façade is two storeys of five bays. Central twin-columned porch with flat entablature. Sash windows with glazing bars. Listing NGR: TL9582185765. Source: *British Listed Buildings*

[3] Rev. Theodore Hilary Child was Rector of Harling E & W, 1947-59; also separately Rector of Bridgham and Roudham from 1950-9. From correspondence with Amanda Hunt, Diocese of Norwich. Child (1909-2000) was married to Ursula Frances Child (1913-2005). From Grave monument in St. Edmund (old cremations) church burial ground, Southwold. At www.gravestonephotos.com

[4] David O'Neale & Tony Dobbin, *Village Life: The Story of Bridgham in Norfolk* (Taverner Publications, 2010)

[5] Stephen George Comyn (1764-1839) was an English naval chaplain who served with Lord Nelson at the Battle of the Nile and the Battle of Copenhagen. He was a close friend of Nelson and is said to have been his favourite chaplain.

[6] The Battle of the Nile on 1 August 1798. The Nelson Society.

[7] Document bequeathed to Norwich Grammar School. *The Times* Wills, 2 January 2004.

[8] O'Neale & Dobbin, ibid. Horatio Nelson William Comyn was born at Bridgham in 1806, being named after the Norfolk hero who had died at Trafalgar the year before. He became curate at Bridgham under his father, the Rev. Stephen George Comyn (Rector 1802-39), who had been Nelson's chaplain on at least three of his ships.

[9] The parish has a long history, and had certainly been in existence for some time by the time of the Norman Conquest, its population, ownership and productive capabilities being set out in the Domesday Book of 1086. Source: www.heritage. norfolk.gov.uk

[10] History of St. Mary's, Bridgham. Source: Diocese of Norwich

[11] The Peddars Way is 46 miles long and follows the route of a Roman road. Others believe that it was an ancient trackway, a branch or extension of the Icknield Way, later used and remodelled by the Romans. The name is said to be derived from the Latin *pedester* – on foot. Source: Donald Maxwell, *Unknown Norfolk* (The Bodley Head, 1925)

Our Lady of Walsingham is a title of the Blessed Virgin Mary venerated by both Roman Catholics and Anglicans, associated with the reputed Marian apparitions to Richeldis de Faverches, a pious English noblewoman in 1061 in the village of Walsingham, Norfolk. Lady Richeldis had a building structure named *The Holy House* built in Walsingham which later became a shrine and place of pilgrimage. See also Francis Blomefield, *Hundred of Shropham: Bridgham*, in *An Essay Towards A Topographical History of the County of Norfolk: Volume 1*, London, 1805 (pp. 436-40) www.british-history.ac.uk/topographical-hist-norfolk/vol1

[12] Harling United Benefice, Diocese of Norwich

[13] Simon Knott, September 2006 at www.norfolkchurches.co.uk. Bridgham has one of the most interesting fonts in Norfolk, made of a white, chalky stone, which has traces of its original colour. It appears eroded as much as defaced, and is remarkable for two of its panels. That to the west shows the Assumption of the Blessed Virgin

[14] From Noel Coward's 1930 play, *Private Lives*:
   Elyot: 'I met her on a house party in Norfolk'.
   Amanda: 'Very flat, Norfolk'.
   Elyot: 'There's no need to be unpleasant'.

[15] Edward Storey, born 1930 at Whittlesey, Isle of Ely

[16] From *Norfolk Notebook* by Lilias Rider Haggard (1892-1968), fourth and youngest child of the British writer Sir Henry Rider Haggard and Mariana Louisa Margitson

[17] Dick Bagnall-Oakeley (1908-74), naturalist and dialect expert

[18] Up until 200 years ago, much of it consisted of open heathland, but the area of Breckland has been substantially reduced in the 20th century by the impact of

modern farming and the creation in 1914 of Thetford Forest. Substantial areas have been preserved, including what is known as the Stanford Battle Area (to the north of Bridgham). The Breckland is one of the few areas in England where the rare and shy (but non-indigenous) golden pheasant may be seen in the wild.

[19] *Breckland Time-Piece*, ibid.

[20] Ibid.

[21] The Malayan Emergency was a guerrilla war between the Commonwealth armed forces and the Malayan National Liberation Army (MNLA), the military arm of the Malayan Communist Party (MCP), from 1948-60. The colonial government referred to the conflict as the 'Malayan Emergency', but the MNLA termed it the Anti-British National Liberation War. The rubber plantations and tin-mining companies had wanted the term 'emergency, since their losses would not have been covered by insurance if it had simply been called a 'war'. See www.coldstreamguards-boro.org and www.malayaaforgottenwar.co.uk

[22] Bridgham, TL 98 NE, 6/19 The Grove, II. House. Early C17 with later alterations. Source: *British Listed Buildings*

[23] In heraldry, *Sable* is the tincture black; bordure is a border; *Ermine* is a 'fur', or varied tincture, consisting of a white background with a pattern of black shapes representing the winter coat of the stoat.

CHAPTER 28

Et in Arcadia ego

The wind of change is blowing through this continent.
Whether we like it or not, this growth of national
consciousness is a political fact.

Harold Macmillan, 3rd February 1960,
addressing the South African Parliament[1]

The news was that Claude's sister-in-law had died on 14th August 1954. Maisie and Charlie had enjoyed a happy life together and her sudden passing knocked him for six. With Christmas on the way, Claude and Elveda were invited to spend the occasion with my grandfather Charlie, my mother and me. The only snag was looking after the ducks, geese, chickens and pigs on which the Oldfields' livelihood now depended. Elveda's brother John and Kathleen Wetherall would have been willing, but Elveda either did not want to prevail upon them, or preferred to spend the time with her own family in Norfolk. In the end Claude came to Golders Green, while Elveda sent good wishes and held the fort in Bridgham.

As always, Claude corresponded regularly, recounting to Elveda on 27th December that he'd accompanied Charlie, Joy and me on Christmas Day to lay flowers on Maisie's grave in Hampstead Cemetery, a resting place she would share with her beloved first-born Peggy – and with theatricals Marie Lloyd and Sir Charles Wyndham and both his wives. It had been 'Very quiet ... just the four of us and old Nellie.' Nellie, the loyal 'retainer' from Abergavenny, had looked after Charlie and Maisie for more than forty years. Although missing Elveda, Claude welcomed a break from the demands of animal husbandry, and London had after all been his home for many years. At Golders Green there was 'plenty of lovely grub and drink', my mother's traditional English cooking producing a sumptuous roast turkey, with pudding, ample cheeses and port to follow; hardly surprising that Claude reported 'turning in quite early – not later

346

than 10'! He also found time to meet with an old friend by the name of Dainton, some of his former colleagues from Rhodesia and his cousin Nellie Hugh-Jones.

Christmas over, Claude took the train back to Norfolk with mixed feelings. Pleased as always to be back with Elveda, at the same time he missed the vitality of London. With luck and persistence the smallholding might provide enough money to visit Charlie more often and possibly treat Elveda to dinner or a show in town. Then one day, seeing an article in *Farmers Weekly* about the fluctuating price patterns known as the pig cycle, he realised that the professionals were doing things on a far larger scale and with modern technology. Scratching around with their handful of livestock at the Rectory, was the game really worth the candle?

Charlie and Maisie Oldfield

Perhaps in time the tranquillity of the Norfolk countryside would make it so, the attractions of London would fade and Claude would settle into a contented if impecunious retirement, happy with a loving wife, simple pleasures, and the occasional excitement of a flutter on the horses. He had spent twenty years in a remote part of Africa and, with the exception of Ndola, far from madding crowds. Norfolk was certainly peaceful, a place in which artists and writers have felt the presence of the sublime. In *The English Landscape*, lifelong inhabitant Raffaella Barker describes 'a vastness in a Norfolk sky and a raw quality to the light' and suggests that 'Norfolk creeps into the heart and soul and inhabits us as much as we inhabit it.'[2]

There was though a crucial difference between Africa and Norfolk. Several years later, Hilary Mantel, who knew both places, would register the contrast through one of her female characters:

> The Norfolk climate gave Anna a bloodless look, tinged her thin hands with violet. Every winter she would think of Africa; days when, leaving her warm bed in a hot early dawn, she had felt her limbs grow fluid, and the pores of her face open like petals, and her ribs, freed from her accustomed tense gauge, move to allow her a full, voluptuary's breath. In England she never felt this confidence, not even in a blazing July. The thermometer might register the heat, but her body was sceptical. English heat is sceptical; clouds pass before the sun.'[3]

Faced with freezing winters Claude might well have pined for Africa. Then there was Dorothy. Did he think about her much? During his recent stay in Golders Green, had he even been tempted to look her up? Curiosity about his old flame seems certain, but acting on it would be another matter, and he was now a married man.

A year after Maisie's death, Charlie suffered a heart attack. With no downstairs 'facilities', Charlie was confined upstairs, relying on the care of my mother. This gave Claude a legitimate reason, if one was needed, to visit London from time to time, accompanied by Elveda when she could get away. Apart from giving my mother some respite, being able to stay for a few nights in Golders Green, meant that Claude could spend time with Charlie, a more agreeable experience for the two brothers with the passing of the years. Claude could also have a night out and in June 1956, enjoyed 'a very pleasant evening at the Connaught Rooms', meeting old friends, and some of the new colonial service boys from Northern Rhodesia

Hippo hunted at Mweru wa Ntipa, 1924

and Nyasaland. In that year he contributed to an ongoing debate in the *Northern Rhodesia Journal* about the fluctuating water levels of Mweru wa Ntipa, the often muddy lake between Mporokoso and Chiengi, which he had first visited in 1913.[4] Digging out his old photographs, he recalled watching the plentiful hippo, crocodiles and beautiful exotic birds – cranes, pelicans and flamingos.

At the time Claude was reminiscing about Northern Rhodesia, the country was also on the agenda in parliament. In a lengthy debate on 5th June 1956, the member for Rugby, James Johnson, reminded the House that the Protectorate:

> does not like the scheme of Federation, under which … it is linked with Southern Rhodesia and Nyasaland. That view is shared by Congress in Nyasaland. They fear that later, in 1962, there will be amalgamation, and they fear, rightly or wrongly, that they will be dominated by Europeans, to their discomfort and handicap … In his last speech, Mr. Harry Nkumbula made some comments on conditions in Northern Rhodesia and on his fears for the future: 'Northern Rhodesia is the darkest spot in the whole of the British Colonial Empire. Its social colour bar, racial discrimination, intimidation and ostracism are worse than those being experienced in the Union of South Africa. Its educational policy and health services cannot be anything but deplorable. The discrepancies in the conditions of service between the European and African Civil

Services and between the European miner and the African miner are shocking.' Not all will share those views in their entirety. Some will say that Mr. Nkumbula paints a lurid picture.[5]

Johnson also pointed out that 'In Northern Rhodesia there are about 2 million Africans disenfranchised there, and of course, disenfranchised here, like all other colonial peoples', and that a parliamentary committee had confirmed the widespread practice of racial discrimination in the country. A comparison was made with the 'enormous change' in Kenya where 'The Norfolk Hotel in Nairobi, the Tors Hotel (*sic*) and the New Stanley Hotel, now admit Africans.' Kenya also remained under colonial rule, and Kenyatta and many others were still languishing in jail. Meanwhile in Northern Rhodesia the moral imperative to end discrimination in shops and elsewhere was, according to Johnson accompanied by commercial considerations: the growing prosperity of black Africans 'many of whom are now earning up to £40 a month – and will shortly earn more – in the copper mines.'[6]

It was Harry Nkumbula, along with Kenneth Kaunda, who had organised a boycott of European premises in protest at discrimination, and the previous year, 1955, both had been imprisoned for two months for distribution of so-called subversive literature. Nkumbula, now leader of the country's African National Congress, had come to London a few months before the debate in question and requested, unsuccessfully, a meeting with the Colonial Secretary:

> unfortunately the Minister, acting upon the advice of the
> Government of Northern Rhodesia, felt unable to see him. I think
> that was a mistake, on many grounds, not least that if the Minister
> sees any leader of a nationalist movement he prevents the leader
> from making false capital out of a Minister's lack of desire to see him.
> Nevertheless, that is what happened.[7]

Whether the Northern Rhodesian Government and the Colonial Secretary expected Nkumbula and his colleagues in the ANC to just leave the matter there, one can only surmise. But by 1957, it had been agreed between the British and Federal governments that a conference would be held to discuss the future of the Federation – but not until 1960 – a three-year delay!

Though the Oldfields had no children of their own, Elveda was always well disposed towards me, encouraging me to come to Norfolk in the

The Grove, Bridgham (taken in 2009)

summer of 1957 in spite of Claude's reticence (described in the opening chapter). I have also not forgotten the welcome from Kathleen Wetherall and our bike ride from the station, the first of many occasions when she would make time for me. On subsequent visits to Bridgham, she welcomed me into her home, often cooking late-night suppers and inviting me to stay at The Grove when Claude was being particularly crabby. Years later, she would relate her first impressions of Bridgham:

> it was just about the outbreak of war … a quiet, lovely little village then, no modern houses, and the old Norfolk labouring type – lovely people and a wonderful rector. I've never known such kindness anywhere and I am very proud and privileged to call them my friends over the many years I've been living here. Village life has changed – it's absolutely incomparable with the old days …[8]

Kathleen, very much involved with church activities at St. Mary's, had a strong Christian faith, and gave generous help to the people of the village. I remember well a summer's outing to Brancaster on the north Norfolk coast, which included visits to both the Anglican and Roman Catholic shrines in Walsingham, where Kathleen enlightened us with her deep affinity with Marian theology.[9]

In August 1959, Claude was in Golders Green looking after Charlie, now turned eighty, whilst my mother took the two of us for a few days' summer holiday. Claude was pleased to record his prowess as temporary housekeeper: 'Charlie complimented me on my batter pudding ... we are getting along together fine and he is very grateful for anything done for him.' Three days later, after seeing *Julius Caesar* at the cinema, with James Mason, John Gielgud and Marlon Brando as Mark Anthony, he reported wistfully that 'I have not been out anywhere today, except with Chris (Charlie's Pekinese) in the Park ... I am getting a bit tired now, & shall be glad to be back with you, sweet.'[10] Still having no luck on the football pools, he appeared to be expecting a cheque from Elveda who, working hard with the livestock and cutting firewood with John, appeared to be subsidising his gambling habit.

When 1960 arrived there was little sign yet of swinging Britain in Bridgham. On 3rd February, Claude would have listened to the reports of Harold Macmillan's memorable speech to the South African Parliament in Cape Town, when he made clear Britain's aversion to the apartheid regime, saying that as:

> a fellow member of the Commonwealth it is our earnest desire to give South Africa our support and encouragement, but ... there are some aspects of your policies which make it impossible for us to do this without being false to our own deep convictions ...The wind of change is blowing through this continent. Whether we like it or not, this growth of national consciousness is a political fact.[11]

The South African Prime Minister, Dr. Hendrik Verwoerd, responded that 'to do justice in Africa means not only being just to the black man of Africa, but also to the white man of Africa.' Many Europeans living in Africa felt that the speech could be interpreted as British abdication in the region, abandoning white settlers, but the reaction from black nationalist leaders in South Africa and further north was naturally much more positive. Albert Luthuli commented that Macmillan had given African people 'some inspiration and hope'.[12]

In 1960, the Monckton Commission concluded that the Federation could not be maintained, except by force or through massive changes in racial legislation. It advocated a majority of black African members in the Nyasaland and Northern Rhodesian legislatures and giving these territories the option to leave the Federation after five years. The Prime Minister of the Federation, Sir Roy Welensky, rejected the report, calling it the 'death knell of federation'.[13] The black nationalists wanted an end to the federation, with independence for their territories on the basis of majority rule.

Claude, recalling some of the able people he had known and worked with, understood the impetus behind 'the wind of change', although he was concerned that so much still needed to be done, especially in the provision of healthcare and education. That summer would bring a red-letter day for him. An envelope landing on the doormat of the Rectory was from the Lord Chamberlain, commanded by Her Majesty Queen Elizabeth to invite Flying Officer and Mrs. Claude Oldfield to an official garden party at Buckingham Palace on 14th July. The invitation included the words: 'Weather Permitting'. How anxiously they must have listened out for the forecast on the Home Service as the day drew near! Fortunately it dawned to blue skies. It would be one of their proudest moments; recognition of Claude's contribution to the colonial service and in WWI in Northern Rhodesia, and in WWII with the RAFVR.

Their invitation card, together with photographs of them in their finery, was framed and hung on the wall of the Rectory. By the following May, Claude was back in Golders Green, writing home that: 'Things are not too difficult, although it is rather a case of "one damn thing after another" … It has been nice having talks and drinks with Charlie and he seems very fond of me these days.'

In the early autumn of 1961 came a very different reminder of the past.

The Lord Chamberlain's Invitation

Claude & Elveda, ready for Buckingham Palace

Just after midnight on 18th September, a plane carrying the UN Secretary-General Dag Hammarskjöld crashed near Ndola. The BBC report sent Claude's thoughts racing back thirty years, recalling the desperate emotional state into which he had spiralled whilst at Ndola. He realized the implications of Hammarskjöld's death for African and world affairs: Cold War opponents America and Russia were vying for influence in the colonial territories now struggling for independence, Hammarskjöld having been on his way to negotiate a cease-fire with Moise Tshombe in the Katanga Province, seceded from the recently-independent Congo. The Albertina, a DC6-B, operated by Swedish Trans Air, had been cleared for landing at Ndola at 12.12am local time on 18th September, but the wreckage was not found until fifteen hours later. Of the sixteen on board, one man, an American from Miami, was found alive, just. Badly burned,

UN Sgt. Harold Julien, managed to tell investigators that Hammarskjöld had ordered the pilot not to land at Ndola, and that there had been a series of explosions.[14] A few days later on 23rd September, Sgt. Julien died from his injuries. Speculation that the crash had not been accidental had already begun.[15]

In 1960 the newly independent Congo had requested UN aid to defuse the complex crisis that had arisen between the Prime Minister, Patrice Lumumba, charismatic young leader of the country's largest nationalist faction and the President, Joseph Kasa-Vubu. Lumumba's reaction had been to seek assistance from the Soviet Union, which promptly sent military advisors and support. In January 1961, a few months before Hammarskjöld's death, Lumumba had been executed by a firing squad. Claude would undoubtedly have pondered the sinister possibilities. He could recollect the ruthless attitudes of the Belgians whom he had encountered in Ndola. Had their successors had a 'cloak and dagger' role in removing both Lumumba and Hammarskjöld?

By early 1962 Claude, scrutinising his morning paper more closely than usual, would have realised that significant change was finally coming to Africa. On 28th February, Colonial Secretary Reginald Maudling announced revised constitutional proposals for Northern Rhodesia, giving some voting rights to Africans. Sir Roy Welensky flew in to London intent on dissuading the government from going ahead. He would find that he was too late, and after meeting Macmillan and lunching with the Queen, he returned home in disappointment the same day.[16]

As my schooldays came to an end, my visits to Bridgham tailed off, but Claude and Elveda continued to stay at Golders Green, usually twice a year, giving my mother a break from caring for my grandfather. In December 1962, Claude and Elveda gave me an unforgettable evening, inviting me to the Odeon Leicester Square for one of the first screenings of *Lawrence of Arabia*. For the whole four hours I was captivated. Looking back, I realise that the occasion must also have been exciting for them, both passionate cinemagoers. This landmark picture, among the first epics made for wide-screen, went on to win seven academy awards, with Peter O'Toole idolised by the public. For Claude, the immense landscapes, the clash of civilisations and crack of gunfire, would all stir memories of his exotic past in distant Africa.

The film still enthrals, thanks not least to David Lean's masterly direction, which in a less impatient age allowed the audience time to appreciate the spectacle, the unfolding scenes a slow burn of suspense. The homosexual overtones, in those pre-Wolfenden days, must have gone way over my head, but the Dera'a scene would long preoccupy students of Lawrence. Alex von Tunzelmann explained that:

> Lawrence wrote in *The Seven Pillars*, and in private letters, that he was imprisoned there by the district governor Hajim Bey and tortured, sexually assaulted and perhaps – his descriptions are elliptical – raped … some historians consider the whole Dera'a incident a fantasy, partly because Lawrence described it sensually – 'a delicious warmth, probably sexual, was swelling through me,' he wrote of being flogged, then kicked in the ribs, and partly because he was seen by witnesses looking unhurt afterwards. In 1924, Lawrence wrote to George Bernard Shaw's wife, Charlotte, confessing that 'to earn five minutes' respite from a pain which drove me mad, I gave away … my bodily integrity.'[17]

Scott Anderson has suggested that Lawrence could have submitted to avoid further torture, and afterwards embroidered his tale with 'the kind of violence that offers an absolution of guilt by making all questions of will or resistance moot.'[18] Whatever the truth about Dera'a, most commentators agree that the film was right to portray the protagonist as psychologically damaged and even more withdrawn afterwards. Tim Bray has tried to establish the facts, referring to Lawrence's two major published works, *Seven Pillars of Wisdom* and *The Mint*, and reading his translations, two volumes of his collected letters, and multiple biographies. Bray concludes that Lawrence is a fascinating historical figure, supported by his compellingly-written accounts of his own exploits, and considers that Lawrence was probably gay but didn't do much about it.[19]

At the end of 1962, elections were held in Northern Rhodesia. Kaunda and Nkumbula were now in rival parties, the former reportedly radicalised by his experience of imprisonment, while the later had become more moderate. Sir Stewart Gore-Browne, knighted in 1945, was a moderate European, who had argued for a government that would work for all races, and now made a bid to return to active politics. Kaunda spoke at over a hundred meetings during the campaign, which was marred by intimidation and an outbreak of violence that killed one ANC official. The final vote gave the legislative council a majority of black African representatives, comprising a coalition that was uneasy but seemed clearly agreed on the need for two things: greater democracy and self-government. Gore-

Browne upheld these aims, but with insufficient support in the elections was obliged to retire once more.

Back in Norfolk the coldest winter since 1946-47 descended. Temperatures fell below zero before Christmas, with up to a foot of snow falling on Boxing Day. December ended with blizzards, deep drifts and chaos, the worst across southwest England and Wales. Outlying roads remained impassable and villages were cut off.[20]

Claude was taking things slowly, his sciatica very painful. The post between London and Norfolk appeared to be getting through, as Charlie and Claude exchanged letters about their ailments and misfortunes. In Golders Green on 17th January, the lounge chimneystack at West Heath Drive had collapsed, and at 3.10am the fire brigade arrived. Then, 'On February 2nd, when Joy went downstairs, she was met with water streaming down the walls, she turned off the mains and did her best to catch the water in bowls. We could not get a plumber till Tuesday, also Wed, so we are OK again. We have no lavatory as this was the cause of the burst pipe …' Countless homes were similarly stricken by the big freeze. I only heard later what had happened at home, as I was living 20 miles away in Hertfordshire gaining a year's practical experience of farming, contending with the snowdrifts while feeding and milking forty Friesians twice a day. Charlie had ended his letter on a positive note, suggesting painkillers for Claude's sciatica, and hoping that their luck would change on the pools.

Nothing however could deter Claude from was his weekly trip to the cinema, and on the evening of Wednesday 20th February, he set out with Elveda and John for their local picture house in Watton. On the way home Claude felt unwell. Thirteen days after his letter about the pipes, Charlie was writing again, but this time only to Elveda, expressing 'our deepest sympathy in the loss of your dear husband … it came as a great shock to both of us (Charlie and Joy), words are a little comfort in times like this … my dear Phil was a wonderful brother to me. We had lots in common, I shall miss him very much.'

Claude had died on the morning of Thursday 21st February 1963, only a few hours after seeing his last film. On 31st December that year the Federation was dissolved, and on 24th October 1964 Northern Rhodesia became the independent Republic of Zambia, led by President Kenneth Kaunda.

Claude's final resting place in Bridgham churchyard

1   *Et in Arcadia ego* (also known as *Les bergers d'Arcadie or The Arcadian Shepherds*) is a painting by Nicolas Poussin (1594-1665), depicting a pastoral scene with idealized shepherds from classical antiquity. The phrase can be translated as 'Even in Arcadia, there am I'.

2   *Daily Telegraph*, 16 October 2000

3   Hilary Mantel, *Change of Climate* (Viking, 1994)

4   F. B. Macrae, 'Mweru wa Ntipa: More about Water Levels', *NRJ*, Vol III, No. 2 (1956), pp 127-30

5   *Hansard*, June 1956

6   *Hansard*, ibid. The correct spelling is *Torrs Hotel*

7   Ibid.

8   O'Neale and Dobbin, ibid., p 226

9   As Anglicans believe that Jesus was both human and God the Son, the second Person of the Trinity, Mary is accorded honour as the 'theotokos' (Greek), literally the 'God-bearer' or 'one who gives birth to God'.

10   This would have been the 1953 film by MGM, adapted from Shakespeare's play.

11   From BBC/onthisday/1950-2005. See also David Harrison, *The White Tribe of Africa* (University of California Press, 1981)

12   Albert Luthuli, 'What I Think of Macmillan's Speech', *Drum* magazine, Johannesburg, March 1960. The reply of the people on the whole is a refusal to be intimidated and in a growing mood to show 'a courage that rises with danger.' Let us look forward to the future with the hope and belief that the centenary anniversary of the Union of South Africa will find our country already a free non-racial democracy. In the meantime let us each and all work … for the consummation of our hope – freedom and democracy for all – at the earliest time possible.

[13] 'Collapsing Bastion', *Time Magazine*, 24 October 1960

[14] 'Explosions on Plane before Dag Crashed', *Vancouver Sun*, 18 September 1961

[15] UN General Assembly, Session 17, 24 April 1962.

[16] 'Sir Roy Welensky in London: The Northern Rhodesian Crisis', *The Illustrated London News*, 10 March 1962

[17] '*Lawrence of Arabia*: a confabulous romp through the desert: Starring Peter O'Toole, this flawed but stunning biopic is a compelling portrait of an enigmatic man', Alex von Tunzelmann, *The Guardian*, 19 December 2013 (Peter O'Toole had died on 14 December)

[18] Scott Anderson, *Lawrence in Arabia: War, Deceit, Imperial Folly and the Making of the Modern Middle East* (Anchor Books, 2013)

[19] Timothy Bray (b. 1955) is a Canadian software developer and entrepreneur, who also co-authored the original XML specification. He is not a professional historian. At www.tbray.org

[20] The Meteorological Office, London

CHAPTER 29

Continua

... the wider life of the Colonies will be much more to Ann's liking than the limited outlook of the English atmosphere

Thomas Jeffreys, writing to his brother, Robert,
28th November 1955

After Claude's death, Elveda continued to live in the Rectory in Bridgham, keeping poultry, surrounded by various pets and sustained by her family. She kept in touch with her brother-in-law, Charlie, in Golders Green, often visiting during the summer. In April 1964, together with 'The Doc' (Charlie's Irish doctor, Leo Nolan), they even won £2 on the football pools.

A letter in February 1966 from Gwen Bourne to Charlie Oldfield broke the tragic news of the sudden death of Elveda's youngest brother, John Law, from an overdose of barbiturates on 8th February. The subsequent inquest concluded that he had intended to take his own life after a row with his friend, Charlie Bobby, who had exasperated John by finding a new girlfriend. John had been devastated. Charlie admitted at the inquest that he had 'slept in the same room' as John and it seems likely that they were in some kind of relationship.[1] With homosexuality a criminal offence prior to 1969, the nature of their friendship had been kept secret. John was only thirty-six. It was a terrible, appalling loss. If it had not been for John's easygoing friendship when I first went to Bridgham aged thirteen, I probably would not have returned for regular holidays over the next five years. John became a very good friend, something like the older brother I never had, and without those school holidays spent with him and his family in Norfolk, I would not have developed a love of the countryside and gone on to study agriculture.

John Law   *Charlie Bobby*

To lose her youngest brother in such circumstances must have been deeply saddening for Elveda who, cheerful by nature, wished for little more than the happiness of those close to her. Soon after John's death, the tenancy at the Rectory ended and Elveda took a bedsit in the home of a female friend at Vicarage Road, Thetford, later moving to a British Legion

flat in nearby Lord Walsingham Court, accompanied by her vociferous mynah bird. Aside from fibrositis, her health remained good for many years, until at the end of November 1998 she was admitted to hospital in Bury St. Edmunds, where she died on 14th December aged eighty-seven. Her funeral was held a few days later at St. Mary's, Bridgham, attended by thirty mourners. Elveda was buried in the same grave as Claude, only a few feet from the ancient walls of the church and close to her brother, John. At her request, the cost of a new joint headstone was paid from her modest estate.

Elveda at Vicarage Road, Thetford, 1972

One must wonder, of course, what happened to Dorothy – and to Robert, Ann and Audrey. Had Claude received any news or tried to find out where they might be living? My own research, attempting to piece together the salient facts, has been quite a challenge, with doors opening unexpectedly to reveal confidences hidden for a couple of generations – but there have also been blind alleys and understandably not everyone wishes to relive distant and sometimes painful memories.

After Claude left Africa in 1932, Robert Jeffreys continued to play a significant part in the colonial administration for eleven more years, being promoted to Police Magistrate in 1934 and Resident Magistrate three years later.[2] Resident magistrates were based at the larger bomas, normally as the most senior official, but in 1939 Robert was seconded to Nigeria as a judge in the Protectorate Court.[3] With the girls still at school, it is likely that Dorothy would have stayed in Northern Rhodesia, and that Robert went to Nigeria alone. His professional life continued to be important to him and he wrote on matters of specialist interest, for example, explaining in *The Leech* in October 1935 that without official records an African's exact age could rarely be confirmed, raising difficulties in certain legal cases.[4] His further deliberations on this subject were published in 1940 in *African Affairs*.[5]

Robert also recorded his observations of witchcraft and discussed these with Gervas Clay (husband of Betty, referred to in previous chapters), when he was DC at Isoka in 1943. Robert's knowledge had been gleaned during the 1920s in Isoka, where he had learnt that kidnapping and killing by strangulation during the early rains of November was the 'observance of customary propitiatory rites for the securing of an abundant harvest'. He believed that the custom continued, albeit in great secrecy.[6] Cases of ritual murder and bloodletting (known as *banyama*) were still being reported in the 1940s.[7] Gervas Clay recommended to his Provincial Commissioner that the assailants in a *banyama* case be convicted of attempted murder, resulting in a memorandum being issued to all districts confirming that *banyama* was ritual murder.[8]

While Robert was grappling with witchcraft, the two girls had been away in Southern Rhodesia, boarding at St. Peter's Diocesan School in Bulawayo, but by the time of his retirement in December 1943, Ann had already been living in South Africa for two years.[9] In 1944, with Audrey having completed her schooling, the rest of the family also moved south to the Cape. Retiring on an annual salary of £920, shortly before his fifty-sixth birthday, Robert had completed thirty years' service and was entitled to a full pension amounting to £606.1s.7d. With the war and the risk to shipping, Dorothy could not be with her mother, Ellen, when she died in Bournemouth in April 1944, aged seventy-five.[10] After the tragic end to her short marriage to Christian, Ellen had not remarried.

In March 1945, with the war not over but the perceived risk to shipping reduced, Robert, Dorothy and Audrey left Cape Town, sailing on the RMS *Andes*, the shipping records list Dorothy as a 'Secretary' and Audrey a 'Student'. After arriving in Liverpool on 25th March, they moved to Belvoir Road in Bideford.[11] Why north Devon? Choosing Charmouth in Dorset for Audrey's birth in 1926 had perhaps whetted their appetite for the West Country, always a popular destination for returning 'colonials'. With its striking coastline, Hartland Point and the Taw and Torridge estuaries, miles of wide beaches and a regular train service to London, clearly Bideford had its attractions.

We are next able to pick up the story of Robert and Dorothy in the 1950s, when they were living at 11 Aubrey Road, Kensington, on the north side of Holland Park. Robert was in regular correspondence with his brother Thomas, who in 1946, after retiring as a mine manager on the copperbelt, had bought the 7,300-acre Chunga ranch near Isoka, for 3s. 6d. an acre, roughly equivalent to £7 per acre today.[12] Having been privileged to view correspondence between Thomas and Robert between 1953 and 1959, it is apparent that the younger two of the four Jeffreys brothers had remained close. The letters contain affectionate reminiscences of their childhood and outings with their first girlfriends. Thomas and his wife Isabella (nicknamed 'Mopes') seemed content with their farming life of 'busy days,

Ann and Audrey in the 1940s (from Ann Jeffreys' collection)

early nights'. They had had successfully raised three children, Michael, Raymund and Janet, who married Desmond Thatcher. Next door was Mbesuma, owned by Frank Rumsey, the despatch rider who in November 1918 had taken the news of the Armistice to von Lettow-Vorbeck.

Thomas tried frequently to coax his brother Robert back to Africa. In November 1956 (when Ann was emigrating to New Zealand), he suggested that Robert could stop off in South Africa and:

> slip up to Chunga for a year or two on the way. Nothing would give us all greater pleasure than to see you walking up the drive, though in actual fact you would hardly drive out from Isoka or Kasama or wherever and then get out of the car simply to give us the pleasure of seeing you walk up the drive, but you know what I mean.[13]

Interestingly there is no mention of Dorothy. Thomas envisaged a long, perhaps permanent stay for his brother, as suggested a couple of months later when he informed him that Mopes has designed a guest annex '… consisting of a room with a sleeping porch and bathroom attached, and an outside lav. We don't run to interior sanitation yet.'[14]

Though never regretting the purchase of Chunga, by 1957 Thomas admitted that farming has become harder, with poisoned cattle and disputes with neighbours, some eventually settled with the help of the local chief, Mubanga. Thomas believed that the Africans were getting 'too full of themselves', that the future of the Federation did not look good, and referred to a recent copy of *Punch*, containing a parody of Kipling's *The English Flag*:

> Never the lotus closes, never the wild-fowl wake,
> But England gives up Something for Somebody else to take
> Only a shout in the market or a swelled tub thumpers frown
> And, deeply apologetic, the English flag comes down[15]

Robert's pension was significantly more than Claude's, but with the rising cost of living after the war, he too would have struggled, and the correspondence indicates that he had difficulty finding work. Dorothy was clearly away for lengthy periods, especially when visiting Ann in New Zealand. Depression and anxiety about both daughters possibly played a part in his inability to get a job. In poor health, the prospect of ever seeing his brother or Africa again faded, and he died in London in December 1959.

Given the challenges faced by Robert and Dorothy's marriage after her long clandestine affair, how did the lives of her two daughters play out? Ann, fleeing the parental nest as fast as possible, had made her life in Cape Town. Her cousin Janet Thatcher recalled that:

> Her first love was an officer in the Royal Navy and his ship was torpedoed … I do not know the man's name but from what Ann told me, I got the impression that no man ever quite matched up to him – or her father. He may have been in the South African Navy but I think Ann said the Royal Navy.[16]

Talking to Michael Trendall, Ann's son-in-law, I was able to ascertain that Ann's first love had been Pierce Thomas de la Garde Grissell. They had met in Cape Town in 1941 when he was on active service on HMS *Dragon*. Writing to Ann on 21st October 1941, he had composed a Sonnet to her:

> When I sit with my love away from care
> And all the noise from life sounds far below
> We use few words, for are they not but air?
> I look into her eyes
> She knows; I know
>
> Drop you no word into the pool of bliss;
> Break not the peace of love with noisy blows
> There is more substance in one quiet loss
> Than in ten thousand words
> I know; She knows
>
> Too deep, too beautiful for humankind
> To understand, to speak of in dull phrase;
> A miracle; two minds become one mind
> Living in oneness till the end of days
> In happiness, in thoughtfulness, in woe
> Single in mind;
> I know; she knows; we know[17]

Less than a year later, tragedy struck. Grissell was drowned when the troopship HMT *Orcades* was torpedoed and sunk by a German U-boat off Cape Town on 10th October 1942, only a day after leaving port.[18] The first two torpedoes did not sink the *Orcades* and an orderly launching of the lifeboats was in progress. The U-boat returned, firing a third torpedo which missed, but a direct hit from the fourth caused substantial damage and the order was given to 'abandon ship'. From a total complement of 1,067 on board, 1,022 survivors were picked up by the Polish SS *Narvik*; Grisell was one of the unlucky forty-five.[19]

In July 1944 Ann met another naval officer, Robert Hodgetts, when his aircraft carrier HMS *Illustrious* docked in Cape Town for a re-fit. Robert had from 1940 been an Observer with 825 Squadron on the aircraft carrier HMS *Furious*. In March 1941, when flying a reconnaissance mission in a Fulmar off the West African coast, he and his crew, having failed to locate their ship, were forced to land in Dakar and were captured. Robert became a PoW, but managed to return to England in 1943. The following year, he joined 810 Squadron of the Fleet Air Arm, operating from HMS *Illustrious*.

Joining him in England, Ann married Robert, six years her senior, at Formby Parish Church in Lancashire on 29th January 1945. Like her mother's marriage in 1923, a special license was required, as neither Ann nor her fiancée had lived in the parish long enough for banns to be read. Robert, then a Lieutenant in the Royal Navy Volunteer Reserve, gave his address as Rosemary Lane, Formby, a modest semi-detached house; Ann, an apartment in the affluent Sea Point suburb of Cape Town. Robert had been offered a quieter posting as an Observer on the shore-based HMS *Urley*, the Royal Naval Air Station at Ronaldsway on the Isle of Man, across the water from Formby, where he served until July 1945.

Ann was soon pregnant and gave birth to Ann Gillian Hodgetts at the Jane Crookall Maternity Home in Douglas on 7th November 1945. Was Ann looking for an idyllic life on the island, as Sir Sampson Sladen and later, Claude and Elveda, had hoped for? West End House on Arbory Street, Castletown, close to her husband's base at the airfield, had given them a roof over their heads, but the relationship did not last long after the war and they divorced.

Returning to the mainland after the war, Robert joined the civil service, becoming an Assistant Principal in the Ministry of National Insurance. He lived in Kew with a Frances Pepper, who he married in July 1949.[20] They had two daughters together, but it seems that Robert was not closely involved with the upbringing of his daughter with Ann.[21]

After the split, Ann returned with her baby daughter to live with her parents at Aubrey Road. By September 1950, aged twenty-six she had married George Budibent, a thirty-seven-year-old divorcee, at the

Kensington Registry Office.[22] An engineer, with a naval background, whose late father had been an Army Colonel, George came with an inheritance and had seemed a safe choice, but only five years later, Ann was writing to uncle Tommy at Chunga, to reveal 'the misguided doings of George and the pending divorce'.[23]

Ann and George had been spending time in Portsmouth, where the Keppel's Head Hotel was a popular meeting place for 'naval types', which Michael Trendall believes led to Ann meeting New Zealander Colin Gardner.[24] A retired naval Lt. Commander and the son of a sheep farmer, he too was a divorcée, six years' older than Ann. They married in Gosport in June 1956, Ann's father again a witness at the ceremony.[25] Having lived initially at Hill Head overlooking the Solent, the couple soon moved out to New Zealand, living first in Gisborne and then in 1963 in Marlborough, on South Island.[26] Ann's uncle felt that after two misadventures, 'the wider life of the Colonies will be much more to [her] liking than the limited outlook of the English atmosphere.'[27]

However, once again this marriage was not to last and in January 1967, at close to forty-three, Ann wed for the fourth time, this time in New Zealand. Her new spouse was David May, with whom she lived in Wellington, although even this relationship drifted to a close, David preferring an 'alternative' lifestyle embracing Buddhism.

Returning to the UK in 1971, Ann lived once again with her mother in Aubrey Road and later in a small house in Parsons Green, increasingly playing the role of the *grande dame*. She appears to have given up on marriage, but started a long liaison with a merchant navy officer, Patrick

Ann in England (c. 1975)

Rattigan, who she had met on the return voyage.[28] For some time, Ann worked in the civil service in London, but in 1976 moved to Liverpool, taking a flat in Princes Park, where Patrick would spend some of his home leave. Having resigned her civil service position, Ann could not find alternative employment and in 1978, Patrick suggested a move to Glossop, buying a 1930s 'semi' in Sheffield Road.[29] Initially it seemed that the relationship was going well, but it became increasingly acrimonious, possibly because Patrick found it difficult to live with Ann's *folie de grandeur*.[30]

Patrick died in January 1999 and left Ann a life interest in the property. She lived alone there, and for a time in Buxton, before returning to Glossop to a house at 25 Princess Street. Becoming unwell over Christmas 2006, Ann died on 2nd January 2007 in hospital at Ashton-under-Lyne, just a few miles from Glossop, having reached the age of eighty-two. Gareth Parkes, related to the Jeffreys family by marriage, recalled visiting her in Glossop, when she described herself as 'cantankerous and pretentious, resulting from my childhood.' Almost certainly, the heart-breaking loss of her first love influenced her attitude to men and romance. Her funeral, with a large congregation, was held in Glossop Parish Church on 18th January, followed by cremation. At the time of her death she was still married to David May.

Ann's daughter (by her first marriage to Robert Hodgetts), also Ann, but known by her second name, Gillian, had accompanied her mother to New Zealand, where she had a strict upbringing and attended Marlborough Girls' College. After school, she lived in Wellington, working as a civil servant.[31] In May 1977, aged thirty-one, Gillian moved back to London, where she met Michael Trendall, an Oxford graduate working in publishing and later, as a German translator. Having married at Kensington Register Office, with Gillian's mother as one of the witnesses, they lived in a flat at 61 Holland Road, ten minutes' walk from Aubrey Road. Michael has described a happy marriage with Gillian having courage and a great sense of humour, in spite of living with systemic lupus erythematosus for much of her life.[32] Michael's work resulted in them moving to Nottingham, but sadly it was to be a short marriage with no children, Gillian dying in Harefield Hospital on 29th March 1991, aged only forty-five.[33]

Fate would take a different course for Ann's younger sister Audrey, who after studying law but not qualifying, became a childcare officer for Kensington social services. In a letter to his brother, Thomas, her father confided that:

> I wanted Audrey to be a doctor just to prove that a doctor can be dependable. She did not take up medicine but studied law and then faded away. I fancy that she has not quite forgiven me for being unable, in the end, to send her to Girton College, Cambridge.[34]

Audrey was in her late thirties, still living at home, when a close friend at work introduced her to David Arkley. Ten years her junior, twenty-seven-year-old David, a manager and buyer in the provisions trade, moved into the Jeffreys' home and married Audrey at Kensington Register Office, on 3rd September 1964, with Audrey's mother and a Mary White as witnesses.[35] Audrey's signature on the marriage certificate is curious, appearing as 'Audery Jefferys' and her father's name reads Robert Sidney (*sic*) Jeffreys. Was the misspelling caused by nerves or a possible sign of dyslexia?

How happy was the marriage? Audrey, David, her sister Ann and their mother Dorothy, all living under one roof, were frequently arguing, and Audrey started drinking heavily. As alcohol took over her life, her health deteriorated and she was admitted to St. Charles' Hospital, North Kensington, where she died on 11th January 1975.[36] She had been married for just over ten years, and was only forty-eight. The inquest gave the cause of death as 'haemorrhage from oesophageal orifices due to alcoholic cirrhosis of the liver'. Audrey had not written a Will, but within three months of her death, her husband, David now living in Putney, had obtained letters of Administration for her Estate amounting to some £4,000.[37]

Audrey's wretched death must have affected the whole family. Her mother, Dorothy, who wrote a new Will within a month of Audrey's death, died of heart failure only four months later, aged seventy-seven, whilst staying in Esher.[38] For Audrey's husband, David, this must have been an exceptionally distressing period. He did not stay in touch with Ann or with her daughter. Remarried, he built a successful career in the expanding computer industry.[39] Claude's death, having come peacefully in Norfolk over a decade earlier, had spared him the possibility of learning the harrowing details of his only child's demise.

Janet Thatcher told me how Ann and Audrey were well aware of the significant difference between them, perhaps partly by instinct, and from conversations with their mother. Janet believed that this explained some of the tensions within the family, especially when Ann and Audrey were both living in Kensington with their parents. Neither sister seems to have had much happiness in marriage. For Audrey we can imagine that the sense of difference was critical, suspecting or knowing that her real father was a man she could only vaguely remember from her childhood, who appeared to take little interest in her mental or physical wellbeing. This could have stirred dark thoughts, frustrations, instability and even resentment towards her parents, possibly being one of the triggers leading her to seek escape through drink.

Claude must have realised that Dorothy and Robert's marriage would be difficult. In a more modern age, perhaps they could more easily have gone their separate ways in a civilised fashion. This could have allowed Claude and Dorothy to be together, but after much anguish, they must have both recognised that it was not to be. Life moved on, Claude left Africa and met Elveda. So much for what might have been.

1   *The Journal*, 18 February 1966

2   *NRBB*, 1924-38

3   St. John's College, Cambridge. Details of R. S. Jeffreys, provided by Fiona Colbert, Biographical Librarian, June 2014.

4   *The Leech* was The Journal of The Students' Medical Council of the University of the Witwatersrand.

5   R. S. Jeffreys, 'The True Age of Africans', *African Affairs*, Vol. XXXIX, pp 170-75, April 1940

6   R. S. Jeffreys to Fallows, Provincial Office, Kasama, 15 April 1944. NAZ/SEC2/429, Native Affairs: Banyama, italics in original. Bemba Christians however reported that killing by strangulation, *ukutweka*, was the way 'seriously ill' chiefs had been killed in the past. Chiefs feared this, and were relieved when missionaries condemned it. Stephen Bwalya, 'Custom and Habits of the Bemba', typescript, Mpika, 1936, Rhodes House, Oxford RH Mss. Afr. 3.1214.

7   Luise White, *Speaking with Vampires: Rumor and History in Colonial Africa* (University of California Press, Berkeley, 2000)

8   Gervas Clay, District Commissioner, Isoka, 'Memorandum Concerning *banyama* and *mafyeka* with Special Reference to the Provincial Commissioner, Kasama's Confidential File on Banyama and to Incidents in the Isoka District during the Latter Part of 1943', 24 January 1944 (National Archives of Zambia, SWC2/429, Native Affairs: Banyama). Gervas Clay, interview, Taunton, Somerset, 26 August 1991. Luise White, ibid.

9   Janet Thatcher, letter of 1 June 2014. St. Peter's Diocesan School was established in 1911 under the influence of the Community of the Resurrection from their base in Grahamstown, South Africa, and was closed in 1977. Janet Thatcher also attended the school in the 1950s.

10 Died on 10 April 1944 at Fairmile House, Christchurch, whilst living at 96 Southbourne Road, Bournemouth. Death registered the next day by W. E. Morgan, the Occupier of Fairmile House. Source: Death Certificate.

11 Their address given is: Armadale, Belvoir Rd, Bideford, Devon. Source: UK Incoming Passenger Lists. *The Andes*, Royal Mail Lines, from Cape Town, via Freetown, Sierra Leone.

12 3s. 6d., equivalent to 17.5p in decimalised currency. Allowing for inflation, about £7 today (2018).

13 Letter from Thomas Jeffreys at Chunga to his brother, Robert, 28 November 1955.

14 Letter from Thomas Jeffreys, 13 January 1956.

[15] First published in the *St. James's Gazette* of 3 April 1891, and the *National Observer* on the next day, both with the title *The Flag of England*.

[16] Thatcher, ibid.

[17] Included in the Order of Service at the funeral of Ann Jeffreys on 18th January 2007 (courtesy of Michael Trendall)

[18] Pierce Thomas de la Garde Grissell, born 1924, was the son of Lt. Col. Thomas and Vera Grissell, formerly of Waterston, Dorset. Pierce had graduated from the Royal Naval College, Dartmouth and at the time of his death was a former midshipman on HMS *Dragon*. http://www.cwgc.org/find-war-dead/casualty/2467976/

[19] HMT *Orcades* at 23,456 tons was one of the largest ships sunk during WWII. She had been built by Vickers-Armstrongs in Barrow-in-Furness for Orient Steam Navigation and was launched in 1937. She was requisitioned for troop transport in 1939. The *Orcades* had sailed from Liverpool in the early autumn of 1942 to Cape Town under the command of Captain Charles Fox. Apparently Fox was unaware that in late August four German U-boats had been despatched to attack the busy sea lanes off Cape Town, although they had orders not to engage in action before 8th October 1942. Leaving Cape Town on 9th October, bound for Liverpool, the *Orcades* carried a complement of 290 crew members, 36 gunners and 741 passengers (mostly service personnel returning to the UK). Of the 45 lost, there were: 27 crew members, two gunners, two civilian passengers, seven naval personnel and seven army personnel. U-172 was a 9C type submarine, commanded by Captain Carl Emmerman. Sources: http://ssmaritime.com/orcades.htm and www.uboat.net/allies/merchants/2258.html.

[20] Marriage Certificate: Robert Bartley Hodgetts, age 30 (formerly the husband of Ann Kathleen Hodgetts, formerly Jeffreys, spinster, from whom he obtained a divorce) and Frances Grace Pepper, age 23 (spinster) at The Register Office, District of Surrey Northern on 30 July 1949, both living at 63 The Avenue, Kew.

[21] Conversation with Michael Trendall in 2018.

[22] George Arnold Ayscough Budibent was born on 27 November 1912. Budibent's first wife was Joan Hardy (1913-82). He married for the second time Helen Dorothy Cuthbert in June 1947. Sources: Marriage Certificates and Budibent and Donnelly Adams Family Trees.

[23] Budibent died in August 1972 in Australia, leaving an Estate in the UK of £31,000 (equivalent to £400,000 today)

[24] The hotel, a landmark on the Hard in Portsmouth, adjacent to the Naval Dockyard, has a long history dating back to 1779. This building was completely destroyed by a fire in 1803, but when rebuilt became a favourite haunt of Sub-lieutenants from the Naval Educational Establishment. The hotel was named after Admiral Augustus Keppel who in 1779 was court-martialled for alleged cowardice in the presence of the enemy, but was acquitted with the charges being found 'malicious and unproved'. http://snippetsfromaportsmouthpast.blogspot.com/2010/09/keppels-head.html

[25] Colin Gardner, born 31 January 1918 in New Zealand. Died 2004 in New Zealand. Source: Moraday and Falkner Family Trees

[26] Electoral Rolls. At 4 Tuahine Crescent, Gisborne in 1957. At 48 Alabama Road, Marlborough in 1963.

[27] Letter from Thomas Jeffreys, 28 November 1955, ibid.

28 Rattigan was an officer with the Vestey family's 'Blue Star Line'.

29 Conversation with Janet Thatcher, March 2014, who had visited Ann in Glossop in 1994 when Patrick was living with her.

30 Conversations with Gareth Parkes in 2012 and 2013 and with Michael Trendall in 2018. The author is also most grateful for help from Tony Wright who knew Ann in her final years and was present at her funeral.

31 Shipping Records for the MS *Rangitane* show Ann (Gillian) Hodgetts (schoolgirl) sailing from Southampton, arriving Auckland 20 October 1958, then aged 13. In 1969, she is listed in the Electoral Roll for 83 Barnard Street, Wellington (Central), NZ as a public servant.

32 Systemic lupus erythematosus, commonly called SLE or 'lupus', is a systemic autoimmune disease that can affect any part of the body. The immune system attacks the body's cells and tissue, resulting in inflammation and tissue damage.

33 The cause of death was given as a ruptured aortic aneurysm as well as systemic lupus erythematosus (Death certificate)

34 Letter from Robert Jeffreys to his brother, Thomas, 24 June 1957

35 David Arkley, born 5 April 1937 in Newcastle-upon-Tyne, although his parents' home was in Edgware, Middlesex. His father was John Blennett Arkley, a male nurse and hospital attendant. In the 1965 Electoral Roll, David, Audrey and Dorothy are all living at 11 Aubrey Road (Robert Jeffreys had died in 1959).

36 Death Certificate

37 Letters of Administration granted 2 April 1975.

38 Death Certificate. Edith Dorothy Anna Christiansen, b. 27 January 1898, died 9 May 1975, age 77, at Hill House, Portsmouth Road, Esher, Surrey. The Informant was James Harry Briscoe, the Occupier of Hill House, but Dorothy's address is shown (probably incorrectly) as 8 Aubrey Road, London W11. Dorothy's Will left her Estate (c.£15,000) between her daughter, Ann and grand-daughter, Gillian. Dorothy had made specific legacies leaving her signet ring and two enamel brooches to Ann; and the remainder of her jewellery, silver and Africana to Gillian. Source: Grant of Probate, 9th May 1975.

39 Conversation with David Arkley

CHAPTER 30

Transition to the New Africa

Endings to be useful must be inconclusive

Samuel Ray Delany

On 11th November 1918 in the Forest of Compiègne, 40 miles north of Paris, the Armistice was signed, marking the end of World War One. In Africa, General von Lettow-Vorbeck, Commander of the German forces, did not receive the news for two days and only formally surrendered two weeks later. Claude Oldfield was part of the Inspection Parade at Abercorn, led by General W. F. S. Edwards, on that historic day, 25th November 1918.

One wonders just what Claude might make of today's world and the huge changes that have taken place in southern Africa. He might have foreseen that many African countries would seek and achieve independence, but could he have imagined Black majority-rule in Southern Rhodesia, that the new Zambia would sink into debt and become known as one of the least-developed nations, and that apartheid in South Africa would end?

Let us consider the key issues that have impacted on both Northern and Southern Rhodesia from the time of Claude's death in 1963 up to the centenary of his birth in 1989.

In 1963, the UK appeared remarkably stable. The Conservative Party had been in government since Churchill's return to power in 1951. Prosperity for many was rising, encapsulated by Harold Macmillan's speech in July 1957 in which he told the nation that 'most of our people have never had it so good.'[1] Macmillan's first government had overseen the start of African independence, the pace of which accelerated under his second government. His 'wind of change' speech in Cape Town in 1960 is still considered a landmark in the process of decolonisation.

Ghana (formerly the Gold Coast) had gained its independence in 1957, but when Iain Macleod was appointed Colonial Secretary to the

UK Government in 1959, the pace of decolonisation greatly accelerated. Macmillan acquiesced to the dissolution of the ill-fated Central African Federation in 1963 and the Government very soon gave independence to Nigeria, Kenya, Tanganyika, Nyasaland and Northern Rhodesia. Independence followed for (amongst others) the Southern Cameroons and Uganda.

This speedy transfer of power was considered by many critics to be premature. Macmillan, wishing to maintain the goodwill of the new nations, overrode the representations and hostility of white minorities and settlers (most notably in Kenya, Northern Rhodesia and Southern Rhodesia), as well as the views emanating from his own party's 'Monday Club'.[2] Nevertheless, South Africa, having become a republic following a referendum in 1960, left the multiracial Commonwealth in protest in 1961.

In spite of all this rapid transformation, any political change in the colonies in southern Africa where white minorities were entrenched, looked improbable. In June 1959, South African exiles in London had started the 'Boycott Movement'. In response to an appeal by Albert Luthuli, a meeting was held in Finsbury Town Hall in London, the key speakers being Julius Nyerere from Tanzania and Father Trevor Huddleston.[3] The massacre at Sharpeville on 21st March 1960, when sixty-nine unarmed peaceful protesters were shot dead by the South African police, strengthened their resolve and soon after the 'Boycott Movement' became the 'Anti-Apartheid Movement' (AAM).

At that time, the UK was South Africa's largest foreign investor and South Africa was the UK's third biggest export market. Initially, the simple objective of the boycott was to ask British people to withdraw their support for apartheid by not buying South African goods. When the boycott was extended to British companies with investments in South Africa, it became clear that an effective boycott would damage the economies of both countries – although many in South Africa, impatient for change, indicated their willingness to bear this burden. The campaign against Barclays Bank, which started in 1970, gained significant publicity, eventually forcing their withdrawal from South Africa in 1986.[4]

As much of the rest of Africa won its independence, the AAM exposed the 'unholy alliance' of South Africa, Rhodesia and Portugal, which refused to give up its colonies of Mozambique, Angola and Guinea-Bissau. The South African ANC (African National Congress) was still committed to peaceful resistance, although the armed struggle began a year later.

Progress was slow. South Africa had supportive regimes as neighbours: the two Portuguese colonies of Mozambique and Angola, as well as Southern Rhodesia – and they administered South West Africa under a League of Nations mandate dating back to Germany's defeat in World War one in 1915.

✳ ✳ ✳

Only twenty months after Claude's death, Northern Rhodesia achieved its independence on 24th October 1964 and became known as Zambia, but the political changes taking place in neighbouring Southern Rhodesia were destined to impact on the whole of southern Africa. The Southern Rhodesian government, made up mainly from the country's white minority (of some five per cent of the population), was angered when, with independence being granted to less-developed African colonies to the north, they were refused sovereignty under the 'NIBMAR' principle (no independence before majority rule).[5] Following four decades of self-government, most white Rhodesians felt that they were due their independence. The British government's refusal resulted from the changing moral view of colonialism and the necessity of introducing democracy, as espoused in Macmillan's 'wind of change' speech; nor did the UK wish to irritate the UN or the Commonwealth. Although the Conservative government, while following a policy of decolonisation, had some sympathies with the Southern Rhodesian position, they decided to give priority to international considerations.

With Labour forming the government after the election in October 1964, independence for Rhodesia without NIBMAR was even less likely. Negotiations between Britain, led by prime minister Harold Wilson, and Rhodesia's Ian Smith, continued through most of 1965. By October, amid renewed rumours of an impending Rhodesian 'UDI' (Unilateral Declaration of Independence), Smith met Wilson in London. These discussions were not productive and, desperate to avert UDI, Wilson travelled to Salisbury to continue negotiations, but still nothing was agreed. Stalemate drew closer, but with the Rhodesian government not prepared for further delay, events appeared to take an inescapable course. *Time* magazine describes how:

> The Prime Minister of Rhodesia stood tall and thin in the cavernous banquet hall of the Meikles Hotel. Before him sat the leaders of

Salisbury society, formally attired. They had raised glasses in a toast to their Queen, but nodded approvingly when he warned that they might soon be leaving her realm. Now they listened silently as Ian Smith, in the flat, nasal accent of the settler, read from the eve-of-battle speech of Henry V: 'That he which hath no stomach to this fight, let him depart. He today that sheds his blood with me, shall be my brother, and gentlemen in England, now abed, shall think themselves accurs'd they were not here.'[6]

UDI was formally adopted by Rhodesia on 11th November 1965. It was the first unilateral break from the UK by one of its colonies since the United States Declaration of Independence nearly two centuries earlier. Britain's initial response to this long-awaited challenge was sanctions. As I watched events from Britain, then part-way through my university degree, it looked as if Smith's government could get away with defying world opinion. For all Wilson's initial bluster, and his prediction that UDI would fail in a matter of 'weeks not months', Rupert Cornwell believed that Wilson would not use force to oust the rebel regime. The sanctions, intended to choke Rhodesia's imports of oil and exports of tobacco, caused inconvenience, but the shared border with South Africa made the measures ultimately unenforceable. Efforts to reach a compromise were started, first with 'talks about talks', followed by a meeting between Smith and Wilson aboard the destroyer HMS *Tiger* in the Mediterranean, in October 1966. The two leaders tried again in 1968, meeting on HMS *Fearless*, off Gibraltar. There was no bridging the basic disagreement over Rhodesia's refusal to abandon UDI and its existing constitution and return to the British fold, pending a settlement acceptable to the black majority.[7]

In spite of almost total international isolation, Rhodesia continued unrecognised, but relatively unscathed, relying on the assistance of only Portugal and South Africa. Guerrilla activities were comfortably contained by the Rhodesian security forces and domestic white opposition had been curtailed by the house arrest of former prime minister Garfield Todd in 1972, and the exile of his daughter Judith.

But the armed struggle had already started, led by Joshua Nkomo of ZAPU (the Zimbabwe African People's Union). Soon a rival group emerged, ZANU (the Zimbabwe African National Union), led by Ndabaningi Sithole and avowed Marxist, Robert Mugabe, with its own strategy for impressing international opinion, undermining white assurance, and achieving a complete breakdown of order.

Events in Europe were to have a major impact when on 25th April 1974, a military *coup* in Portugal overthrew the *Estado Novo*, the authoritarian government in power since 1933. The new regime immediately stopped all military action in its African colonies, declaring its intention to grant them independence without delay. No longer could Rhodesia (or South Africa) rely on support from its close neighbours. The sustainability of Smith's white minority regime was looking increasingly in doubt. Although South Africa's prime minister Vorster was unwilling to make concessions to his own country's black population, he had concluded that white minority rule in Rhodesia was not sustainable in a country where blacks outnumbered whites 22:1.[8]

The guerrilla war continued with increasing audacity. On 3rd September 1978, Air Rhodesia Flight RH825 was shot down by ZIPRA (the Zimbabwe People's Revolutionary Army, the armed wing of Nkomo's ZAPU), using a Russian surface-to-air guided missile. The Vickers Viscount, the *Hunyani*, was flying the last leg of a scheduled service from Victoria Falls to Salisbury, via the resort town of Kariba. On board were fifty-two passengers and four crew; thirty-eight died in the crash, but the insurgents then approached the wreckage, rounded up ten survivors, massacring them with automatic gunfire. Three passengers survived by hiding in the bush, while a further five lived, having gone to search for water. Nkomo claimed responsibility for shooting down the plane, but denied that his men had killed survivors on the ground.

Worse was to follow when on 12th February 1979, Air Rhodesia Flight RH827, the *Umniati*, also flying out of Kariba, was hit by a SAM-7 missile, bursting into flames and crashing into a ravine, killing all fifty-nine on board. At the time, I was working for Brooke Bond Liebig in London. The victims included one of my colleagues, Ron Isitt, who was visiting the Liebig ranches and meat factory at the time, together with two senior managers from the Rhodesian company.[9] Bringing down the two Rhodesian planes demoralised the white population and intimidated the government into submission. An internal settlement led to the creation of Zimbabwe-Rhodesia under a new constitution, which was soon followed by the Lancaster House Agreement, signed on 21st December 1979, which allowed for the creation of the Republic of Zimbabwe. After a period of interim British control, the country achieved internationally-recognised independence in April 1980.

There were terrible losses on both sides during the fifteen-year 'bush' war.[10] According to Rhodesian government statistics, between December

1972 and December 1979, more than 20,000 people were killed, comprising 1,361 members of the Rhodesian security forces, 10,450 guerrillas killed in Rhodesia, and an unknown number in Mozambique and Zambia, plus 7,790 black civilians and 468 white civilians.[11] Robert Mugabe's ZANU-PF party took office on 17 April 1980, following elections in the February.[12] Amazingly, Mugabe remained in power for over thirty-seven years, despite an internal war against Matabele-dominated ZAPU, severe economic decline and seizures of (mainly white-owned) farms, until finally forced from office in November 2017, when Emmerson Mnangagwa was sworn in as Zimbabwe's new president.

✳ ✳ ✳

Claude would have known as well as anyone that at Zambia's independence in October 1964, despite its considerable mineral wealth, the country faced many challenges. There were few trained and educated Zambians capable of administering the Government and the economy was largely dependent on foreign expertise. Kenneth Kaunda's United National Independence Party (UNIP) had won the pre-Independence elections, gaining fifty-five out of the seventy-five seats. Kaunda adopted an ideology of African humanism, not too different in reality from his neighbour Julius Nyerere in Tanzania with African socialism. Economic policies focussed on central planning and nationalisation, notably of the copper mines with the formation of Zambia Consolidated Copper Mines (ZCCM).

In 1968 Kaunda was re-elected president, running unopposed. During the following years Zambia adopted a one-party system and in 1972 all political parties, except UNIP, were banned. This was formalised in a new constitution, adopted in 1973, based on 'one-party participatory democracy'; in practice, this meant that UNIP became the sole political channel in the country.[13] There was dissension to the imposition of a one-party rule, notably from Sylvester Chisembele, the Cabinet Minister for Western Province (previously Barotseland) and Simon Kapwepwe and Harry Nkumbula who, before the declaration of the one-party state, had been leaders of rival political parties. Their attempts to challenge Kaunda's presidency were ultimately unsuccessful and Kaunda was re-elected unopposed in 1973, 1978, 1983 and 1988.

Central planning of the economy initially appeared to be working, but in the mid-1970s there was a drastic economic downturn – from 1975 to 1990, Zambia's economy fell by some thirty per cent. Economists believed that the economic distress could be attributed to a number of factors, including poor trading terms for major exports (principally copper), droughts and other natural disasters. Their analysis also showed an inability to diversify successfully into non-mining activities, such as agriculture and tourism, and delays in applying appropriate policies, even after it had been recognised that central planning and socialism had produced an economic catastrophe.[14]

A more sympathetic view might argue that whilst the goal of greater self-sufficiency was inherently laudable, it was not necessarily practical, as import substitution didn't work. The economy was, of course, heavily dependent on the copper industry, which had been nationalised. During the 1970s, the price of copper sank substantially, partly due to the USSR, the second-largest world producer, flooding the market. Nevertheless, while the population continued to grow, Zambians suffered a drastic decline in living standards with income per head falling by fifty-eight per cent between 1981 and 1999.[15] By 2000, the country was classified as one of the least-developed nations, with around eighty-four per cent of the rural population below the poverty datum line.[16]

Another significant reason for Zambia's economic problems was the political situation of their neighbours. When Southern Rhodesia adopted UDI in November 1965, Zambia had become a key member of the 'Frontline States', those countries close to South Africa which would play a vital role in supporting South Africa's ANC in their efforts to overthrow the apartheid regime.[17] When the ANC was banned in South Africa, its headquarters was moved to Lusaka, from where the activities of *uMkhonto we Sizwe* (the ANC's paramilitary wing) were coordinated. Recruits, who had left South Africa via Lesotho or Mozambique, travelled to Lusaka, before being sent for military training.[18] In 1985, Zambian soldiers were able to protect the ANC from South African attacks during their national conference.[19]

So in 1965, land-locked Zambia, with its previous economic dependence on the white-minority governments of Southern Rhodesia and South Africa, needed alternative solutions for its trade and transport. The Benguela Railway from Lubumbashi (previously Elizabethville) to Benguela (Lobito Bay), on the Atlantic coast, had only limited capacity and was not a reliable substitute due to Portugal's close relations with South Africa and its declared neutrality towards Rhodesia. Realistically, the

Great North Road from Lusaka, running north to the Tanzanian border, and then via Mbeya to the Indian Ocean coast at Dar-es-Salaam, was the principal alternative transport route. Used extensively, the condition of the road became so atrocious that it often took ten days to drive the 1,200 miles – and it became known as 'the Hell Run'.

Zambia spent the next few years diverting its imports and exports from the southern African ports, mainly to Dar-es-Salaam. As time went by, other routes were identified but none of them were satisfactory. The first major project, completed in 1968, was the construction of an oil pipeline from Dar-es-Salaam to the Indeni refinery in Ndola, a distance of over 1,000 miles.[20]

Although the pipeline reduced the pressure on the road, a cheaper route was needed for all other goods and commodities, with a railway line appearing to be the obvious answer. Funding was required, but Britain prevaricated, arguing that the Smith regime would soon be gone. The Chinese, interested in accessing Africa's minerals, stepped in – designing and constructing the TAZARA Railway from Dar-es-Salaam to Kapiri Mposhi in central Zambia, completing the project in 1975.[21] The cost of US$406 million (approx. US$2.56 billion today) was met by the provision of a long-term loan by China.[22]

One-party rule and the declining economy created growing anger and resentment. When strikes were organised in 1981, the government responded by arresting several trade union leaders, among them Frederick Chiluba. Protests broke out again in 1986 and 1987, both in Lusaka and on the copper belt. In 1990, rising food prices triggered riots and more than thirty people were killed. After a failed *coup* attempt in 1990, Kaunda grudgingly recognised the need for reform. The ban on political parties was eventually lifted and the outcome, after elections in 1991, was a new government led by Chiluba's 'Movement for Multiparty Democracy' (MMD), holding 125 of the 150 seats, UNIP the remainder.[23]

Chiluba, despite an unsuccessful *coup* attempt in 1997, was eventually forced to stand down in 2002. The MMD, continued in government, first under Levy Mwanawasa, followed by Rupiah Banda until 2011. That government was replaced by the Patriotic Front, a new opposition party, led by Michael Sata, until his death in October 2011. An interim administration was led by Guy Scott, pending elections in January 2015 when Edgar Lungu, also of the Patriotic Front, was elected. Scott was the first white president of Zambia and the first white president in sub-Saharan

Africa since F.W. de Klerk, South Africa's last apartheid-era president, left office in 1994.[24]

* * *

Over those thirty-odd years from the early 1960s, southern Africa had evolved, at terrible expense in economic terms, with many lost opportunities – and with dreadful loss of life, especially as Zimbabwe was born out of Rhodesia.

Since the 1960s, attitudes have changed massively – way beyond what Claude, or most of his generation – could ever have imagined. Anthony Kirk-Greene asked whether recruits into the colonial service in the 1950s might have foreseen a time when Africa would become independent. Their response would have been: 'Certainly not in my lifetime, probably not in my son's, possibly in a hundred years'.[25] By the late 1950s, as we have noted, that moral shift had started – and it affected how Britain looked at its colonial 'possessions'. The type of recruitment into the colonial service had changed, so that no longer would Claude's Cambridge degree in classics have been an immediate passport to a career in Africa. Many of those who went out in the last few years leading up to independence have written their memoirs, mostly with affection of their time in a changing Africa. One of the more perceptive is that by Callum Christie who joined the colonial service in Northern Rhodesia in 1959.[26] He was not an Oxbridge classics graduate, but had gained a degree in economics from the University of Aberdeen. Having been asked to attend Chibemba language classes at SOAS before his departure, he arrived in Northern Rhodesia to find that his posting was to Barotseland to work with Lozi-speaking people![27]

In *Goodbye Colonialism, Farewell Feudalism*, Christie highlights the wide range of opinions and attitudes which he encountered in Northern Rhodesia in the five years leading up to independence. Writing back to his parents in May 1960, he is amazed that: 'The Mongu Club has just voted to keep it all-white even for the period of the Queen Mother's visit.'[28] Two months later, his impression of his fellow colonial officers gets worse, when Christie asks his DC, David Acheson: 'David, why don't you ever shake the hand of an African?' He is astonished by the response: 'it's because I feel a physical revulsion at doing so. I know that it's wrong but I can't help myself.' This, from a man whose father, Dr James Acheson, had served with the colonial medical service in Northern Rhodesia.[29] It's worth adding that David's younger brother, Denis, was a Rhodes Scholar who was active in the Liberal Party in Northern Rhodesia in the early 1960s.[30] Attitudes can vary even in the same family!

Christie also encountered Gervas Clay (husband of Betty, whose letters home have been mentioned in earlier chapters) who, as Resident Commissioner, advocated returning to long ulendos on foot, as the principal mode of travel between villages, not impressed by the 'modern' trend to use a Land Rover to cover the ground with greater efficiency. Fifty years earlier, Claude – and also his colleague, Cullen Gouldsbury – might have been impressed, but the young Christie was not.[31] Christie was, however, encouraged by the advice of a colleague, Ian Edye: 'Always remember that we are public servants. That means we're here to serve the public, not the other way round.'[32]

Since decolonisation, black Africans have increasingly told their side of the story of the colonial period, often a sobering contrast to the partisan accounts that have previously dominated the canon. A recent example is Danai Gurira's play *The Convert*, set in Southern Rhodesia in 1895, which confronts the links between Christianity and colonialism. The setting is a mission house in Salisbury occupied by Chilford, a black Catholic teacher who has adopted European manners and speech. The focus is on his latest convert, a young Shona-speaking girl, now christened Ester, who has escaped an arranged marriage by converting to Christianity. Forsaking her family, she has become Chilford's protégé and the epitome of devout propriety, but when anti-colonial riots spread from Bulawayo and the mission is threatened, Ester is forced to decide where her loyalties ultimately lie. Gurira's play never shows us the white settlers, but it expresses how easily cultural norms can impose themselves on an established society, tearing families apart.[33]

✳ ✳ ✳

There is never likely to be agreement on the perennial question of whether anything positive remains of the European legacy. Piers Brendon believes that the moral balance sheet of the British empire is a confusing mixture of good and bad.[34]

On the credit side, the British empire was founded on liberal principles expressed by Edmund Burke, who maintained that colonial government was a trust, to be so exercised for the benefit of the subject peoples, who would eventually gain their right to self-rule.[35] This view prevailed for two centuries and was expressed in classical terms by the Conservative, Benjamin Disraeli, in 1879: 'One of the greatest of Romans, when asked what was his politics, replied *Imperium et libertas*.'[36]

Others might claim that Britain played a major part in ending slavery, following David Livingstone's example and calling, and brought order where previously there was turmoil, building an administration staffed by dedicated district officials. It could be contended that the British empire was more humane than those administered by other European nations, of which the Belgians in the Congo probably would surely rank the worst? After World War Two, Britain quickly recognised the need to grant independence to most of its colonies and protectorates, even though at times it was forced by circumstances, with the partition of India causing horrendous carnage. In Africa, lives were lost in the southern Sudan, during the 'Mau Mau' struggles in Kenya – and later in Rhodesia (as discussed earlier in this chapter).

'Empire and Liberty' is, of course, self-contradictory. Three weeks after Disraeli's reference to Roman political thinking, William Gladstone, leader of the Liberal Party, suggested that what the Romans really meant was 'Liberty for ourselves, Empire over the rest of mankind.' He continued his speech – and this was 140 years ago, in 1879, before the British Empire had even reached its zenith – 'modern times have established a sisterhood of nations, equal, independent; each of them built up under that legitimate defence which public law affords to every nation, living within its own borders, and seeking to perform its own affairs'.[37]

Brendon recognises that balance sheets require proper interpretation, but that there is little doubt about his judgement when he suggests that: 'even according to its own lights, the British empire was in grave moral deficit.'[38] Nonetheless, one could maintain that as the empire evolved, colonial societies did become more just, open and fair. The Empire typically introduced a strong legal system and improved education, though often too slowly. Building roads and railways created an infrastructure for developing economies. The common English language and culture, together with a shared history, has encouraged the growth and success of the Commonwealth. In a modest way, Claude's practical contribution helped to support that achievement.

Kenneth Kaunda's May Day address to the Zambian people in 1972 didn't lay blame on his country's colonial history. Even though he was well acquainted with the iniquities of empire, he called for personal and collective responsibility. Taking thoughts on endeavour from Thomas Carlyle, Kaunda began: 'There is a perennial nobleness and even a sacredness in Work'.[39] His lengthy peroration concluded with:

> The destiny of this Nation lies in our hands; we must accept full responsibility for shaping today the Zambia of tomorrow which is our children's heritage. Indeed the real success of our democracy rests in our triumph in breaking the chains of economic and social bondage among the majority of the Zambian people. This is a national cause, as important as the struggle for political independence. It is a daily and continuous challenge for every patriotic worker. This must, therefore, be a day of reflection and rededication to our cause of building a free, strong and prosperous Zambia, through sweat and toil, under our national motto, One Zambia, One Nation'.[40]

Kenneth Kaunda

[1] Harold Macmillan, prime minister, was speaking at a Tory rally in Bedford on 20 July 1957 to mark 25 years' service by Alan Lennox-Boyd, the Colonial Secretary, as MP for Mid-Bedfordshire.

[2] Founded in 1961, in the belief that Macmillan had taken the party too far to the left, the club became embroiled in the debate about decolonisation and immigration.

[3] Albert Luthuli (c. 1898-1967), South African teacher, activist and politician; president of the African National Congress (ANC) from 1952, leading opposition to the white minority government. In 1960, he was awarded the Nobel Peace Prize, the first African to be honoured in this way. Julius Kambarage Nyerere (1922-99). Ernest Urban Trevor Huddleston (1913-98), later Archbishop of the Province of the Indian Ocean, was well known for his strong anti-apartheid views and for his book, *Naught for Your Comfort*.

[4] The campaign started as a result of Barclays' involvement in financing the Cabora Bassa dam in Mozambique. Barclays took the business decision to sell their South African business in 1986. The boycott ended in 1987 once campaigners believed the evidence presented by Barclays about their disengagement from South Africa. Source: AAM Archives

[5] The white population reached a peak of 296,000 in 1975, representing just over 8% of the population. It fell to around 120,000 in 1999, to less than 50,000 in 2002 and approx. 29,000 in 2012.

[6] *Time* magazine, Friday, 5 November, 1965.

[7] Obituary of Ian Smith (1919-2007) by Rupert Cornwell, *The Independent*, 22 November 2007

[8] In 1978, there were 270,000 Rhodesians of European descent and more than six million Africans. From Robin Wright, *The Christian Science Monitor*, 1975, and the Alicia Patterson Foundation.

[9] The two senior Liebig managers were Loris Zucchini, Managing Director (58) and Edward 'Ted' Wigg, Production Director (37), who both lived in Bulawayo. A full list of the names is available at www.rhodesian.com.au/memoriam%20viscounts.php

[10] The Rhodesian Bush War, also known as the Second Chimurenga or the Zimbabwe War of Liberation, lasted from July 1964 until December 1979.

[11] Tor G. Jakobsen, 'The Fall of Rhodesia: Why did the white minority rule end in today's Zimbabwe?' on 19 October 2012 at www.popularsocialscience.com

[12] PF (Patriotic Front) was added an epithet to 'ZANU'.

[13] Gabriel C. Banda, 'Zambia's Independence and Our Elders Pensions', October 2016 (at WordPress)

[14] Presentation by the Government of Zambia to the Third UN Conference on the Least Developed Countries, Brussels, 14-20 May 2001

[15] GDP (Gross Domestic Product) was US$720 in 1981, falling to US$300 in 1999 (GRZ/UNICEF *Mid-Term Review*, 2000)

[16] GRZ/UNICEF, ibid.

[17] The 'Frontline States' (FLS) were a loose coalition of African countries from the 1960s to the early 1990s committed to ending apartheid and white minority rule. They included South Africa's neighbours, Namibia, Botswana, Zimbabwe, Mozambique, Swaziland and Lesotho as well countries further north: Angola, Zambia and Tanzania.

The FLS was disbanded when Nelson Mandela became President of South Africa in 1994.

[18] *uMkhonto we Sizwe* (The Spear of the Nation) was founded in the wake of the Sharpeville massacre on 21 March 1960, representing the ANC's conviction that, in the face of the massacre, the organisation could no longer limit itself to non-violent protest.

[19] Kevin Ritchie, the South African *Sunday Independent*, 26 October 2014

[20] *Nicholas Bariyo, 'Zambian Govt. seeks to recapitalize Tanzania Oil Pipeline' Downstream Today, 29 September 2009.* The Tanzania Zambia Mafuta Pipeline, *mafuta* meaning oil in Swahili, was designed for a throughput of 1.1 million tonnes per annum, but is currently handling about half that volume (in 2009).

[21] Also known as the Great Uhuru Railway or TANZAM Railway. *Uhuru* is Swahili for freedom.

[22] 'Tanzania–Zambia Railway: a Bridge to China?' *The New York Times*, 29 January 1971

[23] Source: African Elections Database. When Kaunda handed power to Chiluba on 2 November 1991, he was only the second mainland African head of state to allow free multiparty elections and to peacefully relinquish power after losing. The first, Mathieu Kérékou of Benin, had done so in March of that year.

[24] Guy Lindsay Scott was born on 1 June 1944 in Livingstone, Northern Rhodesia. His father, Alec Scott was a doctor who had emigrated to Northern Rhodesia from Scotland in 1927; his mother, Grace, had emigrated from England in 1940.

[25] Anthony Kirk-Greene, *Symbol of Authority: The British District Officer in Africa* (I. B. Tauris, 2006) p 207

[26] Callum Christie, *Goodbye Colonialism, Farewell Feudalism: Letters from a District Officer, Barotseland* 1959–62 (Kirkgate Books, Glasgow, 2016)

[27] SOAS, the School of Oriental and African Studies, was founded in 1916 as the School of Oriental Studies. It took its present title in 1938, when it had also established a centre for African Studies. SOAS is a constituent college of the University of London.

[28] When the author was living in Malawi in the early 1970s, the Lilongwe Golf Club (then known as the Lilongwe Gymkhana Club) was effectively 'whites only', apart from one or two 'honorary' African members, such as Norman Kauma, who was an excellent golfer. The President, Dr. Hastings Banda, apparently believed that the European population should not be forced to socialise with Africans! The Club did not elect its first black chairman, Dean Lungu, until 1996, more than 30 years after Independence. Source: Lilongwe Golf Club website

[29] Obituary of Mrs. Maud Acheson, who died aged 102 in Port Alfred, South Africa, records that: 'She married Dr James Alexander Acheson in 1927. She is survived by her sons, David, Michael and Denis, and her daughter Bridget'. Source: *The Herald* (formerly the *Eastern Province Herald*, published in Port Elizabeth), 31 December 2002

[30] Denis Acheson, born in Northern Rhodesia, was a Rhodesian Rhodes Scholar, active in the Liberal Party of Northern Rhodesia in the early 1960s, and later a senior executive of the RST Group. In 2003, he reviewed *Africa: Another Side of The Coin* by Andrew Sardanis. See the *britishempire* website, courtesy of OSPA (The Overseas Service Pensioners' Association)

[31] Christie, ibid, p 52

[32] Ibid., p 294

[33] Written in 2012. See Alice Saville, *Time Out*, 20 January 2017 and Michael Billington, *The Guardian*, 22 January 2017

[34] See Piers Brendon, *The Decline and Fall of the British Empire, 1781-1997* (Jonathan Cape, 2007) and 'A moral audit of the British empire' 6 November 2007. Source: www.opendemocracy.net

[35] Edmund Burke (1730–97) was an Irish statesman, who after moving to London in 1750 served as an MP with the Whig (Liberal) Party.

[36] Benjamin Disraeli, 1st Earl of Beaconsfield (1804-81) was a British politician (Conservative), novelist and essayist and served twice as Prime Minister. At the Guildhall on 9 November 1879, he said: 'One of the greatest of Romans, when asked what was his politics, replied, *Imperium et libertas*. That would not make a bad programme for a British ministry.' Disraeli was referring to *Agricola*, Ch. 3, where Tacitus said of Nerva, 'He joined two things hitherto incompatible, *principatum ac libertatem.*' Meaning the principate (the reign of a single emperor) and liberty.

[37] Speech during the Midlothian campaign (27 November 1879). William Ewart Gladstone (1809-98) was a British statesman of the Liberal Party, who served for twelve years as Prime Minister, spread over four terms between 1868 and 1894.

[38] Brendon, 'Moral audit', ibid.

[39] Thomas Carlyle, *Past and Present*, (Dent, 1843). Carlyle (1795-1881) was a Scottish philosopher, satirical writer, essayist, translator, historian, mathematician and teacher.

[40] Kenneth Kaunda, *The dignity of labour* (Lusaka: The Cabinet Office/The Government Printer, 1972). Printed as being delivered in Lusaka on Saturday 29 April 1972, although it is a May Day speech. The background to the speech is discussed by Lethiwe Nkosi in the *African Yearbook of Rhetoric*, Vol. II, No. 3, January 2011, pp 61-66

The Formal Surrender by the German Schutztruppe, Abercorn, 25th November 1918

In this short appendix, the author has attempted to bring together information on the key people in the Inspection Parade. He gratefully acknowledges the support and assistance of Dr. Anne Samson (historian and co-ordinator of the Great War in Africa Association) and Tim Wright (Chairman of the Northern Rhodesia Police Association), but any errors or omissions are entirely the author's responsibility. Any further information or amendments will be gratefully accepted.

Claude's annotation of the photograph of the parade gives the names of those carrying out the Inspection as:

General Edwards
Col. Dickinson, Northern Rhodesia Regiment
Major Alport, Northern Rhodesia Regiment
Captain Wardroper, Northern Rhodesia Regiment
Captain James, Northern Rhodesia Regiment
C. P. Oldfield, J.P., Political Officer and Magistrate

Tim Wright has pointed out that since the Northern Rhodesia Regiment was not formed until 1932, the officers must have been serving with the Northern Rhodesia Police.

The official report of the surrender states that the 'Guard of honour for General Edwards composed of 25 men (King's African Rifles) and 25 men NRP (Northern Rhodesia Police), all under Captain Lindsay DSO, paraded in Abercorn at 11 hours on the occasion of the official surrender of General von Lettow and his forces. General Edwards and his staff attended by Lt. Col. Hawkins DSO, Major Lambert MC, Lt. Col.

Dickinson, and Capt. Wardroper, received the surrender at 11.30. Each company of Germans grounded arms and laid down their equipment, M Guns and ammunition in turn. The surrender was completed by 15.15 hours. There were, surrendered in good condition, one 7cm Gun, 24 Maxims, 14 Lewis Guns, 1,250 Rifles, 208,000 rounds SAA, English and Portuguese. Enemy confined and their camp under guard.'[1]

Lt. Col. Hawkins is not named as being included in Claude's photograph. There seem to be two possibilities: either a simple mistake in listing the names, or that the parade took place in different stages, through the day. The official report above states that the 'Surrender' took nearly four hours (from 11.30am to 3.15pm)

Key Personalities

Brigadier-General William Frederick Savery Edwards (1872-1941), CB CMG DSO KPM

Born 27th July 1872 at East Budleigh, Devon. Married Evelyn Bingham on 8th August 1902. Commissioned 2nd Lieutenant into 4th Battalion, Devon Regiment, January 1897. Attached to the Sierra Leone Field Force, 1899-1901, and with the Ashanti Field Force, 1900, wounded. South African (Boer) War 1899-1901. Made Lieutenant January 1900, Captain April 1901. Retired July 1901. Brevet-Major and Brevet-Lieutenant for Colonial War Service. Edwards joined the South African Constabulary 1901-06, followed by the Uganda Police 1906-08. He was appointed Lt. Colonel, East African Expeditionary Force from August 1914, and later Brigadier-Commander from 1917.

Whilst in British East Africa (BEA) in 1914, the KAR were deployed on northern frontier security duties, but until Indian Army troops arrived, the KAR were needed to counter German *Schutztruppe* demolition patrols who were targeting the Uganda Railway line and infiltrating across the border from Lake Victoria down to Mombasa.

The BEA Police selected 400 askari to form the Police Service Battalion plus twelve European officers and two Warrant Officers, commanded by Edwards, who was the Inspector General of the East Africa and Uganda Police. Edwards worked his men hard hoping to be deployed against the German threat, but on 11th January 1915, he was ordered to move his Battalion north to deal with Turkana raiders. In early August 1915, the Uganda Police Battalion moved into southern Uganda and north-western GEA to take over positions on the Kagera River Line. Edwards (now Lt. Col.) became responsible for the askari who frequently swam or silently canoed across the Kagera to raid *Schutztruppe* posts or burn down vegetation that provided cover for enemy patrols.

Edwards was then appointed Inspector General of Lines of Communication in East Africa, with the rank of Brigadier-General and in 1918, commanded the 'Edforce' column in Portuguese East Africa, which was in hot pursuit of von Lettow-Vorbeck in October, before finally accepting the *Schutztruppe* surrender at Abercorn on 25th November.

Edward Paice believes that the Surrender was handled sensitively by Edwards, particularly as Article XVII of the Armistice agreement had only stipulated that the German forces in East Africa should be 'evacuated', but the War Office had insisted that evacuation could only be effected if 'unconditional surrender and disarmament' took place. Van Deventer, overall commander of British forces in the region, was clear in his own mind that the British had no real right to demand a surrender.

An unfortunate consequence of the surrender was that both German combatants and their askari became PoWs. The War Office also refused to lend von Lettow-Vorbeck two million Marks that he owed his askari in back pay. Nevertheless, van Deventer insisted that during their journey home, the Germans should be 'granted the honours of war' and treated as ordinary citizens rather than as PoWs.[2]

General William F. S. Edwards should not be confused with **General Sir Alfred Hamilton Mackenzie Edwards (1862-1944) KBE CB MVO**, Commandant-General of the Rhodesian Forces, who had retired from the British Army in May 1907, becoming Chief Constable of the London Metropolitan Police, before his appointment to the Rhodesian Forces. Later, he was appointed Commissioner of the BSA Police as an external appointment from outside the force, retiring in January 1923.[3]

Col. Edward Griffith Dickinson (1883-1947), Northern Rhodesia Police

Educated at King's School, Canterbury. Joined the Natal Police in 1901; Barotse Native Police (and later the NRP) in 1911. In late July 1916, Dickinson led a detachment of Northern Rhodesia Police as they drove the Germans out of Lutego and a month later, on 29th August, his 'C' company seized Iringa without a fight. Dickinson commanded the Service Battalion from 1918-19.[4]

Dickinson was the last Commandant before the Military and Civil Police were divided into separate forces on 1st April 1932, with the Military becoming the Northern Rhodesia Regiment. The establishment of the new Northern Rhodesia Police was seven officers, 35 members of the inspectorate, 40 British constables, 494 uniformed African police and 42 African detectives, all under Captain P. R. Wardroper as Commissioner of Police.[5]

Major Herbert Allport (1884-1964), Northern Rhodesia Police

Herbert Allport was born in Ireland. He had a twin sister, Rhoda and a younger brother, Albert Edward (b.1886).[6] Allport was 'Mentioned in Despatches' in 1917.[7]

Captain Percy Redesdale Wardroper (1892-1942), Northern Rhodesia Police

Joined the BSAC Police in 1912. No details available for service in WWI. Appointed Commissioner of Police, when Lt. Col. Dickinson established the new Northern Rhodesia Police in 1932 (see above). Awarded OBE 1934. In 1935, Wardroper moved his office to Lusaka, the new capital. In 1936, he retired as Commissioner after 21 years in the Force and was succeeded by his deputy, Harry Hart.[8]

Captain Francis Stafford James (1878-1955), Northern Rhodesia Police

Educated Clifton College. Joined the BSAC Police in 1903; then the Barotse Native Police in 1905. James was involved in the abortive attack on Namema in May 1916, when Northey had four columns poised to attack different enemy-fortified locations just across the border in GEA. Murray had divided his column into four sub-units (A, B, C and Reserve) with James commanding the Reserve. Later promoted to Major, James retired from Northern Rhodesia in June 1923 to become Chief Constable of Chesterfield, and then Sheffield (1931-41).[9]

[1] Written by Lt. Col. Hawkins as CiC 1/4 KAR. See *Abercorn Surrender*, Ref. WO 95/5331, pt 13, The National Archives, Kew.

[2] Edward Paice, *Tip and Run: The Untold Tragedy of the Great War in Africa* (Weidenfield & Nicolson, 2007). Various other sources, including www. greatwarforum.org/topic/208049-brigadier-general-f-s-edwards-cb-cmg-dso-kpm; www. kaiserscross.com/188001/188901.html; *Rhodesiana*, Vol.17; Military Keep Museum, Dorchester.

[3] Source: www.bsap.org/hiscommissioners.html

[4] http://www.kaiserscross.com/188001/366822.html

[5] Website for the Northern Rhodesia Police Association (www.nrpa.org.uk)

[6] From Bell family history: http://www.bellsite.id.au

[7] Despatch from Lt.Gen. Sir J.L. Van Deventer, Pretoria, 20 January 1919 published in *The London Gazette*, 3 June 1919

[8] Tim Wright, *The History of the Northern Rhodesia Police* (British Empire and Commonwealth Museum, 2001)

[9] From www.kaiserscross, ibid. Also the Northern Rhodesia Police Association (Tim Wright) and *Rhodesiana*, Vol.17

BIBLIOGRAPHY

Principal references and further reading

The bibliography is divided into sections: UK (General, St. Paul's School, Trinity Hall, Cambridge and Norfolk), followed by Africa and Zambia, and WWI in East Africa. Publishers are based in London, unless stated otherwise.

UK

Nicholson, Virginia, *Singled Out: How Two Million Women Survived without Men after the First World War* (Viking, 2007)

Scott-Fox, Charles, *Holcombe Court: A Bluett Family Tudor Mansion* (private, 2012)

St. Paul's School

Bussey, David, *John Colet's Children: The Boys of St Paul's School in Later Life, 1509-2009* (Gresham Books, Oxford, 2009)

Mackenzie, Compton, *Sinister Street: The First Volume* (Martin Secker, 1913)

McDonnell, Michael F. J., *A History of St. Paul's School* (Chapman & Hall, 1909)

Mead, A. H. *A Miraculous Draught of Fishes: A History of St Paul's School* (James & James, 1990)

Raymond, Ernest, *Mr Olim* (Cassell, 1961)

Raymond, Ernest, *The Story of My Days: An Autobiography 1888-1922* (Cassell, 1968)

Streeton, Richard, *P. G .H. Fender: A Biography* (Faber & Faber, 1981)

The Pauline and websites for St. Paul's School and Old Pauline Lodge

Trinity Hall, Cambridge

Bond, Henry, *A History of the Trinity Hall Boat Club* (W. Heffer & Sons, Cambridge, 1930)

Cook, T. A., *Rowing at Henley* (OUP, 1919)

Crawley, Charles, *Trinity Hall: The History of a Cambridge College, 1350-1975* (Trinity Hall, Cambridge, 1976)

Pagnamenta, Peter (ed.), *The Hidden Hall: Portrait of a Cambridge College* (Third Millennium, 2004)

The *Cambridge Review*

Norfolk

O'Neale, David & Dobbin, Tony, *Village Life: The Story of Bridgham in Norfolk* (Taverner, 2010)

Wesker, Arnold, *Roots* (Bloomsbury, 1959)

Africa and Zambia

Attwater, Donald, *The White Fathers in Africa* (Burns, Oates & Washbourne, 1937)

Bennett, Frank, *Under an African Sun: Memoirs of a Colonial Officer in Northern Rhodesia* (Radcliffe Press, 2006)

Bigland, Eileen, *The Lake of the Royal Crocodiles* (Hodder & Stoughton, 1939)

Blood, A. G., *The History of the Universities' Mission to Central Africa, Vol II (1907-1932)* (Universities' Mission to Central Africa, 1957)

Brelsford, W. V., The Tribes of Northern Rhodesia (Government Printer, Lusaka, 1956)

Brelsford, W. V., Generation of Men: The European pioneers of Northern Rhodesia (Northern Rhodesia Society, Harare, 1965)

Cancel, Robert, *Storytelling in Northern Zambia: Theory, Method, Practice and Other Necessary Fictions* (Cambridge: Open Book, 2013)

Central Africa, Magazine of UMCA (Universities' Mission to Central Africa) (until December 1932)

Chipungu, Samuel N. (ed.), *Guardians in Their Time: Experiences of Zambians under Colonial Rule, 1890-1964* (Macmillan, 1992)

Chuba, Rev. Dr. Bwalya S., *Mbeleshi in a History of the London Missionary Society* (Pula Press, Botswana, 2000)

Clark, J. Desmond, *Kalambo Falls: Prehistoric Site, Vol I* (Cambridge University Press, 1969)

Coe, David G. & Greenall, E. Cyril, *Kaunda's Gaoler: Memoirs of a District Officer in Northern Rhodesia and Zambia* (Radcliffe Press, 2003)

Coquery-Vidrovitch, Catherine, *Africa: Endurance and Change South of the Sahara* (translated by David Maisel) (University of California Press, 1992)

Coupland, Sir Reginald, *Livingstone's Last Journey* (Collins, 1945)

Cunnison, Ian George, *The Luapula Peoples of Northern Rhodesia: Custom and History in Tribal Politics* (University of Manchester Press, 1959

Davidson, Julie, *Looking for Mrs Livingstone* (St Andrew Press, Edinburgh, 2012)

Franklin, Harry, *Unholy Wedlock: The Failure of the Central African Federation* (George Allen & Unwin, 1963)

Franklin, Harry, *The Flag Wagger* (Shepheard-Walwyn, 1974)

Fraser, Kim & Ellison, Gabriel, *Harmony of Hooves: A Celebration of Racing and Polo in Northern Rhodesia and Zambia from 1904-1996* (private, 1999)

Gann, L. H., *A History of Northern Rhodesia: Early Days to 1953* (Chatto & Windus, 1964)

Garvey, Brian, *Bembaland Church: Religious and Social Change in South Central Africa, 1891-1964* (Brill, Leiden, 1994)

Gewald, Jan-Bart, Hinfelaar, Marja & Macola, Giacomo (ed.), *Living the End of Empire: Politics and Society in Late Colonial Zambia* (Brill, Leiden, 2011)

Gibbs, P., Phillips, H. & Russell, N. (eds.), *Blue & Old Gold – The History of the British South Africa Police, 1889-1980* (30 Degrees South, Durban, 2010)

Goddard, Tony, *My African Stories* (The Memoir Club, County Durham, 2005)

Gouldsbury, C. & Sheane H., *The great plateau of northern Rhodesia, being some impressions of the Tanganyika Plateau* (Edward Arnold, 1911) Reprinted by Negro Universities Press (New York, 1969)

Gouldsbury, H. C., *God's Outpost* (Nash, 1907)

Gouldsbury, Cullen, *An African Year* (Edward Arnold, 1912)

Gouldsbury, Cullen, *Songs out of Exile* (T. Fisher Unwin, 1912)

Gouldsbury, Cullen, *From the Outposts* (T. Fisher Unwin, 1914)

Hall, R., *Zambia* (Praeger, New York, 1965)

Harries, Patrick & Maxwell, David (ed.), *The Spiritual in the Secular: Missionaries and Knowledge about Africa*, (Eerdmans, Grand Rapids, 2012)

Hine, Bp., *Days Gone By* (John Murray, 1925)

Hinfelaar, Hugo F., *History of the Catholic Church in Zambia* (Bookworld Publishers, Lusaka 2004)

Hobson, D., *Tales of Zambia* (The Zambia Society Trust, 1996)

Hudson, John, *A Time to Mourn* (Bookworld Publishers, Lusaka 1999)

Jeal, Tim, *Livingstone* (Heinemann, 1973)

Kirk-Greene, Anthony, *Glimpses of Empire: A Corona Anthology* (I. B. Tauris, 2001)

Kirk-Greene, Anthony, *Symbol of Authority: The British District Officer in Africa* (I. B. Tauris, 2006)

Lamb, C., *The Africa House: The True Story of an English Gentleman and His African Dream* (Penguin, 2000)

Lawley, Jonathan, *Beyond the Malachite Hills: A Life of Colonial Service and Business in the New Africa* (I. B. Tauris, 2010)

Lipschutz, Mark R. & Rasmussen, R. Kent, *Dictionary of African Historical Biography*, 2nd edition (University of California Press, 1986)

Lockhart, J. G. & Woodhouse, C. M., *Rhodes* (Hodder and Stoughton, 1963)

Mackinson, Ian, *Footprints in the Dust … to end of Empire and beyond* (Ian Mackinson, 2003)

Macmillan, Hugh, *The Lusaka Years, The ANC in Exile, 1963-94* (Jacana Press, 2013)

Mansfield, Charlotte, *Via Rhodesia: A Journey Through Southern Africa* (Stanley Paul, 1911)

Maynard Smith, Canon, *Frank, Bishop of Zanzibar* (a life of Bishop Weston) (SPCK, 1926)

McCarthy, James (ed.), *The Road to Tanganyika: The Diaries of Donald Munro and William McEwan* (Kachere Series, Malawi, 2006)

McIntyre, C., *Zambia*, 5th Edition (Bradt, 2012)

Milner-Thornton, Juliette, *The Long Shadow of the British Empire: the Ongoing Legacies of Race and Class in Zambia* (Palgrave Macmillan, 2012)

Moore, Henrietta L. & Vaughan, Megan, *Cutting down Trees: Gender, Nutrition and Agricultural Change in the Northern Province of Zambia, 1890-1990* (Heinemann, 1993)

The Northern Rhodesia Journal, later *The Zambia Journal*, Vols I to VI, 1950-65 (Livingstone Museum, Livingstone, Zambia)

O'Brien, Conor Cruise, *Murderous Angels: A Political Tragedy and Comedy in Black and White* (Hutchinson, 1969)

Ogez, Bishop Jean Marie, *Where it All Began: Centenary of the Church in Zambia* (Missionari d'Africa, 1991)

Oliver, Roland, *The Missionary Factor in East Africa* (Longmans, 1952)

Parkyn, Amanda, *Roses under the Miombo Trees: An English Girl in Rhodesia* (Matador, 2012)

Portman, Lionel, *Station Studies: Being the Jottings of an African Official* (Longmans Green, 1902)

Ranger, T. O. & Weller, John (eds.), *Themes in the Christian History of Central Africa* (University of California Press, 1975)

Ransford, Oliver, *Livingstone's Lake: The Drama of Nyasa* (John Murray, 1966)

Ransford, Oliver, *The Dark Interior* (John Murray, 1978)

Richards, Audrey Isabel, *Land, Labour and Diet in Northern Rhodesia: An Economic Study of the Bemba Tribe* (OUP, 1939)

Roberts, Andrew D., *A History of the Bemba: political growth and change in north-eastern Zambia before 1900* (University of Wisconsin Press, 1973)

Roberts, Andrew D., *A History of Zambia* (Africana Publishing Company, New York, 1976)

Rotberg, Robert I., *Christian Missionaries and the Creation of Northern Rhodesia*, 1880-1924, Princeton University Press, 1965

Rotberg, Robert I., *Black Heart: Gore-Browne and the Politics of Multiracial Zambia*, University of California Press, 1977

Rotberg, Robert I., *The Founder: Cecil Rhodes and the Pursuit of Power* (OUP, 1990)

Rotberg, Robert I. & Mazrui Ali I. (Eds.), *Protest and Power in Black Africa* (OUP, 1970)

Rukavina, Kathaleen Stevens, *Jungle Pathfinder: The Biography of Chirupula Stephenson* (Hutchinson, 1951)

Schur, Tony (ed.), *From the Cam to the Zambezi: Colonial Service and the Path to the New Zambia* (Radcliffe Press, 2015)

Shaw, Mabel, *God's Candlelights: An Educational Venture in Northern Rhodesia* (Edinburgh House Press, 1932)

Shurmer-Smith, Pamela, *Remnants of Empire: Memory and Northern Rhodesia's White Diaspora* (Gadsden Publishers, Lusaka, 2015)

Stuart-Mogg, David, *Mlozi of Central Africa: the End of the Slaver* (Central Africana, Blantyre, Malawi, 2010)

Taylor, John V. & Lehmann, Dorothea A., *Christians of the Copperbelt: The Growth of the Church in Northern Rhodesia* (SCM Press, 1961)

Taylor, John V, *The Primal Vision: Christian Presence Amid African Religion* (SCM Press, 1963)

Waller, Horace (ed.), *The Last Journals of David Livingstone, in Central Africa, from 1865 to His Death, Volume II (of 2), 1869-1873, by David Livingstone, Continued By A Narrative Of His Last Moments And Sufferings, Obtained From His Faithful Servants Chuma And Susi* (John Murray, 1874)

Watson, William, *Tribal Cohesion in a Money Economy: A Study of the Mambwe People of Northern Rhodesia* (Manchester University Press, 1958)

White, Luise, *Speaking with Vampires: Rumor and History in Colonial Africa* (University of California Press, 2000)

Williams, Susan, *Who Killed Hammarskjold? The UN, The Cold War and White Supremacy in Africa* (Hurst, 2011)

Wright, Tim, *The History of the Northern Rhodesia Police* (British Empire & Commonwealth Museum, 2001)

World War One in East Africa

Abbott, Peter, *Armies in East Africa 1914-1918* (Osprey Publishing, 2002)

Anderson, Ross, *The Forgotten Front: The East African Campaign 1914-1918* (The History Press, 2004)

Brelsford, W. V. (ed.), *The Story of the Northern Rhodesia Regiment* (Galago, 1954)

Campbell, Frederick Charles Gunning, *Chapters from a Soldier's Life* (private, 1941)

Farwell, Byron, *The Great War in Africa*, (W. W. Norton & Co, New York, 1986)

Foden, Giles, *Mimi and Toutou Go Forth: The Bizarre Battle for Lake Tanganyika* (Michael Joseph, 2004)

Paice, Edward, *Tip and Run: The Untold Tragedy of the Great War in Africa* (Weidenfeld & Nicolson, 2007)

Samson, Anne, *World War I in Africa: The Forgotten Conflict Among the*

European Powers (I.B. Tauris, 2012)

Shorter, Aylward, *Cross & Flag in Africa: The 'White Fathers' during the Colonial Scramble 1892-1914* (Orbis Books, New York, 2006)

Shorter, Aylward, *African Recruits and Missionary Conscripts: The White Fathers and the Great War 1914-1922* (Missionaries of Africa History Project, 2007)

Strachan, Hew, *The First World War in Africa* (OUP, 2004)

Von Lettow-Vorbeck, Paul, *My Reminiscences of East Africa* (Hurst & Blackett, 1920) Published in Germany as *Meine Erinnerungen aus Ostafrika* (Hase & Köhler, Leipzig, 1920)

Yorke, Edmund James, *Britain, Northern Rhodesia and the First World War: Forgotten Colonial Crisis* (Palgrave Macmillan, 2015)

DRAMATIS PERSONAE

This section mainly covers the period spent by Claude Oldfield in Northern Rhodesia (1911-32)

British Government

Secretaries of State for the Colonies

Lewis Harcourt (3 November 1910-25 May 1915)
 1st Viscount Harcourt (1863-1922), Liberal MP, Peterborough, then Poplar
Andrew Bonar Law (25 May 1915-10 December 1916)
 The Right Honourable Andrew Bonar Law (1858-1923), Conservative MP, Bootle
Walter Long (10 December 1916-10 January 1919)
 The Right Honourable Walter Long (1854-1924), Conservative MP, Westminster, St. George's

Governors General of South Africa

Viscount Gladstone (31 May 1910-8 September 1914)
Sydney Charles Buxton (8 September 1914-17 November 1920)
 1st Earl Buxton (1853-1934). Taught by Claude's father, Thomas Smedley Oldfield, at Hewitt's School, Rottingdean.
HRH Prince Arthur of Connaught (17 November 1920-21 January 1924)

Governors of British East Africa

Sir James Hayes Sadler (1905-09)
Sir Edouard Percy Cranwill Girouard (1909-12)
Sir Henry Conway Belfield (1912-1917)
Sir Charles Calvert Bowring (1917-1919)
Sir Edward Northey (1919-20)

Governors of German East Africa

Gustav Adolf Graf von Goetzen (1901-06)
Georg Albrecht von Rechenberg (1906-12)
Dr Albert Heinrich Schnee (1912-19)

Administrators of North-Eastern Rhodesia

Patrick William Forbes (1 July 1895-June 1897)
Henry Lawrence Daly (June 1897-10 July 1898)
Robert Edward Codrington (11 July 1898-24 April 1907)
Lawrence Aubrey Wallace (24 April 1907-January 1909)
Leicester Paul Beaufort (January 1909-16 May 1911)
Hugh Charlie Marshall (16 May 1911-17 August 1911)

Administrators of North-Western Rhodesia

Robert Thorne Coryndon (9 April 1897-8 April 1907)
Hugh Hole (8 April 1907-20 October 1907)
John Carden (20 October 1907-February 1908)
Robert Edward Codrington (February 1908-16 December 1908)
Lawrence Aubrey Wallace (January 1909-16 August 1911)

Administrators of Northern Rhodesia
(following merger of North-Eastern Rhodesia and North-Western Rhodesia)

Hugh Charlie Marshall (9 May 1911-17 August 1911)
Lawrence Aubrey Wallace (17 August 1911-17 March 1921)
Sir Francis Drummond Percy Chaplin (12 March 1921-20 September 1923)
Richard Allmond Jeffrey Goode (20 September 1923-1 April 1924)
Herbert James Stanley (1 Apr 1924-25 July 1927)
Richard Allmond Jeffrey Goode (25 July 1927-31 August 1927)
Sir James Crawford Maxwell (31 August 1927-1 December 1932)
Sir Ronald Storrs (1 December 1932-7 January 1935)

WWI *in Africa*

British Officers

Aitken, Major General Arthur. Commander of the British Indian Expeditionary Force 'B'; dismissed after the rout at Tanga

Alport, Major. Northern Rhodesia Regiment. See Appendix

Edwards, General Sir Alfred Hamilton Mackenzie. See Appendix

Edwards, General William F. S. See Appendix

Dickinson, Col. Edward Griffith. See Appendix

Hawkins, Lt. Col. E. B. B. Battalion and column commander, 4th KAR (1916-18)

Hodson, Col. F. A. Commanded the forces on the GEA border

James, Captain F. S. Northern Rhodesia Regiment. See Appendix

McCarthy, Lieutenant J. J. Northern Rhodesia Police

Murray, Lt. Col. Ronald E. Column commander, 'Norforce' ('Murray's Column')

Northey, Edward. Commander-in-Chief, 'Norforce'; later Governor of British East Africa / Kenya (1919-22)

O'Sullevan. Major J. J. Northern Rhodesia Police

Spicer-Simson, Geoffrey. Senior naval officer, Lake Tanganyika Expedition (1915-16)

Stennett, Major H. M. Northern Rhodesia Police

Wardroper, Captain P. R. Northern Rhodesia Regiment. See Appendix

South African Officers

Crewe, Brigadier-General Charles. Commanding officer, Lake Force (1916); politician and newspaper owner

Smuts, General Jan Christian. Cabinet minister, Union of South Africa (1914-15); Commander-in-Chief, British / South African Forces (1916). later Prime Minister of South Africa (1919-24; 1939-48)

van Deventer, Lieutenant-General Sir Jakobus Louis. Divisional commander, British / South African Forces (1916); Commander-in-Chief, British / South African Forces (1917-18)

Belgian Officers

de Koninck, Major. Belgian officer (Abercorn, 1914-15)
Tombeur, Lieutenant-General Charles-Henri. Commander-in-Chief, Belgian Forces (Force Publique) (1916); captured Tabora in GEA

German Officers

Boell, Ludwig. *Schutztruppe* Company commander/staff officer; unofficial historian
von Lettow-Vorbeck, General Paul Emil. Commander-in-Chief, German forces in East Africa (the *Schutztruppe*)
Looff, Captain Max. Captain of the *Königsberg*; *Schutztruppe* detachment commander
Spangenburg, Walter. *Schutztruppe* company commander
Wahle, General Kurt. Retired officer on holiday in Africa, aged 59, when war was declared; *Schutztruppe* logistics officer (1915); commander *Westruppen* (1915-17); detachment commander (1917-18)

Colonial Service, Northern Rhodesia

Alexander, Adam Murray
Brigham, Harold Loftus
Brooks, Herbert Cecil
Brown, Frank Leslie. Medical Officer
Buxton-Wickins, Edward Hugh
Chapman, Allan Simpson
Chesnaye, Christian Purefoy
Chicken, Rupert Thomas (Tom)
Clough, Eric Duncombe. Medical Officer
Clough, Mrs Grace Margaret. Mistress, European education (1930)
Draper, Christopher Robert Burroughes (Chris)
Draper, Lena Maud. Wife of Chris Draper
Facey, Samuel Dyke
Franklin, Harry

Franklin, Mrs Marie Constance. Mistress, European education (1930)

Franklin, Ms Toni (daughter of Harry & Marie). Later, Mrs. Tilling

Goodall, Edward Basil Herbert

Goode, Richard Allmond Jeffrey. Administrator of Northern Rhodesia (1923-24, 1927)

Gouldsbury, Henry Cullen. Poet and author

Green, Hugh Abbott

Hill, Hugh Charles Norwood

Hillier, Stanley

Jones, Edgar Anderson Averay. Later Mining Commissioner

Lloyd, Stephen Pemberton Lucius

Marshall, Hugh Charlie ('Tambalika'). Administrator of N.E. Rhodesia (1911) then of Northern Rhodesia (1911)

Matthews, Bertram John

Moffat, John Smith

Moffat-Thompson, James

Morton, Gerald Humphrey. Admitted to Mental Home, Cape Town, 1930

Munday, Edward

Murray, James

Otter, Martin John Bruere

Owen, William Elsworthy Montague

Rideal, Guy St. Clair. Won DSC in WWII (*London Gazette*, August 1940)

Sandford, Thomas Frederick

Stevens, Charles G.

Stokes, Geoffrey

Vellacott, Eric William

Wallace, Laurence Aubrey. Administrator of N.W. Rhodesia (1909-11), Administrator of Northern Rhodesia (1911-21)

Woods, H. S. Veterinary Officer

Others (Farmers, Settlers, Missionaries, etc)

Barnes, Father Herbert. Anglican priest

Gore-Browne, Stewart. Settler, builder of Shiwa Ng'andu

Hurlow, Mr & Mrs. Seventh Day Adventists

Leeke, Father Charles. Anglican priest

Lobb, Gordon. Farmer (near Abercorn)

Nutter, Mr & Mrs Cecil & Ada. London Missionary Society
Smith, Lionel. Farmer (near Abercorn)

UK

Beck, Edward Anthony. Master of Trinity Hall (1902-16)
Bourne, Gwen. Lived at The Rectory, Bridgham; cousin of Kathleen
    Wetherall
Hillard, Albert Ernest. High Master, St. Paul's (1905-27)
Walker, Frederick William. High Master, St. Paul's (1877-1905)
Wetherall (Henniker-Wetherall), Kathleen Ada Violet. Friend of Laws
    and Oldfields; lived at The Grove, Bridgham

Various sources, including: Blue Books; www.britishempire.co.uk/
    maproom/northernrhodesia/northernrhodesiaadmin.htm

TIMELINE FOR CLAUDE OLDFIELD (1889–1963)

1889	6 May: Born in Maida Vale, fourth son of Thomas Smedley Oldfield (classics tutor) and Mary Anna Bluett-Knowlman
1902–03	Private tutoring with a 'Mr. Bull' at York Gate, Marylebone
1903–08	St. Paul's School, Hammersmith
1908–11	Studying classics at Trinity Hall, Cambridge Rows for his College 1st Eight at Cambridge and Henley Regatta Graduates in summer of 1911, with a Lower II Class B.A. degree
1911	26 August: Sailed from Southampton. Arrives Abercorn, probably late September or October
1913	February–October: Seconded from Abercorn to assist at Mporokoso
1914–18	During World War One, serves on patrols on border with German East Africa
1915	September: Departs on leave to UK
1916	May: Returns to Abercorn. 12 July: slight earthquake in Abercorn
1917	10 March: 'Mentioned in Despatches', signed Winston Churchill, Secretary of State for War
1918	23 April–3 July: Temporary transfer from Abercorn to Mporokoso 25 November: Joins the inspection parade at the formal surrender of General von Lettow-Vorbeck in Abercorn
1919	8 July: Letter of commendation from Lawrence Wallace, Administrator of NR 30 September: Proceeds on leave to UK (spending three months *en route* to Durban)
1920	In UK, until 14 May. On return, provides leave cover at

Ndola (30 June–12 August). 13 September arrives in Chiengi (new posting)

1922	April: Transfers from Chiengi to Kawambwa
1923	May: Departs on long leave (may have stayed in Africa; cannot find shipping records of any voyages to/from UK) July: Robert Jeffreys returns from UK, having married Dorothy Christiansen on 18 February in London
1924	1 February: Appointed Native Commissioner, Mporokoso 26 March: Robert and Dorothy Jeffreys first child, Ann, born in Kasama 31 March: Claude's eldest brother Robert (Thomas) dies in Adelong, New South Wales, aged 47 28 April: Kenneth Kaunda born near Chinsali
1925	13 August: Claude's father, Thomas Smedley Oldfield, dies at home, aged 81
1926	February: Dorothy Jeffreys pregnant with second child, fathered by Claude October: The Jeffreys sail to UK, Audrey born in Charmouth, Dorset on 26 November 1 November: Claude starts home leave
1927	27 January: Jeffreys family of four leave London to return to NR On his return from leave, Claude provides leave cover at Lundazi (3 August–8 November), then posted to Chinsali
1930	14 February: Departs on home leave 7 September: Provides leave cover at Serenje
1931	27 January: Appointed DC, Ndola, until 10 May, when transferred to Mkushi
1932	21 May: 'Last supper' with Charles Stevens at Mkushi. Departs 'on leave, pending retirement'. 13 June: arrives Southampton on *Balmoral Castle*, aged 43
1933–39	Living in Maida Vale, looking after his mother, who dies on 21 June 1939; and also disabled, older brother, Harold, who dies on 14 February 1937 Meets Elveda Law in 1933, or possibly in 1932. No record of him working during this period

1939	After mother's death, marries Elveda Law in London on 9 August. Moves with her to Laxey on Isle of Man. 3 September: war declared on Germany
1940	Claude and Elveda return to London and live in Maida Vale
1941	Enlists in RAFVR (RAF Volunteer Reserve). Flying Officer with No.4 Mechanised Transport Corps, arranging women drivers' rotas; later at barrage balloon station
1945–53	Joins the Motor Trade Association as Secretary at their offices in Park Lane, Mayfair
1949–51	Living in Bishop's Stortford (birthplace of Cecil Rhodes); commuting to London.
1951–54	Living in Cambridge
1954–63	Retirement to The Rectory, Bridgham, Norfolk (near Thetford), living with Elveda's family
1960	14 July: invited to Buckingham Palace Garden Party
1963	21 February: death at home in Bridgham, Norfolk

Family Tree: Oldfield

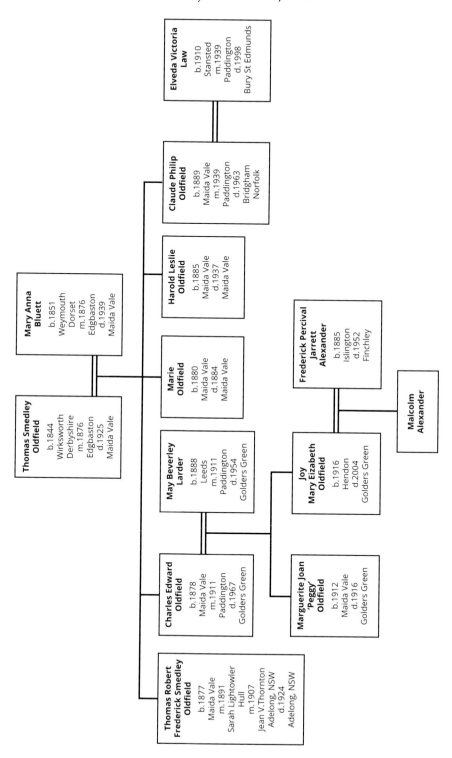

Elveda Victoria Law
b.1910
Stansted
m.1939
Paddington
d.1998
Bury St Edmunds

Claude Philip Oldfield
b.1889
Maida Vale
m.1939
Paddington
d.1963
Bridgham
Norfolk

Harold Leslie Oldfield
b.1885
Maida Vale
d.1937
Maida Vale

Mary Anna Bluett
b.1851
Weymouth
Dorset
m.1876
Edgbaston
d.1939
Maida Vale

Thomas Smedley Oldfield
b.1844
Wirksworth
Derbyshire
m.1876
Edgbaston
d.1925
Maida Vale

Marie Oldfield
b.1880
Maida Vale
d.1884
Maida Vale

Frederick Percival Jarrett Alexander
b.1885
Islington
d.1952
Finchley

Malcolm Alexander

May Beverley Larder
b.1888
Leeds
m.1911
Paddington
d.1954
Golders Green

Joy Mary Eizabeth Oldfield
b.1916
Hendon
d.2004
Golders Green

Charles Edward Oldfield
b.1878
Maida Vale
m.1911
Paddington
d.1967
Golders Green

Marguerite Joan 'Peggy' Oldfield
b.1912
Maida Vale
d.1916
Golders Green

Thomas Robert Frederick Smedley Oldfield
b.1877
Maida Vale
m.1891
Sarah Lightowler
Hull
m.1907
Jean V.Thornton
Adelong, NSW
d.1924
Adelong, NSW

Family Tree: Jeffreys

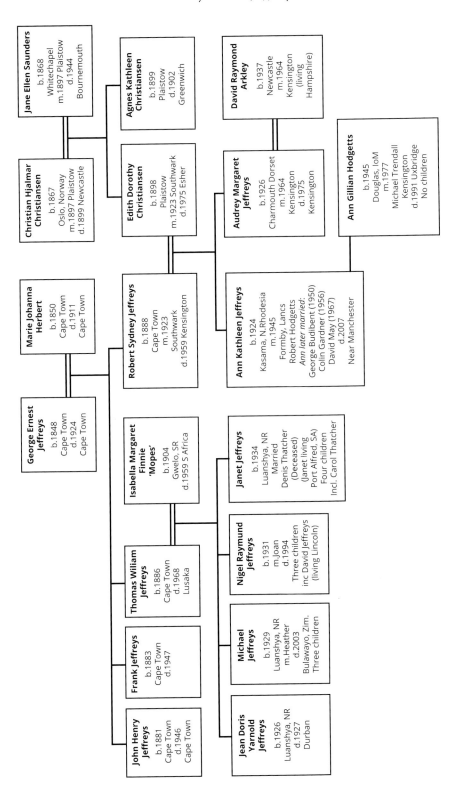

Jane Ellen Saunders
b.1868
Whitechapel
m.1897 Plaistow
d.1944
Bournemouth

Agnes Kathleen Christiansen
b.1899
Plaistow
d.1902
Greenwich

David Raymond Arkley
b.1937
Newcastle
m.1964
Kensington
(living Hampshire)

Christian Hjalmar Christiansen
b.1867
Oslo, Norway
m.1897 Plaistow
d.1899 Newcastle

Edith Dorothy Christiansen
b.1898
Plaistow
m.1923 Southwark
d.1975 Esher

Audrey Margaret Jeffreys
b.1926
Charmouth Dorset
m.1964
Kensington
d.1975
Kensington

Ann Gillian Hodgetts
b.1945
Douglas, IoM
m.1977
Michael Trendall
Kensington
d.1991 Uxbridge
No children

Marie Johanna Herbert
b.1850
Cape Town
d.1911
Cape Town

Robert Sydney Jeffreys
b.1888
Cape Town
m.1923
Southwark
d.1959 Kensington

Ann Kathleen Jeffreys
b.1924
Kasama, N.Rhodesia
m.1945
Formby, Lancs
Robert Hodgetts
Ann later married:
George Budibent (1950)
Colin Gardner (1956)
David May (1967)
d.2007
Near Manchester

George Ernest Jeffreys
b.1848
Cape Town
d.1924
Cape Town

Isabella Margaret Finnie 'Mopes'
b.1904
Gwelo, SR
d.1959 S Africa

Janet Jeffreys
b.1934
Luanshya, NR
Married
Denis Thatcher
(Deceased)
(Janet living
Port Alfred, SA)
Four children
Incl. Carol Thatcher

Thomas Wiliam Jeffreys
b.1886
Cape Town
d.1968
Lusaka

Nigel Raymund Jeffreys
b.1931
m.Joan
d.1994
Three children
inc David Jeffreys
(living Lincoln)

Frank Jeffreys
b.1883
Cape Town
d.1947

Michael Jeffreys
b.1929
Luanshya, NR
m.Heather
d.2003
Bulawayo, Zim.
Three children

John Henry Jeffreys
b.1881
Cape Town
d.1946
Cape Town

Jean Doris Yarnold Jeffreys
b.1926
Luanshya, NR
d.1927
Durban

Family Tree: Law

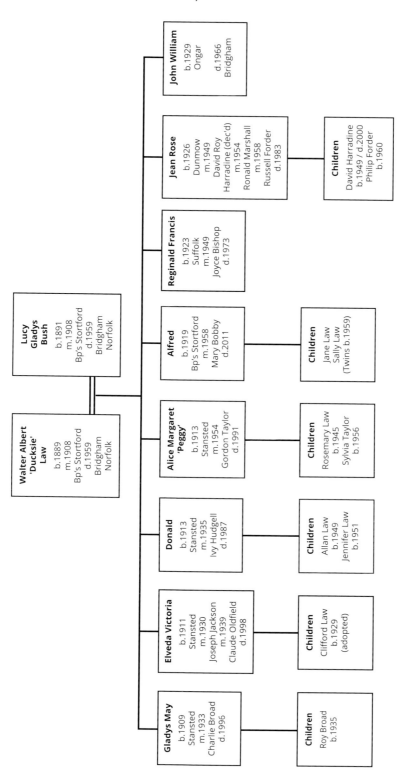

Walter Albert 'Ducksie' Law
b.1889
m.1908
Bp's Stortford
d.1959
Bridgham
Norfolk

Lucy Gladys Bush
b.1891
m.1908
Bp's Stortford
d.1959
Bridgham
Norfolk

Gladys May
b.1909
Stansted
m.1933
Charlie Broad
d.1996

Elveda Victoria
b.1911
Stansted
m.1930
Joseph Jackson
m.1939
Claude Oldfield
d.1998

Donald
b.1913
Stansted
m.1935
Ivy Hudgell
d.1987

Alice Margaret 'Peggy'
b.1913
Stansted
m.1954
Gordon Taylor
d.1991

Alfred
b.1919
Bp's Stortford
m.1958
Mary Bobby
d.2011

Reginald Francis
b.1923
Suffolk
m.1949
Joyce Bishop
d.1973

Jean Rose
b.1926
Dunmow
m.1949
David Roy
Harradine (dec'd)
m.1954
Ronald Marshall
m.1958
Russell Forder
d.1983

John William
b.1929
Ongar
d.1966
Bridgham

Children
Roy Broad
b.1935

Children
Clifford Law
b.1929
(adopted)

Children
Allan Law
b.1949
Jennifer Law
b.1951

Children
Rosemary Law
b.1945
Sylvia Taylor
b.1956

Children
Jane Law
Sally Law
(Twins b.1959)

Children
David Harradine
b.1949 / d.2000
Philip Forder
b.1960

INDEX